# Future Directions in Information

# Chandos
# Digital Information Review Series

Series Editors:

David Baker and Lucy Ellis

Chandos is pleased to publish this major Series of books entitled Digital Information Review. The Series editors are Professor David Baker, Professor Emeritus, Plymouth Marjon University; Director, David Baker Consulting and Dr Lucy Ellis, Honorary Research Fellow, Exeter University; Associate, David Baker Consulting.

The Chandos Digital Information Review Series aims to be a summary and a summation of the key themes, advances and trends in all aspects of digital information and explores the impact on the information world. The emphasis is on both the key current topics and future developments; an international perspective is taken throughout. Each publication in the series has a dynamic set of contents that respond to and, more importantly, anticipate digital information futures. The relevant chapters are written by experts in the field, drawing widely from Europe, North America, Australasia and South East Asia.

New authors - we would be delighted to hear from you if you have an idea for a book. We are interested in short practically orientated publications (45,000 words) and longer theoretical monographs (75,000-100,000 words). Our books can be single, joint or multi author volumes. If you have an idea for a book please contact the publishers or the Series Editors: Professor David Baker (david@davidbakerconsulting.co.uk) and Dr Lucy Ellis (l.ellis3@exeter.ac.uk)

Chandos Digital Information Review

# Future Directions in Digital Information

## Predictions, Practice, Participation

*Edited by*

***David Baker***

***Lucy Ellis***

CP
CHANDOS
PUBLISHING
ELSEVIER
An imprint of Elsevier

Chandos Publishing is an imprint of Elsevier
50 Hampshire Street, 5th Floor, Cambridge, MA 02139, United States
The Boulevard, Langford Lane, Kidlington, OX5 1GB, United Kingdom



**Library of Congress Cataloging-in-Publication Data**
A catalog record for this book is available from the Library of Congress

**British Library Cataloguing-in-Publication Data**
A catalogue record for this book is available from the British Library

ISBN: 978-0-12-822144-0 (print)

For information on all Chandos publications
visit our website at https://www.elsevier.com/books-and-journals

*Publisher:* Glyn Jones
*Editorial Project Manager:* Chiara Giglio
*Production Project Manager:* Surya Narayanan Jayachandran
*Cover Designer:* Miles Hitchen

Typeset by SPi Global, India

# Contents

## Part Three Where formal meets informal

## Part Four Applications and delivery

# Conclusion

# List of figures and tables

## List of figures

# List of tables

# Foreword

Technology will be a huge agent of change in the coming years in a variety of ways. Higher bandwidth and advances in mobile technology will continue to raise the expectations of anything, anywhere, with anytime accessibility. Expectations are manifested in a significant shift by users from *hunter/gatherer*, searching for information, for whatever need, in a variety of physical entities, to the *harvester*, expecting to find all they need from the convenience of their networked device. We will see more remote and virtual working, as social distancing becomes a normal practice. There will be improvements in information delivery services and digital meeting and sharing applications.

Digital and social media have already had an impact on organizational priorities and behaviours. Until now, they have tended to be adjuncts to traditional roles and expectations. Institutions of all types managing and disclosing information for users have to maintain, protect, and develop their collections and be accountable for their actions. Organizations will have to review how they balance their priorities between the physical and the virtual.

However, we should not automatically assume that technology is the solution to every problem: the danger of technical rationality—the extent to which seeking technological solutions dominates future research programmes. Technology is a key component, but research programmes should begin by considering carefully what is the core of the problem faced: problem setting rather than problem solving. The dangers of technical rationality and the need for policy frameworks for the future call for radical change both in the overall management and funding of research programmes and the behaviours and attitudes of institutions. This should take place within limits to set aside organizational identity and accept the value of collective action and advocacy in research and innovation with the aspiration that it will offer services that better meet the future needs of audiences of all types.

The fixed stoic image of a library is no longer fit for purpose. It must be made flexible, modernized, and more accessible to meet the needs and demands of today's users. The sector must not shy away from nontraditional development and collaboration. If technology can perform menial tasks, then this frees up staff to specialize in research and other aspects of the profession, leading to a more useful and efficient front-line service overall.

There should be new approaches to change management. By tradition, library and information services have had a duty to collect, care for, and exploit their collections in whatever form over time. Radical, disruptive change brings with it a significant risk. The incremental approach to change management is likely to be retained for aspects of service management and delivery. However, within the turbulent landscape of the Internet, while rapid change in service propositions has similar risks, there will be occasions when, to deliver effectively, quicker responses to outside forces will be needed. Those leading the innovation and change may sometimes need to operate more as entrepreneurs than conventional public service managers. Flexibility and open-mindedness are key when it comes to developing new approaches. If it does not work, try something else. Different ideas should be explored and monitored to help achieve success.

What will be called for is a far more collaborative and coordinated approach to innovation, where risks can be shared and where ideas can be incubated, and risk managed. It will be necessary to find ways for local institutions to give up some of their independence in service innovation for the greater good for truly effective service development in the digital landscape. Curated and trusted resources should be promoted and advertised by libraries since these are stable and authoritative. By relying on these resources, but managing them internally for delivery, risk is then diminished.

Policy frameworks for future research management must be considered. At the present time, there are only small levels of collaboration to find solutions that might offer service improvements across all or a cadre of institutions. Where technical innovation does take place, it may well have little impact on similar organizations elsewhere. Given increasing user expectation that 'everything' should be accessible anytime, anywhere—the shift from hunter/gatherer to harvester—there will need to be policy frameworks in place to ensure that research and innovation delivers maximum value through cooperation and coordination.

While demonstration of value to the user will be essential, it is highly likely that the scale of use and success will continue to be significant. The future of public funding looks now more uncertain than ever and institutions wishing to protect (and grow) their budgets will have to show value at scale. This will be important in the exploitation of Internet technologies where the possibility exists to reach the widest possible audience. The question of value comes in, which can still be captured online. It will become less about the numbers, especially as user numbers drop when people bypass the library completely in search of online information. Instead it will become more about the quality of the information that the people are using and the uses to which they put this information. Numbers will still play a role, but this will be vastly diminished when it comes to justifying services and projects.

Convenience and point of demand will continue to be the drivers of technological innovation. The 'learning for life' that technology offers presents the greatest opportunities for increased value to individuals and to society at large. Learning literacy (LL—known more formally as heutagogy)—assisting users to understand how they maximize personal benefit from the knowledge and information they find—will become significant: how to interpret, how to test reliability and encourage the value of what they find in ongoing learning journeys, whether in formal education or in everyday life. Supporting LL, understanding the exchange relationship between the online collection resources and the user and modelling the value delivered must be the core activities for library and information services.

Successful delivery of online resources will call for new relationships with users in terms of both the design of new systems and the constant monitoring of how services are received and revised in the light of experience. Success will depend on an organizational shift towards constant monitoring and engagement. It is important that information ethics underpins everything that libraries do, especially if they are offering user training in digital literacy, which should include citizens' rights and duties and training in the good and ethical use of information. They should regularly question their practice and ensure that users do the same. In a world where other digital competencies and websites are questioned, libraries need to set the best possible example of good practice and use data responsibility, so users can learn from their example.

The key factors in future strategies must include making clear how both the virtual and the physical are managed to deliver best value and engagement with collective research and innovation. There should be a preparedness to change significant parts of delivery priorities as external demands change. Sometimes success will require speedy action, sometimes not. Balancing radical change with the traditional incremental approach but ensuring that at all stages the processes of development, innovation, and research engage with current users and potential new audiences will be important.

How can technology be used by all, not just those who are used to it? This includes both users and staff to ensure no one gets left behind. The development of online services should work with the development of in-person resources rather than as a separate thing. It is important to think about those who do not visit libraries in person but do have access to personal technology.

A clear mission and purpose must underpin everything a library service does. Practices and ways of working must evolve to meet both user demands and new technological potential. This should lead to an appraisal of the institution within its environment to establish the external pressures, changes, and opportunities it will face through time. The institution must remain confident in its fundamental purpose and when necessary be fleet of foot, acting like an entrepreneur in responding to external change. The critical challenge of digital projects is the speed of change that can and does take place.

Libraries will continue to collect and enable access to quality sources of information. They will retain authority, organizing and enabling effective search and retrieval for end users, curating, acquiring, and delivering quality information sources for different user groups. They will save users time and effort, provide reassurance about information quality, provide guidance to users on how to make good choices about information, how to use information appropriately, and how to create and disseminate their own content in an appropriate and safe manner.

Libraries are safe places; spaces for comfort and well-being. These characteristics guarantee users the confidence to explore information freely and openly. This is at the basis of the development of ideas that in turn will foster new knowledge for society. They have an indirect impact through education, with a population who are better informed about the world and able to conduct themselves responsibly in the digital environment and more able to make social connections. If libraries continue to focus on free and open information, open buildings, and free services, then they will remain essential.

**The Delphi Group**

# Preface

In Act I Scene 5 of Shakespeare's *Macbeth*, the deadly Lady Macbeth reads letters from her husband telling her of the witches' prophesy that he will be king. These, she describes 'have transported me beyond/This ignorant present'. She prepares herself to conspire with that prediction, and like an electric shock to the soul she declares: 'I feel now/The future in the instant'. The darkness of the ignorant present is held up for stark contrast with a categorically different kind of 'present moment' as something containing, in a blinding instant, the course of a fully formed evil monarchical history.

You could say that, for Lady Macbeth, the future is already happening.

The title of this book is *Future Directions in Digital Information* and we ask our readers to judge if the future is in the 'instant' of the words that it contains. While Part Five of the book deals with 'New Paradigms' and thus answers the explicit brief of predicting the future course of specific aspects of digital information, we contend that future directions are inscribed into the work of all authors by virtue of the fact that they describe their present labours in a field that is characterized by extraordinary levels of vitality. The pace is so fast that the tools, techniques, concepts, and theoretical apparatus in information science and librarianship are becoming the future in the present moment, a situation understood by Lady Macbeth.

By invitation, 34 leaders in the field have contributed chapters for this book, representing work carried out in Australia, China, Denmark, France, Germany, Greece, Mexico, Nigeria, Spain, Sweden, the United Kingdom, and the United States of America. This multinational perspective will be valuable to the reader as it gives an understanding of the organizational characteristics and constraints that information specialists are working with in different countries. Equal access to resources and services remains a challenge in an unequal world. For those who are differently abled, library and information services have to recognize the rights of all to be included on the same terms.

Contributing authors are those delivering digital information services and systems and their papers represent the views and behaviours of subject specialists and academic communities. All are information managers and are required to select, collect, and provide high-quality access to content, facilities, and applications. All are knowledge managers, able to detect and respond to changing information behaviours.

The Chandos Digital Information Review Series, of which this is the latest volume, aims to be a summary of the key themes, advances, and trends in all aspects of digital information and explores the impact on the information world. The two Chandos series that sit alongside it are *Advances in Information* and the *Information Professional* Series. *Digital Information Review* captures the key themes, advances, and trends. It is about the process of adding things together, a methodology for identifying the matters of our time, and the ways of thinking that define us. One such summative methodology can be found in the Delphi study that underpins Chapters 1 and 19 of this book.

The 19 chapters of the book are divided into five parts and a brief overview of each is given here. Chapter 1 introduces the purpose and aims of the book and provides an overview of the content of each chapter in terms of methodological approach and what they tell us about the future of digital information. The discussion of the key themes is reinforced and augmented by the results of the Delphi exercise and by selected thought pieces both of which are presented in text boxes. Thought pieces were commissioned to provide stimulating statements, reflections, predictions, ideas, and viewpoints—sometimes contentious and always pithy—about the future directions digital information is taking. The texture and discourse style of the book is further varied and invigorated by the presentation of the results of a Delphi study conducted specially for this purpose. 'Delphi is a qualitative method of forecasting by developing expert consensus about a topic through a series of anonymous mailed questionnaires…The Delphi method has been employed in technological forecasting, planning, and a variety of other areas' (Baker, 2004, p. 82). A virtual team of nine panellists—from a wide range of backgrounds relating to digital information provision—was selected (see Acknowledgments).

The Delphi panel embraced a wealth of knowledge, skills, and experience in the field of libraries and information science (LIS). The panel comprised members from Europe, Africa, the United Kingdom, and the United States of America. It included a mix of senior figures and newly established talent in higher education (HE), public libraries, national research and teaching associations, publishing and consultancy. Three panel members were library directors at major universities, one being simultaneously a chair of an academic libraries' consortium; one member was a research support librarian and one member a head of acquisitions. The group has amassed substantial experience in both writing for publication and in reviewing premier scholarly journals. Membership and leadership of the major professional associations was represented, alongside specialisms in museums and archives, digital, shared, and data services. One panellist was an experienced advisor to the UK Government, whose work included guidance on digital strategy development and as the lead of a museums and archives development agency for the sector. Many panellists continue to work on research projects of global interest and significance including information literacy, audience analysis and modelling in digital content, digitization strategies, and ICT developments in public libraries. A number of other professional commitments are shared across the panel, notably, research support for the Association of Commonwealth Universities: scholarly communication, professional development and training, demand-driven library acquisitions, and finally e-book and streaming media library acquisitions.

A series of questions were developed according to the main themes of this book and are shown in Appendix: Delphi Questions. The answers to these questions were collated and turned into a series of statements, which were then sent back to the participants for further comment. These responses were then summarized and analyzed. A by-product of distilling the mass of data that came out of the process is the '20 Absolute Truths' about the future of digital information, which can be found at the end of Chapter 19.

Part One: *Strategy and Design* showcases the best in institutional responses to challenges brought about by the increase in digital capability and expectation. Joachim Schöpfel and Otmane Azeroual describe the human dynamics that have brought about a merger of Current Research Information Systems (CRIS) and Institutional Repositories (IR) systems based on an overview of recent papers and surveys and with a comprehensive range of examples to illustrate the challenge for the library. A gloriously architectural and technical treat is in store for readers, made tractable by a good narrative. Adapting to CRIS is good news for librarians where the 'key is metadata, and metadata is part of academic librarians' core competencies. Their expertise with unique identifiers, standard protocols, and data formats is required for the development of both systems, and they will seize the convergence and merger of IR and CRIS as an opportunity for their future development on campus, as a central part of the research service environment'. Deeply committed academic librarians are also at the centre of Gabrielle Wong and Diana Chan's chapter, which takes a radical democratic view of the design of library-based research data management services. It was the Library at Hong Kong University of Science and Technology which was equipped to cultivate and broker a new level of trust and reassurance between the research community and the institution in its ambition to implement research data policies and mandatory workflows. Traditionally, the researchers 'did not need or want help' in managing research data, but through advocacy and expertise the Library was able to build 'support and services emphasizing the value of RDM [Research Data Management] as good practice for research management and academic integrity'. Andy Phippen, Emma Bond and Ellen Buck's chapter provides a wake-up call regarding how institutions should respond to information literacy education. The authors highlight the significant risk to reputations when digital literacy, good identification of authentic sources, and awareness of fake news is assumed to exist among a student population *en masse*. The rot can set in before university starts where 'ad hoc and poorly defined critical digital literacy education in schools result in students frequently bringing poor critical thinking to the online environments'.

Part Two: *Who are the Users?* comprises four chapters dealing with the characteristics, behaviours, and attitudes of users. There is much we can learn from these discussions about the extent to which users are ultimately the centre of our universe and whether this undifferentiated term is as widely used as it is to reflect a necessary lack of regard for the type of information service being provided. Information specialists are mandated to deliver the right interventions and services at the right time to users whose expectations of digital access and citizenship are at an all-time high. How much user data is effective? Should we be worried about hyperutilitarianism and is there an alternative universe where the experts are creating the users and their appetites?

The quality of accessibility statements is brought to the fore by Huw Alexander and Alistair McNaught, who write about the application of a librarian-based crowdsourcing methodology to the real world of e-book publishing. Their work provides much novel information for users and for the first time provides a measure of the success of 'accessible content'. Katarina Michnik's empirical study in Sweden also provides new information about the online public library user; that is, the user who uses online public library services. Who are these people and are they like anyone we already know? We find out that today's online public library services may not be effective in targeting public library nonusers and/or people with low reading skills and information literacy. Moving to Nigeria, a chapter by Stephen Akintunde highlights the importance of cultural context for information user behaviour. In anthropologically informed research which takes into the account the impact of changing kinship structures, we see a clash of cultures which has consequences for users of digital information in higher education (HE). Akintunde stresses that technology and digital information can be employed as a strategy for social transformation and national development in Africa. Finally, to complete this part of the book, Eva Ortoll, Josep Cobarsí, Agustí Canals, and Lynn S. Connaway explore the real issues of online behaviour in an online university. Through a series of focus groups, a variety of user voices is heard, including different approaches to the distinction between human and digital sources of information. Student and faculty alike are shown to be affected by information overload, which affects their behaviour in hitherto unknown ways.

Part Three: *Where Formal Meets Informal* focuses on the current scale and significance of engagement by the formal information world, as found in universities, with the commercial world. Is digital information as the dominant paradigm showing this to be a false dichotomy? The use of social media, mobile phones, and off-the-shelf resources is nothing new, but what exactly is happening now, and are we in a greater position of trust and acceptance than before?

Evgenia Vasilakaki and Valentini M. Papaconstantinou present their research on mobile technology and the use of educational games in HE. There is no doubt that the increasing interest in the use of games is because of their essential characteristics, which provide an architecture for learning. In HE, games are starting to be integrated into the curriculum in order to achieve learning outcomes, presupposing that the line between 'where the fun stops and the learning starts' has been delineated. The authors review the growing relevant literature describing the level of acceptance of, and preference for, this alternative and/or complementary method of teaching and learning. Social media, as another phenomenon associated with the informal world, is the subject of investigation by Daniella Smith as a professional development tool by academic librarians. Social media appear to offer substantial numbers of professionals an economical way of updating skills. What exactly is professional development and furthermore 'What does professional development conducted on Twitter look like?' Much useful data is generated, linking demography and social variables to the use of social media and social media in a library context. In his wide ranging and widely referenced chapter, Mark Dahl considers the formal and informal ecosystem of information in which academic libraries are already operating. In addition to contributing to the conceptual debates, he designs an enlightened and informative plan for how libraries 'might use their purchasing power to support open access, select book and journal content bundles with compelling value and leverage demand-driven purchasing'. This chapter will serve as a valuable reality check for those making high-level decisions.

Part Four: *Application and Delivery* is rooted in the practicalities and creative endeavour of forming necessary bridges from the old order into the new. Catherine O'Connor presents a case study of civic policy designed to generate local digital skills and its relationship to the university agenda. She explores the question of whether HE is the right environment in which to gain these skills beyond the infrastructure it offers of validation, approval, assessment rigour, marketing, programme launch, and funding. A compelling case is made where a co-designed university programme meets the requirements of both specialist content and general digital skills content relevant to the local labour market. Importantly, the work enables students to visualize a digital future for themselves. In a completely different industry context for a librarian, Matthew Naughtin describes an orchestra's seismic cultural transformation as brought about by the advent of digital access to, and sharing of, sheet music. As the librarian of the San Francisco Ballet's orchestra, Naughtin is in a position to observe and describe cultural and copyright issues that can be traced back to Monteverdi and Mozart. In another different type of context, this time an arts university, Karen Carden makes the case for the primacy of the printed book despite the growing demand for digital resources. Shifting formats is the topic of her chapter and she describes the special type of bibliographic activity undertaken by library staff in a creative setting. Sayeda Zain charts a host of transformative digital trends in education covering a comprehensive area of application including special education, new technologies, new pedagogies, and value for money. In the final chapter of Part Three, Juan D. Machin-Mastromatteo contributes an autobiographical chapter about his transition from reference librarian to full-time teacher of information literacy, discussing many salient issues, complexities, and trends along the way, not least those around a career change. Written from the heart, it reports his own work developing instruments to assess the success of IL initiatives and includes practical advice on where and how to use them.

Part Five: *New Paradigms* comprises four chapters dealing with the identification and modelling of upcoming predictions in the use and value of digital information. Martin Hamilton's chapter presents a scenario planning approach to the implications for information professionals of the cutting edge of Education 4.0 and up-to-the-minute digital developments, while propounding a new legal realism in its control of ethical standards. What could the future of education look like for libraries, those who run them, and their patrons? The vivid description of future scenarios for universities includes how libraries would operate as a service within them. Imaginative and futuristic analyzes are carried out. These look at areas such as digital disruption plotted against student mobility, as conceptualized by the author. The next chapter—'Data-driven modelling of public library infrastructure and usage in the United Kingdom'—describes a collaboration between the Alan Turing Institute and the British Library. Flora Roumpani, Maja Maricevic, and Alan Wilson argue that there is poor availability, understanding and use of the public library sector's data. The use of techniques stemming from mathematical modelling, and which are based on 'theories of systems of interest', is described in detail, and drives future planning and development. How can a data-driven model be built which can be used, for example, to understand the effect of closures of libraries? Understanding the demand for a library in an area and whether that may change if a library is closed, is the key factor leading to the design of a simulation for the effects of closures in that area. Anja Toft Ingwersen, Mai Aggerbeck, and Signe Nielsen ask how the specific skills of the librarian in a digital context can be used in the future. Far from librarians and information specialists becoming observers of an asteroidal landscape run by machines, what will really be in demand globally will be these professionals' abundant nonroutine cognitive skills. A scoping review of the literature and personal interviews are presented as the basis for these conclusions. In the penultimate chapter by Carl Gustav Johannsen, researchers as users come under the spotlight; this is a group whose role has fundamentally changed especially in the light of a shift already identified by Johannsen where the needs of research administrative units have been prioritized among the main concerns of the academic library above and beyond providing services. This chapter aims ‘both to consider the use of bibliometric data by research management units at universities and to move one step further and investigate to what extent a new phase of digitization, linked with notions like surveillance society, surveillance state, and surveillance capitalism, has influenced public and academic libraries’. Chapter 19 completes the book by summarizing the main themes of the book, which will have a bearing on the future directions of digital information provision, access, and management. Through presentation of the Delphi material and thought pieces, plus additional commentary, the chapter provides tools with which service leaders can update their knowledge and influence and shape the debate.

We hope you enjoy this book. We anticipate the content and the message to have relevance and scope for a diverse but focused readership of a perhaps unsurprisingly large number of professional groups.

## Descriptive variety in human communication

When we think of digital information, we most often think of it as textual, as opposed to numerical or visual. Textual information falls into the category of written language as distinct from spoken, or its nonspoken correlate, signed language. While writing and speech are different forms of language, they both share the attribute of being characterized by variation. When I was a student of Linguistics in the 1990s in the United Kingdom, variation was the dominant paradigm that covered all the branches of the discipline including phonetics, phonology, syntax, grammar, semantics, pragmatics, and the interdisciplinary subjects such as psycholinguistics and sociolinguistics. Looking back, this educational paradigm was political; you did not consider any variety of anything to be superior or more worthy of study than any other—every variant has equal value and status. There is more than one way of saying the ‘same’ thing; variety is everything (but what does it signify?) and we conduct our research to find out if its outputs are categorical or gradient in nature. Even standard English or its spoken equivalent, Received Pronunciation, was just another variety, albeit with special characteristics to do with it being a standard form.

A major source of variation in spoken language is the pronunciation and dialect variation that represent a region. Written language has less recourse to this and is more restricted being standardized in its grammar, organization, and vocabulary. Having said that, the linguistic variables used in both spoken and written dialects are correlated with social variables such as age, ethnicity, class, and gender of the writer or speaker. Another form of variation in written language is that it can be handwritten or typed. Written language that is typed betrays much less of the person behind the keyboard than the person behind a quill pen and much less still than someone speaking that language. Or does it? With the rise in digital information will we lose an enormous amount of descriptive variety in human communication? In one way, yes, but perhaps not in the sense that we have the technology to record and preserve a great sample of human experience like never before in the form of digital text.

Consider that we also preserve variety in the use of *register* in typed language—varieties determined by the particular purpose or formality of the social context of use. Contrasting registers are evident in this book, notably between a formal academic register adopted in the chapters and the more informal, although 'consultative' register used in the thought pieces and the Delphi commentary.

**Lucy Ellis**
University of Exeter, Exeter, United Kingdom
**David Baker**
David Baker Consulting,
davidbakerconsulting.co.uk

## Reference

Baker, D., 2004. The Strategic Management of Technology: A Guide for Library and Information Services. Chandos, Oxford.

# Contributors

**Mai Aggerbeck** VIA Library, VIA University College, Aarhus, Denmark

**Stephen Akintunde** University of Jos Library, Jos, Nigeria

**Huw Alexander** textBOX Digital Ltd

**Otmane Azeroual** German Institute for Higher Education Research and Science Studies (DZHW), Berlin, Germany

**David Baker** Plymouth Marjon University, Plymouth, United Kingdom; David Baker Consulting, davidbakerconsulting.co.uk

**Emma Bond** University of Suffolk, Ipswich, United Kingdom

**Ellen Buck** University of Suffolk, Ipswich, United Kingdom

**Agustí Canals** Catalonia Open University, Barcelona, Spain

**Karen Carden** University of the Arts London, London, United Kingdom

**Diana L.H. Chan** Hong Kong University of Science and Technology, Kowloon, Hong Kong

**Josep Cobarsí** Catalonia Open University, Barcelona, Spain

**Lynn Silipigni Connaway** Director, Library Trends and User Research, OCLC Research, Dublin, OH, United States

**Mark Dahl** Aubrey R. Watzek Library, Lewis & Clark College, Portland, OR, United States

**Lucy Ellis** David Baker Consulting, davidbakerconsulting.co.uk; University of Exeter, Exeter, United Kingdom

**Martin Hamilton** Principal at martinh.net, Digital Innovation Consultancy

**Anja T. Ingwersen** VIA Library, VIA University College, Aarhus, Denmark

**Carl Gustav Johannsen** University of Copenhagen, Copenhagen, Denmark

**Juan D. Machin-Mastromatteo** Autonomous University of Chihuahua, Chihuahua, Mexico

**Maja Maricevic** The British Library, London, United Kingdom

**Alistair McNaught** McNaught Consultancy Ltd

**Katarina Michnik** University of Borås, Borås, Sweden

**Valentini Moniarou-Papaconstantinou** University of West Attica, Athens, Greece

**Matthew Naughtin** San Francisco Ballet, San Francisco, CA, United States

**Signe Nielsen** VIA Library, VIA University College, Aarhus, Denmark

**Catherine O'Connor** Leeds Trinity University, Leeds, United Kingdom

**Eva Ortoll** Catalonia Open University, Barcelona, Spain

**Andy Phippen** Bournemouth University, Bournemouth, United Kingdom

**Flora Roumpani** The Alan Turing Institute, London, United Kingdom

**Joachim Schöpfel** GERiiCO Laboratory, University of Lille, Lille, France

**Daniella LaShaun Smith** University of North Texas, Denton, TX, United States

**Evgenia Vasilakaki** National Library of Greece, Athens, Greece

**Alan Wilson** The Alan Turing Institute, London, United Kingdom

**Gabrielle K.W. Wong** Hong Kong University of Science and Technology, Kowloon, Hong Kong

**Sayeda Zain** Mont Rose College, London, United Kingdom

# Author Biographies

**Mai Aggerbeck** is a Contact Librarian at VIA Library and is associated with the Health Education in VIA University College. Since 2002, she has been teaching information literacy in the following Health Education programmes: Nursing Therapy and Occupational Therapy. Additionally, she has been teaching PhD students in systematic mapping of a research area combined with publication of research and the issues regarding copyright. From 2020 her area of interest has been the development of the Academic Library, with a special focus on how we can create a better relationship and a greater integration with the educational environment to define new roles and institutional frameworks. This need for re-examination of the library content is based on new learning strategies and new ways to create, collect, and achieve knowledge based on the technological improvement. The result of this can be found in the outcomes of various projects and articles.

**Stephen Akintunde** is Chairman, Nigerian University Libraries Consortium and immediate past University Librarian, University of Jos, Nigeria. He has been a member of the Steering Committee, Supporting Research Community, Association of Commonwealth Universities. He is a reviewer for Information and Learning Science, and Global Knowledge, Memory and Communication. He is a recipient of Outstanding Reviewer in the Emerald Literati Network Awards for Excellence and has published in international journals such as International Information and Library Review, Journal of Librarianship and Information Science, Library Management and African Journal of Academic Librarianship. He has held leadership positions in the Nigerian Library Association and is a member of professional associations such as the American Library Association and the Chartered Institute of Library and Information Professionals.

**Huw Alexander** is the Managing Director of textBOX, a specialist image description company. Huw has worked in the publishing industry for more than 20 years. His passion for promoting accessibility has developed over the last decade through listening to the stories and issues of users and content providers. textBOX was launched in 2018 and he now describes things for a living.

**Otmane Azeroual** is a researcher at the German Institute for Higher Education Research and Science Studies (DZHW) in Berlin, Germany. After studying Business Information Systems at the University of Applied Sciences—HTW Berlin, he is doing his doctorate in Computer Science at the Otto von Guericke University of Magdeburg and at the University of Applied Sciences—HTW Berlin. His areas of research include database systems, information systems, data quality, business intelligence, big data, open data, cloud computing, text data mining, IT security, and Industry 4.0.

**David Baker** was Principal and Chief Executive of what is now Plymouth Marjon University 2003 until 2009, also becoming Professor of Strategic Information Management there in 2006. From 2008 until 2012, he was Deputy Chair of the Joint Information Systems Committee (Jisc). He is Chair of the Board of the Institute for Contemporary Music Performance, Deputy Chair of the Trinity Multi-Academy Trust, Halifax, West Yorkshire and was until recently a member of the Board of Governors of the Universities of Northampton and South Wales. David has written widely in the field of library and information management with 19 monographs (most recently with Chandos Publishing) and with more than 100 articles to his credit. He was also for 4 years Editor of *Information and Learning Sciences* (Emerald). He has spoken at numerous conferences, led workshops and seminars and has undertaken consultancy work in most countries in the European Union, along with work in Ethiopia, Kuwait, Nigeria, South Africa, and the Sudan. He has led a number of large technology-based projects in the LIS sector, both in relation to digital and hybrid library development and content creation for teaching and learning. His other key professional interest and expertise has been in the field of human resources, where he has been active in major national projects.

**Emma Bond** is Director of Research, Head of the Graduate School and Professor of Socio-Technical Research at the University of Suffolk. She has extensive research experience focusing on online risk and vulnerable groups, especially in relation to domestic abuse, revenge pornography, sexual abuse, and image-based abuse. Emma has nearly 20 years of teaching experience on Social Science undergraduate and postgraduate courses and is a Senior Fellow of the Higher Education Academy. Her research on virtual environments, mobile technologies and their risk has attracted much national and international acclaim and she is frequently asked for expert commentary on TV, radio, and print media.

**Ellen Buck** leads the Centre for Excellence in Learning and Teaching, and the Department of Library and Learning Services at the University of Suffolk. Ellen is responsible for implementing the University's Learning, Teaching and Assessment strategy, which includes the development and delivery of progressive learning models, and curricula which are inclusive in design, research informed, and employer engaged. This includes the provision of support, guidance, and a range of blended CPD activities. Ellen began her career as a professional librarian in the civil service before moving into the Higher Education sector. She has extensive leadership experience and has overseen several transformational projects for the University including the review and procurement of the institutional Online Learning Environment and the delivery of new blended learning degree apprenticeships, as part of the HEFCE Development Fund project.

**Agustí Canals** is Associate Professor at the Universitat Oberta de Catalunya in Barcelona, where he is serving as Academic Director of the MSc in Strategic Management of Information and Knowledge in Organizations and leads the KIMO Research Group on Knowledge and Information Management in Organizations. He is also Senior Research Fellow at the I-Space Institute (Philadelphia). He received his MBA and his PhD in Management Sciences from the ESADE Business School and an MSc in Physics from the Universitat Autònoma de Barcelona. He has also held visiting research positions at the Warwick Business School (University of Warwick), at the Wharton School (University of Pennsylvania), and at the Saïd Business School (University of Oxford). His research and professional interests are in the areas of strategic knowledge management, information management, innovation, social networks, and complexity. He has published many research articles in academic journals and several books and book chapters.

**Karen Carden** currently works for the University of the Arts London (UAL) Library Services as Resources & Systems Manager. She manages a team of people who provide centralized library systems and resource procurement alongside technical, bibliographic, and electronic information and accessibility support to all six of our college libraries. She sits on the departmental management team and have a functional responsibility across the service for collections. Prior to this she worked in libraries for almost 15 years. Most of these years were in academic libraries in both pre- and post-1992 institutions—mostly in London. She has been involved in consortia and joint consortia tendering exercises for library-related products and services. Her professional interests include: radio frequency identification (RFID—technical standards and privacy in particular), shared services in higher education, library performance evaluation and measurement, library management systems (proprietary and open source), supply chain efficiency, supplier relations, and resource discovery and systems approaches in libraries.

**Diana L.H. Chan** has been the University Librarian at the Hong Kong University of Science & Technology (HKUST) since 2012. She started her library work in United States and Canada. She received her BBA at the Chinese University of Hong Kong and MLS from San Jose State University. Ms. Chan has published a 3-volume book, 3 book chapters, 14 journal papers, and presented 50 conference papers on various library topics, including strategic management, staff development, space development, Learning Commons, institutional repository, digital libraries, consortia collection development, demand-driven acquisitions, information literacy, research support service, shared ILS, etc. She has served as Chair of JULAC (Joint University Librarians Advisory Committee in Hong Kong) in 2015/16, also in the JULAC Access Services Committee, JULAC Consortiall Committee, Hong Kong Monographic Acquisitions Committee, Hong Kong Public Libraries Advisory Committee, Guangdong Higher Education Library Committee, Hong Kong Library Association, and many university-wide committees.

**Josep Cobarsí** holds a Bachelor's in Telecommunications Engineering and a PhD in Organizations Management. He is Associate Professor of Computer Science, Multimedia and Telecommunication Studies at Universitat Oberta de Catalunya (online university with headquarters in Barcelona, Spain). He was director of the Information Science degree at UOC. He is a researcher at Knowledge and Information Management in Organizations group at UOC. He is UOC representative at Information Schools academic network and Spain country representative of the Association of Information Science & Technology. He undertakes teaching and research activity about digital behaviour, information systems, and disaster management and data science.

**Lynn S. Connaway** is Director of Library Trends and User Research at OCLC Research. She is Past President of the Association of Information Science & Technology and is the recipient of the ASIS&T 2019 Watson Davis Award. Lynn is the Past Chair of the Association of College and Research Libraries Value of Academic Libraries Committee. She held the Chair of Excellence, Departmento de Biblioteconomía y Documentación, Universidad Carlos III de Madrid, was a Visiting Researcher in the Department of Information Studies, University of Sheffield, and Visiting Scholar at the Royal School of Library and Information Science, Denmark. Connaway has received research funding from the IMLS, Jisc, and the Arts and Humanities Research Council. She is coauthor of the 4th and 5th editions of *Basic Research Methods for Librarians* and of the 6th edition, *Research Methods in Library and Information Science*.

**Mark Dahl** is director of the Aubrey R. Watzek Library at Lewis & Clark College in Portland, Oregon. After completing graduate work at the University of Wisconsin, Madison, he began his professional career in libraries in 1998 as a systems and technical services librarian at Central Oregon Community College. He moved to Lewis & Clark College in 2001, where he established the digital initiatives programme and gradually took on greater administrative responsibilities, becoming director in 2012. His interests in the field include digital projects, data services, library space, consortia, library collections, and the changing role of the liberal arts college library. In October 2019, he served as a Fulbright Specialist for strategic planning for the National Library of Kosovo.

**Lucy Ellis** is an Associate of David Baker Consulting and Honorary Research Fellow for the College of Humanities at Exeter University. She is currently working as a consultant in higher education. Her background is as a lecturer, research scientist, and project development consultant. Following a PhD in Instrumental Phonetics in 2000, she worked as a senior lecturer at Plymouth Marjon University on the BSc (Hons) Speech and Language Therapy and the BA (Hons) English Language & Linguistics programme, where she became Programme Leader for BA Human Communication. She was chief investigator and project manager for a National Institute for Health Research (NIHR) study in the speech production strategies of deaf children. She is a reviewer for Information and Learning Sciences (Emerald), Journal of British Institute of Organ Studies, British Academy grants scheme and for the publisher Palgrave. She has been a PhD external examiner and an external assessor for university curriculum approval.

**Martin Hamilton** is a widely published writer, public speaker, strategist, and change agent. His work focuses on helping people and organizations to understand the impact of near future trends and technologies. Martin has worked extensively with senior teams in a wide variety of organizations to help them develop their innovation strategy and supported a large number of start-ups to scale up their business. Martin has worked in and around the intersection of research and industry for some thirty years, doing everything from researching next-generation Internet protocols to running a supercomputer centre.

**Anja T. Ingwersen** is a Contact Librarian at VIA Library and is associated with the Health Education and Educational Programmes in VIA University College. Since

2004, she has been teaching information literacy to students and VIA employees. In addition, she has been working on a variety of projects aimed at supporting learning processes both within IL and other study skills, as well as innovation and entrepreneurship.

**Carl Gustav Johannsen** is Emeritus Professor at the University of Copenhagen. He has written and contributed to more than 20 books and several international articles, conference papers and reports on different public, academic, and special library issues. Recently, he has, in particular, focused on innovative staff design, like the staffless or open public library model and also on the many different roles that the users today play in modern public library environments as clients, citizens, guests, customers, and creative partners. He has also contributed to the library history literature, especially, on special library issues.

**Juan D. Machin-Mastromatteo** is a full-time professor and researcher at the Universidad Autónoma de Chihuahua (UACH) in Mexico and member of the National Researchers System. His qualifications include a PhD in Information and Communication Science, a Master's in Digital Library Learning, and a Bachelor's in Library Science. He has more than 18 years of work experience in archives, libraries, higher education, and professional development. He has excelled in different roles: cataloguer, database developer, reference librarian, instructor, collection developer, designer of library promotion materials and multimedia resources, coordinator of information literacy programmes in higher education institutions, scientific production analyst, consultant, and peer reviewer for scientific journals. His lines of research are: information literacy, action research, evaluation of scientific production and bibliometrics, open access, information architecture, and digital libraries. He has published more than 50 peer-reviewed and indexed articles, five books, 15 book chapters, has presented his papers in more than 54 international conferences, and has facilitated more than 16 workshops for training researchers. He is the Associate Editor for the scientific journal Digital Library Perspectives (Emerald), as well as a member of the editorial boards for The Journal of Academic Librarianship (Elsevier) and for Information Development (SAGE). In the latter journal he has published, since 2015, a regular column Developing Latin America. He is a peer reviewer for 17 scientific and indexed journals within the fields of information science and education, for which he has evaluated more than 150 manuscripts.

**Maja Maricevic** is Head of Higher Education and Science at the British Library, responsible for the development of strategic relationships, policy and partnerships with higher education and science sectors. Maja's research focuses on the research functions in heritage organizations, including libraries—how these organizations support research, how have such functions developed over time, their future and key enabling policies as well as barriers. This also means looking at different aspects of digital research and infrastructures and policies that underpin them. Maja is currently Co-Investigator on the Living with Machines project, a 5-year collaborative project between the Alan Turing Institute and the British Library investigating history of the Industrial Revolution using data-driven approaches. Maja is an Advisory Board

Member for the Arts and Humanities Research Council and a board member of the Knowledge Quarter. She has previously worked in universities, government departments, and as a professional consultant for PricewaterhouseCoopers.

**Alistair McNaught** has spent 20 years as a mainstream teacher committed to developing students' skills and independent learning. This led to early adoption of e-learning, which in turn paved the way for an abiding interest in making teaching and learning content more accessible to more students. Alistair spent 10 years as a senior advisor for TechDis—a national advisory service for technology and disability—followed by four years as an accessibility specialist at Jisc before setting up McNaught Consultancy. He was one of the earliest members of the Publishers Association Accessibility Action Group and has worked for more than 10 years to help suppliers, librarians, disabled students, and assistive technologists understand one another.

**Katarina Michnik** has a PhD in Library and Information Science. The focus of her doctoral thesis is how the social legitimacy of public libraries may be challenged and strengthened in digital contexts. Katarina has a special interest in the role and use of public libraries in digital societies, alongside with an interest in the concept of literacy and information searching, dissemination, and evaluation through different social media. As a part of this interest, she is a member of two research groups at the University of Borås: Libraries, Culture and Society and Social Media Studies.

**Valentini Moniarou-Papaconstantinou** is an Emeritus Professor at the department of Library Science and Information Systems of the Technological Educational Institute of Athens now Department of Archival, Library and Information Studies, University of West Attica, Athens, Greece. She taught information organizations management and collection management and gave lectures on these topics in courses organized by various organizations in Greece. Her research interests include a theorization of changes in the information field and information services management, LIS students' educational choices and their learning careers, as well as the understanding of information technology acceptance by LIS students. She has given talks and presentations at several international conferences and her research publications have appeared in international journals such as *Education for Information, Aslib Journal of Information Management, Library and Information Science Research, New Library World, Library Management, Program, Library Review, and Journal of Librarianship and Information Science.*

**Matthew Naughtin** was born in Omaha, Nebraska in 1947, Matthew Naughtin is a composer, author, violinist, programme annotator, and music librarian. He was awarded a Bachelor's degree in Music Performance in 1970 by Northwestern University in Evanston, Illinois. He then taught and performed in the Chicago area for several years before returning to Omaha in 1977. There he played in the Omaha Symphony Orchestra and served as the Symphony's Music Librarian, Program Annotator, Resident Composer, and Musical Arranger. He was appointed Music Librarian of the San Francisco Ballet in 1997 and now lives and works in San Francisco. He has also served as Music Librarian with the Peninsula Music Festival, Colorado Music Festival, San Francisco Conservatory of Music, San Francisco Symphony, and San Francisco Opera. Matt's original orchestral compositions and arrangements have gained wide recognition, and he has written *Ballet Music: A Handbook*, a reference work on ballet music published by Rowman & Littlefield in 2014.

**Signe Nielsen** is a Contact Librarian at the VIA Library and is associated with the Social Studies programmes at VIA University College (Social Teacher and Social Worker). Since 2004, she has been teaching students information literacy, and additionally PhD students in systematic mapping of a research area combined with publications of research.

**Catherine O'Connor** is Head of the School of Business, Communication and Law at Leeds Trinity University. She is University Lead for Learning, Teaching, and Employability and has led work to engage with employers around labour market issues in Leeds. She has developed a number of projects designed to look at how skills gaps can be addressed and presented on this in both academic and professional forums. Prior to joining Leeds Trinity in 2007, she spent 15 years working in local news media. Her research interests focus on how universities work with both students and employers to address labour market issues and how students can be given a voice as key stakeholders in this agenda.

**Eva Ortoll** is Associate Professor at the Information and Communication Science Department of the Universitat Oberta de Catalunya in Barcelona. She holds a PhD in Information Sciences from Universidad de Zaragoza (Spain). Her research is around: information behaviour, competitive intelligence, and information management. She is member of the KIMO Research Group on Knowledge and Information Management in Organizations. She was director of Information Science Degree at UOC. She was director of the University Health Science Library at Universitat Rovira i Virgili in Spain.

**Andy Phippen** is a Professor of Digital Rights at the Bournemouth University and is a Visiting Professor at the University of Suffolk. He has specialized in the use of ICTs in social contexts and the intersection with legislation for more than 15 years, carrying out a large amount of grass roots research on issues such as attitudes toward privacy and data protection, Internet safety, and contemporary issues such as sexting, peer abuse, and the impact of digital technology on well-being. He has presented written and oral evidence to parliamentary inquiries related to the use of ICTs in society, has widely published in the area, and is a frequent media commentator on these issues.

**Flora Roumpani** is a Research Associate in the Alan Turing Institute (UK's national institute for data sciences and artificial intelligence) and previously a fellow at the British Library, working on urban analytics. She is also a Visiting Lecturer at the Royal College of Art in the Environmental Architecture MSc. She holds a PhD and an MRes from the Centre for Advanced Spatial Analysis in Bartlett UCL and has a diploma on Architecture Engineering from the Department of Architecture in the University of Patras. She has worked as an urban planner in Doxiadis Associates, for the design and analysis of cities in Greece and abroad and she is a registered architect in the United Kingdom. Her areas of expertise include urban analytics and simulations in 3D environments, spatial analysis and visualization, and urban-regional planning and design. Areas of interest also include projects involving creative technology, public engagement, and exhibitions.

**Joachim Schöpfel** is Associate Professor in Information Sciences at the University of Lille, France, and researcher at the GERiiCO laboratory. He is consultant in scientific communication at the Ourouk Consulting Bureau, Paris. His research field is scientific information and academic publishing, research data, and open science.

**Daniella Smith** is an Associate Professor in the Department of Information Science at the University of North Texas. She has been a faculty member since 2010 and is the current Associate Director of the Information Science PhD programme. She is the author of the book *Growing Your Library Career with Social Media* from Chandos Publishing (2018).

**Evgenia Vasilakaki** is a Project Manager at National Library of Greece. She was awarded a doctoral degree in May 2011 from the Department of Information & Communications at Manchester Metropolitan University, Manchester, UK on Multilingual Information Retrieval and Users' Information Seeking Behaviour. Over the last 10 years she has taken part in research projects in various contexts (i.e. business administration, public/private sector, cultural heritage, and refugee crisis); ranging from national (i.e. THALIS DOC-CULTURE, Consultant to Greek Ministry of Education) to European level (i.e. CrossCult H2020, Erasmus + Lib(e)ro, Europeana 'Rise of Literacy'), in different positions (i.e. member, coordinator, team and working package leader, deputy to management board) and responsibilities. Her research interests lie on information seeking behaviour, LIS roles and information services offered, information literacy, multilingual information retrieval, and access. She has published in international peer-reviewed journals, namely: *Library and Information Science Research, New Library World, Library Management, Program, Library Review*.

**Alan Wilson FBA, FRS** is Director, Special Projects at The Alan Turing Institute (Chief Executive, 2016–2018). Until recently, he was Executive Chair of the Ada Lovelace Institute and Chair of the Home Office Science Advisory Council. In his research, as a mathematician and geographer, he works on the science of cities, building computer models that have applications in both planning and commercial sectors. He was Professor of Urban and Regional Systems in CASA, UCL from 2007 to 2018. He was Vice Chancellor of the University of Leeds from 1991 to 2004 when he became Director-General for Higher Education in the then DfES. From 2007 to 2013, he was Chair of the Arts and Humanities Research Council and from 2013 to 2015 of the Government Office for Science Foresight Project on The Future of Cities. He is a fellow of the British Academy and of the Royal Society. He was knighted in 2001 for services to higher education.

**Gabrielle Wong** is the Head of Research Support Services at the Hong Kong University of Science and Technology Library (HKUST Library). Before taking the current position, she was responsible for managing teaching and learning space, including the Learning Commons in HKUST Library. She is active in research, with interests covering information literacy teaching, instructional design, intellectual development, and communication skills. Her publications span over these topics as well as learning space assessment and library services for research support. She is also an EdD candidate. Her thesis topic is leadership development of academic librarians. In this area, she has published three journal papers, including a literature review, a case study, and a conceptual paper. Gabi obtained a BSc at the University of Hong Kong, and her MLIS at McGill University, Canada.

**Sayeda Zain** has been working in higher education for more than 20 years. She worked for the British Council in Pakistan for 7 years as a UK Education Manager. She is currently working as Dean of Studies at Mont Rose College of Management & Sciences in London. She has four Master's degrees: PGCert Learning and Teaching from Anglia Ruskin University UK, 2019; MSc International Management from University of Wales Newport UK, 2008; MSc Strategic Human Resources Management from University of Glamorgan, UK, 2007; and MBA from Al-Hajvery College of Business Administration, 1994. She has Level 8 qualifications in Strategic Direction and Leadership from the Chartered Management Institute and is also a Fellow of Advance HE. She recently completed a High Impact Leadership course from the University of Cambridge Institute for Sustainability Leadership. She is a member of the Mont Rose College Board of Governors and the Academic/Quality Assurance Board. She initiated the formation of the College Research Centre and the associated research journal, published biannually since 2015.

# Acknowledgments

The editors are especially grateful to all who made this book possible: the authors of the chapters for their contributions and their enthusiasm for the project; to all those who contributed Thought Pieces, to Kathleen Yoell, Zachary Smith, and to the Delphi Panellists: Stephen Akintunde, Chris Batt, Eileen Breen, Paul Kelsey, Sara Marsh, Hannah Myers, Tatiana Sanches, Claire Sewell, and Tim Wales.

We would also like to thank Glyn Jones for his support in establishing the book proposal and to Michelle Fisher, Chiara Giglio, Surya Narayanan Jayachandran, and Sheela Josy at Elsevier for their help in the preparation and production of the book.

**David Baker**
**Lucy Ellis**

# Abbreviations

| | |
|---|---|
| **ACRL** | Association of College and Research Libraries |
| **AI** | artificial intelligence |
| **AIED** | AI in Education |
| **AKABER** | academic reporting |
| **ANT** | actor network theory |
| **APA** | American Psychological Association |
| **API** | application programming interfaces |
| **APPG** | All-Party Parliamentary Group |
| **AR** | augmented reality |
| **ARA** | Archives and Records Association |
| **ASAs** | Academic Skills Advisors |
| **ASPIRE** | Accessibility Statements Promoting Improved Reader Experiences |
| **AUSSE** | Australian Survey of Student Engagement |
| **BBC** | British Broadcasting Corporation |
| **BESA** | British Educational Suppliers Association |
| **CASRAI** | Consortia Advancing Standards in Research Administration Information |
| **CERIF** | Common European Research Information Format |
| **CILIP** | Chartered Institute of Library and Information Professionals |
| **CIPFA** | Chartered Institute of Public Finance and Accountancy |
| **CLAIT** | Computer Literacy and Information Technology |
| **CMU** | Carnegie Mellon University |
| **COVID-19** | coronavirus disease 2019 |
| **CRIS** | current research information systems |
| **DAI** | Digital Author Identification |
| **DAW** | digital audio workstation |
| **DCC** | Data Curation Centre |
| **DCMS** | Department for Digital, Culture, Media and Sport |
| **DDA** | demand-driven acquisitions |
| **DEAH** | Doctorate in Education, Arts, and Humanities |
| **DH** | digital humanities |
| **DL** | digital literacy |
| **DMP** | data management platform |
| **ECTS** | European Credit Transfer and Accumulation Scheme |
| **EDI** | electronic data interchange |
| **EPUB** | electronic publication |
| **ETL** | extract, transform, load |

| | |
|---|---|
| **EUNIS** | European University Information Systems organization |
| **FAANG** | Facebook, Apple, Amazon, Netflix, and Google |
| **FAIR** | Findable, Accessible, Interoperable, Reusable |
| **FE** | further education |
| **FTE** | full-time equivalent |
| **GDS** | Government Digital Services |
| **GIS** | geographic information system |
| **GO-Science** | Government Office for Science |
| **HAL** | Hyper Articles en Ligne |
| **HE** | higher education |
| **HEFCE** | Higher Education Funding Council |
| **HEI** | Higher Education Institution |
| **HEPI** | Higher Education Policy Institute |
| **HKUST** | Hong Kong University of Science and Technology |
| **ICD** | Information Culture Development |
| **ICPSR** | Inter-University Consortium for Political and Social Research |
| **ICR** | InterCoder Reliability |
| **ICT/s** | Information and Communications Technology/ies |
| **IFLA** | International Federation of Library Associations |
| **IFTTT** | if this then that |
| **IL** | information literacy |
| **ILDLs** | Information and Learning Development Librarians |
| **IMSLP** | International Music Score Library Project |
| **IOC** | International Olympic Committee |
| **IR** | Institutional Repositories |
| **IT** | Information Technology |
| **JISC** | Joint Information Systems Committee |
| **JSTOR** | Journal Storage |
| **LA** | local authority |
| **LEO** | Longitudinal Education Outcomes |
| **LGBT** | lesbian, gay, bisexual, and transgender |
| **LIS** | Library and Information Science |
| **LL** | learning literacy |
| **LMS** | Library Management System |
| **LTU** | Leeds Trinity University |
| **MIE** | Master in Educational Innovation |
| **MIT** | Massachusetts Institute of Technology |
| **MOLA** | Major Orchestra Librarians' Association |
| **MOOC** | Massive Online Open Course |
| **MP** | Member of Parliament |
| **NARCIS** | National Academic Research and Collaborations Information System |
| **NTU** | Nanyang Technology University |
| **NUC** | National Universities Commission |
| **OA** | Open Access |
| **OA** | Output Area |
| **OAI-PMH** | Open Archives Initiative Protocol for Metadata Harvesting |

| | |
|---|---|
| **OCLC** | Online Computer Library Center |
| **OECD** | Organization for Economic Cooperation and Development |
| **OER** | Open Educational Resources |
| **OfS** | Office for Students |
| **OLE** | Online Learning Environments |
| **ONS** | Office for National Statistics, UK |
| **OS** | Ordnance Survey |
| **PCs** | personal computers |
| **PDF** | Portable Document Format |
| **PISA** | Programme for International Student Assessment |
| **PLN** | Personal Learning Network |
| **PRC** | Portal de la Recerca de Catalunya |
| **QAA** | Quality Assurance Agency |
| **RCD/KDSF** | German Research Core Dataset |
| **RDM** | Research Data Management |
| **RDS** | Research Data Services |
| **RFID** | radio frequency identification |
| **RGC** | Research Grant Council |
| **RQ** | research questions |
| **RSS** | Really Simple Syndication |
| **RUSA** | Reference and User Services Association |
| **SCONUL** | Society of College, National and University Libraries |
| **SIM** | spatial interaction model |
| **SM** | social media |
| **SNS** | social networking sites |
| **SOM** | Society, Opinion and Media |
| **SPSS** | Statistical Package for the Social Sciences |
| **SSRN** | Social Science Research Network |
| **STEM** | Science, Technology, Engineering, and Mathematics |
| **SUPC** | Southern Universities Purchasing Consortium |
| **SWOT** | Strengths, Weaknesses, Opportunities, and Threats |
| **TAM** | Technology Acceptance Model |
| **TDD** | Telecommunications Device for the Deaf |
| **TEF** | teaching excellence framework |
| **TPACK** | Technological Pedagogical Content Knowledge |
| **TTY** | teletypewriter |
| **UAL** | University of the Arts London |
| **UN** | United Nations |
| **UNESCO** | United Nations Educational, Scientific, and Cultural Organization |
| **UOC** | Universitat Oberta de Catalunya |
| **URL** | Uniform Resource Locator |
| **VAT** | value added tax |
| **VIVE** | The Danish Centre for Social Science and Research |
| **VLE** | virtual learning environment |
| **VR** | virtual reality |
| **ZORA** | Zurich Open Repository and Archive |

# Future directions in digital information: Scenarios and themes

# 1

*David Baker*[a,b] *and Lucy Ellis*[b,c]
[a]Plymouth Marjon University, Plymouth, United Kingdom, [b]David Baker Consulting, davidbakerconsulting.co.uk, [c]University of Exeter, Exeter, United Kingdom

## 1.1 Introduction

In his foreword to the last *Digital Information Review*, Nick Poole (Poole, in Baker and Evans, 2016, p. xvii) wrote that, while *Digital Information Strategies: From Applications and Content to Libraries and People* was a book about the future, the origins of the disruptions which it described were rooted in the past. This first chapter, then, aims to summarize and analyze the present state of the art, and the origins, of digital information provision. It does this by synthesizing Chapters 2–18. Chapter 19 is a summation of the themes discussed and explored throughout *Future Directions in Digital Information: Predictions, Practice, and Participation.* Both chapters are underpinned by the results of the Delphi exercise that David Baker undertook and the thought pieces that he and Lucy Ellis commissioned. This material always appears in text boxes. Where there is no attribution, the text is a synthesis of the Delphi participants' responses; otherwise, the content is an authored thought piece.

## 1.2 COVID-19

The world is already much changed from when *Future Directions in Digital information* was first conceived and contracts signed. It will no doubt be further transformed before the Coronavirus epidemic is a memory; or rather a whole series of memories that will need to be preserved for the future. As far as possible the current and likely future impacts of COVID-19 are discussed: longer-term implications are considered in the last chapter; emerging trends (as far as they can be discerned) are referred to in this chapter. It has long been a self-evident truth that 'the more things change, the more they can never be the same' (Allan Veaner, quoted in Baker, 2017, p. 2). The present global crisis confirms this, as further considered in Chapter 19.

### Public memory

While academic biographies and fictional books in contemporary settings will offer future generations some idea about life in our era, it is the general public—which naturally includes library

**Future Directions in Digital Information. https://doi.org/10.1016/B978-0-12-822144-0.00001-X**

users—having lived through the reality of the situation, that is an invaluable source of data. Several projects, such as the Mass Observation Archive which is part of the University of Sussex's Special Collections, have already implemented this notion: collecting diaries, written memories, and photographs from participants, for posterity.

Different generations have different views and have undergone different experiences. Those who lived through the Second World War, for example, will have had a different childhood from the current youth; even with the COVID-19 pandemic bringing about government measures unseen since that earlier era. People of a similar age living in different areas and economic zones will have greatly varying experiences from one another.

By interacting with the public through workshops, interviews and other memory gathering projects, libraries and education bodies will help ensure this 'lived' data is not lost forever with the passage of time.

***Hannah Myers***
**Walker Morris, Leeds, United Kingdom**

## 1.3 Environments and ecosystems; digital disruption and paradigm shifts

Vitality, unpredictability, rapidity; instability, turbulence: words that describe the environment in which digital information is being provided, managed, stored accessed, applied, and exploited. All the evidence points to this being true regardless of Coronavirus, both now and for the foreseeable future. 'Digital ecosystems evolve organically… like any ecosystem, this can result in unplanned complexity' (Chapter 5). As Mark Dahl writes in Chapter 10, 'over a quarter century since the advent of the World Wide Web… libraries remain in a state of transformation', not least because, while much of the engagement with information—across all sectors and every part of the globe—is primarily online, as discussed in Chapter 3, we are dealing with 'a highly complex and complicated network of people, things, devices, software and digital content and activity, carried out within rapidly changing socio-political, technical and cultural contexts', which, according to Mark Hamilton (Chapter 15) are likely to be driven especially by digital disruption, climate change impacts and tensions between national and global trends.

Schöpfel and Azeroual's chapter talks of the 'fourth paradigm': 'data-intensive scientific discovery, a new way of doing science based on information and communication technology'. They and others argue that the interdisciplinary nature of education necessitates new paradigms. Will there be 'Education 4.0' as a result of the Fourth Industrial Revolution, discussed later in this book? While Martin Hamilton (Chapter 15) rightly advises caution when it comes to technologies that are at the 'peak of the hype cycle', there is little doubt—as evinced by the chapters, thought pieces and Delphi responses—that there will be disruption if not an outright revolution in library and information provision in the coming years, not least because societies themselves will be subject to rapid and radical change.

Society will be open to disruption in social relationships as technology is, apparently, more socially disruptive than previously thought, leading to changes in the traditional systems of kinship. Technology has great power to increase socialization, albeit in new ways, rather than breaking it down. Websites allow you to share thoughts and hobbies with people across the globe. Social media are playing a significant role in enabling families and friends to stay closely in touch. People would feel much more isolated without the various video and audio channels now freely available to communicate. There will be more mobility, more distance communication, more knowledge between cultures, greater collaboration in commerce and industry, more optimization in research and potentialization of new discoveries.

Society's needs change and develop over time, so the library's objectives need to be revisited and reflected on periodically to ensure they are still valid and workable. The challenge comes when the library wants to collaborate and offer a service for all (economies of scale, increase access to information), while the parent institution is in competition with others and needs the library to contribute to giving the parent institution an edge over others.

Chapter 8 focuses on the major area of distance education and online information behaviour. As Eva Ortoll and colleagues point out, remote learning demands ubiquitous access to digital information resources and, if done well, improving users' digital empowerment in the process. The Digital Visitors and Residents conceptual framework is used 'to explain how people deal with technologies and the digital environment and why... according to this framework, digital behaviour can take place in a resident or a visitor mode. Individuals with a visitor mode of engagement use technology and information in a functional way, as a tool, to solve a problem without leaving a trace of their actions. In contrast, individuals with a resident mode of engagement see technology, the Internet and digital information as a way of life'. Chapters 9 and 11 reinforce this latter concept, with reference to the development and adoption of mobile learning, the use of games and social media in education and training at all levels as a means 'of distilling new knowledge and/or making sure this knowledge is understood and thus used by the learners'.

## Games and education

Video games have often been decried as the 'enemy' of learning: a distraction for children and teenagers, taking them away from homework and leading them to stare at a screen for minutes or hours at a time. Yet the appealing mechanics of video games, that addictive element that brings players back for more, is being implemented by educational apps to lure in learners. Education itself is being 'gamified'.

One example is the language learning app, Duolingo. As an educational tool, it breaks down several languages into bite-sized lessons that are easy to work through, utilize your phone's microphone and auditory technology to test speaking and listening in addition to reading and writing (or rather, typing). However, to help players form a daily studying habit, game elements are added. The app keeps track of how many days in a row you study: your 'streak'. You are enrolled in leagues, with the chance of progression if you earn enough points through your studies. Players earn treasure for meeting goals, which can be spent on rewards such as a 'streak freeze', little outfits for the app's mascot, or even wagered against yourself that you'll maintain your current streak for so many days. These additions elevate the app beyond being a simple electronic workbook. They make learning more fun and encourage you to push yourself that little bit harder: to take an extra lesson to reap the rewards. Ultimately, this reward is both increased knowledge of a language as well as the game-style bonuses, justifying their existence. Even mainstream video games on other platforms offer educational potential. Minecraft, the immensely popular world builder often talked about in school playgrounds, can be used to teach the coding language Python, opportunity libraries have seized by offering workshops. The game offers a familiar, recognizable environment for children to learn this new skill, taking away the pressure of the classroom and encouraging learning through enjoyment. With the video game market unlikely to fade away any time soon, librarians and educators should continue to explore their appealing elements to benefit their learning activities.

***Hannah Myers***
**Walker Morris, Leeds, United Kingdom**

Digital and social media have already had an impact on organizational priorities and behaviours. Until now they have tended to be adjuncts to traditional roles and expectations. Institutions of all types of managing and disclosing information for users have on the one hand to maintain, protect, and develop their collections and be accountable for their actions. Given the increasing user expectation that 'anywhere, anytime' is the default position, organizations will have to review how they balance priorities between the physical and the virtual.

## 1.4 Collections and services

It has long been clear (Baker, 2004) that the Internet, and pervasive connectivity to it, is responsible for the complete and irrevocable transformation of whole industries. Education, in all its forms, levels and sectors, is being changed—though not yet out of all recognition—by information and communications technology—though, as many of the authors in this book comment, there is limited time for library and information services to prepare for the future, let alone to shape it. Chapter 10 stresses that 'the library's role as gateway to information through its discovery service, research databases, and reference tools has been disrupted by search engines for well over a decade. The library's role as provider of scholarly information through book and journal collections is being challenged by openly accessible information resources on the Internet… [users] can begin their research on [the Internet] and often click through to sources to complete it without ever touching their… library'. As a result, libraries must 'embrace the messy, multifaceted information ecosystem in which they find themselves', as Dahl urges, in order to ensure that they continue to have a vital role and influence over developments.

Libraries and information services need to constantly review their priorities and be prepared to stop or pause them as context changes. Sometimes structures must change to better adapt and modernize. To be sustainable, libraries must find a way to be critical to their broader institutions. The priority is always dependent upon the perceived needs of the user and supporting institutions. Solutions and change will need to be directed at a wide audience, regardless of collections or other traditional services. There will be a need for a new approach to change management, whether short-term or strategic. In the past, libraries and information services could not radically change their service propositions without putting at risk existing priorities or the integrity of their major asset—the collection. The result is a style of change management that has been called *technical rationality*, where a problem is defined, and a technical solution developed. That approach will not work so well if there is a recognition that each individual problem must fit into a wider context of activities in other institutions, plus greater engagement to produce solutions that are able to maximize the benefit to the widest possible audiences.

To maintain and increase the relevance of library and information services, there will need to be a fundamental reappraisal of service priorities and approaches to collections management and delivery. Service innovation will have to begin with a close study of audience trends and engage users in the design and creation of new services. The engagement of users in the design and introduction of innovation will be a constant need because of the need for service 'consumption'. Digital is now becoming 'first' with the traditional as an adjunct. Academic libraries have made a significant shift towards online content while maintaining print collections because they continue to be valued by users. Access will replace the concept of building and maintaining collections and will become the Gold Standard for libraries and other providers. Point of demand access and service to constituents will be more important than traditional research and building and preserving traditional collections.

Only online publication will become the norm for academic publications, with print on demand as a secondary option. This will have an impact on both the physical library space and the services and training that are offered to library users. It will place a demand on library managers to provide more access services such as devices and spaces for digital resources rather than shelf space. Libraries should be able to innovate and put that free space to good use, offering specialist spots such as quiet study zones or creative areas. We will continue to see more electronic information for point of demand needs, but print will not disappear. We will still see print books being published and purchased by libraries. Many users still prefer print, especially in public libraries. Print books offer an aesthetic element, and both older and younger users still like to read books.

---

Libraries are fast moving to digital-first if not digital-only. This is certainly the case in academic libraries in the western world and, increasingly, second and third world countries. E-journals and e-books have replaced hard-copy collections in many subject areas; their many advantages—and their occasional disadvantages—are discussed later in this book. The move from print to digital can only hasten in the light of the 2020 pandemic and its likely aftermath. Where print collections remain part of core provision, their existence and value will require justification, alongside any other services and content offered.

---

The current COVID-19 pandemic is already acting as a catalyst for change in forcing remote use of online library resources at the expense of inaccessible print resources. This may, in turn, lead to a radical cull of print collections as senior managers start to question (much sooner than predicted) the need for print holdings and associated infrastructure at their institutions in the light of actual online assessment experiences in 2020 with only a few designated national or research libraries retaining hard copies for the benefit of the nation.

Access and use of digital content will become the norm and library services will be digitally enabled because of the increased use of technology by users. Physical library collections will become more archival because of the availability and preference for digital content. Library services will continue to evolve, even in a digital environment. People will still visit libraries to study and to socialize, and the public library will continue to be a gathering place for recreational needs. Academic libraries will remain places for students to study, even though on-demand access to digital information will be the premium service. There will always be the need for professional skills to manage the digital collections and to review and revise services to ensure that they are truly focussed around user need and are trusted.

Libraries will have to work harder than ever before to develop services and add value to their traditional product—print and digital resources—perhaps through increased curation of specialist resources. Although access will be easier, users could be overwhelmed by choice and the librarian will work to connect the right user with the right resource. The unknown is whether the interface will remain mainly human in a fixed location or the human skills will be embedded in the delivery interface. E-books should be praised for their adaptive qualities: they can be made far easier to read for those with disabilities or learning difficulties.

## 1.5 Users, usage, e-valuation

Today's users are those who traditionally use the library—students at all levels working on assignments/qualifications, independent researchers looking for more in-depth materials and academics who are preparing classes or carrying out research. This user group will expand to include more casual users who would not normally think about using a library: life-long learners, commuters, transfers. Library services, both physical and digital, will be used by a general public who want to check the latest research for themselves, carry out their own research and read up around issues that are part of the public consciousness/news. Many of these users will not know that they are accessing library services as resources move increasingly online and access becomes more seamless.

Expectations are manifested in a significant shift by users from *hunter/gatherer*, searching for information, for whatever need, in a variety of physical entities, towards the *harvester*, expecting to find all they need from the convenience of their networked device. People who lack research skills or familiarity with library systems and have a reliance on search engines become harvesters almost by default. Often, what they want is the hunter's ability to pin down one vital piece of information in a quicker, more efficient way.

Every edition of *Digital Information Reviews* has used phrases such as 'the Google generation', generations X and Y, millennials, 'digital immigrants', and 'digital natives' as a way of categorizing types of user and their particular backgrounds and needs. A number of authors in this book regard such conceptualizations as unhelpful, in that they oversimplify reality. Several authors in this book argue that real life is far more complicated and are able to cite numerous case studies and examples to demonstrate that. And yet, in some instances, notably in the case of Stephen Akintunde's Africa, the basic tensions between those who were 'born digital' and the older generations for whom technology has had to be embraced later in life, give a validity to such a simple divide and meaning to the concomitant cultural implications, which are still being worked through. What is interesting about modern-day users of all kinds, is the increasing shift, as noted in the text box above, from hunter/gatherer to harvester of information.

More usage data exists than ever before, and the science of bibliometrics continues to develop, as evinced by discussions in this book. Andy Phippen and colleagues (Chapter 3) discuss the realities and the possibilities for analytics in the context of learning delivery in a digital landscape; Carl Gustav Johanssen argues in Chapter 18 that, at a time when 'surveillance capitalism' is a growing trend, library and information services should 'take care that its use of all kinds of user data from transactions and from other sources should be transparent to its users'. But he also suggests that library professionals might be able to turn such approaches to advantage for the benefit of their users.

---

A 'now' assessment is needed to understand user needs and behaviours and to track trends and changes in user demand. In terms of how that takes place, there will be a need to consider the changing priorities for the parent institution(s), influenced both by institutional needs and the wider policy framework set by the government. Some institutions will have a body of potential users within the institution itself—school, university, for example, whereas others will have wider less-defined audiences—public museums, public libraries, archives, and record offices. Whereas research on information seeking behaviour can assist in projecting user needs, institutional library and information services will be localized and may not give value for money. A more global understanding of discoverability and access to information will attract more digitally savvy users.

Policy frameworks for future research management must be considered. At the present time, there are only small levels of collaboration to find solutions that might offer service improvements across all or a cadre of institutions. Where technical innovation does take place, it may well have little impact on similar organizations elsewhere. Given increasing user expectation that 'everything' should be accessible anytime, anywhere—the shift from hunter/gatherer to harvester—there will need to be policy frameworks in place to ensure that research and innovation deliver maximum value through co-operation and co-ordination.

Integrated use of learning analytics will be commonplace as all library support and content is likely to be digital and the value of library interactions can, therefore, be measured at every stage of the student journey. This will be relevant to the academic/education sector but will not be directly transferrable to other forms of publicly funded collection institutions. Libraries need to ensure they are listening to users and monitoring statistics to ensure funding and time is being spent on the most used and useful services. It is important to be clear about value-added, such as what did the library do versus what the user could do independently: Collect, organize, present, mediate, pay for content; provide user education/digital literacy, teach new skills; support self-creation of content; support dissemination of content. Then assess the impact of any of these in relation to user experience.

In an increasingly networked society, many libraries and information services find themselves no longer able to operate as though they are monopolistic services. The evaluation must be a mechanism to demonstrate the value delivered against the purposes defined in the mission statement. In the commercial world, the return on investment is the balance between product out and money in. For the library or information service, the return is less tangible. It is the value that is delivered across the boundary exchange between the service and the user. A more granular and reflective approach may be necessary. There need to be performance indicators which are gauged on a regular basis and the results used to inform future plans and action.

---

It is clear that the user is key in the future of library and information services. But who are the users? As Katarina Michnik notes in Chapter 6, 'a recurring theme in public library research today is [their] role… in a world with an increasing number of services and activities provided and accessed online'. The same could be said of academic libraries, as 'social media are increasingly used for gaining information', and 'partial or full displacement' of traditional services therefore occurs. Experience in Sweden suggests that, at least in the public sphere, online provision is only reaching those who would be using library services anyway, with digital replacing hard copy, with footfall reducing as logins increase. At the same time, the increased and ever more diverse expectations of those who do patronize the facilities makes it harder for library managers to determine priorities. Chapter 16 offers data-driven geographical modelling as a way of maximizing the impact of public libraries as they strive to manage a reducing resource base.

The use of technology provided by the library means that the technology could either attract users into the library or keep them at bay; it may be the decider of the future of the physical library space. Innovative responses to the dynamics of learning will be critical to the relevance of library and information service provision in the future because current users are already discovering other means of accessing resources. How to design a service proposition that continues to reflect the needs of the user community and how to justify that proposition to parent organizations and funding agencies will be crucial.

Library and information managers should deliberately involve users in the design of new interfaces and at the same time, the perception of library staff on the relevance of their services in meeting the needs of users should be considered. It seems simple to design content and services around what our users actually want but decisions are too often taken in meeting rooms based on what librarians think they want. It is also important to ask the staff what they think about how things are designed.

Service change needs to reflect the needs and behaviours of users. Public collecting institutions no longer hold a monopoly on access to knowledge and are often in competition with online service propositions from external agencies. At the simplest level, for much information, the source of choice (and immediacy) will be the smartphone rather than the library: the hunter-gatherer/harvester paradigm shift.

The library must be at the forefront of technological innovation in the provision of services to attract users to either physical or virtual library spaces. The future of libraries will depend on the ability of the profession to change and to conform to new and changing learning styles. Users are already discovering other means of accessing resources, but how many of these are being provided by the library or institution without the user realizing it? Libraries still have an opportunity to offer unique services if they provide technology currently not commonly available in homes, such as advanced printing and scanning, 3D priNters, stop-motion animation cameras, etc. They can become places of digital learning, helping users to acquire modern creative skills.

## 1.6 Discovery and convergence: Improved quality and reduced cost

Just as e-publications have transformed the concept of the library collection, so discovery tools such as Google and Amazon have changed the ways in which information and content are discovered and utilized beyond recognition, much as described and forecast in the last edition of this series. While terms such as 'information overload' and 'data deluge' are perhaps less prevalent than 4 years ago, the need for convenience and simplicity of access—as for example through one-stop search mechanisms—remains as important, not least for library and information services. The convergence of systems and services is 'more than a marginal phenomenon and reflects a strategic choice made by an increasing number of… institutions. This evolution is likely to continue because of benefits such as reduced costs… improved data quality and the users' general preference for simple procedures' (Chapter 2).

Information overflow/overload will be a push factor in finding solutions to multiple platforms. One-stop solutions will become inevitable as individuals and organizations may no longer be able to cope with searching multiple sites. The focus will continue to be on making information easier for customers to use and manage. We may see companies streamline and simplify by offering discovery in specialized areas and fields. It is easier to develop a specialized product for specific information or discipline, and probably more useful for practitioners.

Convenience and point of demand will continue to be the drivers of technological innovation. The characteristics of technological systems that are common today in social networks and in major online service providers, such as personalization and the use of sophisticated algorithms to respond to users, could become more dominant in catalogues and discovery services. The trend away from multiple usernames towards using, for example, a Google or ORCID sign-on or possibly biometrics could be significant for access to other services.

## 1.7 Digital and information literacy

Digital literacy (DL) is a crucial skill which will become more important. Without extensive training in information literacy and digital fluency, users will not be able to access resources nor take advantage of them. DL should involve the ability to evaluate information. Just because our users can find it does not mean that it is correct or reliable. If we are producing digitally literate users they should be able to evaluate the suitability of the information to their current need. With growing open access publications and more creative ways of displaying information and gathering data, it is imperative that information literacy (IL) be taught to give the most appropriate strategies for information search, evaluation and use across platforms and disciplines.

As everyday tasks increasingly and exclusively move online, more and more of the population will need to be able to demonstrate at least a basic level of DL in order to function in society and avoid potential scams. It should be taught by independent bodies such as libraries who are not affiliated to any one company or brand. Poor DL is a serious risk to individuals and organizations (identity fraud, cybersecurity, phishing attacks) and this will always be the case as people will always be on a spectrum of new/experienced user, new/established service, new/outdated technology, with hackers always one step ahead. Services need to be as secure and idiot-proof as possible, but without putting barriers in the way of usability, as it just leads to work-arounds and greater risk. DL needs to include information security and keeping yourself and others safe online, at every level and appropriate to the user group, children, students, or older people.

This book makes many references to literacy in general and digital and information literacy in particular. Andy Phippen and colleagues (Chapter 3) stress the centrality of information literacy to learning and to developing lifelong learning. Users may be ever more digitally engaged but they are not necessarily digitally *aware*. Library and information services, and, where relevant, their parent institutions, have a 'duty of care' to ensure that, especially in an age of 'fake news', users are appropriately supported and assisted to navigate the global information environment. Martin Hamilton (Chapter 15) therefore stresses the need to 'understand how technologies develop, how people use them, and the implications that they have on learning spaces and social cohesion' as a crucial element in 'developing critical digital literacies... in order to address rising concerns in relation to wider aspects of digital citizenship'. Juan Machin-Mastromatteo's action research self-study relates his own experiences and observations as a librarian and university teacher focusing on his design and delivery of information literacy programmes.

### A new information literacy (IL)

Interdisciplinary engineering challenges require a new information literacy (IL) mindset which will affect the engineering education paradigm. Interdisciplinary problems such as sustainability challenges in connection with engineering design, are major issues in all engineering research and will continue to be so in the future. Higher education engineering curricula need a paradigm shift so that students increasingly engage in interdisciplinary research activities. These activities require independent information seeking and use. It is essential to guide students to understand that in their research tasks they are using literature with the aim of finding a solution to a problem. To find suitable information, they need information literacy skills. In addition to search skills, students learn to observe their research problem from an interdisciplinary viewpoint. IL education, which is integrated into the subject curriculum, enhances students' diverse vision of their research projects, and thus promotes their ability to search for information and find solutions to the problems.

***Marja Talikka***
**Lappeenranta University of Technology, Lappeenranta, Finland**

### The future of adult learning

When I started work at an FE college in Nottingham, UK in the late 1980s, my department was called Adult Literacy and Numeracy. Over the years the name changed to Adult Basic Education, Adult Basic Skills, and then Skills for Life. What didn't change, however, were our students who came from a variety of backgrounds and with a much wider range of skills than those names suggest. With an age range of 16–70 plus, they came to classes for many reasons, including enjoyment, companionship, and of course self-improvement.

In the early 1990s, we started using computers—at first the Mackintosh, later changing to PCs. I was an early adopter, and, armed with my CLAIT qualifications, was soon responsible for designing first our IT and later ICT courses and preparing others for their qualifications too.

It was a time of great change and optimism as many hundreds of students across the whole ability range learned how to use the new technologies and saw the benefits for personal enjoyment and skills development. It gave me much personal satisfaction to see, for example, an older lady emailing her son who lived in California, or a former boxer finding he could access details of his fight records online.

However, since 2010 there has been a decline in funding, with, according to the Institute for Fiscal Studies, a decrease of 47% government spending on adult education, excluding apprenticeships, between 2010 and 2019. A survey released in early 2020 by the Learning and Work Institute shows the number of adult learners has fallen by almost 4 million since 2010. Many classes have disappeared just when they are most needed to help people acquire the skills required to use everyday technology safely. In a post-Brexit world, this decline in adult learning must be reversed to ensure that everyone can achieve their potential. The UK Government's announcement of a £3 billion National Skills Fund in the 2019 election Manifesto is welcome and I hope that some of that funding could be made available to run classes, led by experienced paid tutors, specifically targeted at these groups. Provision of Adult Community Learning Centres has been mentioned, but in the meantime, libraries, traditionally places of inclusion and equality, are the ideal setting in which to provide training in all kinds of literacy—digital, learning and information, perhaps making use of widely available mobile technology.

*Kathleen Yoell*

**David Baker Consulting, https://davidbakersnovelfactory.com/ davidbakerconsulting.co.uk/**

## 1.8 Digital divides

Nowhere is 'the digital divide' more evident than in Africa, as Stephen Akintunde demonstrates in Chapter 7. But many other divides need to be tackled if information inequity is to be reduced.

The question of a continuing digital divide needs to be considered more closely. The 2019 edition of the Oxford Internet Survey (Perceived Threats to Privacy Online: The Internet in Britain. Oxford Internet Institute) states that almost everyone under the age of 50 uses the Internet and that nearly 50% of those 65 and above are also regular users. In 10 years, those heading for 50 in 2019 will be thinking about retirement in 2029 so that more retired/elderly people could be expected to maintain their digital skills and use of online services. That same survey makes clear that those on low incomes and those with low educational attainment are less likely to use IT, so it will be of the essence that the specific needs of disadvantaged groups are understood and built into the design of new systems and hardware. There is also a divide between traditional students and nontraditional, e.g. commuters, part-timers, transfer students, etc.

There is still a digital divide based on wealth, age and more or less-well-developed economies. Authors from poor developing economies will not be able to afford publication fees and will be joined by authors from more developed economies advocating for free publications in an open-access era. The population is ageing and there are significant numbers of people in later life not easily able to use modern technology, either through lack of dexterity, cognitive ability or willingness. It would be good if this drove change in terms of adapting devices to make them easier for older people to use.

Developments in technology have the potential to increase already significant divides. Many people wrongly assume that others enjoy the same level of access to technology, but this is not always the case. It is important to remember the potential for further divide when implementing any new technologies. Current technology developments make members of society respond differently: those who easily adopt, those who are hesitant, and some who are phobic. The divide in digital literacy (DL) will lead to misinformed citizens and reduced citizen engagement. There will be a greater need for filtering and quality control. Increasingly, it is assumed that people have access to social media (as it is also assumed, they have access to the Internet more generally) but this is not the case, so messages disseminated this way may fail to reach a proportion of the population. People will be left behind either due to financial constraints or a lack of knowledge on how to use these tools. This has the potential to result in a two-tier system: the haves and have nots of knowledge.

## Diversity and inclusiveness

Currently, within the library and information science landscape (LIS) in the United Kingdom, there is increasing discourse around the diversity and inclusiveness of libraries. In the wider profession, the Chartered Institute of Librarians and Information Professionals (CILIP), the UK professional body for library and information professionals, redefined their role within the LIS landscape and pledged to take a more activist stance to issues around social justice, including issues around diversity and inclusion within the profession (CILIP, 2019). In higher education (HE) libraries within the United Kingdom there is an increasing shift in focus to issues such as decolonization and diversification of collections. A key part of this work inevitably has to start by asking ourselves a number of questions.

*Whose information is included?*

HE libraries have an obligation to ensure our users have access to collections that include representation from marginalized groups and therefore offer a wider range of perspectives. In terms of impacting change within the curriculum, librarians can work with academics and students to critically evaluate material being put on reading lists and checking the diversity represented within these lists. Librarians are in a position of responsibility for finding alternative sources of information which can inform alternate readings for the curriculum.

*How are we representing information?*

HE librarians must also scrutinize the classification scheme used in our libraries and which subject terms are used for marginalized groups within our catalogues. For example, there has been work done to highlight the biased nature of the Library of Congress schema when classifying gender, race and LGBT+ records (Ros, 2018). To make collections more inclusive of the communities they represent it is essential to critically engage with de-marginalizing these from biased classification schemes.

*Who are our information professionals?*

In 2015 CILIP and the Archives and Records Association (ARA) workforce mapping project found that 96.7% of the LIS profession in the UK identified as white (CILIP and ARA, 2015). This was higher than the national average across other sectors. It's becoming increasingly important to ask how we as information professionals can meet the information needs of the diverse communities we serve when the UK LIS workforce is lacking in diversity itself. The profession needs a more representative staff that is diverse at all levels of the profession if it is to drive real change.

***Heena Karavadra***
**University of Leicester, Leicester, United Kingdom**

### References

CILIP, 2019. Diversity Within the Profession—Speech to CILIP West Midlands Members Day. https://www.cilip.org.uk/page/DiversitywithintheProfession. (Accessed 20.05.20).

CILIP and ARA, 2015. A Study of the UK Information Workforce. https://www.cilip.org.uk/page/Workforcesurvey. (Accessed 20.05.20).

Ros, A., 2018. The Bias in Your Library's Catalog. https://oaktrust.library.tamu.edu/handle/1969.1/166418. (Accessed 20.05.20).

## 1.9 Training, education, and development

Because so much is changing and will continue to change, skills building and capacity development will be crucial to the development of professionals in the future, as Wong and Chan demonstrate in Chapter 4 and as evinced in the ASPIRE project (Chapter 5). Chapter 12 is a case study focusing on the Leeds City Region (UK) and how Leeds Trinity University is engaging with local employer communities to bridge the current significant digital skills gap. 'It reflects on the positive outcomes of working in partnership with employers to respond to labour market issues and considers the position of students as stakeholders in such an agenda'. Training, education, and development will be just as important for library and information services staff, as emphasized by a number of Delphi participants, both here and in Chapter 19. Chapter 12 is especially valuable in this respect, being an in-depth study of Juan Machin-Mastromatteo's journey from librarian to academic. This detailed biography looks in detail at career structures (or the lack of them) and the challenges and opportunities offered by a career change, underpinned by a continuing focus on the teaching of information literacy.

### Librarianship and information work: training and the digital revolution

Technological advancements such as online courses and work submission, streamed lectures and access to research and statistical databases have made training and education opportunities available to a greater number of people and facilitated the act of studying in a greater number of places. The library and information sector is no exception to this.

For example, the CILIP Certification process—the first step for information assistants to pledge commitment to and learn more about their profession—is now submitted as a document online. This portfolio can include a wealth of evidence ranging from typed experiences and summaries to workshop materials, photographs, and social media posts. Solely from a practical point of view, digital forms of these materials are easier to collate and merge together into one document, such as a PDF, which generally preserves formatting and structure excellently, and is a commonplace file type readable by most computers. Creating a PDF is far easier, and arguably a better overall presentation, than clipping together printed papers and other odds and ends to create your portfolio. Digital submission is faster, being almost instantaneous, and work can also be easily backed up, with a copy stored safely elsewhere, such as in cloud storage or on a USB drive ahead of submission, in the extremely unlikely event it gets lost in the system. A paper copy sent in the post, however, does not offer that same security and assurance.

Digital access to resources also makes matters easier for those who need to work alongside studying. Databases allow those undertaking qualifications to access articles, statistics, and other useful information online, rather than losing potential working hours travelling to various libraries or museum reading rooms to gather up what they need. Communication with your mentor or tutor is also far easier: if you do not live near each other, or have regularly conflicting schedules, it is far easier for both parties to discuss your progress through a webcam session that it is to arrange a face-to-face meeting. Digital documents also speed up and simplify the exchange of assignment drafts and feedback between both parties.

Beyond courses and qualifications, continuing professional development also benefits from the digital revolution. For those unable to attend workshops and sessions in person, possibly due to work commitments or funding restraints, webinars and online courses—which can be programmed to offer certificates of completion by way of evidence—are an ideal alternative. Even social media allows ease of regular communication and the sharing of news and development between those employed in the information sector; a user's profile tailored to reflect the level of formality and professionalism they wish to convey.

In academia, particularly at the university level, digital submission and research are becoming increasingly commonplace as part of undergraduate and postgraduate degree studies. As one employed in the library sector, utilizing similar methods to undertake your own training gives a person a valuable insight into the student experience, making them more understanding of potential issues students may face, and thereby better equipped to help them.

***Hannah Myers***
**Walker Morris, Leeds, United Kingdom**

## 1.10 Ready for the future?

Much of this book is about the future. But are library and information services ready for the disruption and the turbulence? Will they be able to embrace Education 4.0, for example, and, as Hamilton urges when he cites Davies et al. (2017), to ensure that 'changes to delivery are driven by educational considerations rather than… balance sheets… If we accept that the opportunity exists for significant disruption, is it even possible for slow moving and often bureaucratic large organizations to embrace this, or will the future belong to agile innovators operating much more like Internet startups?'

But it will not be easy; much determination, energy, and imagination will be needed in the process, as evinced by Wong and Chan's careful, well-thought out, strategic yet pragmatic, bottom-up approach (Chapter 4) to developing research data management (RDM) services at Hong Kong's University of Science and Technology (HKUST). The most important lessons learned must surely be that trust has to be earned and engagement is a continuous process. Risk must be managed, and people supported through failure, as required. Long-term success tends to be achieved when mistakes may have been made, but the necessary lessons learned from them. HKUST's overarching roadmap offers much to library and information service leaders planning to negotiate and perhaps create the future.

Another encouraging exemplar can be found in Chapter 5, where 'a group of volunteers with no budget and limited influence created a credible data source that positively influenced the practices of major suppliers' in terms of accessibility, with special reference to print-disabled users. It is a story 'of collaboration and community'.

### Radical thinking required

Information overload is nothing new and identifying strategies for navigating the plethora has long been the domain of librarians. The advent of the online library catalogue was huge in terms of how we went about finding the information we sought, so too was the introduction of discovery layers that enabled searches across multiple formats and platforms. There is another seismic shift occurring in how we can discover and link information, with artificial intelligence, machine learning, and the like, making connections that would not be immediately obvious or possible using traditional library discovery methods and metadata schema. This is a radical departure from traditional systems, categorizations, schemas, and search strategies. How we seek, discover, and connect information is changing. These are exciting times that call for a departure from established thinking and approaches, but are we ready to embrace this brave new world, and will the 'traditionalists' be convinced this transformation is for the better?

***Trish Wilson***
**Te Herenga Waka, Victoria University of Wellington, Wellington, New Zealand**

### Commitment to the edges and frontiers

Situated in the fast-changing technology landscape, the ongoing higher education transformation has accelerated with big data evolution, smart infrastructure innovation, and advanced artificial intelligence. Along with these, there are security, transparency, and accountability issues, challenges, and controversies. Together, these forces are reshaping academic enterprise and reconfiguring knowledge spaces. To stay relevant, the library and information field will need to transcend its existing constraints and boundaries to effectively integrate into the transformative enterprise. That is why, as an information scholar and practitioner, I am committed to the edges and frontiers of the academic infrastructure by exploring new modes of information inquiry and new ways of data exploration and interaction in the evolving intelligent infrastructure landscape. When engaging in the transformative process and shifting enterprise, we need new leadership, creative thinking, and inclusive efforts to forge new pathways of development.

***Yi Shen***
**Virginia Tech, Blacksburg, VA, United States**

The rest of this book suggests that many library and information services and their leaders and managers are not only preparing for discontinuous change (with some continuities in specific areas) and radical and rapid disruption but also that they are setting trends and creating new futures.

## References

Baker, D., 2004. Strategic Technology Management. Chandos, Oxford.

Baker, D., 2017. Making sure things can never be the same again: innovation in library and information services. In: Baker, D., Evans, W. (Eds.), Innovation in Libraries and Information Services. Advances in Libraries and Information Services, vol. 35, pp. 1–44.

Baker, D., Evans, W., 2016. Digital Information Strategies: From Applications and Content to Libraries and People. Chandos, Oxford. Davies, S., Mullan, J., Feldman, P., 2017. Rebooting Learning for the Digital Age: What Next for Technology Enhanced Higher Education? Higher Education Policy Institute (HEPI) Report 93. https://www.hepi.ac.uk/wp-content/uploads/2017/02/Hepi_Rebooting-learning-for-the-digital-age-Report-93-02_02_17Web.pdf (accessed 29.04.20).

# Part One

# Strategy and design

# Current research information systems and institutional repositories: From data ingestion to convergence and merger

2

*Joachim Schöpfel*[a] *and Otmane Azeroual*[b]
[a]GERiiCO Laboratory, University of Lille, Lille, France, [b]German Institute for Higher Education Research and Science Studies (DZHW), Berlin, Germany

## 2.1 Introduction

Current research information systems (CRIS) and institutional repositories (IR) were developed as clearly distinguished systems, with different objectives and functionalities, with different standards and data models, and for different needs and user groups. IR have been described as 'a set of services that a university offers to the members of its community for the management and dissemination of digital materials created by the institution and its community members … including long-term preservation where appropriate, as well as organization and access or distribution' (Lynch, 2003). CRIS, on the other hand, stand for a family of information systems (databases, decision support systems, and so forth) to store and manage data about research conducted at an institution (Joint, 2008). While academic librarians are often deeply committed to the management of open access and IR, they are less involved and familiar with research evaluation and CRIS.

Both systems are part of the 'fourth paradigm' (Hey et al., 2009), data-intensive scientific discovery, a new way of doing science based on information and communication technology. After a period of an 'alleged dichotomy' (de Castro et al., 2014), separate implementation and discussion on data ingestion, data exchange and interoperability, both systems started to converge and even to merge. Today IR often fulfil the requirements of monitoring and assessment of institutional research performance while CRIS, beyond the processing of metadata, begin to process, store, and disseminate research papers.

Our chapter tries to make this evolution understandable for academic librarians, based on an overview of recent papers and surveys and with examples to illustrate the challenge for the library. What are the benefits and what are the risks and potential barriers of this convergence? Special attention will be paid to the role of data quality and of user acceptance, and to the implications for the academic librarian.

**Future Directions in Digital Information. https://doi.org/10.1016/B978-0-12-822144-0.00002-1**

## 2.2 Institutional repositories

Institutional repositories (IR) are part of the green road to open access (OA) through author self-archiving of their papers in university-driven online collections or databases (Harnad et al., 2004). Being part of the OA movement, they are a new vector of scientific information which 'have no counterpart in the traditional landscape of scholarly communication' (Suber, 2012, p. 52). OpenDOAR, the global directory of OA repositories lists close to 4000 IR in 2019 (Directory of Open Access Repositories, 2019). There are other kinds of open repositories, governmental, disciplinary, or aggregating. Yet IR are the most important category, representing 87% of all open repositories. Many are from European institutions; others are from the Americas and other parts of the world. Many of the highest-ranked universities have their own IR, like Harvard, Columbia, MIT, Oxford, or Cambridge.

Often, IR have been implemented as standalone systems, as a platform on an institutional server more-or-less connected with other systems. Some IR have been launched with a regional or national infrastructure, for instance as a portal on a governmental open repository. Many IR are based on open software, like DSpace, EPrints, Islandora, or WEKO; some of them are designed for a specific national environment, like OPUS or MyCoRe in Germany or HAL in France (Hyper Articles en Ligne, 2001). Other IR are launched with commercial software, like Digital Commons, or are in-house developments.

The initial and main functions of IR are direct communication: immediate and open dissemination and preservation of the institutions' scientific output, which means the papers and data produced by their affiliated researchers. Generally, IR are initiated in compliance with the goals of the global OA movement, to increase the accessibility and findability of scientific knowledge, for other researchers, for the industry, and for society as a whole. Also, most IR have implemented a standard metadata format, compliant with the Dublin Core, and a standard protocol for harvesting and other aggregating services, and especially the OAI metadata harvesting protocol.

Academic librarians are most often (if not always) deeply involved and committed to IR, from the very start of the project on to the administration, maintenance, and development of the system, to content updates, metadata curation, and staff training. Now, research managers and policy makers, in particular, ask for indicators of institutional research performance in order to assess scientific excellence and international competitiveness; also, they identify IR as potentially relevant data sources for in-house statistics and indicators. Over the years, IR adapted to the requirements of monitoring and assessment of institutions' scientific output, with new functionalities and services. This new (secondary) function impacts the IR twice. Firstly, monitoring requires metadata, not the deposit of text or data files. Therefore, for instance, the number of documents in the French HAL repository declined over time to only 33% of the total because research structures increasingly upload metadata without deposits, for needs of evaluation. Secondly, as monitoring requires reliable and comparable information sources, this new function fosters standardization of metadata formats, of persistent identifiers like DOI and ORCID for resources, authors, institutions and so on, and of terminology (nomenclature) for disciplines, subjects, methodology, countries, towns, and other relevant categories. IR are often hosted and run by academic libraries; the fact that academic librarians are used to norms and standards contributed to this process in a helpful way.

Initially designed for articles and preprints, IR contain other resources, like theses and dissertations, conference papers, unpublished reports, or working papers; increasingly IR also contain courseware, software, image files, AV materials, and data sets. However, we must be careful with the meaning of 'contain'; more and more, IR do not only accept author self-archiving of papers and other items but allow the creation of metadata records without the document or data files, for the reason mentioned above. Therefore, many IR are today a kind of 'mix' of OA repositories and bibliographic databases, with a more-or-less important section of freely accessible resources, along with metadata records linking to other platforms (articles) or repositories (data) via persistent identifiers or URLs.

## 2.3 Current research information systems

Research information includes all metadata that arises in connection with research activities, such as information about publications, project data, and persons involved. Because this information is often stored in multiple systems, current research information systems (CRIS) are needed to bundle the information in a structured way, to simplify the creation of reports and to enable value-added services. Academic institutions can be supported by the provision of CRIS (see Fig. 2.1). A CRIS is a database or federated information system, representing research management information (Jeffery, 2012). 'The CRIS provides a single portal bringing corporate and academic research activity together, reducing duplicate data entry, increasing data quality, identifying authority sources of information and recording complex relationships between researchers, projects, outputs and impact' (Clements and Proven, 2015).

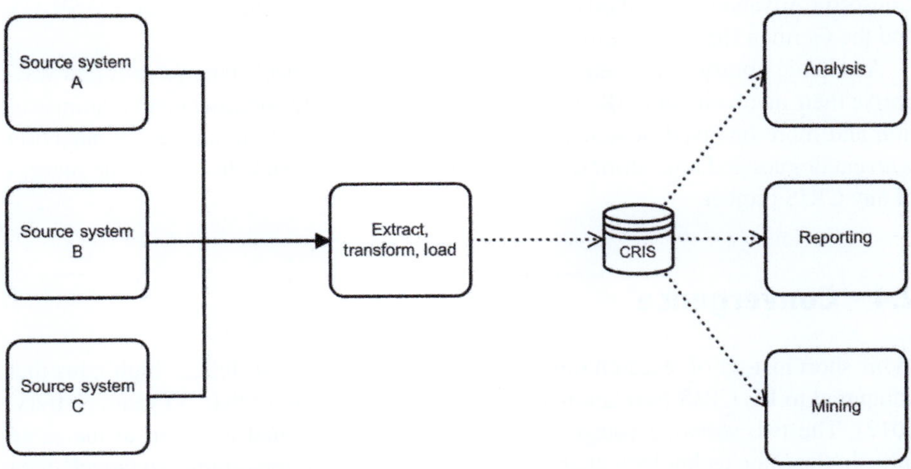


**Fig. 2.1** Architecture of a CRIS.

Relevant research information in a CRIS database is for instance data on people (name, job title, affiliation, skills, etc.), organizations and research facilities (name, type, country, etc.), projects (name, duration, funding, programme, etc.) and outputs (publications, research data, patents, etc.).

Research information should not be confused with research data (research output). With the help of CRIS, the entire research process in academic institutions can be supported and the research context documented. For example, CRIS should be able to link projects with funding and research results and allow for evaluation and assessment within an institution and comparison with other institutions. Furthermore, a CRIS can be used to manage research projects, research results, research resources, and research funding.

CRIS are facing a certain challenge, as for example divergent user expectations. From the perspective of the administration of a CRIS, research information should be presented as uniformly as possible in order to be able to make comparisons and assessments quickly and easily. CRIS, as a central database of all research relevant high-quality information of an institution, make it possible for prospective customers and cooperation partners to easily find the responsible persons and contact information as well as provide an overview of the research activities and services. Researchers, on the other hand, need a precise description of their research profile, taking into account specific criteria for evaluating the activity of the respective discipline, or they want to find exact information and use the subject-specific research information of other researchers. CRIS can also support auxiliary functions for researchers, such as the creation of CVs and publication lists.

Another challenge facing CRIS, from an international perspective, is the compatibility and interoperability of research information coming from different systems. In Europe, USA, China, and other countries, the trend towards the emergence of international CRIS can be observed, which requires standardization in the field of research information. Standardization is key, and different initiatives support the standardization of CRIS, like the Common European Research Information Format (CERIF), the Consortia Advancing Standards in Research Administration Information (CASRAI), and the German Research Core Dataset (RCD/KDSF).

Academic librarians are generally involved in CRIS projects but in a different way, unlike their involvement in IR. They are less involved in development and administration and more involved in standardization issues, data curation, and interconnection with catalogues and repositories. Nonetheless, they are key stakeholders in the success of any CRIS project.

## 2.4 Convergence

In his short history of research information management, Keith Jeffery highlights that compared to IR, CRIS have a longer history, going back more than 50 years (Jeffery, 2012). The two software categories have not been developed together, at the same time, in the same technological environment. When institutions started to launch open repositories, CRIS—at least some kind of research information software—often were already there. The first impact was, therefore, that CRIS discovered IR as a new source of potentially relevant information.

### 2.4.1 Data from IR to CRIS

A CRIS needs relevant, reliable, and valid information on scientific publishing as one part of research output (results). For instance, it needs information about the type and status of publication, the date, and the publisher, and it needs information about the relationship between this output and persons (authors), projects, organizations (affiliations), and other outputs (patents, data and so on). Insofar as this kind of information is stored in institutional repositories, CRIS managers have identified IR as a relevant data source for CRIS, as one of the 'source systems' in Fig. 2.1, similar to bibliographic databases and library catalogues.

Fig. 2.2 shows the example of the dataflows of the ZORA repository of the University of Zurich (Zurich Open Repository and Archive, 2019). The dataflow from IR to CRIS is on the right-hand side, from ZORA to the research information system AKABER, shown in *blue*. The content of the flow is bibliographic data. The purpose is academic reporting. Because of this dataflow, the AKABER system has a near 100% coverage of the academic output, with library curated data and a high proportion of papers in open access.

A CRIS is a kind of gateway to knowing where all the relevant resources are (Jeffery, 2012). For instance, when a new CRIS was implemented at the Free University of Bozen-Bolzano, it ingested data from four information systems: human resources, purchasing, the national Italian publication database from Cineca and the local IR; the CRIS maps the attributes of the uploaded data and saves them into the corresponding CRIS tables. Yet, as the CRIS was designed as the unique data entry point for the researchers' publication data, it also transferred data back to the IR (Siciliano et al., 2014).

### 2.4.2 Data from CRIS to IR

On the other side, institutions, and especially academic libraries, identified CRIS as a source of valid information on research output (articles, books, dissertations, and conference papers) to improve the quality of metadata (missing or erroneous data) and the coverage (missing records). IR data is not always consistent, especially because of self-archiving, and the usually high degree of standardization makes CRIS potentially interesting for the improvement of the IR quality. CRIS 'have given a great boost to open access repositories' (Joint, 2008).

The Norwegian national CRIS has been developed as a 'single point of entry for all research' (Wenaas et al., 2012). Authors are invited to upload their publications on the CRIS platform; but as the CRIS also receives metadata from databases and journal platforms, it can enrich the local IR and inform institutions and authors about potential uploads (legal deposits allowed by publishers), which means that 'there is a potential to increase holdings in the IR and also identify the large portion of Norwegian research results that are candidates for self-archiving'. The article submission form on the CRIS platform is easy and user-friendly, and it is the starting point for an invisible 'highway' to the IR.

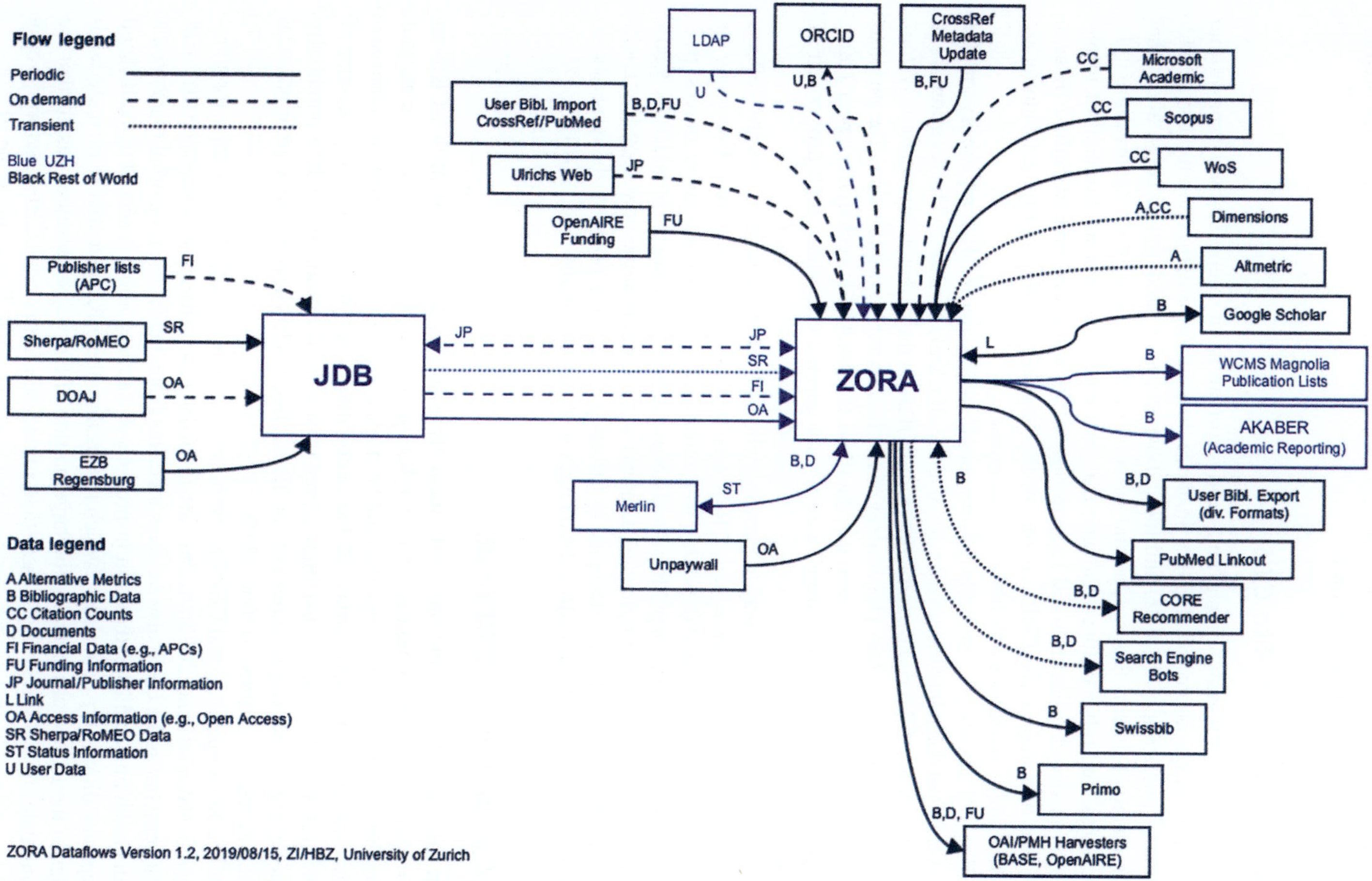


**Fig. 2.2** Dataflows of the ZORA repository, University of Zurich.
*Source*: Martin Brändle, UZH.

Ivanović et al. (2014) present plugins for the export of data on published results, in particular PhD dissertations, and conferences via standardized (OAI-PMH, SRU) and nonstandardized XML protocols and in different formats (Dublin Core, MARC21, ETD-MS) to various systems, including their local IR but also a national government gateway (Serbia), OpenAIRE (European projects) and DART-Europe (European dissertations). The key is standardized metadata and common formats and protocols, including shared and centralized identifiers. Here, a local CRIS is feeding local, national, and international systems with new data about scientific output.

The OpenAIRE gateway to European research output illustrates this. OpenAIRE was launched in 2009 as a follow-up project of the DRIVER infrastructure and aggregator of European IR (OpenAIRE, 2018a). Since 2015, OpenAIRE provides guidelines for CRIS managers 'to expose their metadata in a way that is compatible with the OpenAIRE infrastructure (i.e. to support) the inclusion and therefore the reuse of metadata in their systems within the OpenAIRE infrastructure' which is described as being 'itself a CRIS system' (OpenAIRE, 2018b).

Along with new bibliographic information for updates, CRIS also contain useful information to enrich or disambiguate existing IR metadata, especially about the authors and institutions (for example spelling, identifier, or address), but also about projects (project name, funding body or project tender).

### 2.4.3 Impact on both systems

A recent survey from EUNIS and euroCRIS, with 84 institutions from 20 European countries, shows that 65% of institutions have linked their CRIS and IR (Ribeiro et al., 2016). The communication between IR and CRIS and their gradual convergence impact both systems, but in different ways. On the one hand, CRIS must take into account and adjust to the library and open access standards. Clements and Proven (2015) describe the evolution of an institutional CRIS 'from [its] traditional role as a tool managed by the Research Office to manage and assess research towards more widespread uses within institutions, in particular within the Library, to facilitate Open Science'. For this reason, a CRIS is increasingly the primary bibliographic record of the scientific output and must be compliant with the usual bibliographic standards and procedures. Clements and Proven (2015) observe that a similar role is emerging for research data and that CRIS become the primary source of research data records, which means that CRIS must also be compliant with data repository standards, such as generic and discipline-specific metadata formats for research data.

This convergence also impacts the IR. The first and principal impact is on the workflows and the functions of IR, the gradual replacement of self-deposits in the IR by data (document files) and metadata (records) imported out of the CRIS, from different origins (self-deposits in the CRIS, library catalogues, metadata from publishers), contributing to a 'complex two-way exchange of data' between CRIS and IR (MacGregor, 2019). Beyond this fundamental change of workflows and functions, the interconnection with a CRIS may have other effects on the local IR. 'Progressively, repository architectures are merging and co-evolving with CERIF-CRIS' (Jeffery, 2012). Siciliano et al. (2014) describe how the integration of both systems can require a new and much more detailed hierarchical organization of collections and communities in the repository to allow a consistent mapping with the CRIS. More generally, as the purpose of the standard CRIS format CERIF is to represent research information and to transfer it between systems, it can improve the interoperability and compliance with the FAIR principles, of repositories and other digital archives (Engelman et al., 2018).

### 2.4.4 From local to regional or national systems

If CRIS and IR converge first and foremost on a local level, within the framework of the institutional architecture of information systems, the process can also be observed on a larger, regional, or national level. We already mentioned the case of the national CRIS in Norway and the national gateway to publications in Serbia. In the Netherlands, the Dutch national portal of research information, NARCIS (National Academic Research and Collaborations Information System, 2007) aggregates data and metadata from both repositories and research information systems (Dijk et al., 2006). Based on information imported from local CRIS and IR, NARCIS provides information on research institutes (profiles, addresses, projects, and publications), researchers (expertise, addresses, research projects, and publications), research activities (research projects and programmes), publications (metadata and full text), data sets (metadata), and news (web pages). The main problem of NARCIS is data quality, especially the matching of the researchers' names from different sources (library catalogues, CRIS, IR), and for this reason, the Netherlands have developed a national digital author identification (DAI), for all systems and levels.

The NARCIS infrastructure was the model for the launch of PRC (Portal de la Recerca de Catalunya, 2020), a similar research portal in Catalonia. The PRC portal receives information from the local CRIS of Catalan universities and research organizations. It is based on DSpace-CRIS but it does not include documents, just metadata. Here, the convergence remains on the local level, at least for the moment.

## 2.5 Merger

Clearly, there are 'overlapping areas in the tasks that (both systems) perform and there has been a gradual convergence of these two types of systems', through systematic metadata transfer or 'by allowing one of them to take over the features of the other one, thus delivering a single-system integrated functionality' (de Castro et al., 2014). This opens the door for further convergence to a gradual merging of both systems, not only at the user interface but also in the back office. The EUNIS/euroCRIS survey reveals 'CRIS acting as repositories, repositories with extended data models, a wide range of interoperability features between co-existing CRISs and repositories and even a new species in the ecosystem that claims to be both a repository and a CRIS' (Ribeiro et al., 2016). This can be described in two ways.

### 2.5.1 CRIS with IR functionalities

First, we can observe how CRIS have developed functionalities usually attributed to IR; 'CRIS acting as repositories', in some way or other. For instance, some CRIS allow the deposit of documents, a service which is a basic feature of open repositories. Labastida i Juan (2015) describes the bridge between the IR (DSpace) and the in-house developed CRIS at the University of Barcelona (Catalonia). Authenticated researchers self-archive their publications not in the IR but in the CRIS. After validation, the CRIS transfers the documents in PDF with standardized metadata (Metadata Encoding and Transmission Standard) to the IR which attributes a persistent identifier (handle) to each deposit and communicates this identifier to the CRIS. The CRIS also controls embargo periods and reuse rights (licensing). Interoperability through standardization is the key to making the two operating systems communicate with each other. Since 2015, the quality of the transferred information has been improved, for instance, by linking projects with outputs in order to get the project metadata, including a controlled thesaurus for subjects or trying to get better control of authorities; however, IR and CRIS remain two distinct systems (personal information from Labastida i Juan, October 2019).

One of the leading commercial research information management solutions, Pure, from Elsevier, is perhaps the best example of this evolution. Initially developed by the Danish start-up Atira as a 'normal' CRIS, with all required functionalities such as evaluation and reporting, identification and dissemination of expertise, and interconnection with national assessment frameworks. Pure moves progressively towards a 'single content management system on campus', explicitly labelled as a repository (Elsevier Pure, 2020). Pure offers the possibility to ingest and store not only the data on research but also the related content and documents—the scientific output itself—such as publications, data sets, and awards, press clippings, 'narrative data around projects' and so forth. 'With Pure, you can store your institution's manuscripts, data sets, and other research artifacts in a single place where they are linked to your researchers' profiles and other research data'. Thus, central IR functions have been transferred to the CRIS, upstream of the workflow, leaving to the IR the preservation and dissemination of the documents and records, along with the attribution of a persistent document identifier (see also the case study by de Castro, 2018). The researchers interact with the CRIS for the deposit, creation of metadata, and evaluation, while the IR remains available for the retrieval of papers (Fig. 2.3).

Some CRIS provide the required conditions for the dissemination (harvesting) of data and metadata via the OAI-PMH protocol and/or import metadata and files from commercial databases, like Scopus, with a focus on journal publishing. Thus, they can play the role of an operational IR, from the ingestion of content to its dissemination. Sometimes, 'an independent IR (remains) in operation for disseminating other kinds of institutional output such as dissertations and/or grey literature' (de Castro et al., 2014). But the potential for a kind of vertical integration between CRIS and IR on the local level is real. The challenge is organizational rather than technical: repositories are mostly hosted by academic libraries while CRIS are not. Another challenge is shared with many IR: how can CRIS guarantee the long-term preservation of deposited contents?

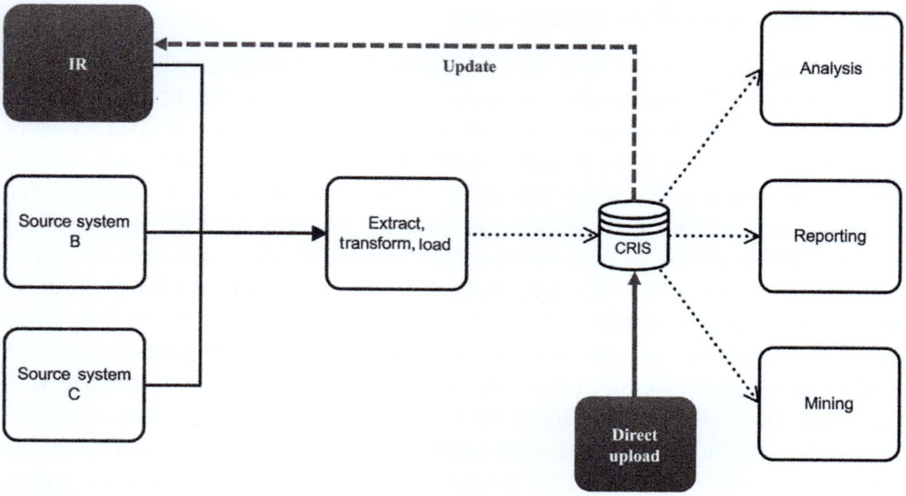


**Fig. 2.3** CRIS with IR functionalities.

## *2.5.2 IR with CRIS functionalities*

Second, we can observe how open repositories begin to develop functionalities and services usually attributed to research information management, such as scientometric assessment of the scientific production of individual researchers, institutions and departments, the generation of individual CVs, the linking between funded research projects, publications and patents, and so on.

The Polish Omega-Spir software is one example. Initially developed as an IR, from 2013 on its functionality 'went beyond the typical functionality of institutional repository towards the functionality of CRIS … due to applied intelligent tools (acquisition tools, reporting functionalities), the maintenance efforts of Knowledge Base are essentially reduced compared to the typical solutions. The process of moving the system to the university level was already simpler, as the team had experience with organizational and training issues at the faculty level' (Rybinski et al., 2018). The authors mention two major benefits, no costs in excess of usual IR maintenance and a single unique interface. A third benefit should be added: complete institutional control over the whole process and content, without outsourcing.

The successful extension of DSpace, the free open-source software for repositories for research information management is another example of this merger. 'Differently from other [commercial] CRIS… DSpace-CRIS has the institutional repository as its core component, providing high visibility on the web to all the collected information and objects' (DSpace-CRIS, 2019). The flexible data model of DSpace-CRIS is compliant with the CERIF standard and the ORCID identifier and allows for the configuration of different data models and metadata schemas, according to local requirements. The DSpace-CRIS wiki indicates more than 100 installations worldwide, mainly in Europe (Italy, Germany, Spain) and Asia.

HAL is a third example. Initially launched as an open repository based on self-archiving of research papers by French academic communities, HAL developed into a platform with a high number of institutional portals and other collections. Answering the institutional need for scientific monitoring and evaluation, HAL adds features and plugins useful for scientometrics and the assessment of research output. This development has two main effects on HAL: the increasing use of national and international standards and identifiers (nomenclature of publication types, DOI, ORCID), and the number of records without the document files (though only 24% of the HAL metadata provide access to the document).

## 2.6 Data quality

Research information is often spread across different systems within an institution. This results in increased administrative overhead, inconsistent and incomplete data, and unreliable reports that negatively impact business decisions. Therefore, the users of the CRIS require high-quality data. Increasing data quality is an important and still problematic task for many organizations. Although effective quality management should occur as early as possible in the data flow (as e.g. in manual data collection), quality deficiencies often only become visible in the CRIS (Azeroual and Schöpfel, 2019). The data quality can be measured based on certain criteria such as completeness, correctness, consistency or timeliness (Azeroual et al., 2018b) and can be positively influenced during the phase of data acquisition and integration, for example, when transferring research information from various data sources into the CRIS. Proactive data quality management means not only the removal of random errors but also

- the identification and elimination of sources of error,
- constant control of the research information and its quality,
- preventive measures (such as proactive measures) to prevent further errors, and
- the regular clean-up of new data errors (e.g. using data cleansing).

It is not enough to clean-up the research information only when it is integrated into the CRIS, but it is necessary to communicate errors to the appropriate places so that they are already remedied in the source system, such as IR, catalogues, human resources, and accounting. This not only prevents the occurrence of the same errors the next time the data is loaded from the respective system into the CRIS by Extract, Transform, Load (ETL) process (Azeroual et al., 2019a) but also sensitizes the responsible persons, for example, when manually entering research information.

Whether research information can achieve high quality in CRIS depends on the quality of the respective data sources. It is easy to overlook the question of whether a data source is trustworthy at all and whether it has a high-quality database from the outset (Azeroual et al., 2019b). However, if the data quality is taken seriously, one should also rate the data sources according to their trustworthiness. In order to analyze research information, it must first be sensibly selected with regard to the intended use. The amount of data selected should be as large as necessary and as small as possible. The right choice of research information is a first step towards high data quality. A general statement about which research information should be selected for integration cannot be made. This depends on the individual needs of a particular organization.

The problem with IR is that they are often not exhaustive and that they may contain incomplete or erroneous records. This may not be a crucial issue for IR insofar as their goal is dissemination, and therefore recall sensitivity (retrieving most of the relevant content) seems more important than precision. However, this is unacceptable for CRIS where precision of information retrieval is essential. Eliminating erroneous research information when integrating it into a CRIS is often a cumbersome but important process for creating high data quality. Therefore, a workflow of data cleansing should be provided for organizations so that they can correct the occurring quality problems and ensure the quality in their system (Fig. 2.4). This has advantages for the organizations, both internally and externally. Establishing a data quality model is sustainable, which means quality ensures the quality of service and knowledge available in organizations. It helps to bundle important know-how and keep it in organizations, independently of people.

The key elements of this workflow can be described as follows:

**(1)** For records that cannot be corrected from the outset, their preliminary deletion in the integration process should be considered. For example, this may be the case of missing or incorrect key attributes or other unique identifying attributes such as part numbers and descriptions. Such a master data record may not be clearly identified without this information and has no value in the CRIS. Such records must first be corrected or re-entered in the respective department.

**(2)** Missing or incorrect data records can be corrected by publication data. For example, if there is only a unique article number without an article description, it is usually possible to determine the associated article description from it and insert it into the attribute provided for this purpose.

**(3)** Similar to the replacement of research information from publication databases, certain values in data integration can be derived from calculations or other logic for missing or erroneous values.

**(4)** Using meaningful default values instead of missing data can prevent null values and improve data quality. Examples of this would be date fields, which by default are set to the current date or any other specified day when not filled. It is important to define the default values in advance in such a way that all possible cases and exceptions are recorded and no further errors result from incorrect insertion logic (which are in hindsight difficult to identify).

**(5)** Any redundancies that have arisen or been identified as part of the integration of research information should be treated as part of the data cleansing. A good way to do this is to consolidate (summarize) multiple records into a single correct one. It is always important to find a balance between effectiveness (finding as many redundancies as possible) and efficiency (keeping runtime as short as possible).

**(6)** If records are composed of nonrelated attributes, they must be separated and stored in two different records. Such erroneous data sets can occur, for example, in the automated summary of redundancies. A manual check or automated comparison with correct comparison values should be done in such cases.

**(7)** After the research information has been corrected, as a last step it should be checked to see whether there are already groups for the newly added data records in the CRIS into which they can be added. If not, check whether the new records form a separate group. Examples of this are articles or author classes, which do not exist yet and are recognized only during the data integration. The modeled workflow examines both cases with the involvement of the respective departments.

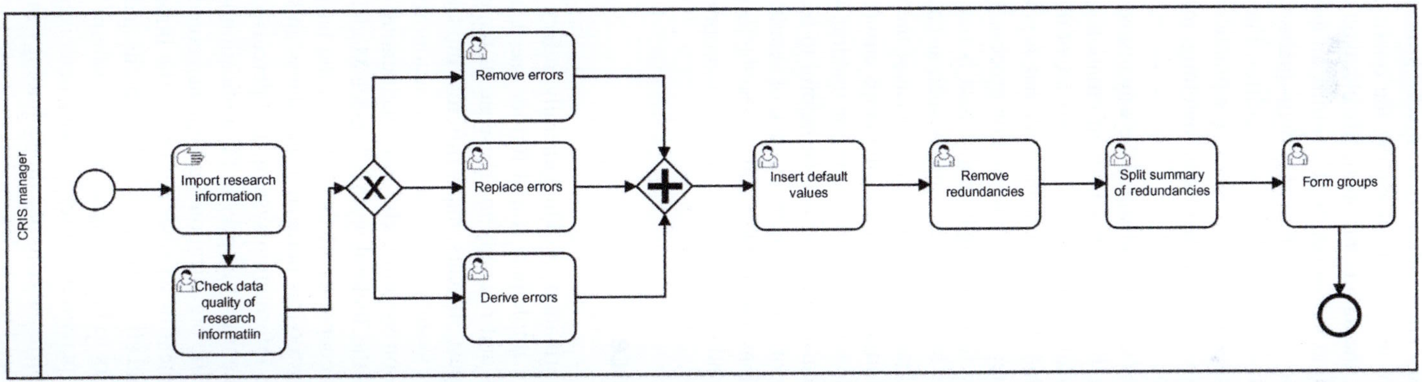


**Fig. 2.4** Workflow of data cleansing.

Data cleansing activities are limited to relatively simple but sometimes time-consuming activities. Also, instead of improving the quality of data, further errors may occur if, for example, the data is automatically changed and there is insufficient manual control of the changes subsequently. Therefore, an iterative process is recommended during the clean-up. To ensure that only high-quality data is sent to a CRIS, a data cleansing tool must be used at CRIS-using facilities. For more detailed information on how the data cleansing processes work using a practical example in the context of CRIS (such as syntax errors, standardization, matching, merging, and enrichment, see Azeroual et al., 2018a).

The rapid development of CRIS has changed the way research organizations capitalize on research information. Because of this high information dependency, the effective management of data quality and ensuring data integrity are of the highest priority. If data quality issues are not detected and validated early, the risk is poor research information. Data cleansing is the first step in the data preparation process. It identifies and corrects errors in a record to ensure that only high-quality data is transferred to CRIS. When research information comes from multiple sources, such as catalogues, databases, and repositories, the need for cleansing data increases because the sources have redundant data or incompatible data formats. Data cleansing helps ensure data accuracy, so only high-quality data is available for analysis and decision making. Whenever the erroneous data are from an IR, the cleansing process will be helpful to increase the quality of the repository itself, in the case of systematic errors, lack of standardization, etc. However, as MacGregor (2019) mentions, the problem can also be the lack of open standards and protocols, interoperability, and support by a commercial, proprietary CRIS.

## 2.7 User acceptance

The acceptance of an information system generally refers to users' decision on whether they should buy or implement it and further use it in the long term, in the sense of active willingness and not only in the sense of reactive toleration (Arnold and Klee, 2016). Over the past 30 years, many different models have been developed to describe and link people, systems, and contextual factors with potential impact on the acceptance of information systems. The most influential, most tested, and best-operationalized approach is the Technology Acceptance Model (TAM) (Davis, 1989).

The TAM explains the acceptance of the CRIS on the basis of cognitive factors. Cognitive factors are understood as perceived usefulness and perceived ease-of-use operability of the examined information system. The perceived usefulness refers to a user's assessment of how the use of a specific IT application improves the execution of work tasks within a specific organizational acceptance context. The perceived ease of use relates to the assessment of whether the use of the information system can be learned without difficulty and effort. The higher the benefits and ease of use of a CRIS, the more likely it is for users to be willing to use the system. In the TAM, the interaction of the two factors—perceived usefulness and perceived ease of use—results in an intention on the part of the user to use the technology in question (behavioural intention to use) which can lead to a real, actual system use (Schöpfel et al., 2019).

Perceived usefulness and perceived ease of use are both valid indicators for the acceptance and use of CRIS. Yet both factors are impacted by other independent variables such as culture, job position and function, data quality, and system security (Azeroual et al., 2019c). Following different studies (Kollmann, 1998; Lucke, 1995; Venkatesh et al., 2007), in Western cultures, the perceived usefulness seems to be more important in determining the intentions and actual use, while ease of use appears to be the key in non-Western cultures. Communication regarding the introduction of the CRIS, such as training manuals and direct contact with the CRIS developer, should, therefore, carry different messages, depending on the culture in which the CRIS is to be used.

As for the job positions and functions in the academic environment of CRIS and IR, at least five internal user groups must be distinguished: researchers (scholars), students, administrators, scientific bodies (councils and similar), and university managers responsible for research strategies. As Rybinski et al. (2017, 2018) observe, the needs and expectations of these groups vary significantly, and in many cases, they may even be contradictory. And then there may be external stakeholders with other needs and requirements, such as entrepreneurs, funding bodies, and government authorities.

Introducing a CRIS to people working with library holdings, digital libraries, and repositories may be a challenge. 'In every community, any change and innovation in consolidated procedures and workflows is considered with suspicion' (Siciliano et al., 2014); Rybinski et al. (2018) had to cope with 'scepticism from the researchers', from the beginning of their CRIS project. Reluctance, suspicion, and scepticism may result not only from fear of change, but also from issues of control and evaluation, personal data, and ethics. Faced with a CRIS project, some academic librarians may experience helplessness, loss of control, and lack of skills; also, they 'must come to grips with the role of repositories within the CRIS environment' (Joint, 2008). Siciliano et al. (2014) admit they initially had underestimated problems related to privacy and copyright and their impact on the validation process. Traditional library ethics include the promotion of open access and transparency, nondiscrimination, respect of privacy, confidentiality, commitment to neutrality and personal integrity (IFLA, 2016) while CRIS have more to do with performance, competition, assessment, evaluation, and management. This may create conflicts.

How do we deal with these potential barriers? Acceptance is the key, especially by researchers and librarians. A good partnership between librarians and IT staff is required, just as a trusting relationship between librarians and researchers is necessary. IR are generally much lighter and easy to configure platforms than CRIS (de Castro et al., 2014), which implies more need for acceptance of CRIS than IR.

The experience of immediate usefulness may contribute to acceptance. For instance, in the Polish CRIS project, researchers could, at an early stage, 'immediately observe their profiles, so that they gradually turned to be more and more keen to contribute to the process of the (knowledge) database maintenance' (Rybinski et al., 2018). The Italian team tried another way to achieve a faster and easier acceptance of the new CRIS: 'we decided ... to feed it with project and publication data produced [in the last 17 years] before committing it to the research community ... we are confident that this valuable critical mass of research outcomes easily searchable and reusable in the system [will] improve its acceptance' (Siciliano et al., 2014). This may mean additional work for the implementation team; but the implementation of a CRIS and the convergence of CRIS and IR will show other benefits, improved quality, reliability and reusability of metadata and less work, avoiding duplicated inputs in the two systems.

## 2.8 Future perspectives

According to the EUNIS/euroCRIS survey, 18% of the responding institutions already use the same software application for both CRIS and IR (Ribeiro et al., 2016). The convergence of both systems is more than a marginal phenomenon and reflects a strategic choice made by an increasing number of universities and other research institutions. This evolution is likely to continue because of benefits such as reduced costs for implementation, hosting and maintenance, improved data quality, and the users' general preference for simple procedures ('one input, many outputs'), unique gateways, and single points of contact. The ongoing vertical integration of data services in the information industry (Chen et al., 2019) will foster this development.

This development may take different paths, at a different pace, in different regions. de Castro et al. (2014) observe that there were some geographical areas in the world with a 'fairly well-established open access repository network, very little CRIS implementation, and barely any mechanisms in place yet for ensuring CRIS/IR interoperability'. Perhaps, in these regions, 'convergence' means that their repositories will develop new features that meet their research information management requirements; perhaps they will turn 'their eyes to open source CRIS when comprehensive research reporting starts to be perceived as an institutional need'. Then, convergence takes place.

For academic librarians, this convergence is a challenge insofar they are usually working with repositories and digital libraries while 'representing research management information, CRIS are an integral part of the ICT environment providing the context for the day-to-day work of the researcher – or research manager, innovator or the media' (Jeffery, 2012). But this challenge can be an opportunity for academic librarians to develop new services and skills, to demonstrate their mastery of metadata, curation, and standards, and to improve their relationships with academic communities and research management. They have little choice and must adapt to CRIS, as 'when it comes to interoperability with legacy systems such as Finance and HR, CRIS are the preferred system to link to because of the data and information contained in them; CRIS will become more important than IR' (Ribeiro et al., 2016). CRIS are here to stay.

For this reason, the real challenge for academic libraries is data quality and standards. They can build on a long tradition and practice with cataloguing and bibliographic standards and rules. They have a good knowledge of academic users' needs and behaviours. And they have experience with service levels and developments. In the words of one of the leading figures of the CRIS community, Keith Jeffery, the vision of the future development of CRIS 'requires a user model, a processing model and a data model providing consistent services underpinned by a resource model'

(Jeffery, 2012). The key is metadata, and metadata is part of academic librarians' core competencies. Their expertise with unique identifiers, standard protocols, and data formats is required for the development of both systems, and they will seize the convergence and merger of IR and CRIS as an opportunity for their future development on campus, as a central part of the research service environment.

## Acknowledgments

The authors would like to thank Dragan Ivanovic (University of Novi Sad) and Martin Brändle (University of Zurich) for helpful comments and advice.

## References

Arnold, C., Klee, C., 2016. Akzeptanz von Produktinnovationen: Eine Einführung. Springer Fachmedien Wiesbaden GmbH, https://doi.org/10.1007/978-3-658-11537-1.

Azeroual, O., Schöpfel, J., 2019. Quality issues of CRIS data: an exploratory investigation with universities from twelve countries. Publications 7 (1), 14. https://doi.org/10.3390/publications7010014.

Azeroual, O., Saake, G., Abuosba, M., 2018a. Data quality measures and data cleansing for research information systems. J. Digit. Inf. Manage. 16 (1), 12–21. https://arxiv.org/abs/1901.06208. (Accessed 04.05.20).

Azeroual, O., Saake, G., Wastl, J., 2018b. Data measurement in research information systems: metrics for the evaluation of data quality. Scientometrics 115 (3), 1271–1290. https://doi.org/10.1007/s11192-018-2735-5.

Azeroual, O., Saake, G., Abuosba, M., 2019a. ETL best practices for data quality checks in RIS databases. Informatics 6 (1), 10. https://doi.org/10.3390/informatics6010010.

Azeroual, O., Saake, G., Abuosba, M., Schöpfel, J., 2019b. Solving problems of research information heterogeneity during integration—using the European CERIF and German RCD standards as examples. Inf. Serv. Use 39 (1–2), 105–122. https://doi.org/10.3233/ISU-180030.

Azeroual, O., Saake, G., Abuosba, M., Schöpfel, J., 2019c. Quality of research information in RIS databases: a multidimensional approach. In: International Conference on Business Information Systems, BIS 2019. vol. 353, pp. 337–349, https://doi.org/10.1007/978-3-030-20485-3_26.

Chen, G., Posada, A., Chan, L., 2019. Vertical integration in academic publishing. connecting the knowledge commons—from projects to sustainable infrastructure. In: The 22nd International Conference on Electronic Publishing–Revised Selected Papers. OpenEdition Press, Marseille, pp. 15–40.

Clements, A., Proven, J., 2015. The emerging role of institutional CRIS in facilitating open scholarship. In: LIBER Annual Conference 2015, London, June 25th, 2015. https://dspace-cris.eurocris.org/handle/11366/393. (Accessed 04.05.20).

Davis, F.D., 1989. Perceived usefulness, perceived ease of use and user acceptance of information technology. MIS Q. 13 (3), 319–340. https://www.jstor.org/stable/249008. (Accessed 04.05.20).

de Castro, P., 2018. The role of Current Research Information Systems (CRIS) in supporting Open Science implementation: the case of Strathclyde. ITLib (5), 21–30. https://doi.org/10.25610/itlib-2018-0003.

de Castro, P., Shearer, K., Summann, F., 2014. The gradual merging of repository and CRIS solutions to meet institutional research information management requirements. In: CRIS 2014, 13–15 May 2014, Rome, Italy., https://doi.org/10.1016/j.procs.2014.06.007.

Dijk, E., Hogenaar, A., van Meel, M., 2006. NARCIS. Integrating CRIS, OAI and web crawling. In: CRIS2006: 8th International Conference on Current Research Information Systems (Bergen, May 10–13, 2006). https://dspacecris.eurocris.org/handle/11366/328. (Accessed 04.05.20).

Directory of Open Access Repositories, 2019. Jisc, Digital Resources, Open Access. https://v2.sherpa.ac.uk/opendoar/. (Accessed 03.05.20).

DSpace-CRIS, 2019. https://wiki.lyrasis.org/display/DSPACECRIS/DSpace-CRIS+Home. (Accessed 03.05.20).

Elsevier, 2020. Elsevier Pure. Research Information Management System. https://www.elsevier.com/solutions/pure/features. (Accessed 03.05.20).

Engelman, A., Enkvist, C., Pettersson, K., 2018. A FAIR archive based on the CERIF model. In: CRIS2018: 14th International Conference on Current Research Information Systems (Umeå, June 13–16, 2018)., https://doi.org/10.1016/j.procs.2019.01.076.

Harnad, S., Brody, T., Vallières, F., Carr, L., Hitchcock, S., Gingras, Y., Hilf, E., 2004. The access/impact problem and the green and gold roads to open access. Ser. Rev. 30 (4), 310–314. https://doi.org/10.1016/j.serrev.2004.09.013.

Hey, T., Tansley, S., Tolle, K. (Eds.), 2009. The Fourth Paradigm: Data-Intensive Scientific Discovery. Redmond, WA, Microsoft.

Hyper Articles en Ligne, 2001. https://hal.archives-ouvertes.fr/. (Accessed 03.05.20).

International Federation of Library Associations and Institutions (IFLA), 2016. Code of Ethics. https://www.ifla.org/publications/node/11092. (Accessed 03.05.20).

Ivanović, D., Ivanović, L., Dimić-Surla, B., 2014. Multi-interoperable CRIS repository. In: CRIS 2014, 13–15 May 2014, Rome, Italy., https://doi.org/10.1016/j.procs.2014.06.014.

Jeffery, K., 2012. CRIS in 2020. In: CRIS2012: 11th International Conference on Current Research Information Systems (Prague, June 6–9, 2012). http://dspacecris.eurocris.org/handle/11366/119. (Accessed 04.05.20).

Joint, N., 2008. Current research information systems, open access repositories and libraries. Libr. Rev. 57 (8), 570–575. https://doi.org/10.1108/00242530810899559.

Kollmann, T., 1998. Akzeptanz innovativer Nutzungsgüter und -systeme: Konsequenzen für die Einführung von Telekommunikations- und Multimediasystemen. Gabler Verlag, Springer Fachmedien Wiesbaden GmbH, Wiesbaden, https://doi.org/10.1007/978-3-663-09235-3.

Labastida i Juan, I., 2015. Managing the bridge between institutional repositories and CRIS: Universitat de Barcelona. In: EuroCRIS Strategic Meeting, Barcelona, 10th November, 2015. https://dspacecris.eurocris.org/bitstream/11366/412/1/Eurocris_Labastida.pdf. (Accessed 08.05.20).

Lucke, B., 1995. Akzeptanz: Legitimität in der 'Abstimmungsgesellschaft'. VS Verlag für Sozialwissenschaften, Springer Fachmedien Wiesbaden GmbH, Wiesbaden, https://doi.org/10.1007/978-3-663-09234-6.

Lynch, C., 2003. Institutional repositories: essential infrastructure for scholarship in the digital age. Libr. Acad. 3 (2), 327–336. Project MUSE, https://doi.org/10.1353/pla.2003.0039.

MacGregor, G., 2019. Repository and CRIS interoperability issues within a 'connector lite' environment. In: OR 2019 14th International Conference on Open Repositories, Hamburg, June 10–13, 2019. https://pureportal.strath.ac.uk/en/publications/repository-and-cris-interoperability-issues-within-a-connector-li. (Accessed 04.05.20).

National Academic Research and Collaborations Information System (NARCIS), 2007. https://www.narcis.nl/. (Accessed 03.05.20).

OpenAIRE, 2018a. OpenAIRE History. https://www.openaire.eu/history. (Accessed 03.05.20).

OpenAIRE, 2018b. Guidelines for CRIS Managers 1.1. https://zenodo.org/record/2316420. (Accessed 03.05.20).

Portal de la Recerca de Catalunya (PRC), 2020. https://portalrecerca.csuc.cat/?locale=en. (Accessed 03.05.20).

Ribeiro, L., de Castro, P., Mennielli, M., 2016. EUNIS—EUROCRIS Joint Survey on CRIS and IR (Final Report). EUNIS, Paris. http://www.eunis.org/wp-content/uploads/2016/03/cris-report-ED.pdf. (Accessed 04.05.20).

Rybinski, H., Skonieczny, L., Koperwas, J., Struk, W., Stepniak, J., Kubrak, W., 2017. Integrating IR with CRIS—a novel researcher-centric approach. Program 51 (3), 298–321. https://doi.org/10.1108/prog-04-2017-0026.

Rybinski, H., Kubrak, W., Skonieczny, L., Koperwas, J., Struk, W., 2018. Omega-Psir—Institutional CRIS at Polish Universities. ITlib (5), 36–44. https://itlib.cvtisr.sk/archiv/2018/5/omega-psir-institutional-cris-at-polish-universities.html?page_id=3532. (Accessed 04.05.20).

Schöpfel, J., Azeroual, O., Saake, G., 2019. Implementation and user acceptance of research information systems. Data Technol. Appl. 54 (1), 1–15. https://doi.org/10.1108/DTA-01-2019-0009.

Siciliano, L., Schmidt, S., Kinzler, M., 2014. BoRIS and BIA: CRIS and institutional repository integration at the Free University of Bozen-Bolzano. In: CRIS 2014, 13–15 May 2014, Rome, Italy. vol. 33, pp. 68–73, https://doi.org/10.1016/j.procs.2014.06.011.

Suber, P., 2012. Open Access. MIT Press, Cambridge, MA. http://mitpress.mit.edu/books/open-access. (Accessed 04.05.20).

Venkatesh, V., Speier, C., Morris, M.G., 2007. User acceptance enablers in individual decision making about technology: toward an integrated model. Decis. Sci. 33 (2), 297–316. https://doi.org/10.1111/j.1540-5915.2002.tb01646.x.

Wenaas, L., Karlstrøm, N., Vatnan, T., 2012. From a national CRIS along the road to green open access—and back again: building infrastructure from CRIStin to institutional repositories in Norway. In: CRIS 2012. 11th International Conference on Current Research Information Systems, June 6–8, 2012, Prague, Czech Republic. https://dspacecris.eurocris.org/handle/11366/116. (Accessed 04.05.20).

Zurich Open Repository and Archive (ZORA), 2019. https://www.zora.uzh.ch/. (Accessed 03.05.20).

# Effective strategies for information literacy education: Combatting 'fake news' and empowering critical thinking

3

*Andy Phippen*[a], *Emma Bond*[b], *and Ellen Buck*[b]
[a]Bournemouth University, Bournemouth, United Kingdom, [b]University of Suffolk, Ipswich, United Kingdom

## 3.1 Introduction

Broad and inclusive information literacies have been important for the university sector for a considerable time but are increasingly becoming understood as *digital* literacies in the contemporary society. They are a crucial aspect of graduate employability and a key component of the broader expectation that universities exist to develop global citizens capable of functioning in a connected, liberal society. In drawing upon learning analytics from a UK higher education institution (HEI), this chapter outlines how the nature of student engagement with information is changing, with far greater accessing of e-books and online journal systems, and the general expectation of most institutional engagement to have some level of online interaction. At the same time, we are seeing increasing concerns across the higher education (HE) sector in relation to online abuse, harassment, and hate crime, with universities struggling to effectively respond and support students (Phippen and Bond, 2020). It is, therefore, 'essential to understand how technologies develop, how people use them, and the implications that they have on learning spaces and social cohesion in the HE environment' (Bond and Goodchild, 2013, p. 122). This we argue is crucially important in developing critical digital literacies across the contemporary HE milieu in order to address rising concerns in relation to wider aspects of digital citizenship.

This chapter critically considers the wider context of students' technological landscapes and everyday experiences in a digital society to suggest that universities need to take a more holistic approach to supporting students in developing ethical digital literacies in the 21st century. We argue that ethical digital literacies are not simply showing students how to use information resources effectively, but to understand how digital technology can be used, and abused, in a broader social context. Although we have recently seen a significant shift across the university sector to make use of information and communication technologies (ICTs) for learning environments and pedagogic tools, we have also simultaneously witnessed (e.g. through the abuse of plagiarism detection systems and learning environments that report on a student's engagement with a given course) such tools being used negatively to monitor and control students, potentially impacting on their human rights.

**Future Directions in Digital Information. https://doi.org/10.1016/B978-0-12-822144-0.00003-3**

The majority of this generation of students, the post-millennials, will have grown up with more access to ubiquitous technologies than those cohorts of students before them. Yet, there is an evidence across the sector that the assumption that all students are already fully equipped to engage with information systems—the 'digital natives' hypothesis (see Prensky, 2001)—is both misleading and unhelpful as it lends itself to a false conjecture that there is a little need to develop educational strategies around digital literacies. This chapter explores philosophically the concept of the digitally literate student and what it means practically for an institution. We consider the risk to the institution in not developing effective strategies for digital literacy education, from both being capable of delivering an effective student learning experience, but also more widely as to whether they are failing in their duty of care to equip students with the knowledge to both exploit the online world and also protect themselves from harm and we suggest that universities need to strive to develop ethical digital literacies across the sector.

## 3.2 Delivering learning

Any consideration of using technology in everyday life reveals a highly complex and complicated network of people, things, devices, software and digital content, and activity, carried out within rapidly changing sociopolitical, technical, and cultural contexts (Bond, 2014). Thus, as universities are charged with ensuring students are 'career ready' for the immediate and longer-term futures, so the learning delivered must support the development of required competencies. The 'transnational', 'value added' graduate needs to be equipped with a global mindset and transcultural and digital literacy skills for cross-cultural communication (Wyburd, 2017) and interpreting and decoding the role digital texts play in the digital economy 'should be a key element of what it means to be literate in contemporary society' (Pangrazio and Selwyn, 2019, p. 427).

Not only is this achieved by knowledge acquisition through curricula but also through the ways in which the university applies this knowledge to its own practices; in short, leading and delivering learning through whole-environment design. For service providers such as librarians and academic skills advisors this often means moves to extensively digital collections (Casselden and Pears, 2019), a needed increased focus on a broad, beyond-library conceptualization of information literacy and an understanding of how technologies such as plagiarism detection tools can themselves become tools for learning. Academics must respond to the need to evolve their pedagogic practices, drawing on team based (Sibley et al., 2014) and flipped learning (Jenkins et al., 2017), maximizing the technological affordances (Johnston et al., 2018) delivered in part through online learning environments (OLE).

With this technological shift, there is an increasing amount of data available to monitor 'usage'. While usage data may become a proxy for measures of engagement, often gathered and reviewed through learner analytics platforms, it should help universities and practitioners understand the changing approaches students are taking to information, what it means to deliver learning in a digital landscape. The following examples, on the use of learning environments, pedagogical tools and online literature, are taken from practice at the University of Suffolk, UK.

## 3.3 Learning environment

Typically, university learning environments have been understood as physical or virtual. The physical classroom has been the primary space for learning; with the virtual environment being used as a 'bolt on' activity, a holding pen, or repository for learning resources. Recent changes in the platform used have enabled the university and its educational practitioners to reimagine the spaces. Online spaces have become integral to the learning experience as Dezuanni (2015, p. 436) proposes: 'digital forms of communication are ubiquitous and vernacular, and students deserve the opportunity to learn to participate with these technologies that will enhance their life opportunities'. Thus, no longer the 'bolt on', the OLE becomes the hub for learning from which seamless connections can be made to other learning spaces (home, workplace, and transport), taking learning to the learner.

The recent development of a blended learning degree apprenticeship has provided colleagues with an opportunity to see the impact of these changes on learning behaviours. This development coincided with the implementation of a new OLE for the university, one which would offer a 21st-century learning experience.

The BSc (Hons) Nursing degree apprenticeship blended learning programme has been fully instructionally designed, scaffolding self-directed learning and promoting social learning activities. In itself this approach helps students to develop collaborative approaches to learning, problem solving, and team working; competencies which are invaluable for future graduates. This course runs alongside its sibling course with a more traditional mode of delivery, focusing on face-to-face delivery.

As the two courses have been delivered over the last academic year, it has been possible to begin to review the data that the OLE is providing in relation to measures of usage and engagement with resources for two identical content modules across the different modes of delivery.

The blended learning programme has 44 enrolled students. The traditional programme has 79. The larger size of the cohort on the traditional delivery course is reflected in the number of platform logins, but the data appear to show an explicit difference in the information and resource usage behaviours from November 2018 to August 2019 between the two student groups. The data are presented in Table 3.1.

It might be assumed that students on a blended learning course would spend more time in the OLE and those going there to revisit face-to-face delivered resources, for example, lecture PowerPoint slides. These data appear to be telling a different story, however; the number of log-ins per student is fewer (124:174 on average) but the time spent in content, engaging with it, and responding to it is far greater and far more consistent.

**Table 3.1** Comparing blended and traditional access to case study courses.

| | Module 1 | | Module 2 | |
|---|---|---|---|---|
| | **Blended** | **Traditional** | **Blended** | **Traditional** |
| No. log-ins | 5457 | 13,591 | 5487 | 13,891 |
| Time spent in module (h) | 52 | 24 | 106 | 60 |
| Average page access per student | 30 | 8 | 55 | 23 |

In the blended learning delivery students are asked to engage in learning activities, develop reflective practice through e-portfolios, and share learning through conditional-release activities, commenting on the contributions of their peers. Alongside the knowledge acquisition aligned to the learning outcomes, students are having to develop their online identity in a context which is similar to, but different from, social media. There is a need for students to understand these differences, and to be able to develop the skills needed in a learning social network (Kennedy et al., 2017).

## 3.4 The creative use of pedagogic tools

The creative use of classroom technologies and tools to enhance the learning experience and increase engagement and retention of students is well established (Blessinger and Wankel, 2013) but there are also tools, for example, plagiarism detection tools, which can also be used to enhance and promote learning.

Plagiarism detection software is often perceived as a punitive tool, working to catch students trying to cheat the system, and pass off the work of others as their own. Reports produced by the tool can be difficult to interpret with a potential to result in increased cases of academic misconduct. The wider digital learning environment in which students have to learn to operate, 'require the development of digital literacies both on the part of learners and educators' (Helm, 2014, p. 46). Work by Academic Skills Advisors (ASAs) has recently shown how this tool can be used to develop and use higher-order cognitive skills, using information more effectively.

Academic referencing is central to academic integrity, but it is also a skill which causes a considerable degree of anxiety. ASAs frequently encounter students who want to be able to reference correctly to avoid penalty or accusations of academic misconduct. With students focused on the mechanics of referencing such as the commas, italics, and quote marks, the power of appropriate and effective referencing as a tool is lost. In a digital learning environment, students can be taught how to use technologies to enhance and increase the impact of the narratives they build through research and information.

This is certainly true of plagiarism software. Rather than using software to better evade detection, plagiarism reports and 'match reports' provide a student with invaluable data which, with guidance, can be used to enable academic voice and argument. In context, the report can indicate where poor academic practice results in 'red flags', ones which can be omitted through appropriate and effective referencing. Developing skills in this way helps to demonstrate the power that information, used in the correct way, can have, and conversely what happens when information is misused. However, as with all things algorithmic, they can sometimes be blunt tools, whose accuracy for detecting plagiarism can vary as expressed so eloquently by Weber-Wulff (2019):

> *Software cannot determine plagiarism; it can only point to some cases of matching text. The systems can be useful for flagging up problems, but not for discriminating between originality and plagiarism. That decision must be taken by a person.*

## 3.5 Information provision

It is increasingly recognized that engagement with libraries and library resources is an indication of both engagement with learning and student outcomes (Australasian Survey of Student Engagement [AUSSE], 2012; Soria et al., 2013). E-books and e-journals have become a silver bullet for university libraries. Notwithstanding the challenges they may bring to librarians (Frederick, 2015), 'e' is understood by library patrons to both be ubiquitously accessible, device agnostic and, importantly, customizable through assistive functionality.

In the last 3 years, this university library has invested primarily in a 'digital first' approach to collection development. This investment responds to a large body of commuter students, long periods of placement, and students studying across multiple campuses. Nationally, the average number of e-books accesses per full-time equivalent (FTE) user was 77% higher in 2016–2017 than 2013–2014 (SCONUL, 2018a) and this trend is also reflected locally. Data submitted to SCONUL's annual statistics return show that in 2015–2016 full-text article requests were at 377,977, while in 2017–2018 this had increased to 525,035. E-book section requests increased from 817,552 to 1,210,626 in the same period (SCONUL, 2016, 2018b). At the same time, the loan of physical books, excluding renewals, decreased from 58,653 to 47,854.

Looking at individual titles, it was possible to see dramatic differences in usage data, one title had over 8000 section requests in 2017–2018, with only 63 loans. Liaison Librarians challenged the data, arguing that students would not be using the books in the same way. There was a belief that print books were being read cover-to-cover, while e-books were being dipped in and out of multiple times. The types of use were not considered truly comparable.

> *Academic libraries have invested heavily in electronic resources and made them accessible via the information systems embedded in their library web portals.*
>
> *Chen (2014, p. 263)*

Understanding what that means for information seeking behaviours for students on courses is challenging to those adjusting to the change in format. Students often prefer using Google and Google Scholar (Zhao, 2015), and the integration of library collections with tools such as Google Scholar normalizes academic research; discovery tools enable students to hone their research skills using 'google-esque' search boxes. While finding information remains a fundamental skill, understanding what the information is, its provenance, in an increasingly digital learning landscape with blurred boundaries, becomes even more critical.

## 3.6 Information literacy

Over the past few decades, academic libraries in universities have become providers of information literacy (IL) training (Chen and Lin, 2011) and while there is often confusion between IL skills and information technology (IT) skills amongst academics and students (Ellis et al., 2016), IL is central to learning and to developing lifelong learning (Chen, 2014; Mnkeni-Saurombe, 2015). Education has always been intertwined with material technologies and actor network theory (ANT) offers a valuable lens with which to understand this interconnectedness (Fenwick and Edwards, 2012). IL is viewed as a key aspect of digital literacy, and Dezuanni (2015, p. 420) draws on ANT to propose that information literacies 'are produced by negotiations within networks as students and teachers interact with digital technologies, concepts and materials'. Furthermore, as Foucault (1991) observes, such [learning] environments are produced within the specific yet arguably broader social, cultural, temporal, political, and technological spaces of which they are part. By understanding the broader context, the intricate and mutually constitutive character of the human and the technical becomes apparent. As such, student learning and students' interaction with learning materials needs to be understood in this wider sociotechnical context and the diversity of student experience is central to developing realistic understandings.

Unhelpful conceptualizations associated with notions of the 'digital native' rhetoric (see Prensky, 2001), we argue, hide the reality of the diversity of students' lived experiences, leads to unhelpful assumptions that universities are currently populated by cohorts of 'the digital' or 'Internet' generation and undermines their right to education, help, and support to develop critical digital literacies. Such notions are highly problematic as there is a wealth of evidence that young people are growing up not as a homogenous digital generation but with digital diversity. As stark digital divides across socioeconomic, gender and geographic clusters remain (ONS, 2019), there is, in reality, a considerable diversity in young people's ability to use information sources, knowledge of the Internet, and their opportunities to access and interact online. Furthermore, digital literacy is too often oversimplified and needs to include creation, critical thinking, and ethical reasoning and as digital technologies continue to influence teaching, learning, and research, colleges and universities should be developing and expanding digital literacy programmes to ensure that students can not only use digital tools but also critically consume and create a variety of content (Feerrar, 2019). Pangrazio and Selwyn (2019, p. 422) assert that:

> *The field of media and communication offers a more nuanced approach to data literacies, where the focus is upon developing critical understandings of the language audience and representations of data.*

While such perspectives are not new but rooted in previous educational responses to digital media that promote critical understanding (see e.g. Buckingham, 2003), we suggest that it would be helpful to draw on such approaches when developing and evaluating digital literacy programmes in the HE sector.

## 3.7 Ethical literacy

Using an ANT approach, we understand learning, agency, ethical literacies, and resilience as network effects in themselves, as being produced by the ongoing interactions of human and nonhuman actors in the network. Such conceptualizations are also helpful in considering the UK Government White Paper (2019) on online harms, which outlines how policy makers are increasingly concerned about developing more joined up approaches to responding to online risk.

> *Although most university students' experiences of technology are useful and positive, where online harassment does occur, this can have severe and long-term repercussions for physical, emotional and mental wellbeing and affect academic achievement and future career prospects. Yet, the evidence also shows that for many young people, online harassment is embedded in their digital lives and to some extent is normalised and expected, emerging as part of a wider dynamic of their peer group and intimate relationships. Understanding this is important for universities when developing strategies and interventions to challenge such behaviour.*
>
> *UUK (2019, p. 6)*

However, many universities are unaware of, or fail to acknowledge the role of, digital technologies and social media in students' everyday lives and a lack of understanding of their rights, legislation, and social behaviours continue to place students at risk of online harms (Phippen and Bond, 2020).

Thus, as the debate has shifted towards critical digital literacy which involves both 'critical and practical understanding of digital technologies in socio-cultural settings, where people are creators as well as observers' (Alexander et al., 2016, p. 1), we have simultaneously seen rising concerns in how universities are responding to the wider sociotechnical contexts of students' everyday lives. Hauck (2019, p. 202), for example, proposes a better understanding of the importance of critical digital literacy in relation to the characteristics of the 21st-century graduate and suggests that what is missing from the current debate on digital literacy is 'the critical dimension of digital literacy as reflected in awareness of the socio-cultural contexts of technology use beyond education systems'. We, therefore, argue that universities have a wider duty of care towards their students than providing IL support and encouraging critical digital literacy, and that by adopting a more holistic approach, universities should be striving to support the development of ethical digital literacies across the HE sector.

As Professor Debra Humphries, writing in the UUK (2019) report cited above, argues:

> *Education is the key tool in arming all students with the knowledge of how to stay safe online and how to report offensive content. Universities are ideally placed to support students to engage with the Internet safely and to raise awareness of the potential harms from online harassment, including the impact on physical and mental health, academic success and potential career prospects.*

We also argue that universities have a vital role to play in developing educational programmes and resources for students embedded across the curriculum to enable meaningful and critical engagement with digital society. Rather than simply viewing IL as an isolated skill required for academic success (or even survival), it should be seen as one of the actants (see Callon and Latour, 1981) in the complex network of people (students, educators, and associated others); technological tools; the learning setting (the HEI) and the wider global, political, economic, and technological environment. Therefore, we suggest that a more holistic approach to developing not only IL and digital literacies but also to developing critical digital literacies is required across the HE sector. In understanding the development of such literacies as a part of the wider everyday experiences of students, which includes the challenges and risks they face, we can better facilitate a shift towards developing ethical digital literacies across the HE milieu.

## 3.8 The continuum of digital risk in HE

Universities cannot assume that students arrive at university with a strong appreciation of information literacy or how to present an argument in an evidence-based manner. There is much discussion in the literature around digital literacy in HE (e.g. Jones and Shao, 2011; Gaston, 2006) that embraces the unhelpful discourse around 'digital natives', already dismissed earlier in this chapter, as well as other literature (Kennedy et al., 2008) that questions the legitimacy of the term in relation to higher education students. The idea that, simply as a result of being born in a given year or beyond, somehow an individual would have an innate ability to navigate the digital landscapes in a manner not possible by those born before this year (1980 apparently being the year the change occurred) has been roundly discredited, and fails to acknowledge the disparate nature of the teaching of information literacies in schools.

We have, in our experience working on policy projects related to online abuse and harassment, observed these unhelpful terms being used, along with assumptions that, as 'digital natives', the current generation of students come to university equipped with a set of digital skills, which means the institution need not worry about addressing this core skills need—'don't they learn about all of this sort of thing in schools?'

However, perhaps the most reliable source of evidence on the teaching of digital literacy in schools is the UK Safer Internet Centre's annual analysis of the 360 Degree Safe self-review tool, a software platform that allows schools to perform a thorough audit of their online safety policy and practice. Among the aspects of practice considered in the tool is digital literacy, described in the tool thus:

> *This aspect describes how the school develops the ability of young people to find, evaluate, use, share, and create digital content in a way that minimises risk and promotes positive outcomes.*

The tool allows schools to rate themselves from level 1 (outstanding) to level 5 (no practice whatsoever). In 2018 (Phippen, 2019), data from almost 8000 schools, from both primary (aged 5–11) and secondary (aged 11–18) settings in the United Kingdom would suggest the vast majority of schools have 'some' level of information literacy but it does not go beyond the fundamental teaching at an ad hoc level as defined in the tool as level 3:

> *Pupils/students are taught in some lessons to be critically aware of the content they access online and how to validate the accuracy of information. They have an understanding of research skills and the need to avoid plagiarism and uphold copyright regulations. There is evidence that functional skills to operate online in a safe and appropriate way are taught.*

While the majority of schools (43%) disclose this aspect at level 3, 19% of schools fall below that level and 38% are above.

So, for the majority of schools surveyed, at best we can assume that digital literacy has been addressed to 'some' level, but nothing beyond a few lessons. There is little in the national curriculum that provides guidance on digital literacy, as highlighted in the recent UK Government's Science and Technology Committee investigation into young people's use of social media and impact on mental health (Science and Technology Committee, 2017) which made clear calls for more effective digital literacy, and co-ordination within the national curriculum, to ensure this education was delivered in a progressive and uniform manner. However, currently within the UK education system, HEIs assume good levels of digital literacy at their peril.

A key facet of the challenges in engaging with ethical digital literacy is the 'so what?' question: what are the issues that might arise if the HE sector does step up to the plate regarding ensuring a 21st-century digital literacy among their student bodies. We would argue that there lies a continuum of digital risk upon which various problematic digital behaviours sit, and equally we might suggest that the severity of the risk will vary between the individual (the student) and the organization (the university). We can place activities such as plagiarism, fake news, unauthorized access, abuse, and harassment on this continuum, and we would argue that critical thinking, alongside an appreciation of what is both legal and ethical, are fundamental factors in tackling all on the continuum. We need to move away from unhelpful typologies such as those defined in the Online Harms White Paper (Science and Technology Committee, 2017) and focus instead on the underlying knowledge that will mitigate these risks and protect institutions.

What is also clear is that the days of institutional immunity to the actions of the student body are fading quickly, and we are beginning to see far more debate around what 'duty of care' looks like for a university (Sladdin, 2018). We only need to consider that perennial challenge for the digital literacies in the higher education—plagiarism—to appreciate this.

We have, in the HE sector, invested for many years much research and curriculum time into tackling the plagiarism issue. There are clear reasons for addressing these concerns so robustly. Most obviously, there are issues of academic dishonesty and the quality of achievement for a student associated with a given institution. There have been a number of reputationally damaging news article (Ali, 2016) across the sector related to 'paid for' degrees. However, there is also a clear institutional risk associated with a student plagiarizing in a piece of work (e.g. a dissertation or PhD thesis) that becomes a public document. While we invest time and policy in protecting the institution from associated damages that might arise from such behaviour (e.g. a disclaimer at the start of the document that the student signs to state it is all their own work), there are still concerns that an institution could become liable if the accused student claims they were not made aware of plagiaristic practice and their legality (Littlemore, 2012) (i.e. the university failed to deliver effective information literacy to the individual and the student cannot, therefore, be judged to have behaved in a dishonest manner). With clear implications for both reputation and legal challenge, it is no surprise that plagiarism has been a key focus for institutions for a number of years. We see policies in place and in general universities will labour the point about the student's responsibility to not plagiarize and the disciplinary implications if they do. Moreover, we see the rise in 'plagiarism detection software', which claims to make the detection of plagiarized content more straightforward and easier to detect.

The logical extension to plagiarism is what is sometimes referred to as fake news—defined on Wikipedia (Wikipedia, n.d.) as:

> *Fake news (also known as junk news, pseudo-news, or hoax news) is a form of news consisting of deliberate disinformation or hoaxes spread via traditional news media (print and broadcast) or online social media.*

The use of Wikipedia for this definition is both deliberate and somewhat mischievous, in that there is much academic debate about its relevance and accuracy for academic writing (e.g. Eijkman, 2010). In this case, we feel it provides a reasonable definition of fake news.

We can consider these two types of misuse of information as parts of the continuum of digital risk; while one makes claims of ownership over information that are not justified, the other is the use of information to justify a position, argument, or opinion and presents, again, a risk to academic credibility as a result. While the academy has invested considerable resources into plagiarism and plagiarism detection, it is only beginning to struggle with fake news. We have, at this stage, few feasible approaches in making use of algorithms to detect fake news sources. Indeed, when Facebook announced their 'fake news' strategy (Facebook, 2017), it was clear that it was more targeted at account-level identification and exclusion than identifying authenticity through textual analysis.

From a digital literacy point of view, fake news is poor uses of information resources to make unfounded claims. We might argue similarity with unintentional plagiarism for those with poor information literacy, who do not understand either the proper use of citation or appreciating how to source quality information resources. And while fake news is challenging to tackle with technical interventions, both can be tackled with information literacy that asks some fundamental questions such as:

- From where did you source the information?
- Who was the author?
- Is there any means to check the validity of the claims they make?
- Are you referring to it correctly?
- Are you presenting the information as fact or opinion?

There are some basic skills we can instill in students around presenting an evidence-based argument, where that evidence is rigorous and well considered. In this era of 'post truth' (McIntyre, 2018) and poor role modelling around rigorous fact checking, it is crucial that students do not start to draw on fake news sources and can make a distinction between an opinion and an evidence-based position. While academic sources might demonstrate different perspectives on an argument, they will, one would hope, at least have an evidence base or theoretical perspective to underpin this.

In moving further along the continuum, we get into an area when digital literacy becomes more than just understanding sources and resources, to appreciating the ethical use of, and access to, devices and resources. We would argue strongly that an institution consider what ethical digital literacy might look like for the needs of their student body to consider these more behavioural aspects, which can result in legal challenge, potentially on university estate and equipment. From an institutional perspective, this does not make them directly liable. However, it is still something we need to consider with the 'digital student' arriving at the university with a poor grasp on what is, and is not, unacceptable behaviour. As stated in the recent Universities UK guidance on online harassment and abuse (McIntyre, 2018):

> *Should a student become the subject of abuse, or at risk of abuse, within an online environment provided by their university, the institution needs to be able to demonstrate due diligence, for example through the use of well-defined acceptable usage policies, appropriate monitoring approaches and effective staff training to recognise and support those students who are at risk.*

Issues related to digital behaviour differ in terms of both act and severity. We know, through our own teaching of students over many years, that a lot of these might be dismissed as 'banter'. For example, a student taking a mobile device from another, who may have left the device unlocked or not have a means of authenticated access enabled, might then use the device to send a joke message or social media post, masquerading as the device's owner. In general, there is little harm that arises from these antics, but, by the letter of the law (specifically *section 1 of the Computer Misuse Act 1990*—UK Government, 1990) they have engaged in illegal activity. While we would not suggest that an institution should generally involve law enforcement in these sorts of behaviours, it is worthwhile to be sufficiently ‘digitally aware’ about the legislation in the event of more abusive behaviour that might result from the unauthorized access to a device.

Recent media stories have shown how digital technologies might be used by students to abuse, and defame; also, how universities have struggled to address these problems. For example, there have been stories where an institution has a society using group chats to post up messages clearly contravening hate crime legislation (BBC News, 2018). While the university response was swift, what was clear from the reporting was that the institution had not defined policy to address these sorts of issues prior to the incident. While group chats using platforms such as WhatsApp (as was used in this case) are not public or easily accessed from those beyond the group, neither can they be considered private communications (in that they are seen by more than two people).

However, perhaps the most well-known incident (BBC News, 2019) recently that highlighted the nature of online abuse in universities, and a poor institutional response, occurred when a female student was shown a long and extensive Facebook group chat, where male students were making extreme and graphic threats of sexual violence towards their peers. When a complaint was made, and when some of those in the group’s chat were subject to disciplinary action, some were allowed to continue with their studies alongside those to whom threats have been made. The outcome of this is an ongoing case of negligence brought by two of the students against the institution, and much negative publicity in the press.

The result of these cases is that there is far more of a focus around what a duty of care looks like from institutions when concerned with the digital literacy of their students, and how they respond when issues such as academic dishonesty or abuse arise as a result of digital technology. If we are to take a legal position, while duty of care is, of itself, a term reliant on case law when related to the tort of negligence, there is a more general moral duty that one might expect in the student/institutional contract. We have already taken note of the Office of the Independent Adjudicator for Higher Education stating that institutions have a role to play in ensuring students are aware of the nature of plagiarism and why it is important. Equally, we see growing numbers of cases (albeit without established case law) that are moving us towards a clearer picture of what form this duty of care might take, and when an institution might be considered negligent.

We have shown in this discussion that there is little evidence to expect students to arrive at an institution with a uniform and complete knowledge of what we have referred to as ethical digital literacy, and there is no defence in saying ‘we assumed they already knew this’. We would argue that these ethical literacy skills are now fundamental for future employability and to be able to make an effective contribution to the society, which one might imagine would further motivate institutions into tackling the poor digital literacies of their students. However, our recent research (BBC News, 2019) would highlight that universities are, in general, playing catch-up when considering students’ use of digital technologies, with the majority not even having a policy in place to tackle this.

We cannot expect a university to be able to produce ethically digitally literate students if it cannot demonstrate such capabilities of itself. There is a fundamental need within the university sector for institutions to not simply provide online learning platforms as a way of demonstrating its literacy, but to have effective policy in place, alongside well-trained staff and effective, responsive reporting routes that give students confidence that their institution is aware of both the capabilities of digital technology and also the risk, and how to mitigate against them.

## 3.9 Conclusion

Developing a student body that is digitally literate can no longer be considered simply equipping them with the skills to use the learning platforms we provide. We have shown that students are clearly becoming more and more digitally engaged, and also that we cannot expect students to arrive at our institutions with a full-rounded knowledge of what it means to be digitally literate. Whether we call these principles digital literacy, online safety or virtual resilience, we need to move beyond looking at specific issues and developing a framework of critical thinking that can tackle both current and future online risks.

We have also argued that there are strong institutional drivers for universities to engage in the development of ethical digital literacies for their student body, and to show leadership in this area. Ethical digital literacy encompasses a duty of care such that institutions act reasonably in students' best interests, to protect their well-being and provide appropriate support, while providing them with knowledge that will be useful for both their time at university, their careers beyond, and their everyday lives.

## References

Alexander, B., Adams Becker, S., Cummins, M., 2016. Digital Literacy: An NMC Horizon Project Strategic Brief. vol. 3.1 New Media Consortium, Austin, TX.

Ali, A., 2016. UK Universities in 'Plagiarism Epidemic' as Almost 50,000 Students Caught Cheating Over Last 3 Years. https://www.independent.co.uk/student/news/uk-universities-in-plagiarism-epidemic-as-almost-50000-students-caught-cheating-over-last-3-years-a6796021.html. (Accessed 29.04.20).

Australasian Survey of Student Engagement (AUSSE), 2012. Australasian University Executive Summary Report. https://www.acer.org/files/AUSSE_2012_Australasia_University_Executive_Summary.pdf. (Accessed 08.05.20).

Blessinger, P., Wankel, C., 2013. Increasing Student Engagement and Retention Using Classroom Technologies: Classroom Response Systems and Mediated Discourse Technologies. Emerald, Bingley.

BBC News, 2018. 'Racist' Law Society Disbanded by University of Exeter. https://www.bbc.co.uk/news/uk-england-devon-46565444. (Accessed 29.04.20).

BBC News, 2019. Inside the Warwick University Rape Chat Scandal. https://www.bbc.co.uk/news/uk-48366835. (Accessed 29.04.20).

Bond, E., 2014. Childhood, Mobile Technologies and Everyday Experiences. Palgrave, Basingstoke.

Bond, E., Goodchild, T., 2013. Challenges of teaching with technology in HE: towards a new third space? In: Cases on Higher Education Spaces: Innovation, Collaboration, and Technology. IGI Global, pp. 121–139.

Buckingham, D., 2003. Media Education: Literacy, Learning and Contemporary Culture. Policy Press, Cambridge.

Callon, M., Latour, B., 1981. Unscrewing the big leviathan: how actors macro-structure reality and how sociologists help them to do so. In: Knorr-Cetina, K., Cicourel, A.V. (Eds.), Advances in Social Theory and Methodology: Toward an Integration of Micro- and Macro-Sociologies. Routledge, Boston, pp. 277–304.

Casselden, B., Pears, R., 2019. Higher education student pathways to ebook usage and engagement, and understanding: highways and cul de sacs. J. Librariansh. Inf. Sci. https://doi.org/10.1177/0961000619841429.

Chen, Y., 2014. Testing the impact of an information literacy course: undergraduates' perceptions and use of the university libraries' web portal. Libr. Inf. Sci. Res. 37, 262–274.

Chen, K., Lin, P., 2011. Information literacy in university library education: towards a working model. Inf. Res. 12 (4), 399–418.

Dezuanni, M., 2015. The building blocks of media literacy: socio-material participation and the production of media knowledge. J. Curric. Stud. 47 (3), 416–439.

Eijkman, H., 2010. Academics and Wikipedia: reframing Web 2.0+ as a disruptor of traditional academic power-knowledge arrangements. Campus-Wide Inf. Syst. 27 (3). https://doi.org/10.1108/10650741011054474.

Ellis, C., Johnson, F., Rowley, J., 2016. Promoting information literacy: perspectives from UK universities. Library Hi Tech 35 (1), 53–70.

Facebook, 2017. Working to Stop Misinformation and False News. https://www.facebook.com/facebookmedia/blog/working-to-stop-misinformation-and-false-news. (Accessed 29.04.20).

Feerrar, J., 2019. Development of a framework for digital literacy. Ref. Serv. Rev. 47 (2), 91–105.

Fenwick, T., Edwards, M., 2012. Researching Education Through Actor-Network Theory. Wiley, London.

Foucault, M., 1991. Discipline and Punish: The Birth of the Prison. Penguin Books, London.

Frederick, D.E., 2015. On eBooks in academic libraries: an article based on a presentation at the Library 2.014 Conference. Library Hi Tech News 32 (5), 12–15.

Gaston, J., 2006. Reaching and teaching the digital natives. Library Hi Tech News.

Hauck, M., 2019. Virtual exchange for (critical) digital literacy skills development. Eur. J. Lang. Policy 11 (2), 187–210.

Helm, F., 2014. Developing digital literacies through virtual exchange. eLearning Papers 38, 1–10.

Jenkins, M., Bokosmaty, R., Brown, M., Browne, C., Gao, Q., Hanson, J., Kupatadze, K., 2017. Enhancing the design and analysis of flipped learning strategies. Teach. Learn. Inq.: ISSOTL J. 5 (1), 1–13.

Johnston, B., Macneill, S., Smyth, K., 2018. Conceptualising the Digital University: The Intersection of Policy, Pedagogy and Practice. Palgrave Macmillan.

Jones, C., Shao, B., 2011. The Net Generation and Digital Natives: Implications for Higher Education. http://oro.open.ac.uk/30014/1/Jones_and_Shao-Final.pdf. (Accessed 29.04.20).

Kennedy, G.E., Judd, T.S., Churchward, A., Gray, K., Krause, K.L., 2008. First year students' experiences with technology: are they really digital natives? Australasian Journal of Educational Technology 24 (1).

Kennedy, E., Neumann, T., Rowett, S., Strawbridge, F., 2017. Digital education and the connected curriculum: towards a connected learning environment. In: Carnell, B., Fung, D. (Eds.), Developing the Higher Education Curriculum: Research-Based Education in Practice. UCL Press, London, pp. 188–202.

Littlemore, S., 2012. Universities Need to Tell Students the Rules About Plagiarism, Says Adjudicator. https://www.theguardian.com/education/2012/jun/11/universities-students-rules-plagiarism-adjudicator. (Accessed 29.04.20).
McIntyre, L., 2018. Post-Truth. MIT Press.
Mnkeni-Saurombe, N., 2015. Information literacy: a cornerstone for open distance learning at the University of South Africa. J. Librariansh. Inf. Sci. 42 (2), 156–165.
ONS, 2019. Exploring the UK's Digital Divide. https://www.ons.gov.uk/peoplepopulationandcommunity/householdcharacteristics/homeinternetandsocialmediausage/articles/exploringtheuksdigitaldivide/2019-03-04. (Accessed 29.04.20).
Pangrazio, L., Selwyn, N., 2019. "Personal data literacies": a critical literacies approach to understandings of personal digital data. New Media Soc. 21 (2), 419–437.
Phippen, A., 2019. UK Schools Online Safety Policy and Practice. 2018 Annual Report. https://swgfl.org.uk/assets/documents/uk-schools-online-safety-policy-and-practice-assessment-2018.pdf?_=1553703046. (Accessed 29.04.20).
Phippen, A., Bond, E., 2020. Online Harassment and Hate Crime in HEIs. Report from FOI Request. https://www.uos.ac.uk/sites/www.uos.ac.uk/files/FOI-Report-Final-Jan-2020-rgb.pdf. (Accessed 29.04.20).
Prensky, M., 2001. Digital natives digital immigrants. On the Horizon 9 (5), 1–6.
Science and Technology Select Committee, 2017. Impact of Social Media and Screen-Use on Young People's Health. https://publications.parliament.uk/pa/cm201719/cmselect/cmsctech/822/82202.htm. (Accessed 29.04.20).
SCONUL, 2016. SCONUL Annual Library Statistics 2015-2016. https://www.sconul.ac.uk/page/sconul-annual-library-statistics-2015-16. (Accessed 30.11.19).
SCONUL, 2018a. Commentary on the SCONUL Annual Statistical Return 2016-2017: The Continuing Evolution of Academic Libraries. https://www.sconul.ac.uk/sites/default/files/documents/The_continuing_evolution_of_UK_academic_libraries.pdf. (Accessed 30.11.19).
SCONUL, 2018b. SCONUL Annual Library Statistics 2017-2018. https://www.sconul.ac.uk/page/sconul-annual-library-statistics-2017-18. (Accessed 30.11.19).
Sibley, J., Ostafichuk, P., Michaelsen, L.K., Roberson, B., Franchini, B., Kubitz, K., 2014. Getting Started With Team-Based Learning. Stylus Publishing, LLC, Sterling.
Sladdin, J., 2018. Duty to Care for Student Mental Health Has Legal Implications for Universities. https://www.pinsentmasons.com/out-law/analysis/duty-to-care-student-mental-health-legal-implications-universities. (Accessed 30.11.19).
Soria, K.M., Fransen, J., Nackerud, S., 2013. Library use and undergraduate student outcomes: new evidence for students' retention and academic success. Libr. Acad. 13 (2), 147–164.
UK Government, 1990. Computer Misuse Act 1990. Available at: http://www.legislation.gov.uk/ukpga/1990/18. (Accessed 30.04.20).
UK Government, 2019. Online Harms White Paper. Available from: https://www.gov.uk/government/consultations/online-harms-white-paper. (Accessed 30.11.19).
UUK, 2019. Changing the Culture: Tackling Online Harassment and Promoting Online Welfare. https://www.universitiesuk.ac.uk/policy-and-analysis/reports/Pages/tackling-online-harassment.aspx. (Accessed 30.11.19).
Weber-Wulff, D., 2019. Plagiarism detectors are a crutch, and a problem. Nature 567, 435.
Wikipedia, n.d. Fake News. https://en.wikipedia.org/wiki/Fake_news (Accessed 30.11.19).
Wyburd, J., 2017. Transnational graduates and employability: challenges for HE language departments. In: Álvarez-Mayo, C., Gallagher-Brett, A., Michel, F. (Eds.), Innovative Language Teaching and Learning at University: Enhancing Employability. Online Research-publishing.net.
Zhao, J.C., 2015. Making information literacy instruction relevant: a needs assessment approach at McGill University. Sci. Technol. Libr. 32 (3), 241–256.

# Designing library-based research data management services from bottom-up

4

*Gabrielle K.W. Wong and Diana L.H. Chan*
Hong Kong University of Science and Technology, Kowloon, Hong Kong

## 4.1 Introduction

In the past 10 years, research data management (RDM) support has been emerging as a new genre of service among academic libraries. Research institutions and funding agencies worldwide have become more aware that research data are a valuable asset, which deserves proper management. Moreover, effective curation, preservation, and sharing of research data are the core to research accountability and integrity. Considering this, academic libraries started to show increasing interest and strong intention to develop new capability that supports researchers in managing data.

However, RDM support cannot be provided by libraries alone. Research data management is a complex and multifaceted issue. It spans the whole research cycle, from proposal stage, production stage, to publishing and beyond; the nature of data and best practices differs from discipline to discipline. Within a university, effective RDM support often requires the joint efforts of researchers, research administrators, the IT department, and the library. Collaboration within and beyond an institution is also essential.

While many libraries are building RDM services, they take on very different development paths, and come in a diverse range of service models and levels. This is because the formation of RDM services depends on a lot of factors that may vary from country to country and institution to institution. Major factors include the amount of resources a library can have, the expertise and knowledge among staff members, the structure of institutional research administration, existing data practices in the research community, and many other complex contextual factors. Although it is a global movement to help researchers making RDM a norm, how it works in their daily workflow is very much a localized issue.

One core factor that heavily determines a library's approach to RDM services is whether there is any research data policy imposed by the institution or major funders. Data policy or mandates are arguably the most powerful driving force for researchers to adopt RDM good practices. That creates a top-down RDM environment for a library to offer support services. Without any policy or mandates, a library would have to build support services from bottom-up.

How do academic libraries position themselves in such a bottom-up context? This chapter describes and reflects on the experience at the Hong Kong University of Science and Technology (HKUST) and proposes a framework that depicts the dynamics of service design when building library-based RDM services from scratch.

**Future Directions in Digital Information. https://doi.org/10.1016/B978-0-12-822144-0.00004-5**

## 4.2 Literature review

Literature about RDM as a library service has become prominent in the recent years. A keyword search of 'research data management' in the database lens.org conducted on November 8, 2019 retrieved over 460 papers published in journals, conferences, and reports. The number of publications picked up after 2010, reaching a plateau in 2014 (Fig. 4.1).

### *4.2.1 RDM support as a new library service*

Research data management (RDM) is a complex issue involving multiple activities carried out by various actors 'addressing a range of drivers and influenced by a large set of factors' (Pinfield et al., 2014, p. 26). In a research university, the library is one of the actors, carrying out a wide range of activities relating to supporting researchers in their community in RDM.

While many libraries have begun to investigate and develop RDM services, the nature and scope vary. Tenopir et al. (2014) surveyed the research data services (RDS) in academic libraries in the United States and Canada. The study categorized data services as technical/hands-on RDS (e.g. operating an institutional data repository and helping researchers write data management plans) and informational/consulting RDS (e.g. helping users find a repository or data source). While many services were in a planning stage at the time of study, informational RDS was more common than technical. A later study on research libraries in Europe found similar patterns in service planning and range: library-developed research data services tended to focus on advisory and support services, more than technical services such as ingesting and preserving

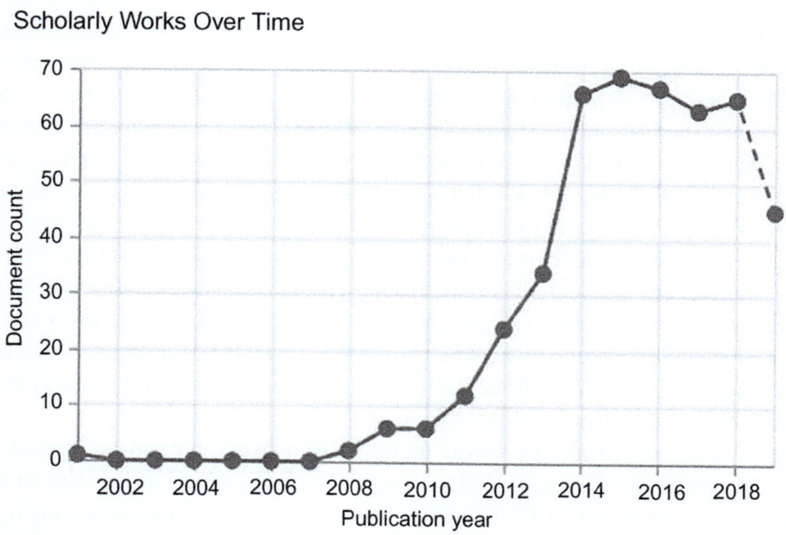


**Fig. 4.1** Number of RDM publications in Lens.org.

data sets. In addition, it revealed that almost all libraries which were studied collaborated with other organizations inside their institutions, or with outside organizations in developing service policies (Tenopir et al., 2017).

Some studies and service models provide more detail than the dichotomy between technical RDS and information RDS. Pinfield et al. (2014) built a library-oriented model in institutional RDM with four components: the drivers, programme components, influencing factors, and stakeholders. Library was one of the stakeholders in the model. Librarians can use the model to systematically approach their service by considering all these components when designing their RDM support.

An international survey of RDM activities and services in libraries used a 'landscape maturity model' to position current and planned practice in academic libraries. The model demonstrated that different activities and services were at varying stages of service maturity (Cox et al., 2017). In another survey on users' RDM needs and behaviours at a research university, the researchers framed RDM assistance using 9 types: data management platform (DMP), data collection, data refinement, analysis, documentation, visualization, finding data sets, finding repository, and meeting mandates (Joo and Peters, 2019).

## 4.2.2 Researchers' perception of and practices in RDM

Library RDM service design should directly respond to users' needs and behaviours. To understand researchers' current perception and practices on managing their data, librarians conducted various types of survey. Some studies targeted researchers' perception of library services on RDM support; others aimed to describe researchers' data practices, or to explore their concerns in data sharing. Their findings point to a range of areas that the library should consider in developing their RDM services.

Ragon (2019) studied a group of biomedical researchers. It was found that traditional service models of Health Sciences libraries aligned best with the beginning and end phases of a research cycle but were insufficient to meet researchers' needs of support in the conducting phase of research. Joo and Peters (2019) found that the researchers they surveyed had little experience using RDM services offered by the library; their perceived need varied significantly by discipline. There is a gap of skills in using metadata standards; libraries should offer more training in this aspect.

Majid et al. (2018) surveyed RDM knowledge and practices among faculty and researchers at the Nanyang Technology University (NTU) in Singapore, where a data policy and depositing mandate was in place. Most researchers at the NTU had a positive attitude towards research collaboration and data sharing; however, they had concerns for data sharing, especially on legal and ethical issues, misuse, and misinterpretation. These findings pointed to the need for library efforts in addressing these concerns through awareness campaigns and training.

Van Tuyl and Michalek (2015) described a detailed picture of the RDM practices of faculty at the Carnegie Mellon University (CMU), USA. Their results presented the types and quantity of data produced at the CMU, which offered guidance for the library to build a suite of services for their research community.

### 4.2.3 Library roles in RDM

While various user studies highlighted different functions a library can serve in meeting their researchers' RDM needs, how do academic libraries play their roles in this complex service environment?

Most researchers, especially graduate students, indicated that RDM skills are important; but where RDM education is insufficient in the curriculum, librarians can help fill this gap in assisting researchers in their knowledge creation process, leading to long-term preservation and access to scientific information (Pasek and Mayer, 2019). They can offer support and education in the areas of data planning, organization, metadata, and preservation; and help to ensure that data sets are better indexed and accessible in open access repositories.

Developing courses appeared to be a popular access point for libraries to establish their roles in the RDM support landscape. An Issue Brief by ITHAKA described the service development at the Health Sciences Library at the New York University (Rambo, 2015). Librarians there first developed a stand-alone introductory data management class for postdoctorates, then built on the programme with additional elements. The experience was later expanded to librarian workshops. Their approach was to build up services one by one; while it looked piecemeal and haphazard, it followed a path based on the best information about local needs and opportunities. Whitmire (2015) also shared how they developed the graduate-level RDM credit course. Southall and Scutt (2017) explained how the Oxford University incorporated RDM training into their existing iSkills programme.

Engagement is another important role the library can play. In a recent publication, Clare et al. (2019) compiled 24 case studies, illustrating how libraries in research institutions of different sizes engaged their users in pushing RDM forward. As they explained in the introduction, 'in order to implement good RDM practice throughout research communities a culture shift is necessary, and effective engagement with researchers, who are the main data producers and re-users, is essential for this shift to happen' (p. 2). Petters et al. (2019) reported an interesting case of engaging collaboration between the library and a research group at the Virginia Polytechnic Institute and State University. Through consultative research data management support from the library, and the research group's effort to improve data management systems, the quality of research data was improved substantially in terms of coding consistency and data accuracy. Supporting emergent data communities is a new mechanism for conceptualizing and supporting research data sharing. Librarians working closely with formal or informal groups of scholars can provide effective support, which maps to research practices and changing needs (Cooper and Springer, 2019).

## 4.3 RDM planning at HKUST Library

The Hong Kong University of Science and Technology (HKUST) is one of the eight publicly funded universities in Hong Kong. It is a research-intensive university maintaining a competitive position in global rankings. The majority of funding which supports research among the public institutions in Hong Kong is managed by the Research Grant Council (RGC), which has not issued any mandates on research data management. Naturally, the awareness of data management among researchers in Hong Kong is not high.

At the HKUST, our community collects many data sets in their research processes with little attention to their management. HKUST Library has envisioned providing an RDM service to its community as early as 2014. This was also the time when much discussion and sharing of RDM practices appeared in the literature and conferences. However, we had little knowledge and skills on research data management among library staff. To start, the Library's internal Scholarly Communications Committee had begun to explore this service, and to study how to build capacity for our librarians. Committee members first went through some online resources, including MANTRA (https://mantra.edina.ac.uk/) at the University of Edinburgh and the Data Management Course at the University of Minnesota (https://sites.google.com/a/umn.edu/data-management-course_structures/home-1). We also actively sought training opportunities locally and overseas for our librarians. In 2015, the HKUST hosted the Data Curation Spring Institute, co-organized by the Graduate School of Library and Information Science, University of Illinois, and the University of Hong Kong. In the following years, librarians attended various local and overseas conferences and workshops for further development. After self-study and programme training, our instructional librarians applied their learning in offering workshops on finding data repositories, data citation, and basic data file management skills.

As with many academic libraries starting their RDM support, HKUST Library also created web guides to provide advice and resources for researchers on how to manage research data. In 2015, the library systems team built up a data repository, using Harvard's open source software Dataverse. It was tested and populated with a few research data sets from researchers and the Library.

In 2018, the Library went through an organizational realignment process to consolidate the coordination of various kinds of research support effort. The department of Research Support Services was formed. Three librarians and two staff members were redeployed from other departments. Designing and providing the RDM service in a more coherent and systematic manner became a charge to this department along with support from subject librarians. Then, a series of initiatives were launched, resulting in a workable service planning roadmap formulated around June 2019.

### 4.3.1 Consultation with research administrators

Among the first steps that the Library took was to consult with key administration units and decision makers relating to research activities in the University. We talked with the Director of the Research Office, and the Associate Vice President for Research & Development; with the aim of understanding the feasibility and complexity of developing the University's policies on RDM. One piece of advice that we collected from different discussions pointed to first setting up data policies for research postgraduates. If the Library were to pursue this strategy, we should submit a proposal to the University's Committee of Postgraduate Studies, recommending postgraduate students to submit a data management plan, and deposit data in the thesis submission process. However, after further exploration, the Library was aware of concerns and potential resistance from thesis supervisors and students. Understanding that our research community may not have been ready for implementing research data policies and mandatory workflows, the Library was advised to first build support and services emphasizing the value of RDM as good practice for research management and academic integrity. Meanwhile, building up awareness and support for institutional policies can be positioned as a longer-term goal.

### 4.3.2 Funding

In 2018, around the same time that the Library created the new Research Support Services department, it also prepared a project proposal seeking seed funding from the University to support research data services. This project would help to kick-start the Library's effort in developing data services that are on par with best practices and which cater for disciplinary diversity. Such services would prepare the researchers to meet future funders' requirements and the trend towards open science. Two major components in the proposal were: librarians' capacity building and engagement with the HKUST research community. The funding request was subsequently endorsed, enabling the Library to invite speakers and trainers, organize workshops, engage research students, and acquire software.

### 4.3.3 Strategic planning

Although HKUST librarians had been learning about RDM through self-study, workshops, and conferences, since 2014, building a library-based RDM service imposed challenges at various levels. With the help of the project funding, the Library involved RDM experts from the Data Curation Centre (DCC) in spring 2019 to guide librarians making a service plan. In a 2-day programme for HKUST librarians, the DCC speakers facilitated discussion on service options, institutional maturity, priorities on RDM, and strategies on community engagement. After the programme, library staffs were able to fine-tune the strategic plan and chart the RDM service. The resulting roadmap consisted of several objectives in three areas:

- Data management planning infrastructure, policy, and support
  - Develop a DMP online platform to help researchers make data plans
  - Advocate for embedding/requiring DMP in postgraduates research process
  - Develop guiding tools and advisory service on writing DMP
- Data stewardship
  - Develop a data archive
  - Unify research output submission interface
- RDM advocacy and engagement
  - Increase awareness of RDM and advocate for good practices
  - Update HKUST community of publishers' data practices
  - Engage faculty champions for support, use cases, and advice
  - Organize research data training

To translate the objectives to an implementation plan, each objective was laid out with impacts, actions, milestones or deliverables, responsible staff, and target date. The roadmap became a guiding document for the Library to build an RDM service from bottom-up.

The three areas in the roadmap are interrelated. The first one focused on helping young researchers on developing DMP via a platform managed by the Library. The platform will be a key component in the data set submission workflow, which also involved the data stewardship infrastructure being built by the Library. For this, the Library planned to construct our research data archiving infrastructure with a 'dark archive' component in addition to the existing Dataverse repository. The third area, advocacy and community engagement, was essential to make the first two areas relevant to our researchers.

### 4.3.4 Project status in spring 2020

After the roadmap was drawn up in mid-2019, we focused our effort on developing the DMP template and platform. A working group of five librarians studied the literature and examples of DMP, including machine actionable DMP standards; we came up with a draft, and we involved a small team of research postgraduates to test and give comments. At the same time, the library systems team worked on a simple web platform to mount the DMP. The web form is intended to be a part of an integrated submission system to be released in fall 2020 for electronic thesis submission.

At the time of writing, the Research Support Services team was rounding up the DMP template. We are planning to have some internal testing rounds in December 2019, and to roll out the service in spring 2020 as a pilot phase. Education and promotion activities will include RDM and DMP workshops for research postgraduates. While we highlight the service being a pilot, we aim to be receptive to users' comments, on the relevance of the template questions, and how DMP can fit in researchers' workflow in a constructive manner rather than an administrative burden.

## 4.4 Points of reflection

Having been leading the research data service planning and development from the very beginning at the HKUST, the authors went through many ups and downs, and observed how various factors played out in the process. We reflect on our experiences of building RDM services from scratch, in an institutional environment where research data mandates and policies are still lacking. The following analysis should be able to provide some reference points for libraries, which take the bottom-up approach to building their RDM services.

### 4.4.1 Challenges and opportunities

Traditionally, research data have been handled almost exclusively by researchers themselves; they did not need nor want help. At the same time, data management was completely out of libraries' service zone, and librarians did not have and did not need to have knowledge and skills in research management. Therefore, the first hurdle most research libraries face when building RDM services from the ground up are researchers' doubts about our role, and the general lack of librarians' competencies. Related to researchers' perception about the role of the library in RDM is the attitude of a university's administration towards the library taking on this challenge. If they share the same doubts as many researchers, they may not entrust the library with the charge, nor allocate the resources needed.

At the HKUST, the Library has established a good reputation for service quality. There is in general a high level of trust towards most of the Library's initiatives, especially from the University administration. This proved to be a great help when we first proposed the research data endeavour and requested funding support in 2018. The fact that there was no existing research data policy on the one hand might imply that our research communities were indifferent to the issue; however, on the other hand, this 'ground zero' was also an opportunity for the Library to raise awareness and advocate the value of RDM.

Nevertheless, trust from the research community must be substantiated by demonstrated expertise. Although HKUST researchers may know we have services that support their RDM, they may not think that we can really help (Wiley and Mischo, 2016). Library staff's ability to deliver relevant services and meaningful help is of the utmost importance. Academic libraries worldwide have been recruiting librarians with data skills and finding training opportunities for their existing staff. HKUST Library did not have the option to create additional positions for new recruits; yet, the library director managed to redeploy existing staff to create the new department of Research Support Services. The department further coordinated learning resources and training programmes for librarians, while we gradually planned out our services.

### 4.4.2 Capacity building for library and librarians

'To successfully and sustainably launch and maintain data services in libraries, data curation programmes must be tailored to a library's existing capacity' (Yoon and Donaldson, 2019, p. 1).

A library's ability to create and sustain RDM services is not limited to librarians' knowledge and skills. To take a more comprehensive view of a library's capacity on RDM, one needs to stocktake the extent of existing organizational agility, human resources, technology infrastructure, and financial resources. Yoon and Donaldson (2019) conducted a national survey in the United States on data curation capability of libraries. They looked at six capacity dimensions at an organizational level:

- Value: a library's ability to develop a shared vision, goal, and mission on data services
- Administrative: to develop and draw on daily management, workflow, strategic plans, and policies
- Human resources—ability to deploy human capital; these include librarians' knowledge, skills, motivation, attitudes, as well as those behaviours that influence organizational culture and data curation
- Financial resources
- Technical infrastructure
- Network: the ability to draw on relationships with relevant stakeholders

Focusing on the capacity of individual librarians designing and offering services, the competency profile for RDM (Schmidt and Shearer, 2016) covers a broad range of knowledge and abilities in three areas:

- Providing access to data: knowledge of data infrastructure and analysis tools; understanding data organization and IP issues
- Advocacy and support for managing data: knowledge of funders' policies, RDM best practices, data publishing requirements, options, and citation; understanding research practices and disciplinary norms; ability to articulate benefits of data sharing and to assess data
- Managing data collections: knowledge of metadata standards, discovery tools, data linking, and storage; ability to select and appraise data sets, undertake digital preservation and curation

In order to develop skills, formal training, informal training, mentoring, and support networks are all important. Librarians need to have an in-depth knowledge of research processes in specific discipline areas in order to be able to contribute as a full partner in research activity (Brown et al., 2015). Some libraries develop training programmes to help other librarians initiate new services (Read et al., 2019; Sewell and Kingsley, 2017).

As described in a previous section, HKUST librarians started learning RDM using online, self-paced modules in 2014. While almost all librarians at the HKUST were novices in managing research data, we had a strong and visionary team in library systems and technology. The team set up a data repository using the Dataverse platform in 2015. However, without the capacity to develop services that support research data workflow, the uptake of the data repository has been slow. The scenario was changed in 2018, when the Library formed the department dedicated to research support and obtained the RDS project funding from the University. These measures boosted our data curation capacity at the organizational level. Subsequently, individual librarians enriched their knowledge and understanding of RDM through working on the DMP template and learning from fellow librarians and researchers. When we observe and reflect on how our librarians grew in capacity, we learn that it takes a long time and persistent effort for librarians to get to know RDM. Most librarians are not researchers; they are information experts but may not understand research processes well. Their RDM proficiency picks up faster when they design and deliver services. The lesson is that we need to give time for colleagues to learn, and we can expect learning and service delivery to happen simultaneously.

### 4.4.3 Environment scan for leverage points

It is important for a library to start its RDM service planning by conducting environmental scans in order to find institutional leverage points. Brown et al. (2015) specified key drivers of an RDM service including compliance with funding agency requirements, senior administrators who recognize the potential value of data as an asset, a practical need in the institution to improve data management, and an enterprise need to manage the risk of data loss. Such environment scanning can be conducted via surveys or assessment tools such as the Data Assessment Framework developed by the

Digital Curation Centre. Whether a formal or informal assessment method is used, the main purpose of the exercise is to find out:

- If there is any existing data policy or mandates that drives data management
- If existing facility, infrastructure, and data services are in place; they may be scattered in different units already
- Which campus units are interested in RDM best practices

HKUST Library did not conduct a formal survey; instead, we collected environmental information through different channels. We clarified the existing requirements on data imposed by the research funders in Hong Kong; we reached out to the campus Research Office, the office that manages postgraduate affairs, and officers at school level, in order to map out if there were any data practices in place. As we expected, current RDM awareness was low in general, but they support the Library and were interested to be kept updated of the service development. At the same time, we talked directly with senior administrators, often as face-to-face visits. A formal survey would have resulted in more structured data; yet, our dispersed information gathering mode has been keeping our dialogues with stakeholders open and continuous. Apart from reaching out to offices and administrators, it was also important to communicate with researchers.

Through these communications, we secured support from research administrators. In particular, the Vice President of Research Development advised us to build up RDM practices among researchers first, and then plan to put forward a mandate or policy proposal at the next stage. We also attracted interest from administrators who manage research postgraduate developmental courses. They became eager to have RDM workshops counted into their course credit hours.

### 4.4.4 Engagement as a continuous process

The dialogues with the research community do not have to be limited to locating leverage points at the start-up phase. Community engagement should continue into later stages including service piloting, implementation, adjustment, and assessment. In fact, talking with researchers is an excellent learning channel for librarians; they can enrich their understanding of research data formats, types, data cycle, disciplinary norms, and many other necessary competencies for librarians offering RDM services. For example, in spring 2019, we organized an RDM workshop for researchers. While the speakers explained the Findable, Accessible, Interoperable, Reusable (FAIR) principles and the repository, the attendees also shared their data practice with the group. The session turned into a learning opportunity for librarians too.

### 4.4.5 Service design priorities and strategies

For libraries to build RDM programmes from the bottom-up, a resource guide suggested a two-step approach (Erway et al., 2016). The idea is to start with tasks that involve lower skill thresholds, then build up further. Step 1 includes needs assessment, informational subject guides, and various ways to raise awareness and promote RDM.

Step 2 moves into a more rigorous needs study, defining policies, institutional and departmental strategies, a variety of service, and outreach activities. Many librarians can find this resource guide helpful with these sensible step-by-step suggestions.

Nevertheless, some libraries may detour from this advice to craft their own steps according to their institutional context and service capacity. Each library may prioritize their service design differently. At the HKUST, when we considered our RDM technology support, we chose to prioritize building a data repository early on in 2015. It was because our library had the human resources—the library systems team, which had the knowledge and experience in building a repository based on open source platforms. Providing space and computing facilities for data analysis and visualization is another main type of technology support; however, HKUST Library did not prioritize this for a number of reasons. One important reason was a lack of compelling need. Most of the software, facilities, and expertise in research data analysis are discipline specific; in our community engagement and environment scan, we got the understanding that software provision and support were met by departmental resources.

The next technology support we are building is a web platform for DMP. Most HKUST researchers do not have specific mandates to comply with; our strategy is, therefore, to promote the value of DMP as a tool for research management and research integrity. A previous study revealed that most of our researchers were not likely to make a specific data plan, partly because they lacked the knowledge (Parham and Doty, 2012). Therefore, once the DMP platform is up for service as a pilot phase, we will follow-up with advisory services, starting with hands-on workshops. While librarians collect questions and feedback from researchers, we are literally learning from them about their data practices and data needs. As librarians' capacity grows during the development process, we should be able to offer more in-depth consultation services on DMP writing.

In fact, conducting instructional workshops for early-career researchers was one area in which HKUST librarians were more confident when it came to development. Since 2015–2016, our instructional team has been offering two postgraduate data workshops regularly. The two topics are 'data discovery' and 'data disaster prevention'. On top of these two, we will add new workshops on DMP and FAIR data. The four topics will form a solid programme in spring 2020 for researchers, especially postgraduate students.

### 4.4.6 Flexibility and failure tolerance

RDM support is very contextual; there is no standard service model for libraries to support their researchers because each institution is different. This is especially the case for libraries which need to take the bottom-up approach, where service components must be built one by one, with a lot of trial and testing. In developing such new services which are different from previous experience, we learn that a high degree of flexibility is important. Librarians who participate in the service development are learning along the way; they need to be given autonomy as well as permission to fail.

## 4.5 A service design framework

For institutions that do not yet have any research data policy or mandates, libraries can exert the power of a change agent. To cause a change in practice, policy and culture takes a considerable amount of time; libraries working from the bottom-up need patience and strategies. When we reflect on our efforts at building RDM services at the HKUST, we are aware that changes happen slowly and subtly. The subtle progress at the same time allows us to strengthen our RDM support capacity gradually. Our approach to communicate closely with the community, starting with research administrators, proved to be instrumental; it helps the Library focus on those actions that work best in our environment. With the support of senior administrators on our service direction and strategies, and support from postgraduate programme managers in embedding RDM workshops in course credit hours, we are confident that we have established a good foundation on which we can build further RDM service components.

Fig. 4.2 sums up the experience of HKUST Library at planning an RDM service from the bottom-up. The Library works with various research administration offices of the University in advocating RDM as a research management practice that ultimately should deserve to be formalized as institutional policy and mandates; we also communicate the value of having RDM practices embedded in researchers' workflows. At the same time, we promote RDM to researchers as a research management tool, developing supportive services, including DMP and repositories.

In this approach, creating a cultural change is a longer-term goal. A campaign for an institutional policy and mandate is not our short-term priority. We expect that our efforts will gradually change the research culture in our community, where research data are valued as an intellectual and organizational asset, and RDM best practice is a norm rather than perceived as a chore. We believe that when the research community accepts RDM as an essential component in research workflows, advocating for establishing policy and mandates will be a natural step.

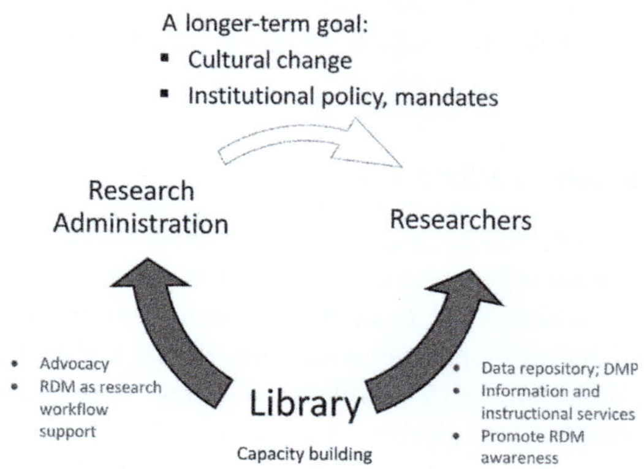


**Fig. 4.2** A bottom-up design approach for RDM services.

## 4.6 Conclusion

Many academic libraries have been developing capacity and services to support research data management throughout a research cycle. However, there is no single-service model nor development path; each institution has its unique context that creates special challenges and opportunities for the library. One key force in this context is whether there is any institutional policy or mandate that requires researchers to manage their data to specific standards. Without a top-down policy or mandate, researchers may see RDM as unappealing and unnecessary extra work. In such an institutional context, a library would need to take a bottom-up approach to promote RDM best practices to, and develop services for, the research community.

HKUST Library started to look into RDM in 2014, created a data repository in 2015, and obtained funding support in 2018 to embark on RDM service planning. Yet, with no top-down institutional requirement on data management, and apparently low awareness of RDM among our research community, the Library explored ways of building up services by capacity building, engaging research administrators, locating leverage points, introducing DMP, and providing practical support to early researchers through workshops and guides. With this approach, the goal is to create cultural change in research practices, which, in time, will result in institutional data policies beneficial to researchers, the institution, and scholarship at large.

## References

Brown, R.A., Wolski, M., Richardson, J., 2015. Developing new skills for research support librarians. Aust. Libr. J. 64 (3), 224–234.

Clare, C., Cruz, M., Papadopoulou, E., Savage, J., Teperek, M., Wang, Y., Witkowska, I., Yeomans, J., 2019. Engaging Researchers with Data Management: The Cookbook. Open Book Publishers, S.L.

Cooper, D., Springer, R., 2019. Data Communities: A New Model for Supporting STEM Data Sharing. https://doi.org/10.18665/sr.311396.

Cox, A.M., Kennan, M.A., Lyon, L., Pinfield, S., 2017. Developments in research data management in academic libraries: towards an understanding of research data service maturity. J. Assoc. Inf. Sci. Technol. 68 (9), 2182–2200. https://doi.org/10.1002/asi.23781.

Erway, R., Horton, L., Nurnberger, A., Otsuji, R., Rushing, A., OCLC Research, 2016. Building Blocks: Laying the Foundation for a Research Data Management Program. http://www.oclc.org/content/dam/research/publications/2016/oclcresearch-data-management-building-blocks-2016.pdf. (Accessed 05.05.20).

Joo, S., Peters, C., 2019. User needs assessment for research data services in a research university. J. Librariansh. Inf. Sci. https://doi.org/10.1177/0961000619856073.

Majid, S., Foo, S., Zhang, X., 2018. Research data management by academics and researchers: perceptions, knowledge and practices. In: Dobreva, M., Hinze, A., Žumer, M. (Eds.), Maturity and Innovation in Digital Libraries. 11279, pp. 166–178, https://doi.org/10.1007/978-3-030-04257-8_16.

Parham, S.W., Doty, C., 2012. NSF DMP content analysis: what are researchers saying? Bull. Am. Soc. Inf. Sci. Technol. 39 (1).

Pasek, J.E., Mayer, J., 2019. Education needs in research data management for science-based disciplines. Issues Sci. Technol. Librariansh. (92). https://doi.org/10.29173/istl12.

Petters, J.L., Brooks, G.C., Smith, J.A., Haas, C.A., 2019. The impact of targeted data management training for field research projects—a case study. Data Sci. J. 18 (1), 43. https://doi.org/10.5334/dsj-2019-043.

Pinfield, S., Cox, A.M., Smith, J., 2014. Research data management and libraries: relationships, activities, drivers and influences. PLoS One 9 (12). https://doi.org/10.1371/journal.pone.0114734.

Ragon, B., 2019. Alignment of library services with the research lifecycle. J. Med. Libr. Assoc. 107 (3). https://doi.org/10.5195/jmla.2019.595.

Rambo, N., 2015. Research Data Management: Roles for Libraries. Ithaka S + R.

Read, K.B., Koos, J., Miller, R.S., Miller, C.F., Phillips, G.A., Scheinfeld, L., Surkis, A., 2019. A model for initiating research data management services at academic libraries. J. Med. Libr. Assoc. 107 (3). https://doi.org/10.5195/jmla.2019.545.

Schmidt, B., Shearer, K., 2016. Librarians' Competencies Profile for Research Data Management. Joint Task Force on Librarians' Competencies in Support of e-Research and Scholarly Communication. https://www.coar-repositories.org/files/competencies-for-RDM_June-2016.pdf. (Accessed 18.10.17).

Sewell, C., Kingsley, D., 2017. Developing the 21st century academic librarian: the Research Support Ambassador Programme. New Rev. Acad. Librariansh. 23 (2–3), 148–158. https://doi.org/10.1080/13614533.2017.1323766.

Southall, J., Scutt, C., 2017. Training for Research Data Management at the Bodleian Libraries: national contexts and local implementation for researchers and librarians. New Rev. Acad. Librariansh. 23 (2–3), 303–322. https://doi.org/10.1080/13614533.2017.1318766.

Tenopir, C., Sandusky, R.J., Allard, S., Birch, B., 2014. Research data management services in academic research libraries and perceptions of librarians. Libr. Inf. Sci. Res. 36 (2), 84–90.

Tenopir, C., Talja, S., Horstmann, W., Late, E., Hughes, D., Pollock, D., Schmidt, B., Baird, L., Sandusky, R., Allard, S., 2017. Research data services in European academic research libraries. LIBER Q. 27 (1), 23–44. https://doi.org/10.18352/lq.10180.

Van Tuyl, S., Michalek, G., 2015. Assessing research data management practices of faculty at Carnegie Mellon University. J. Librariansh. Sch. Commun. 3 (3), eP1258. https://doi.org/10.7710/2162-3309.1258.

Whitmire, A.L., 2015. Implementing a graduate-level research data management course: approach, outcomes, and lessons learned. J. Librariansh. Sch. Commun. 3 (2), eP1246. https://doi.org/10.7710/2162-3309.1246.

Wiley, C., Mischo, W.H., 2016. Data management practices and perspectives of atmospheric scientists and engineering faculty. Issues Sci. Technol. Librariansh. (85).

Yoon, A., Donaldson, D.R., 2019. Library capacity for data curation services: a US national survey. Library Hi Tech. https://doi.org/10.1108/LHT-12-2018-0209.

# Part Two

# Who are the users?

# The power of accessible knowledge: Universities, suppliers, and transparency in the information age

5

*Alistair McNaught[a] and Huw Alexander[b]*
[a]McNaught Consultancy Ltd, [b]textBOX Digital Ltd

## 5.1 Introduction

The growth of digital content has had a far-reaching impact on users, university libraries, and the broader publishing industry. The potential benefits of digital content for print-disabled students create a framework for building a more inclusive learning environment based on the accessible content available to all. The emergence of digital content creates opportunities for innovative approaches and platforms that address the accessibility needs of users and enhance learning outcomes. However, the digital ecosystem is still nascent and the benefits that the medium facilitates are not always fully realized. The wide variety of digital file formats and platforms have resulted in inconsistencies in quality and usability and a subsequent negative impact on learning outcomes. It can also be confusing for end users to know the relative benefits of different formats.

This chapter outlines our attempts to identify and quantify the issues that are being experienced by users and the efforts of content providers to mitigate these issues. The chapter traces the evolution of the first-ever digital content audit from a crowdsourced endeavour driven by volunteers to a fully realized, responsive service for the industry.

## 5.2 The potential of digital text

### *5.2.1 For users*

By its nature, digital text has the potential for being highly adaptable. Users should be able to adjust the font size (without text spilling off the page), personalize colours and contrasts, navigate the text via headings and subheadings, change margin widths or line spacing, and have text read out to them using text-to-speech tools.

These flexibilities benefit readers with disabilities who may need to magnify text, change colours, or access content using assistive technologies such as text-to-speech tools and screen readers. In addition, many other readers benefit from text that can be personalized. People reading on smart phones or tablets want to increase font size without

**Future Directions in Digital Information. https://doi.org/10.1016/B978-0-12-822144-0.00005-7**

the penalty of left-to-right scrolling. Readers working in extreme light conditions (either very bright or very dark) benefit from changing colours and contrasts. Anybody who needs access to a section of the content benefits from navigation by heading level.

Digital text is a powerful tool for both productivity and inclusion. The potential benefits of digital content for all users should, therefore, be clearly signposted for the advantage of both users and content providers.

### 5.2.2 For business

Digital content creates new opportunities for content creators and providers to innovate and experiment. The development of high-quality digital technologies has opened the door to enhancing the discoverability of content and the promotion of inclusivity within education. User-focused design impacts all users through the creation of intuitive reading platforms that seamlessly transition across different types of devices. The evolution of digital content has influenced pedagogy, and this has resulted in new methods of approaching teaching, from advanced video content and more sophisticated interactivity and assessment to personalized learning and gamification.

For content providers, this creates opportunities and challenges. On the one hand, digital offers the chance to reach new markets, streamline workflows, and make cost savings. On the other, digital creates new complexities within the market and places demands on traditional publishers and aggregators to change their mindsets and introduce new skill sets and thinking within their workforce.

The potential of digital content is vast and harnessing that potential will be critical for the continued success of content providers. Managing the complexities of this evolving space has proven difficult and it is the reality of the current environment that we address in these pages.

## 5.3 The reality of digital text

Unfortunately, the reality of digital text can be far removed from the promise. The reasons behind a poor digital experience are varied, and this variability has a significant impact on end users. Depending on which books they access, in which format, from which publisher—and on which platform—the experience can range from frictionless efficiency to clunky frustration or complete exclusion. The variables leading to unpredictability for users are as follows:

- Production: the workflows, tools used, author expectations (e.g. heading structure, link descriptions, and image descriptions), production skill sets, and quality assurance standards influence the accessibility of the base digital file.
- Formats: HTML, PDF (in all its flavours), or EPUB (in various versions) have different accessibility potentials and pitfalls.
- Delivery platform: the way the publisher file is delivered to the end user has profound effects on the accessibility of the final experience. Delivery platforms may cause accessibility attrition, in some cases taking highly accessible EPUB files and converting them to semiaccessible PDFs.

- Reading options: many delivery platforms offer alternative ways of reading. This is likely to include reading online through a bespoke interface, downloading a chapter, downloading the whole book, or downloading as PDF or EPUB. The PDF can be read in the browser or downloaded locally to read in Adobe Reader or Adobe Digital Editions. Equally, an EPUB could be read in Adobe Digital Editions or other reading tools such as Thorium, Calibre, Bluefire Reader, and Kobo reader. Each of these reading platforms has a completely different suite of accessibility pros and cons. These pros and cons are rarely, if ever, described to the end user.

In addition, there are other variables such as **institutional choices** (which reading tools are made available on the network?), **institutional guidance** (do library services provide advice that would allow disabled students to match their requirements to a recommended format or reading tool?), and the **students' own skill set**. Disabled students are rarely as technically savvy as people suppose because they are often informed by support teams who are, themselves, technically underconfident.

At the outset of the project in 2016, we were unaware of the full scope of issues that users were facing. We only knew that getting accessible e-book experiences for disabled students was proving difficult, and that there had not been a concerted effort to identify and address these issues.

## 5.4 Unearthing the reality, part 1: The 2016 Ebook Accessibility Audit

Librarians are not, by nature, very militant, but by 2016 some university library services were recognizing that the experience of disabled students was unlikely to improve without raising their concerns and pushing back against current practices within the publishing industry. Unfortunately, nobody had any firm data or evidence on current practices to support the changes that were perceived to be necessary.

A series of fortuitous conversations brought together Alistair McNaught (then an accessibility specialist at Jisc) with library staff at the Leeds Beckett University, Manchester Metropolitan University, the University of Kent, the University of Liverpool, and York St John University. We discussed the potential of a crowd-sourced project, but first we needed to source a crowd. To this end, Ruth MacMullen at York St John and Sue Smith at Leeds Beckett set-up the LIS-Accessibility JiscMail list (Jiscmail, 2019). The list grew quickly (369 subscribers by October 2019 and around 30 messages, questions, and requests per month) and became a vibrant hub for accessibility issues and advice. As such, it formed an excellent base for the next stage of the project, which was auditing e-book accessibility directly using frontline library staff.

### *5.4.1 User perspectives, not technical standards*

Technical standards are important for providing good user experiences, but they do not lend themselves to purchasing conversations. If neither the library procurement team nor the supplier sales team have a full understanding of the technical standards, it becomes very difficult to prove compliance. Furthermore, code-level compliance can fail to translate to positive user experience, as has been entertainingly demonstrated by Matuzovic's inaccessible 'accessible' website (Matuzovic, 2019).

Our focus was to provide meaningful, demonstrable criteria for librarians or disability staff. The audit was not designed to compete with existing standards, but to be a tool to determine whether the claimed standards compliance translated to a positive user experience. The testing would rely on many frontline library staff without technical backgrounds. We needed simple tests that were easy enough for nonspecialists to check but meaningful enough to cover the majority of accessibility use cases. If a platform scored well in our audit, it was likely to have good credentials in terms of the Web Content Accessibility Guidelines (W3C, 2019), but we did not formally map to these guidelines (Fig. 5.1).

This **reader-focused** testing for the official Ebook Accessibility Audit was undertaken by 33 universities and 5 suppliers (suppliers were invited to audit their own platforms). In total, 44 platforms were tested, covering 65 publishers with nearly 280 e-books tested. The tests conducted were tailored to require minimal technical skills and no expensive software.

#### *5.4.1.1 Robust and representative?*

A crowdsourced approach has a particular advantage—it includes a wide range of tester skill and experience. This is representative of many disabled users in further and higher education who will be using an e-book platform for the first time and accessing it with assistive technologies, which may also be relatively new to

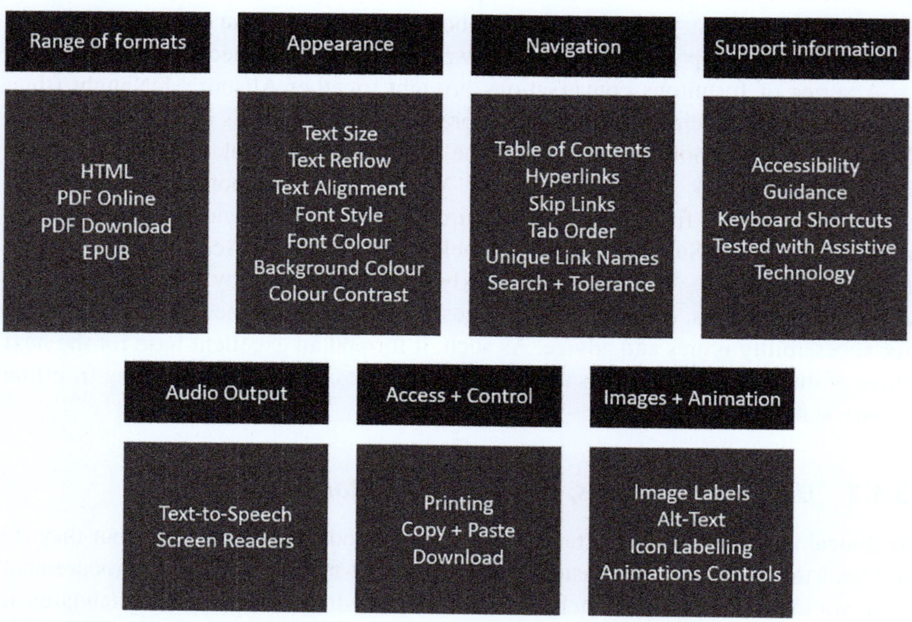


**Fig. 5.1** The criteria for the Ebooks Accessibility Audit.

them. However, crowdsourcing also introduces inconsistencies of interpretation. To reduce these, we created detailed training resources to accompany the survey (GoogleDoc, 2016a).

#### 5.4.1.2 Sampling approach

Prior to starting the survey, we created a presurvey questionnaire to ask higher education library and disability staff to nominate the publishing platforms they were most interested in assessing. Using the questionnaire results, we were able to prioritize the most frequently used platforms. Participants were invited to sign up to assess specific platforms. We attempted to get each platform assessed by a minimum of two organizations, but this was not easy to achieve as different universities subscribe to different suppliers. They could only download and test content to which they were subscribed. This means popular platforms were overrepresented in the sampling, while other more specialist collections were underrepresented. As a result, 41% of the platforms and 38% of the publishers sampled were scored on the basis of a single audit.

#### 5.4.1.3 Incidental benefits

As the audit proceeded, it became clear that, for many library staff, this was their first venture into exploring e-book accessibility. A follow-up survey of testers showed that over 70% were 'first-time testers' who had no prior experience of accessibility on e-book platforms. The project impacted these testers in terms of enhancing skill levels, improving confidence, and establishing empathy with disabled learners (GoogleDoc, 2016b). The postaudit survey received 45 responses from the 69 testers, a high response rate of 65% that demonstrated the high level of commitment within the library community to the aims of the audit.

The results show positive impacts, both amongst those who self-identified as inexperienced and those who self-identified as experienced in accessibility testing. But there was a further, more subtle, benefit that was to be an important philosophical principle within our subsequent work. The data collected by the e-book audit were processed by Susan Smith and Jamie Phillips at the Leeds Beckett University. They were aware that spreadsheet interpretation can be daunting for many people, so they worked hard to produce an interactive dashboard that would allow users to explore the data using different priorities based on their user requirements. If 'text-to-speech' or 'magnification with reflow' was your key user requirement, you could weight each feature more strongly. The supplier's rank order would thus change accordingly. The key recognition here is that the core question for a user is not 'is this accessible?' in some absolute, theoretical, and fundamentalist sense. The key question for each and every user is: 'is this accessible to *me*?' It is an important distinction that shifts the focus away from the elements a supplier may struggle to instantly change (like the underlying accessibility of their product) to something they can improve in an afternoon at low or even zero cost—the ***information*** that would let a user know whether they will be able to use this product or whether they need to request an alternative format to meet their needs.

#### 5.4.1.4 The end of the beginning

The key achievements of this first survey were less about the data and more about community and conversations (E-Book Audit, 2016). We now had a library staff in 33 universities sensitized to accessibility issues around their e-book collections. They were confident in testing the basics, more aware of the disabled student experience, and more confident at questioning suppliers as to the accessibility features of their digital content and platforms.

For their own part, suppliers had responded positively with 'critical friend' input from SAGE, Elsevier, Oxford University Press, Cambridge University Press, VitalSource, Bloomsbury, and Pearson. The Publishers Association Accessibility Action Group (Publishers Association, 2020) were also supportive of the project. The e-book Accessibility Audit won a national award (NAG, 2017) and was shortlisted for an international award (Hub, 2017). Many of the project team were invited to speak at library conferences and contribute to blogs or journals. Several suppliers approached the audit group for support or to tell us what they were doing to improve. We received multiple requests to retest supplier scores in order to reflect improvements they had made to their accessibility provision.

It was evident that there needed to be a follow-up but there were fundamental flaws in the approach that would need to be addressed if a new audit was going to be sustainable for library staff and practical for suppliers.

## 5.5 Unearthing the reality, part 2: The 2018 ASPIRE project

We had learnt many lessons from the original Ebook Accessibility Audit project. It was clear we needed a follow-up project to reflect the effort and investment of responsive suppliers. It was also clear that we needed to be realistic about how rapidly the publishing industry could respond to these challenges. Changing a production workflow is a major investment that can take years to plan and fully implement. We needed to find a different measuring tool, something that was relatively quick and straightforward for suppliers to implement or improve, but still useful for end users and straightforward for librarians to assess.

As noted above, accessibility *information* was a promising new perspective. Although the ultimate goal is fully accessible content, the reality is that most students with disabilities have relatively modest requirements. One may need magnification and reflow, while another may need to change colours, and yet another may need text-to-speech compatibility. If a librarian or disability support team has access to up-to-date information on the 'accessibility profile' of publisher files or aggregator platforms, they can rapidly triage different student needs. This saves a huge amount of time and frustration in on-site testing, allowing them to focus efforts on more challenging cases, where students may need significantly more accessibility support. As a result, we decided to design the 2018 follow-up project around assessing the accessibility ***information*** provided by suppliers on their websites.

**Fig. 5.2** The range of testing criteria for the ASPIRE project.

### 5.5.1 Building on lessons learned

The initial e-books Accessibility Audit project had taught us a variety of crucial lessons. Despite its positive impact on the library sector and some suppliers, and despite the awards, conference workshops, and journal articles, we were aware that crowdsourced data are always open to challenge, especially when sample sizes are small. We were also aware that the original data provided little more than a 'counsel of despair' for suppliers locked into legacy workflows that they could not afford to rapidly improve, despite the best of intentions. The new focus on accessibility *information* had benefits for both the auditors and the audited. For auditors, finding and scoring an accessibility statement based on a detailed template of ASPIRE criteria (see Fig. 5.2) is considerably easier than downloading and auditing an e-book file or a platform interface. For suppliers, improving deficiencies in accessibility information is significantly quicker and more cost effective than improving deficiencies in product workflows or interfaces.

A follow-up project gave us a wide range of opportunities to do things differently in order to maximize the overall impact. One of the frustrations of the original project was being asked by suppliers to reaudit their product so they could see how they had improved. We wanted to transfer responsibility so that suppliers were able to self-assess and self-improve. This meant partnership had to be at the core of the project. The guiding principles in designing the follow-up project are explored below.

## 5.6 Community building—Purpose and process

We wanted to ensure this was as positive an experience as possible for suppliers. This was an opportunity for suppliers to tell their accessibility story and highlight the work and investment they had made. We all had the same goal: more people reading more content, more happily. We organized a launch meeting, sponsored by the Publishers Association and hosted by Springer Nature in January 2018, where nearly 30 attendees, representing librarians, disability support staff, publishers, and platform providers took part. A key part of the meeting was to form small, mixed, groups, and simply discuss the issues faced by each part of the supply chain. From this initial meeting, we invited volunteers to be a part of an informal steering group for the new audit project.

The steering group consisted entirely of volunteers with representatives from libraries, disability teams, publishers, and platform providers. There was no budget available for the new project, so all communication was conducted online using free tools. We set-up a Jiscmail discussion list (JiscMail, 2020) for easy communication and met on a regular basis using Doodle scheduling and a free Zoom video conference call account. A shared GoogleDoc stored meeting notes and actions and allowed the wider community to comment where relevant. Working remotely in this way made us agile, more productive, and cost effective.

## 5.7 Light touch survey

Since our focus was on the quality of the accessibility statement, we needed to identify what an ideal accessibility statement would look like from an end-user perspective. Library and disability staff described the information they needed to support their print-disabled students. Publishers and platform providers gave commentary on how easy (or otherwise) such information was to provide. As a result of these discussions, it soon became clear that we needed to devise different surveys to reflect the different constraints and influences of platform providers and publishers.

The publisher audit focused on the information provided about files, formats, digital rights management and compatibility with assistive technologies (for instance, accessibility tags and image descriptions), and alternative format provision. The platform audit focused on the information provided about the accessibility features of the platform interface and online reading experience as well as the extent to which accessibility features in the file were surfaced in the platform.

## 5.8 Statistically significant

With so many different stakeholders contributing to the auditing process, we needed to manage the data and ensure better statistical validity than we had in the previous project. This was easier because our focus on accessibility information (rather than e-book content) meant it was possible to audit suppliers to whom you did not subscribe, simply by exploring their website for the appropriate information.

To maximize coverage and minimize low sampling rates, we created two sign-up sheets—one for testers auditing publishers (GoogleDoc, 2018a) and one for those auditing e-book platforms (GoogleDoc, 2018b). This gave us a much greater spread of final samples with an average of 4.5 audits per publisher and 3.9 per platform provider.

## 5.9 Positively oriented

This was, to our knowledge, the first-ever crowdsourced audit of supplier accessibility statements. We wanted to ensure that the audit was a positive experience that would benefit both end users and the content and platform providers themselves. Several suppliers were involved in the steering group and had an opportunity to improve their own accessibility statements prior to the testing phase. We also wanted to give the same opportunity to others, so we launched the audit questionnaires at the London Book Fair in April 2018, over 3 months ahead of the planned audit date in July/August.

Huw Alexander, then at SAGE, provided the acronym ASPIRE (Accessibility Statements Promoting Improved Reader Experiences) to help with the marketing and outreach. We created the ASPIRE website (ASPIRE, 2016) with background information, sign-up sheets for selecting publishers/platform providers to audit, and links to the separate publisher and platform audit tools. At the request of colleagues in the publishing supply chain, we created a business case for senior management, explaining why this was important to their customer base and requesting their support for their colleagues to get involved. Our hope was that giving as much information and help as early as possible would help raise the final audit scores. The ultimate aim for the ASPIRE project is to have all suppliers achieve a 100% for their information score. If accessibility information is full and transparent, then the market can compare between suppliers and decide how much accessibility they are willing to pay for.

## 5.10 Staff development

As with the previous e-book audit, the ASPIRE project provided an excellent opportunity for staff development. Within the university context, librarians could be more confident about the needs of disabled students and disability support teams could better understand the potential of e-books to support their learners. Within the supply chain, publishers and platform providers began to understand their mutual dependencies. It became clear that the accessibility investments in one part of the supply chain could be undermined by lack of investment in another part.

### *5.10.1 The ASPIRE results: Information silence*

The overarching theme of the ASPIRE results was missing information within the accessibility statements. On average, publishers were missing 87% of the information required and platforms were missing 78% of the information required. This missing information is critical to procurement decisions and the effective use of the digital content, and it clearly illustrated that content providers are failing to tell the whole story of their content (Fig. 5.3).

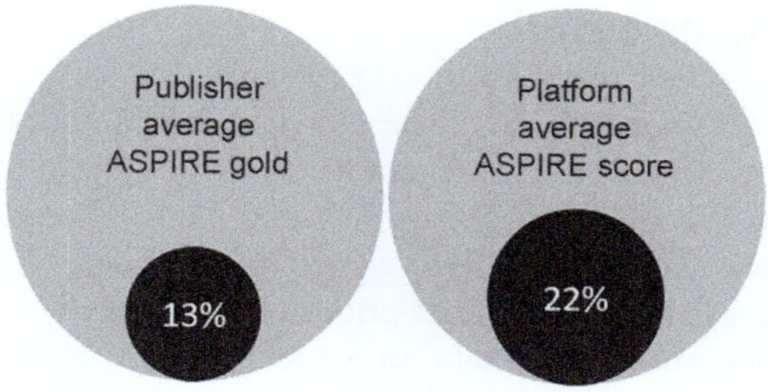


**Fig. 5.3** The average publisher and platform ASPIRE scores.

## 5.11 Publishers

The ASPIRE results for publishers were underwhelming with an average ASPIRE score of 13% across the 87 publishers surveyed. The highest score was achieved by Palgrave Macmillan with 56%, the only publisher to post a score above 50%. Fig. 5.4 illustrates the level of missing information within the publisher accessibility statements, with even contact information failing to be provided in 61% of cases and copy/print policies missing from over 95% of statements.

## 5.12 Platforms

The performance of platforms in the ASPIRE survey was slightly more positive with an average ASPIRE score of 22% across 54 platforms. High scores were recorded by EBSCO (85%), Kortext (81%), VitalSource (76%), and Cambridge Core (61%). However, Fig. 5.5 illustrates the level of missing information across all criteria, with no criterion achieving a 50% score.

### *5.12.1 Key takeaways from the ASPIRE project*

The three key findings from the ASPIRE data were as follows:

- Most suppliers provide far less accessibility information than a university or college requires in order to support their learners efficiently.
- Most suppliers are missing a significant marketing opportunity because their digital products almost invariably have accessibility benefits (compared to hard copy print) that could—and should—be marketed.
- Even when a supplier has an accessible product and useful accessibility information, the information is often hard to find or is spread across unrelated parts of the website, creating a big variability in end-user experience.

The ASPIRE project highlighted the lack of information made available by content providers, but it should be noted that it does not necessarily reflect the work and resources that are being invested in accessibility. A common response from content providers was that the survey was eye opening as they now realized that they were not

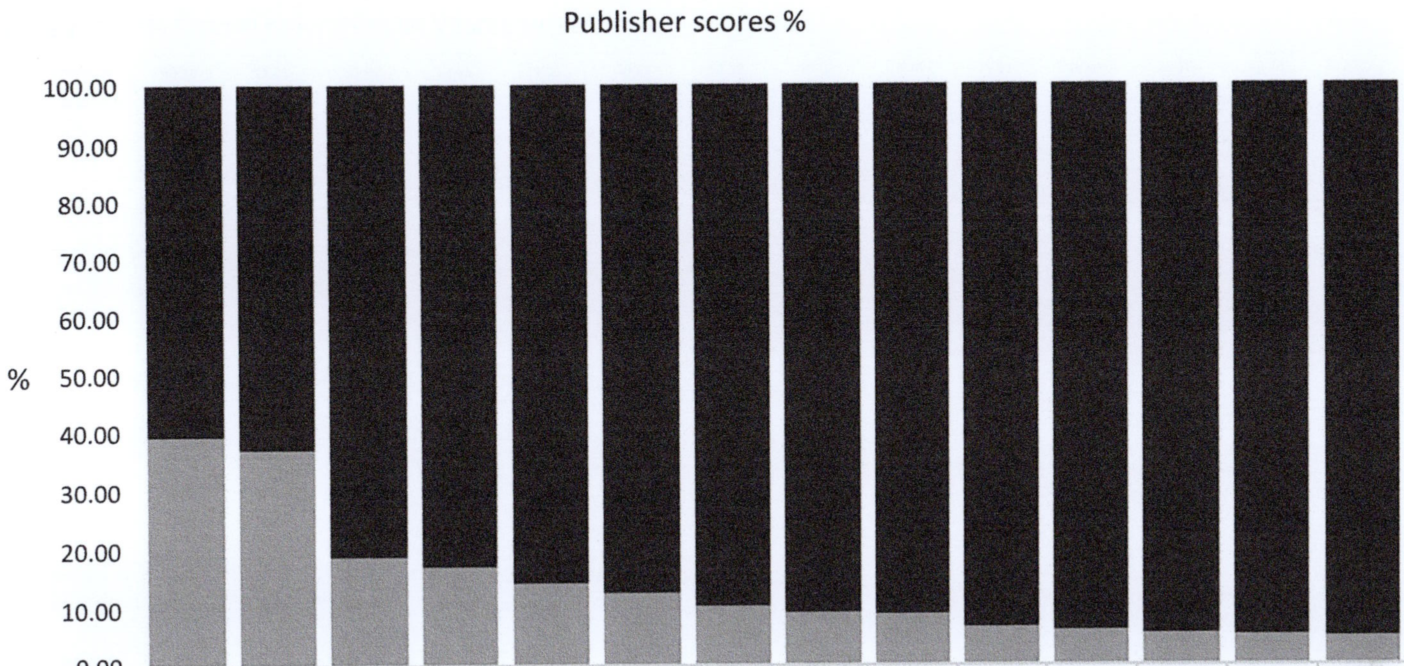


| | Contract details | Discoverabi lity | Engagement with accessibility services | Available formats | DRMfree requests | Licences | Privacy | Currency | DRM information | Magnificati on and reflow | Image description | Response times | Navigation | Copying and printing |
|---|---|---|---|---|---|---|---|---|---|---|---|---|---|---|
| Missing | 60.52 | 62.75 | 81.20 | 83.01 | 85.78 | 87.57 | 89.78 | 90.98 | 91.31 | 93.61 | 94.07 | 94.66 | 95.02 | 95.17 |
| Score | 39.48 | 37.25 | 18.80 | 16.99 | 14.22 | 12.43 | 10.22 | 9.02 | 8.69 | 6.39 | 5.93 | 5.28 | 4.98 | 4.83 |

**Fig. 5.4** Average publisher scores across the ASPIRE criteria.

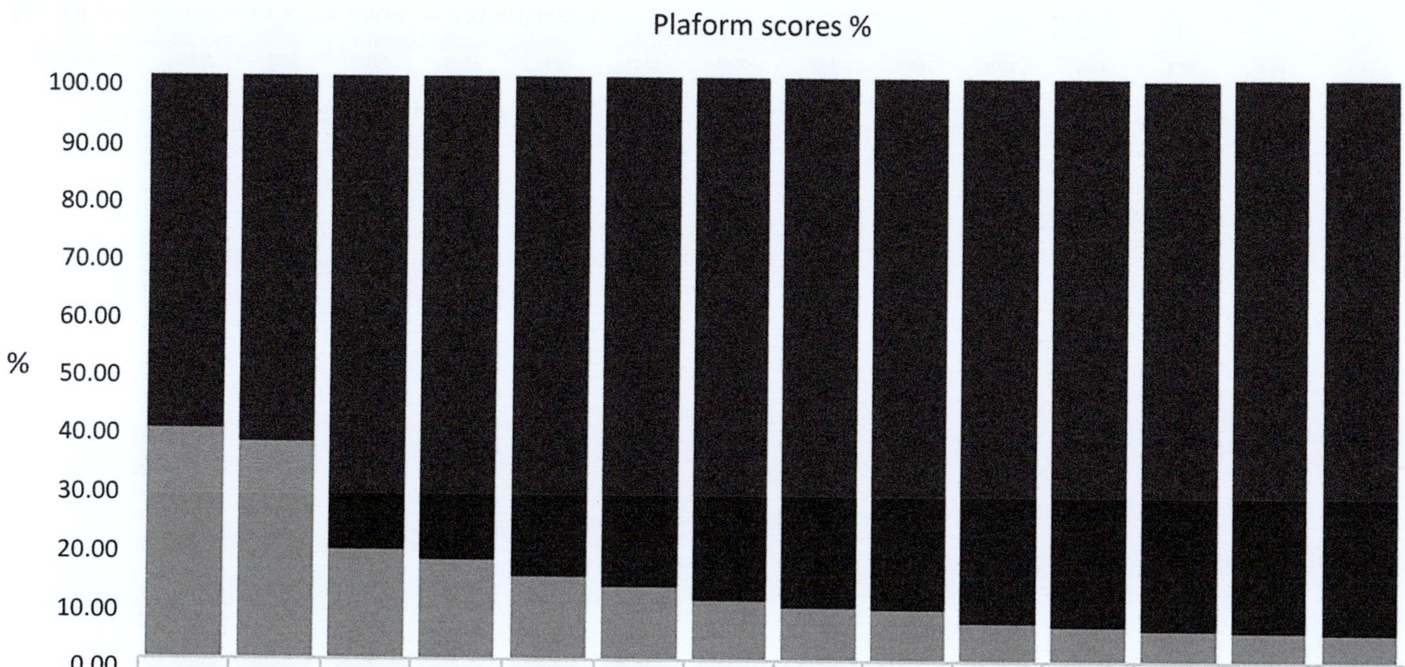


| | Discoverabi lity | Contract details | Screen reader compatibility | Navigation | Magnificati on and reflow | Colours and contrasts | Currency | Image descriptions | Text speech compatibility | Advice on reading options | Copying and printing | DRM-free requests | DRM information | Response times |
|---|---|---|---|---|---|---|---|---|---|---|---|---|---|---|
| ■ Missing | 50.25 | 57.33 | 67.34 | 74.28 | 75.93 | 79.42 | 79.74 | 79.97 | 80.90 | 81.97 | 85.93 | 86.82 | 86.87 | 93.40 |
| ▦ Score | 49.75 | 42.67 | 32.66 | 25.72 | 24.07 | 20.58 | 20.26 | 20.05 | 19.10 | 18.03 | 14.07 | 13.18 | 13.13 | 6.60 |

**Fig. 5.5** Average platform scores across the ASPIRE criteria.

telling the story of the work they had dedicated to establishing inclusive publishing practices. An accessibility statement helps to promote this work and this marketing opportunity is being overlooked in the majority of cases. As Vanessa Boddington of VitalSource stated, 'the audit helped us refine the information we present to the public. Whilst we had focused on making our content as technically accessible as possible… how would users know how we can help unless we tell them?' (ASPIRE, 2018). In the face of the data, content providers across the board were realizing that their message was not being heard.

### 5.12.2 *Raising awareness*

The ASPIRE project was a grassroots initiative built on volunteer time and expertise. As such there was no budget available for outreach and marketing. The project team thus had to be creative and inventive to raise the profile of the project within the publishing ecosystem.

## 5.13 Website

The website was built using free web tools from Learning Apps (Learning Apps, 2012). The website contained a wealth of guidance and data to help content providers address their ASPIRE scores and served as a hub for the project (Fig. 5.6).

## 5.14 ASPIRE awards

To raise the profile of the project and reward content providers who had excelled in the inaugural audit, the project team worked with BookMachine to host an awards ceremony (BOOK MACHINE, 2019). The awards recognized the work of content

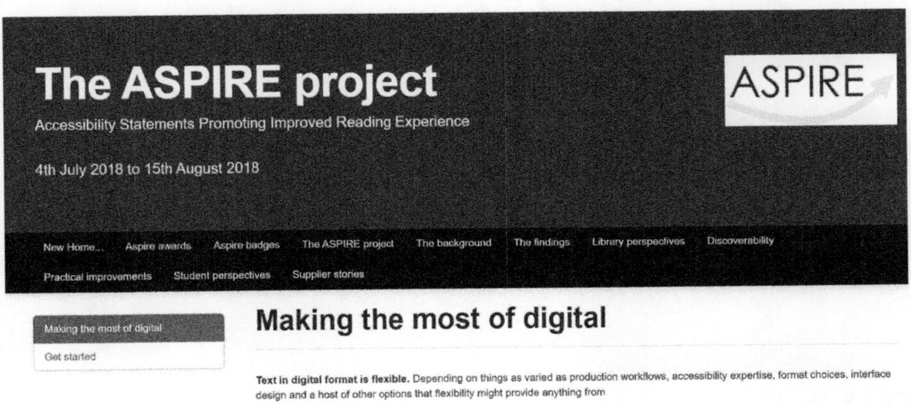


**Fig. 5.6** The 2018 ASPIRE website homepage.

providers and the essential contributions of librarian testers to the audit process. The night was made possible by sponsorship from early supporters of the ASPIRE project, VitalSource, ProQuest, and textBOX, and was complemented by an evening of talks on the importance of implementing accessible practices in the publishing workflow (Figs. 5.7 and 5.8).

**Fig. 5.7** The ASPIRE awards. From left to right: Georgia Parks (Red Globe Press), Alistair McNaught, Vanessa Boddington (VitalSource), and Jo Greig (Policy Press, part of Bristol University Press).

**Fig. 5.8** The ASPIRE awards. From left to right: Alistair McNaught, Tash Edmonds (ProQuest), Jessica Wykes, James Atkinson, Anne Watson, and Dita Krauz (City University).

## 5.15 Conferences, journal articles, and blog posts

In addition to the awards, the steering group presented at numerous conferences and online events, such as UKSG (UKSG Webinar Slides, 2018; UKSG Webinar Invitation, 2018), Jisc (JISC Webinar, 2018), VitalSource's Digital Days (VitalSource, 2019), and the London Book Fair (London Book Fair Presentation, 2019) to draw attention to the ASPIRE results. These conferences were supplemented by a series of articles and blog posts to promote the ASPIRE message and encourage involvement across the industry (Articles and blog posts: McNaught, 2019a,b; Wykes, 2018; Clover and Watson, 2018; Moore, 2018; EBSCO, 2018).[a]

### 5.15.1 *Seeking transparency: The challenges faced by content providers*

Subsequent conversations with content providers as a part of the promotion of the ASPIRE results also unearthed a further complication for the provision of transparent accessibility statements. Website copy was often the purview of the marketing department, whereas compliance with accessibility regulations was overseen by the legal department. This division of responsibility had led to tension in some cases, with legal concerns inhibiting marketing transparency. Creating a balance between these two areas is key to providing meaningful information for customers and this has become even more critical due to the legal changes in the recent times.

### 5.15.2 *A changing legal landscape*

The ASPIRE project started in January 2018 and the results became publicly available in October of the same year. In the meantime, in September 2018, the United Kingdom adopted the EU Directive on Public Sector Web Accessibility (European Commission, 2018a) into UK law. This new legislation (Legislation.gov.uk, 2018) applies to all publicly funded organizations in the United Kingdom, including further and higher education institutions. It introduces two key elements as legal obligations:

- Meeting the 'accessibility requirement'
- Requiring accessibility statements

#### 5.15.2.1 *Meeting the accessibility requirement*

The web accessibility legislation states that (Part 3.9.1.a)

> *A website of a public sector body will be presumed to be in conformity with the accessibility requirement to the extent that it meets harmonised standards, the*

[a] All posts available at: https://www.learningapps.co.uk/moodle/xertetoolkits/play.php?template_id=1856 (Accessed 14.12.19).

> *references to which have been published in the Official Journal in accordance with Regulation (EU) No 1025/2012(1).*
>
> *European Commission (2018b)*

At the foot of that page is a link to 'Implementing Decision on the Standards for the Directive', stating that the updated version of EN 301 549 V2.1.2 (2018-08) will be used. This is aligned to WCAG 2.1 Level AA for web pages. Nonweb documents and applications are also mostly aligned as well.

Organizations that comply with WCAG 2.1 AA will fulfil the accessibility requirements for the regulations. This is why the gov.uk pages refer to WCAG 2.1 AA (GOV.UK, 2018a).

#### 5.15.2.2 Requiring accessibility statements

This new requirement applies to all areas of the digital estate within a university or college. In meetings with Government Digital Services (GDS) (GOV.UK, n.d.), we specifically asked about e-books since the legislation states that 'third-party content that is neither funded nor developed by, nor under the control of, the public sector body' is exempt. The view of GDS was that if you pay for or subscribe to content you are 'funding' it and, therefore, you are responsible for it meeting accessibility standards, as well as being responsible for providing an accessibility statement.

The model accessibility statement (GOV.UK, 2018b) provided by GDS contains more than would be expected from a commercial supplier but the key elements relevant to both the supplier and the university/college are as follows:

1. An explanation of those parts of the content that are not accessible and the reasons why
2. A description of any accessible alternatives
3. Contact information

These are all covered—explicitly or implicitly—by the ASPIRE scoring checklists. Consequently, suppliers providing the kind of user-focused guidance that would give them a high ASPIRE score will also be creating the core of an accessibility statement that a university or college could rely on to meet their own obligations.

Under the Public Sector Web Accessibility legislation, the universities and colleges are responsible for information being available, not the supplier. Yet, it makes no sense for 150 UK universities and nearly 400 colleges to duplicate efforts by trying to explore the accessibility credentials of every platform to which they subscribe. Suppliers should be providing this information. They should know what works, what does not work, and what alternatives and workarounds are possible. Crucially, they know when they improve workflows and, therefore, update their accessibility information. By providing up-to-date accessibility statements suppliers are providing an accurate reflection of their products and services, to their own benefit and to the benefit of their customers.

### 5.15.2.3 Implications for procurement

#### Library view—University of Liverpool

Jane Cooke, Associate Director, Collections, Content, and Discovery at the University of Liverpool, has supported the project since 2016. This is her perspective from a library procurement viewpoint:

> Most Higher Education Institutions (HEIs) purchase content via consortia in order to receive favourable pricing and standardized services. This saves time for library services and ensures minimum quality standards for the HEIs while ensuring pricing and services are fairly and transparently provided for auditing purposes.
>
> Over recent years, further detailed requirements have been added to the consortia agreements as HEIs have developed their own requirements to meet their institutional needs, driven by both external and internal factors. For example, an external factor that HEIs are currently responding to is the legal legislation for accessibility statements.
>
> The current consortia agreement for England—Books, e-books, Standing Orders and Related Material—Inter-regional Agreement (LIB4035 SU)—is led by Southern Universities Purchasing Consortium (SUPC). The format of this agreement breaks down content into seven lots. The lots focus on different formats of books and access models. For e-books the question that suppliers would be judged on regarding accessibility lacked specificity:
>
>> 'Please outline your compliance with the Equalities Act and SENDA and compatibility with assistive software (no more than 250 words)'.
>
> This makes comparing suppliers' answers far harder as the information provided is inconsistent or vague therefore making judgements very difficult. Attempting to provide clearer criteria at a consortium level supports HEIs in gaining a standardized service from suppliers and provides suppliers with standardized criteria to meet. Providing clearer guidelines and requirements for suppliers at the start of the next agreement would be a welcome development that HEIs could then systematically assess and then select suppliers as they do for other criteria.

### 5.15.2.4 Publisher view—Kogan Page

Suppliers also have a vested interest in providing accurate accessibility information because, in the complex ecosystems of digital publishing, the more accurate you are about your own accessibility credentials, the more you can shield your reputation against barriers that might be added further along the supply chain. The publishers, Kogan Page, switched to EPUB 3.2 workflow which creates high-quality accessible content. They also rewrote their accessibility statement using the ASPIRE criteria and leaping from a score of 11%–93% and taking the top position.

McNaught Consultancy organized a reality check afternoon in a university library where the production team could experience their highly accessible books as a disabled student would—after they are delivered through a third-party aggregator and downloaded for off-line reading in Adobe Digital Editions. It was a salutary experience because their highly accessible EPUB 3 was delivered by some aggregators as poorly accessible PDFs, completely undermining their accessibility efforts. But the accessibility statement at least shows where the issue lies. From a reputational point of view that is an important starting point. It also helps encourage other players in the supply line to provide their own. When libraries begin to consider a supplier's accessibility statement in their procurement process, every part of the supply chain will need to be honest. Honesty and transparency allow purchasers to make intelligent, informed purchases. Accessibility then has a marketable value and those who invest can reap rewards.

## 5.16 Lasting impact

The data from the ASPIRE project are informing the decision-making processes of librarians across the United Kingdom. The feedback we have received from librarians, publishers, and platforms has been universally positive and network of support is developing between the publishing and university communities. This positive culture will lead to more transparency within the market and ultimately to better content and improved learning outcomes. Here are a few comments on the impact of the ASPIRE project:

> *We use the ASPIRE scorings when comparing platforms and providers as part of our resource evaluations for retention and renewal. Having one centralized place to check accessibility information saves time within an institution and across the sector and provides a level of confidence as to the consistency of the evaluation and scoring.*
>
> *Julie Cleverley, Leeds Beckett University (textBOX, 2019a)*

> *The ASPIRE scores make it easy for us to see which vendors we should be working with, who will give us value for money.*
>
> *Melissa Steiner, Birkbeck University (Steiner, 2019)*

> *The ASPIRE scores and breakdown enables me to dig deeper into the accessibility of e-book platforms to identify if particular features will be available to meet the needs of our disabled students.*
>
> *Sue Smith, Leeds Beckett University (Smith, 2019)*

> *The ASPIRE project was an essential tool to ensure our work is accessible to as many people as possible.*
>
> *Jessica Lovett, Intellect Books (Lovett, 2019)*

> *Providing clear, useful, and centralized information about accessibility is of critical importance regardless of the actual state of a product's accessibility; openly stating known abilities and limitations saves end users and librarians hours of trial and error.*
>
> *EBSCO (textBOX, 2019b)*

> *The first step was to publish a new Accessibility Statement on our website. This clearly spells out what accessibility features our content supports and on what online platforms it is available. It also demonstrates our commitment as a business to accessibility and invites print impaired readers to get in touch for further information via a dedicated mailbox address.*
>
> *Kogan Page (Klopstock and Thompson, 2019)*

## 5.17 Building a sustainable future for the ASPIRE project

Although feedback for the project from all parties was overwhelmingly positive, there was one question that was repeatedly put to the team: 'we've been inspired to update our accessibility messaging and we'd like to be re-audited to reflect the work we have done'. An initiative of the ambitious size and scope of the ASPIRE project is difficult to maintain, based on a crowdsource model, and we had initially anticipated the project to be an annual undertaking. If we were to meet the demands of the market, we realized that we would need to develop a robust, sustainable model to meet the publishing industry's increased focus on accessibility.

After extensive research and discussions with the steering committee members, it was proposed that the ASPIRE project should be recalibrated as a paid accreditation service for content providers under the wing of textBOX, one of the steering committee members for the initial ASPIRE project. The new service, launched in August 2019, is responsive to the needs of content providers and provides a complete ASPIREreview within 5 business days (textBOX, 2018). With this shift in focus to a fully fledged accreditation service for the publishing industry, ASPIRE can now more truly reflect the work of content providers and provide a window on their content for librarians and content purchasers.

A new improved service offers librarians the ability to deep dive into content provider data through the revamped ASPIRElist and offers extensive guidelines to help publishers and platforms to improve their scores. This is perhaps best reflected by the new highest score for ASPIRE by Kogan Page (Kogan Page, 2019) who recorded a 93% score in October 2019, an incredible 67% improvement on the previous leading publisher (Fig. 5.9).

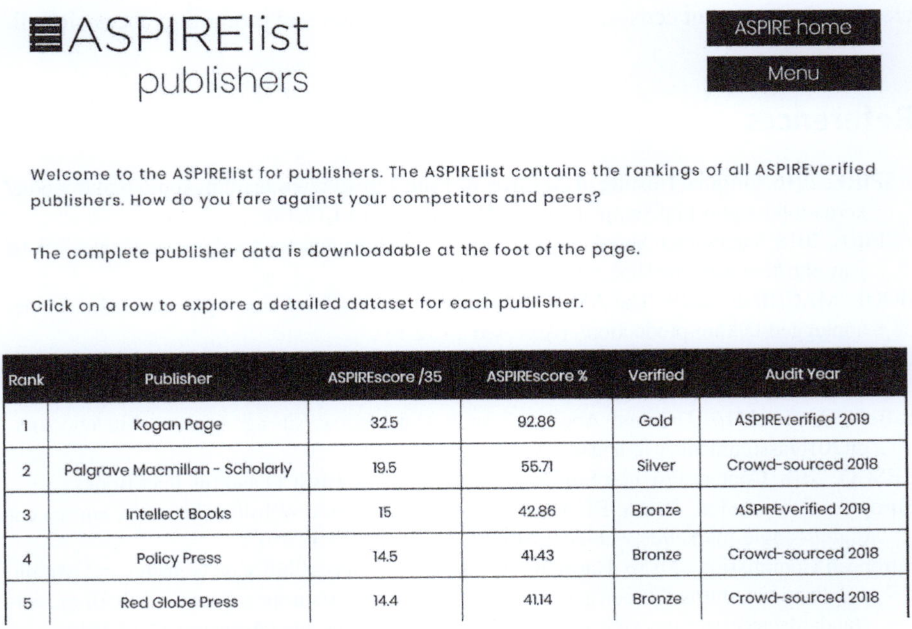
ASPIRElist
publishers

ASPIRE home

Menu

Welcome to the ASPIRElist for publishers. The ASPIRElist contains the rankings of all ASPIREverified publishers. How do you fare against your competitors and peers?

The complete publisher data is downloadable at the foot of the page.

Click on a row to explore a detailed dataset for each publisher.

| Rank | Publisher | ASPIREscore /35 | ASPIREscore % | Verified | Audit Year |
|---|---|---|---|---|---|
| 1 | Kogan Page | 32.5 | 92.86 | Gold | ASPIREverified 2019 |
| 2 | Palgrave Macmillan - Scholarly | 19.5 | 55.71 | Silver | Crowd-sourced 2018 |
| 3 | Intellect Books | 15 | 42.86 | Bronze | ASPIREverified 2019 |
| 4 | Policy Press | 14.5 | 41.43 | Bronze | Crowd-sourced 2018 |
| 5 | Red Globe Press | 14.4 | 41.14 | Bronze | Crowd-sourced 2018 |

**Fig. 5.9** The new ASPIRElist page on the textBOX website.

The new website also offers librarians, publishers, and platforms the opportunity to share their ASPIRE story and aims to become a source of advice and inspiration within the publishing community. To further encourage accessible practices, we are also donating 10% of all profits from the new service to the UK Literacy Association Donkey Library scheme (UK Literacy Association, 2020).

## 5.18 Conclusion

The e-books Audit and the ASPIRE project are both stories of collaboration and community. The project teams were tight knit, dedicated, and passionate. We had identified an issue—the quality of accessibility content and information—that needed to be addressed and used the skills within the pool of volunteers to develop a unique and powerful collection of data. The implementation of a crowdsourced approach enabled us to generate scale and the positive outlook of the team created a sense of goodwill and community. The final results created a valuable reference source for both universities and content providers alike and facilitated the measurement of accessible content and information for the first time. The projects created an opportunity for honest communication and discussion and created a positive environment that will serve to improve the user experience in the long term. Some publishers and platforms have invested significant time and resources into creating better content accessibility: it is important there is a way of publicly recognizing these investments. The ASPIRE project gives them an opportunity to tell that story and engage with their customers and users. It has been a long journey from those early conversations, but one that has blossomed into a sustainable service that makes a difference. It is a small step towards creating a transparent ecosystem for digital information and promoting access for all.

## References

ASPIRE, 2016. Original Hosting of ASPIRE Website. https://www.learningapps.co.uk/moodle/xertetoolkits/play.php?template_id=1856. (Accessed 14.12.19).

ASPIRE, 2018. VitalSource Supplier Story. https://www.learningapps.co.uk/moodle/xertetoolkits/play.php?template_id=1856. (Accessed 14.12.19).

BOOK MACHINE, 2019. The ASPIRE Awards. https://bookmachine.org/event/bookmachine-unplugged-talking-production/. (Accessed 14.12.19).

Clover, D., Watson, B., 2018. Discoverability: University of East London and University of Kent.

E-Book Audit, 2016. Use and Abuse of Audit Data. https://sites.google.com/site/ebookaudit2016/assignments/use-abuse. (Accessed 14.12.19).

EBSCO, 2018. Content Provider Stories From VitalSource. EBSCO and Intellect Books.

European Commission, 2018a. EU Directive on Public Sector Websites. https://ec.europa.eu/digital-single-market/en/web-accessibility. (Accessed 14.12.19).

European Commission, 2018b. Harmonised Standard on Accessibility of Websites and Mobile Applications. https://ec.europa.eu/growth/single-market/european-standards/harmonised-standards/accessibility-websites-and-mobile-applications_en. (Accessed 14.12.19).

GoogleDoc, 2016a. Hints and Tips Training Resources for Auditors. https://docs.google.com/document/d/1LSo6eubwWTO_ydg3EKIESpG6f-gZrDthsKCH2N41PaE/. (Accessed 14.12.19).

GoogleDoc, 2016b. Follow Up Auditor Survey Results. https://docs.google.com/forms/d/10Z-F5o0IuknfNoIgDqgphEltnQLgfwUyBwIOFNZMR4cY/viewanalytics. (Accessed 14.12.19).

GoogleDoc, 2018a. Audit a Publisher Sign-Up Sheet. https://docs.google.com/spreadsheets/d/1XW_EDAy_oLKTF5LHnOWuk2NSjYne5BoxmWa2e0fL46Q/edit?usp=sharing. (Accessed 14.12.19).

GoogleDoc, 2018b. Audit a Platform Sign-Up Sheet. https://docs.google.com/spreadsheets/d/1-DPq8x0VzufImAI6mXwq3N0wkN8PANfKX8E5lKXeai0/edit#gid=0. (Accessed 14.12.19).

GOV.UK, 2018a. Understanding New Accessibility Requirements for Public Sector Bodies. https://www.gov.uk/guidance/accessibility-requirements-for-public-sector-websites-and-apps. (Accessed 14.12.19).

GOV.UK, 2018b. Model Accessibility Statement on gov.uk Website. https://www.gov.uk/government/publications/sample-accessibility-statement/sample-accessibility-statement-for-a-fictional-public-sector-website. (Accessed 14.12.19).

GOV.UK, Government Digital Service. https://www.gov.uk/government/organisations/government-digital-service. (Accessed 14.12.19).

Hub, 2017. Accessible Books Consortium 2017 International Excellence Award. https://hub.londonbookfair.co.uk/lbf-international-excellence-awards-2017-shortlist-revealed/. (Accessed 14.12.19).

JISC Webinar, 2018. The ASPIRE E-Book Audit—Online Briefing. https://www.jisc.ac.uk/training/the-aspire-e-book-audit. (Accessed 14.12.19).

Jiscmail, 2019. LIS Accessibility. https://www.jiscmail.ac.uk/cgi-bin/webadmin?A0=LIS-ACCESSIBILITY. (Accessed 14.12.19).

JiscMail, 2020. https://www.jiscmail.ac.uk/. (Accessed 14.12.19).

Klopstock, M., Thompson, A., 2019. Accessibility in Publishing. A Case-Study from Kogan Page. Inclusive Publishing. https://inclusivepublishing.org/blog/accessibility-in-publishing-a-case-study-from-kogan-page/. (Accessed 14.12.19).

Kogan Page, 2019. Accessibility Page. https://www.koganpage.com/page/accessibility. (Accessed 14.12.19).

Learning Apps, 2012. Solutions. https://learningapps.co.uk/solutions. (Accessed 14.12.19).

Legislation.gov.uk, 2018. The Public Sector Bodies (Websites and Mobile Applications) (No. 2) Accessibility Regulations 2018. https://www.legislation.gov.uk/uksi/2018/952/made. (Accessed 14.12.19).

London Book Fair Presentation, 2019. Accessible Publishing and the Marrakesh Treaty. https://www.londonbookfair.co.uk/en/Sessions/71765/Accessible-Publishing-and-the-Marrakesh-Treaty-Are-You-Ready. (Accessed 14.12.19).

Lovett, J., 2019. The Intellect Books Story. https://www.textboxdigital.com/intellect-story. (Accessed 14.12. 19).

Matuzovic, M., 2019. https://www.matuzo.at/blog/building-the-most-inaccessible-site-possible-with-a-perfect-lighthouse-score/. (Accessed 14.12. 19).

McNaught, A., 2019a. Accessibility Statements Promoting Improved Reading Experience. https://www.jisc.ac.uk/rd/projects/aspire. https://www.linkedin.com/pulse/accessibility-statements-food-labelling-digital-world-mcnaught/. (Accessed 14.12.19).

McNaught, A., 2019b. Accessibility Statements and Student Ebook Experiences. https://accessibility.jiscinvolve.org/wp/2018/05/14/accessibility-statements-student-e-book-experiences/. (Accessed 14.12 19).

Moore, A., 2018. The Student Perspective: University of Sussex.

NAG, 2017. National Acquisitions Group Award for Excellence. https://nag.org.uk/nag-award-for-excellence/. (Accessed 14.12.19).

Publishers Association, 2020. Accessibility Action Group. https://www.publishers.org.uk/activities/accessibility/. (Accessed 14.12.19).

Smith, S., 2019. The Leeds Beckett Story. https://www.textboxdigital.com/leeds-beckett-story. (Accessed 14.12.19).

Steiner, M., 2019. The Birkbeck University Story. https://www.textboxdigital.com/birkbeck-story. (Accessed 14.12.19).

textBOX, 2018. The New ASPIRE Website. https://www.textboxdigital.com/aspire-home. (Accessed 14.12.19).

textBOX, 2019a. The ASPIREstory Webpage. . https://www.textboxdigital.com/aspire-stories. (Accessed 14.12.19).

textBOX, 2019b. The EBSCO Story. https://www.textboxdigital.com/ebsco-story. (Accessed 14.12.19).

UK Literacy Association, 2020. Donkey Library. https://ukla.org/international/books_for_africa/. (Accessed 14.12.19).

UKSG Webinar Invitation, 2018. Accessibility Aspirations: The Outcomes of the ASPIRE Audit of E-Book Accessibility Statements and Their Implications for Libraries. https://www.uksg.org/event/free-uksg-webinar-accessibility-aspirations-outcomes-aspire-audit-e-book-accessibility. (Accessed 14.12.19).

UKSG Webinar Slides, 2018. Accessibility Aspirations: The Outcomes of the ASPIRE Audit of E-Book Accessibility Statements and Their Implications for Libraries. https://www.slideshare.net/UKSG/uksg-webinar-accessibility-aspirations-the-outcomes-of-the-aspire-audit-of-ebook-accessibility-statements-and-their-implications-for-libraries-with-alistair-mcnaught-jisc. (Accessed 14.12.19).

VitalSource, 2019. Digital Day Presentation. Aspirational Thinking. https://events.vitalsource.com/digital-discovery-day-london-2019. (Accessed 14.12.19).

W3C, 2019. Web Content Accessibility Guidelines. https://www.w3.org/TR/WCAG21/. (Accessed 14.12. 19).

Wykes, J., 2018. The Library Perspective: City University.

# Who is the online public library user?

6

*Katarina Michnik*
University of Borås, Borås, Sweden

## 6.1 Introduction

This chapter focuses on the so-called online public library user; by this is meant a user who accesses online public library services. A public library service is considered as an online service if it is accessed remotely and does not require a physical public library visit. Examples of online public library services may be e-book lending and online access to databases. These online services should not be confused with services that are online related but are provided on site at the public library, such as Internet use training (e.g. Bertot, 2016). Furthermore, the terms *online* and *digital* are not synonyms; online is understood as something happening on the Internet, whereas digital is about the format. This means that an online user is someone who is doing things on the Internet, a digital user is someone who is operating in a digital form, for example, as an avatar figure. When it comes to users who are visiting the public library physically and accessing the services on site, the term *public library visitor* is used.

This chapter has a traditional structure. The introductory section presents the focus, including the research questions. These questions are explained further in the second section. The empirical data and the analysis methods are presented in the third section—the method section. The outcome of the analysis is presented and discussed in the fourth section. The chapter ends with a concluding section.

A recurring theme in public library research today is the role of public libraries in a world with an increasing number of services and activities provided and accessed online. According to the research reviews of this area (Audunson et al., 2019; Carlsson, 2015; Choi and Harper, 2019), approaches vary and include studies of the use of specific digital tools within both online and off-line library activities, studies of librarians' attitudes towards digital technologies, and studies with an organizational focus. Despite this heterogeneity, there are some blind spots. Carlsson (2015) writes that there is a lack of empirical studies of the consequences of social media use, studied from a public library perspective.

From earlier studies, we have information about the use of, and attitudes towards, social media in a public library context. According to Kronqvist-Berg (2014), public library users are generally not interested in communicating with library staff through social media. Even if these library users are social media users, they prefer face-to-face communication with library staff. One reason for this lack of interest can be that librarians do not communicate with their users in the 'right' way when it comes to social media. Joo et al. (2018) have found that public library users engage in different

Future Directions in Digital Information. https://doi.org/10.1016/B978-0-12-822144-0.00006-9

ways, depending on the kind of posts the library staff publishes on Facebook: for example, community news posts received more likes and comments than posts about books and authors. Another study stresses the importance of interaction with library users on social media and argues that the presence of libraries on Facebook should not be about announcing upcoming library events but should instead contribute to community engagement (Joo et al., 2019). An interpretation of this may be that public libraries' online activity, including public libraries' social media activity, should not be used to support the physical public library by, for example, announcing what is going to happen on site at the public library. Instead, public libraries' activity online should have its own purpose and value.

When discussing consequences of social media use from a public library perspective, one issue is whether social media platforms will replace public libraries in the future. There are studies stating correlations between public library visits and Internet use in general (Vakkari, 2012), and social media use specifically (Eriksson and Michnik, 2019; Sin and Kwon, 2017). Social media use is characterized by a high level of interactivity; social media users have the possibility to both generate and share information (e.g. Kaplan and Haenlein, 2010). This described use of social media differs from public library use; traditionally, public libraries have been mainly used for gaining information and not for sharing user-generated content. One could, therefore, say that social media and public libraries have been fulfilling different information needs. But now there is a trend shift in social media use; Sin and Kwon (2017) write that social media are increasingly used for gaining information. This may in time result in partial or full displacement of public libraries since traditional information services in physical public libraries can be considered as less accessible than information gained through social media (Shah and Kitzie, 2012). Public libraries strive to improve their availability by offering services online, as, for example, e-book lending and databases. The use of online public library services is rising (Eriksson and Michnik, 2018, 2019) but it is unclear who is using these services. If the online public library user is also the public library visitor, then public libraries have not succeeded in improving their availability alongside the social media use. Therefore, the main question of this chapter is: 'who is the online public library user?' In this chapter, the online public library user is studied in terms of demography and different forms of reading and Internet use.

Traditionally, the public library has been associated with collections of printed books (Carlsson, 2013; Ranganathan, 2006). Today, online public library services enable access to e-books and audiobooks, next to printed books. Is this visible in the online public library user's reading habits? Today, we have new information supply options online. Earlier studies show that these options have not replaced public library visits, but what does the online public library user's use of these options look like? With this in mind, the main question was broken down into the following three research questions:

RQ1: What is the demographic profile of the online public library user?

RQ2: What is the relationship between different forms of reading and the online public library user?

RQ3: What is the relationship between the public library visitor and the online public library user and how does each category search for information online and engage in social media?

## 6.2 Background information

Today, we are familiar with the demography of public library visitors: people from higher socio-economic groups tend to visit public libraries to a larger extent than people from lower socio-economic groups. One reason for this is that public libraries may be perceived as targeting middle-class citizens; citizens from lower social classes may feel that public libraries are not relevant to them (Griffis and Johnson, 2014; Muggleton, 2013; Willett and Broadley, 2011; Williment, 2009). We also know that different groups use the public library in different ways and to varying extents, as for example parents of small children using the public library more than teenagers (Jochumsen and Rasmussen, 2000). Our knowledge of the demography of the online public library user is more limited. This is the reason for including RQ1.

The fact that some groups use public libraries more than others is the subject of recurring discussions in the public library world. The main question is how to persuade people who currently do not use public libraries to do so. One reason for the unevenly distributed use of public libraries is that they may be strongly associated with printed books and reading, meaning that people who have difficulties with reading may feel that public libraries are not relevant to them (Kann-Christensen and Andersen, 2009). According to a statistical survey of activities offered at Swedish public libraries, it is evident that printed books and reading, and literature-related activities are prominent (Michnik, 2018). Previous studies show a statistically strong relationship between public library visits and printed book reading; the more frequently a person visits the public library, the higher the probability is that he or she reads printed books (Eriksson and Michnik, 2019). The question is what kind of relationship exists between online public library use and printed book reading. If this relationship looks different compared to that between *public library visits* and *printed book reading*, exploiting this connection could potentially enable a more heterogeneous public library image. At the same time, public libraries' online services include potential access to new media formats such as e-books (e.g. Bertot, 2016; Wallin, 2019). Therefore, more formats than just the printed book are relevant when talking about the relationship between *online public library use* and *reading*, resulting in the following formulation:

> RQ2: What is the relationship between different forms of reading and the online public library user?
> RQ3: What is the relationship between the public library visitor and the online public library user and how does each category search for information online and engage in social media?

This last question covers the fact that Internet-based media enable behaviours and attitudes among users that may differ from those behaviours and attitudes related to traditional physical media. What characterizes digital development and distinguishes it from previous technological developments during the 20th century is the changed relationship between the user and 'providers of cultural products' from the creative, arts, and entertainment activities sectors. As a result of technological developments during the last century, a so-called culture-consuming structure was created. This structure is characterized by a few culture producers and/or providers who target a broad culture-consuming public. The media developed during this period, for example, radio, TV, and video, illustrate conditions for experiencing cultural products through mainly the act of consumption (Lessig, 2008). With digital developments, the structure of cultural consumption shifted to co-production, where the public was no longer just a consumer but also a co-producer, a so-called 'prosumer' (Jochumsen et al., 2015; Lessig, 2008). Since public libraries developed largely during the 20th century and are built upon a more centralized culture-consuming structure (libraries have a small group of providers, the librarians, who target a wide audience, the public), digital developments can be a huge challenge for public libraries. For example, Hansson (2015) states that digital development can lead to fundamental changes in the public library sector since '…librarians are no longer primarily responsible for providing information and culture through collections of documents, but instead for teaching and offering guidance on the world of the Internet and digital documentation' (Hansson, 2015, p. 10). This may change the currently prevalent relationship between librarians and users. It is no longer obvious that the former should be a provider and the latter a consumer. Instead, libraries might invest in a relationship based on co-creation. Even though the co-producing structure is not new in a public library context and does not require digital technology (Rasmussen, 2016), new digital tools have significantly increased opportunities for co-production.

Previous studies show that there is a growing relationship between public library visits and information searching online. Frequent online searching increases the probability of visits at the public library (Eriksson and Michnik, 2019). Information searching on the Internet can be described as 'looking up facts or definitions and pursuing topics of interest' (Blank and Groselj, 2014, p. 426). This activity is characterized by a low level of interaction, the focus is 'locating documents that already exists within the traditional Web' (Sin and Kwon, 2017, p. 170). This behaviour is like traditional (public) library use based on a culture-consuming structure. The link between public library visits and sharing and gaining information, many times user-generated, on social media looks different: even though it is more probable that social media users will visit the public library, this relationship does not become stronger with increased social media use, as measured by Eriksson and Michnik (2019). Another study indicates that public library visitors opt out of library activities based on co-production (Kronqvist-Berg, 2014). Social media can be defined in different ways, though a popular definition is that the media are based on co-production or participatory creation. An oft-cited definition is Kaplan and Haenlein's (2010), which defines social media as a 'group of Internet-based applications that build on the ideological and technological foundations of web 2.0 and that allow the creation and exchange of user-generated content' (p. 61). Hence, an explanation for the identified difference between the relationships *public library visits-information searching online* and *public library visits-social media use*, could be that information searching online is based on the same structure as traditional (public) library use, whereas social media is not. With this in mind, it can be fruitful to study the relationships between online public library use and information searching online and social media use, and how these relationships compare to links between public library visits and these two online activities. RQ3 reflects this concern: 'what is the relationship between the public library visitor and the online public library user and how does each category search for information online and engage in social media?'

## 6.3 Method

The empirical data with which the research questions have been answered have been collected and provided by the Society, Opinion and Media (SOM) Institute. SOM has an authoritative reputation in Sweden, and its data are mainly used by researchers, students, and journalists:

> *The SOM Institute is an independent survey research organization at the University of Gothenburg. The Institute collaborates with researchers from a range of disciplines, aiming to explore Swedes' attitudes and habits in a range of areas and to understand the evolution of the Swedish society.*
>
> *SOM Institute (2016)*

Every autumn, the SOM Institute surveys Swedes' attitudes and habits within different areas such as culture, environment, and media. The survey questions that were central to this chapter were about the frequency of Internet use, library visits, and reading during the last 12 months. In the first questions discussed here, respondents were asked about how often they had searched for information, used social media, and performed library errands online. There were seven response options to choose from: 'never' to 'daily'. In the other two questions referred to in this chapter, respondents were asked about how often they had visited the library and how often they had read fiction as audiobook, e-book, and printed book during the last 12 months (hereafter the term *reading* and not *fiction reading* is used). In both cases, there were seven response options from which to choose: from 'never' to 'several times a week'.

In order to describe the online public library user in terms of demography, and different forms of reading and Internet use, correlations between selected dependent and independent variables were studied. In Section 6.4, clarification is given on which variables are dependent and which are independent. Correlations can be observed by using different forms of analysis. For this chapter, cross tables and binary logistic regression analysis were used. Cross tables were used in order to analyze the correlation between online public library use and demographic variables such as educational level and age. Since ordinal variables were included in the analysis, Spearman's rho was used as the correlation coefficient. The value of a correlation coefficient ranges from $-1$ to $+1$; 'a correlation of 0 indicates no relationship at all, a correlation of 1 indicates a perfect positive correlation, and a value of $-1$ indicates a perfect negative correlation' (Pallant, 2016, p. 137). Binary logistic regression analysis was used in order to analyze the effect of different forms of reading and Internet use on online public library use. When performing a logistic regression analysis, a central value is the so-called odds ratio, Exp($B$). This denotes 'the change in odds of being in one of the categories of outcome when the value of a predictor [the independent variable] increases by one unit' (Tabachnick and Fidell, 2013, p. 461). If Exp($B$) is above 1, there is an increased probability for the studied relationship. The higher the odds ratio, the higher the probability. S.E. stands for standard error. The significance level was 0.05 in both analysis methods. To be able to say something about a possible change, the results from 2018 were compared with the results from 2013.

The empirical data used have four limitations: first, this chapter is based on the secondary analysis of data provided by the SOM Institute. This means that the survey questions used were not formulated in accordance with the research questions in this chapter. Instead, the research questions were modified to suit the available empirical data. Second, it is unclear what kind of activities should be included in the term *library errands online*. Since this term was not explained in the survey, there is always a risk that respondents have interpreted it differently, which may have affected their answers. Third, some groups are excluded from answering this survey for practical reasons. The questionnaire is sent out to a sample of the Swedish population. To be included in the sample, you must be a registered resident, but you do not need to be a Swedish citizen. However, people who do not know enough of the Swedish language and people who do not have a fixed address will probably not answer this survey. Fourth, the response rate was 53% in 2018 (1797 responses were submitted) and 54% in 2013 (1706 responses were submitted). Although these surveys were carried out in a Swedish context in the year 2018 and 2013, the study results may be useful in other national contexts.

## 6.4 The online public library user—Results and discussion

Online access is high in Sweden. The Swedish Internet Foundation annually publishes *The Swedes and the Internet*. According to the study from 2019, '98 per cent of households have access to the Internet, and 95 per cent of the population state that they use the Internet' (The Swedish Internet Foundation, 2019). However, there are groups, in total about one million Swedes, who do not have full online access.

National library statistics show a downward trend when it comes to public library visits and loans of printed books. At the same time, e-media and online public library use is increasing (Eriksson and Michnik, 2019; Wallin et al., 2019; Wallin, 2019) and the proportion of online public library users has consistently increased in the past few years (Eriksson and Michnik, 2018, 2019). This rise does not yet compensate for the decline in public library visits. A majority of the respondents who have answered the SOM survey have stated that they do not use online public library services.

According to the values in Table 6.1, there is a relationship between educational level and online public library use: the largest proportion of online public library users are people with a high educational level. In 2018, 23% of the respondents who completed a university degree answered that they use online public library services at least once a month. The corresponding proportion for people with a low educational level is 7%. This value increases with the level of education. When comparing values from 2018 with values from 2013, it appears that the percentage of online public library users has increased most among people with a medium-high education: in 2013, 9% stated that they use the public library's online services at least once a month; in 2018, this value was 19%. Among people with a low educational level, there has been a small increase during the last 5 years: from 6% using the public library's online services at least once a month (2013) to 7% (2018). Correspondingly, we can see that the

**Table 6.1** Correlation between educational level (independent variable) and online public library use (dependent variable).

| Educational level | Online public library use | | | | |
|---|---|---|---|---|---|
| | **Weekly (once a week or more often)** | **Once a month** | **Once every 6 months—once a year** | **Never** | **Total** |
| Low | 3% (2018)<br>4% (2013) | 4% (2018)<br>2% (2013) | 7% (2018)<br>6% (2013) | 87% (2018)<br>87% (2013) | 100% (2018)<br>100% (2013) |
| Medium-low | 5% (2018)<br>4% (2013) | 6% (2018)<br>3% (2013) | 15% (2018)<br>13% (2013) | 74% (2018)<br>80% (2013) | 100% (2018)<br>100% (2013) |
| Medium-high | 6% (2018)<br>3% (2013) | 13% (2018)<br>6% (2013) | 21% (2018)<br>14% (2013) | 60% (2018)<br>76% (2013) | 100% (2018)<br>100% (2013) |
| High | 6% (2018)<br>4% (2013) | 17% (2018)<br>12% (2013) | 27% (2018)<br>23% (2013) | 51% (2018)<br>61% (2013) | 100% (2018)<br>100% (2013) |

*Low educational level* means graduation from primary school, *Medium-low level* means graduation from high school, *Medium-high educational level* means a posthigh school education but without a degree from university, and *High educational level* means graduation from university. Calculation of correlation coefficient: Spearman's rho=(−) 0.256 (2018). Spearman's rho=(−) 0.212 (2013). The values are statistically significant.

proportion of respondents with a high level of education who replied that they do not use public library online services has diminished from 61% in 2013 to 51% in 2018. This proportion has not changed at all when it comes to people with a low level of education (87% in both cases). It should also be noted that the calculated correlation coefficient, Spearman's rho, indicates a stronger correlation between the level of education and online public library use in 2018 than in 2013, although the difference is not large.

Table 6.2 shows that young people tend to be online public library users to a larger extent than older people. In 2018, 23% of the respondents aged between 16 and 29 years answered that they use the public library's online services at least once a month, while the corresponding percentage among people in the categories 50–64 years and 65–85 years was 11% and 13%, respectively. Although the proportion of older people (65–85 years) accessing public libraries online is increasing, the major changes occur among the youngest respondents, the category 16–29 years. The proportion of these respondents who answered that they use online public library services at least once a month increased by 10 percentage points, and the proportion of nonusers decreased by 16 percentage points between 2013 and 2018. The corresponding value among people in the category 65–85 years is a 5 percentage points increase of respondents using online public library services at least once a month and a 6 percentage points decrease of nonusers during the same period.

Long distances may be one reason why a smaller proportion of people in rural areas visit public libraries (Eriksson and Michnik, 2018; Höglund, 2017). Online resources can be one way to reduce this geographical divide. There are plenty of studies of the role of the public library that focus on digital and online literacy and inclusion among inhabitants in rural areas. For example, public libraries provide access to different kinds of online resources, and e-media such as e-books (e.g. Bertot, 2016). But

**Table 6.2** Correlation between age (independent variable) and online public library use (dependent variable).

| Age | Online public library use | | | | |
|---|---|---|---|---|---|
| | **Weekly (once a week or more often)** | **Once a month** | **Once every 6 months—once a year** | **Never** | **Total** |
| 16–29 years | 7% (2018) | 16% (2018) | 28% (2018) | 50% (2018) | 100% (2018) |
| | 3% (2013) | 10% (2013) | 21% (2013) | 66% (2013) | 100% (2013) |
| 30–49 years | 6% (2018) | 13% (2018) | 26% (2018) | 55% (2018) | 100% (2018) |
| | 4% (2013) | 9% (2013) | 21% (2013) | 66% (2013) | 100% (2013) |
| 50–64 years | 3% (2018) | 8% (2018) | 16% (2018) | 73% (2018) | 100% (2018) |
| | 3% (2013) | 4% (2013) | 12% (2013) | 80% (2013) | 100% (2013) |
| 65–85 years | 5% (2018) | 8% (2018) | 10% (2018) | 77% (2018) | 100% (2018) |
| | 3% (2013) | 5% (2013) | 9% (2013) | 83% (2013) | 100% (2013) |

Calculation of correlation coefficient: Spearman's rho=0.212 (2018). Spearman's rho =0.160 (2013). The values are statistically significant.

there are some barriers: in his report on public library activities in sparsely populated municipalities, Hansson (2019) highlights some challenges to the adoption of public library online services in rural areas. For instance, inhabitants may be cautious when it comes to learning how to use new forms of media, or public library resources can be limited, which may hamper their ability to develop new online services. According to Table 6.3, there is a difference between large cities and the countryside when it comes to online public library use.

**Table 6.3** Correlation between place of residence (independent variable) and online public library use (dependent variable).

| Place of residence | Online public library use | | | | |
|---|---|---|---|---|---|
| | **Weekly (once a week or more often)** | **Once a month** | **Once every 6 months—once a year** | **Never** | **Total** |
| Countryside | 3% (2018) | 5% (2018) | 16% (2018) | 77% (2018) | 100% (2018) |
| | 3% (2013) | 3% (2013) | 9% (2013) | 86% (2013) | 100% (2013) |
| Smaller urban area | 6% (2018) | 6% (2018) | 15% (2018) | 74% (2018) | 100% (2018) |
| | 3% (2013) | 8% (2013) | 13% (2013) | 77% (2013) | 100% (2013) |
| City or larger urban area | 5% (2018) | 13% (2018) | 20% (2018) | 62% (2018) | 100% (2018) |
| | 4% (2013) | 7% (2013) | 18% (2013) | 72% (2013) | 100% (2013) |
| Large cities | 8% (2018) | 16% (2018) | 23% (2018) | 53% (2018) | 100% (2018) |
| | 6% (2013) | 8% (2013) | 19% (2013) | 67% (2013) | 100% (2013) |

'Large cities' means the three largest cities in Sweden: Stockholm, Gothenburg, and Malmö. The other alternatives *Countryside*, *Smaller urban area*, and *City or Larger urban area* are not defined in the SOM survey. Calculation of correlation coefficient: Spearman's rho=(−) 0.169 (2018). Spearman's rho=(−) 0.123 (2013). The values are statistically significant.

People living in large cities tend to use the online services of their public library more than people living in the countryside; 24% of the former answered in 2018 that they use public library online services at least once a month, compared with 8% among respondents living on the countryside. The difference between large cities and the countryside has increased since 2013. In 2013, the difference was 8 percentage points, which grew to 16 percentage points 5 years later. Here, the following two factors should be noted: first, the difference between online library use in the countryside and in large cities is equal to the difference between those with a higher education and those with a lower educational level (see Table 6.1), and higher than between the oldest and the youngest respondents (see Table 6.2). A cautious interpretation could be that socio-economic factors are of greater impact when it comes to online public library use, compared to age. This may be a significant point for public librarians to think about when planning for online-related training. Second, there has been a noticeable change among people who live in the countryside and use the public library's online options once or twice a year. The proportion of this user group has increased from 9% in 2013 to 16% in 2018.

When it comes to gender, there is a difference between women's and men's online public library use: women are online public library users to a larger extent. However, the gap between the proportion of female and male online public library users seems to have increased between 2013 and 2018. Among those who use their public library online services at least once a month, the difference between genders was 4 percentage points in 2013 (12% of women and 8% of men used these services at least once a month). In 2018, this difference had increased to 6 percentage points (19% of women and 13% of men used online services at least once a month).

When summarizing the content in Tables 6.1–6.4, it becomes clear that groups which tend to use the online services of their public library seem to be the same groups that visit the public library: well educated, young, living in cities, and women. The fact that more highly educated people, younger people, and women, tend to use public libraries to a higher extent is nothing new (Berelson, 1949; Vakkari, 2012). The opportunity to use online public library services seems to have reinforced rather than changed these trends. Table 6.5 confirms that the online public library user is largely also a public library visitor.

**Table 6.4** Correlation between gender (independent variable) and online public library use (dependent variable).

| | Online public library use | | | | |
|---|---|---|---|---|---|
| **Gender** | **Weekly (once a week or more often)** | **Once a month** | **Once every 6 months—once a year** | **Never** | **Total** |
| Women | 7% (2018)<br>4% (2013) | 12% (2018)<br>8% (2013) | 20% (2018)<br>17% (2013) | 61% (2018)<br>71% (2013) | 100% (2018)<br>100% (2013) |
| Men | 4% (2018)<br>3% (2013) | 9% (2018)<br>5% (2013) | 18% (2018)<br>14% (2013) | 69% (2018)<br>78% (2013) | 100% (2018)<br>100% (2013) |

Calculation of correlation coefficient: Spearman's rho=0.093 (2018). Spearman's rho=0.086 (2013). The values are statistically significant.

**Table 6.5** Correlation between public library visits (independent variable) and online public library use (dependent variable).

| Has visited the library... | Online public library use | | | | |
|---|---|---|---|---|---|
| | **Weekly (once a week or more often)** | **Once a month** | **Once every 6 months—once a year** | **Never** | **Total** |
| ...weekly (once a week or more often) | 41% (2018)<br>26% (2013) | 32% (2018)<br>22% (2013) | 11% (2018)<br>9% (2013) | 16% (2018)<br>43% (2013) | 100% |
| ...once a month—once a quarter | 8% (2018)<br>3% (2013) | 32% (2018)<br>20% (2013) | 30% (2018)<br>29% (2013) | 31% (2018)<br>48% (2013) | 100% |
| ...once every 6 months—once a year | 2% (2018)<br>1% (2013) | 4% (2018)<br>5% (2013) | 34% (2018)<br>26% (2013) | 61% (2018)<br>68% (2013) | 100% |
| Has not visited the library | 1% (2018)<br>2% (2013) | 1% (2018)<br>1% (2013) | 6% (2018)<br>7% (2013) | 92% (2018)<br>90% (2013) | 100% |

Calculation of correlation coefficient: Spearman's rho=0.600 (2018). Spearman's rho=0.497 (2013). The values are statistically significant.

Clearly, there is a strong relationship between public library visits and online public library use: people who visit public libraries tend to use the online services of their public library. Among those who have answered in 2018 that they visit the public library weekly, 73% report that they access the public library online at least once a month. The corresponding value in 2013 was 48%, which indicates a substantial increase in online public library users. A small minority of the nonvisitors have answered that they access the public library online at least once a month: 2% in 2018 and 3% in 2013.

An argument for online public library services is the expectation that they can be a way to reach out to new potential public library users (Michnik, 2016). But if the online public library user is to a large extent the public library visitor, this is not a workable strategy. There are several different barriers to public library use. A question which cannot be fully answered in this chapter is why online public library services will be able to overcome these challenges when physical services on site at the public library cannot. One such barrier is the perception among some groups that public libraries are not relevant to them. This may be because public library activities are not adapted to these groups, but this can also be because these groups have a limited view of what public libraries are providing. Kann-Christensen and Andersen (2009) point out that book-related public library activities may seem uninteresting and irrelevant to people who are not interested in reading or have difficulties with it. In order to broaden its appeal, the public library might highlight activities unrelated to reading. The following section addresses this possibility, with a focus on online public library use.

## 6.5 The online public library user's reading

The empirical material used in this chapter addresses the relationship between online public library use and different forms of reading, namely the reading of printed books, e-books, and audiobooks (Tables 6.6–6.8).

Overall, the probability of online public library use is higher among readers than among nonreaders. This is not surprising and may be a sign that public libraries are still associated with books and reading. If this is the case, the adoption of technology online may not enable a more heterogeneous public library image, meaning that the institution will also probably not become more attractive to nonreaders even as online services are adopted (cf. Kann-Christensen and Andersen, 2009). At the same time, the tested relationships look different depending on the form of reading. The strongest relation is found between e-book reading and online public library use. The probability for using a public library online increases with the frequency of e-book reading. On the other hand, this relationship has weakened compared to 2013. In 2013, the probability values that e-book readers used public library online services were clearly higher than the corresponding values for readers of printed books. In 2018, these values were at a more comparable level.

Furthermore, there is a clear link between printed book reading and online public library use. According to the data collected in 2018, the probability of online public library use does not increase with the frequency of printed book reading, which was the case in 2013. Now, it is more probable that people who read printed books once a month or once a quarter will use online public library services, in comparison to people who read printed books more often; the probability for *online* public library use is, therefore, highest among those who read printed books less frequently. This can be compared to the positive relationship between public library visits and reading of printed books; the most frequent printed book readers are also the most frequent public library visitors (Eriksson and Michnik, 2019).

**Table 6.6** Relation between printed book reading (independent variable) and online public library use (dependent variable).

| **Has read printed books…** | **S.E. (2018)** | **Exp(*B*) (2018)** | **S.E. (2013)** | **Exp(*B*) (2013)** |
|---|---|---|---|---|
| …weekly (once a week or more often) | 0.157 | **3.889** | 0.193 | **3.672** |
| …once a month—once a quarter | 0.159 | **4.387** | 0.197 | **3.487** |
| …once every6 months—once a year | 0.165 | **3.071** | 0.210 | **2.534** |
| Has not read printed books | Reference category | | Reference category | |

The dependent variable is binary: *uses the public library online—does not use the public library online*. Exp(*B*) is the odds ratio and predicts the probability that readers of printed books use the public library online. The higher the odds ratio, the higher the probability. Exp(*B*) and S.E. are explained in the method section. The values are statistically significant.

**Table 6.7** Relation between e-book reading (independent variable) and online public library use (dependent variable).

| Has read e-books... | S.E. (2018) | Exp(*B*) (2018) | S.E. (2013) | Exp(*B*) (2013) |
|---|---|---|---|---|
| ...weekly (once a week or more often) | 0.265 | **4.996** | 0.510 | **12,366** |
| ...once a month—once a quarter | 0.249 | **4.071** | 0.333 | **4.243** |
| ...once every 6 months—once a year | 0.202 | **4.176** | 0.274 | **5.526** |
| Has not read e-books | Reference category | | Reference category | |

The dependent variable is binary: *uses the public library online—does not use the public library online*. Exp(*B*) is the odds ratio and predicts the probability that readers of e-books use the public library online. The higher the odds ratio, the higher the probability. Exp(*B*) and S.E. are explained in the method section. The values are statistically significant.

The weakest relationship is between audiobook reading and online public library use; for 2018, the probability of online public library use does not increase with the frequency of audiobook reading. Instead, it is more probable that people who read audiobooks once a month or once a quarter will use the public library's online services, compared to people who read audiobooks weekly, though the difference is not large. What is interesting is that the relationship *online public library use—audiobook reading* changed in the same way as the relationship *online public library use—printed book reading* between 2013 and 2018. In 2013, the probability of online public library

**Table 6.8** Relation between audiobook reading (independent variable) and online public library use (dependent variable).

| Has read audiobooks... | S.E. (2018) | Exp(*B*) (2018) | S.E. (2013) | Exp(*B*) (2013) |
|---|---|---|---|---|
| ...weekly (once a week or more often) | 0.174 | **2.581** | 0.271 | **2.851** |
| ...once a month—once a quarter | 0.199 | **2.857** | 0.231 | **2.483** |
| ...once every 6 months—once a year | 0.160 | **2.617** | 0.182 | **1.542** |
| Has not read audiobooks | Reference category | | Reference category | |

The dependent variable is binary: *uses the public library online—does not use the public library online*. Exp(*B*) is the odds ratio and predicts the probability that readers of audiobooks use the public library online. The higher the odds ratio, the higher the probability. Exp(*B*) and S.E. are explained in the method section. The values are statistically significant.

use increased as both audiobook and printed book reading increased. In 2018, it was not the most frequent readers but those who read once a month or once a quarter who would most probably use the online services offered by their public library.

## 6.6 The online public library user vs the public library visitor, and their different types of Internet activity

So, what does the relationship look like between public library visits and online public library use, when it comes to information searching online and social media use?

As the odds ratio in Table 6.9 indicates, the probability of online public library use increases with the frequency of online information searching: the more frequently a person searches for information online, the larger the probability is that this person will use online public library services. This relationship looks the same in both 2018 and 2013, though the tested probability for using public library online services is larger in 2018 than it was in 2013—the odds ratio is higher in 2018 compared to 2013. A similar relationship can be noted when it comes to the correlation between online information searching and public library visits, although this relation is weaker than the relation *information searching online—online public library use*. To conclude, increased online information seeking increases the probability of online use of public libraries and public library visits, though the probability for the former is higher than for the latter.

According to the values presented in Table 6.10, the probability of online public library use is higher for those who use social media than for those who do not. At the same time, the following three observations must be noted. First, the identified probability does not increase as the frequency of social media use increases. For 2018, it seems to be most probable that those who use social media once a month or less will use the online public library or visit its physical iteration. Second, the relation *social media use—online public library use* and *social media use—public library visits* looked different in 2013; then, it was more probable that the daily social media user would use the online public library services or visit the public library than people who more seldom used social media. Third, the relationship *social media use—online public library use* is stronger than *social media use—public library visits*. Here, there is a higher probability that social media users will use the public library's online services than visit the public library.

The finding that it is more probable that least frequent social media users will use the public library aligns with findings in earlier studies. Sin and Kwon (2017) have found a similar link: 'in several instances, weekly social media users used library services more than daily social media users…' (p. 175). This observation is explained by Sin and Kwon as an indication that social media displaces public library use, meaning that frequent social media users choose to spend time on gaining information from social media actors rather than going to the public library. There are previous studies demonstrating that this is happening: for example, Tóth and Audunson (2012) write that readers may use specific websites targeting readers instead of public libraries.

**Table 6.9** Result of two binary logistic regression analyses: (a) relation between information searching online (independent variable) and online public library use (dependent variable), and (b) relation between information searching online (independent variable) and public library visits (dependent variable).

| Has searched for information online… | Online public library user | | | | Public library visitor | | | |
|---|---|---|---|---|---|---|---|---|
| | **S.E. (2018)** | **Exp(*B*) (2018)** | **S.E. (2013)** | **Exp(*B*) (2013)** | **S.E. (2018)** | **Exp(*B*) (2018)** | **S.E. (2013)** | **Exp(*B*) (2013)** |
| …daily | 0.733 | **10.815** | 0.527 | **6.798** | 0.222 | **3.312** | Not significant | |
| …once or several times a week | 0.736 | **6.978** | 0.527 | **3.650** | 0.223 | **2.755** | Not significant | |
| …once a month or more seldom | Not significant | | Not significant | | Not significant | | Not significant | |
| Has not searched for information online | Reference category | | | | Reference category | | | |

The dependent variables are binary: *uses the public library online—does not use the public library online* and *visits the public library—does not visit the public library*. Exp(*B*) is the odds ratio and predicts the probability that information online searchers use the public library online and visit the public library. The higher the odds ratio, the higher the probability. Exp(*B*) and S.E. are explained in the method section. The values which are not marked as 'Not significant', are statistically significant.

**Table 6.10** Result of two binary logistic regression analyses: (a) relation between social media use (independent variable) and online public library use (dependent variable), and (b) relation between social media use (independent variable) and public library visits (dependent variable).

| Has used social media… | Online public library user | | | | Public library visitor | | | |
|---|---|---|---|---|---|---|---|---|
| | **S.E. (2018)** | **Exp(*B*) (2018)** | **S.E. (2013)** | **Exp(*B*) (2013)** | **S.E. (2018)** | **Exp(*B*) (2018)** | **S.E. (2013)** | **Exp(*B*) (2013)** |
| …daily | 0.173 | **3.579** | 0.156 | **2.909** | 0.075 | **1.621** | 0.071 | **1.588** |
| …once or several times a week | 0.202 | **3.366** | 0.179 | **2.220** | 0.094 | **1.766** | 0.086 | **1.339** |
| …once a month or more seldom | 0.272 | **3.700** | 0.233 | **2.365** | 0.139 | **1.773** | 0.118 | **1.456** |
| Has not used social media | Reference category | | | | Reference category | | | |

The dependent variables are binary: *uses the public library online—does not use the public library online* and *visits the public library—does not visit the public library*. Exp(*B*) is the odds ratio and predicts the probability that social media users use the public library online and visit the public library. The higher the odds ratio, the higher the probability. Exp(*B*) and S.E. are explained in the method section. The values which are not marked as 'Not significant', are statistically significant.

One explanation for social media's possible displacement of public library use is the fact that social media is increasingly used to find information (Sin and Kwon, 2017); social media can be perceived as faster and more efficient when it comes to the amount of available information, although the public library is often described as offering higher-quality information with greater relevance (Shah and Kitzie, 2012).

At the same time, Sin and Kwon (2017) state that there is a strong positive relationship between information searching online and public library use (this is also reflected in Table 6.9). It is worth stressing that the relationship *information search online—public library online use* strengthens with a higher frequency of information searching; in addition, this link has strengthened between 2013 and 2018. So, if social media is going to be used to a larger extent for information searching, this does not automatically mean that it is a threat to public libraries. On the other hand, in 2013 it was more probable that daily social media users would use the public library's online services than less frequently social media users. Five years later, we can see a shift in this relationship; it is now slightly more probable that monthly social media users will use online public library services. This can be seen as a sign that frequent social media users are opting out of public library use.

The relationship between new forms of media and earlier media can change as the use and distribution of the former changes and evolves. In a brief overview of studies that focus on the Internet's relationship to traditional media, Sin and Kwon (2017) write:

> *[t]hese studies reported that the Internet had a substitution effect on broadcasting services but a complementary effect on newspapers in the early diffusion stages. This initial relationship changed as the Internet became a more universal service. The effect of the Internet on broadcasting appears to be complementary, whereas its effect on newspapers has changed to be more competitive.*
>
> *(p. 175)*

One of Sin's and Kwon's conclusions is that with an increased array of social media services, a consequence may be that these will be chosen instead of those of the public library. At the same time, the influence of social media may look different for different public library activities; in Sin and Kwon's (2017) study, public library *online* services seemed not to be displaced by social media use, unlike the activities that take place at the public library. The fact that the relationship *social media use—online public library use* is stronger than *social media use—public library visits* (see Table 6.10), is suggesting that online public library services may be important to the legitimacy of public libraries in future in which social media is widely spread and used.

## 6.7 Conclusion

In the introduction of this chapter, a reference was made to Carlsson's (2015) argument that the public library research field lacks empirical studies on what consequences the use of social media may have for public libraries. One step in this direction can be to focus on the character of the online public library user, a key goal of this chapter. Here, it is stated that the reader, the information seeker, and the social media user tend to use online public library services. Hence, the online public library user seems to be the same user who visits the public library. This indicates that online public library services, at least for the moment, are not a successful way to reach new public library user groups. Instead, these online services seem to reinforce the public library visit trends and the image of public library as book and reading related.

The fact that the same groups are using the public library in its online and physical forms could be a sign that the provided online activities and the ones provided on site at the public library relate to the same areas of interest, rather than offering different activities. According to the earlier studies, online public library services can facilitate access to activities performed in the physical public library (Michnik, 2016) or inform about activities taking place in the physical space of the public library (cf. Joo et al., 2018). This indicates that online public library activities seem to be a means of strengthening activities taking place on site at the public library. Two possible consequences for public libraries may be identified here: first, nonusers will probably not become interested in public library services if the online services are foremost linked to what is happening at the physical public library; these residents have already decided, consciously or unconsciously that they are not interested in these on-site activities. Second, in the long run, a consequence might be that if online and on-site public library services are more or less equivalent, there is a risk that they will not complement each other but instead replace each other (cf. Sin and Kwon, 2017), simply because public library users may choose the form that is perceived as faster and more accessible (cf. Shah and Kitzie, 2012). We already see that while online usage is increasing, on-site use, in the shape of public library visits, is declining (Eriksson and Michnik, 2018).

According to the previous research, a growing challenge for public libraries is the conflict between the various functions that it is supposed to provide. For instance, the public library's role as a meeting place can be hard to combine with that of being a quiet room for reading and studying (Eriksson et al., 2013; Rasmussen, 2016). Maybe a solution here could be that some activities could focus on the online iteration of the public library and others at the physical public library? Today, given the wide variety of activities the public library is supposed to offer, it is hardly difficult for public libraries to fill online and physical arenas with different kinds of activities. Perhaps, the online and the physical public library could complement each other in this way.

## References

Audunson, R., Aabø, S., Blomgren, R., Evjen, S., Jochumsen, H., Larsen, H., Rasmussen, C., Vårheim, A., Johnston, J., Koizumi, M., 2019. Public libraries as an infrastructure for a sustainable public sphere: a comprehensive review of research. J. Doc. 75 (4), 773–790.

Berelson, B., 1949. The Library's Public. Columbia University Press, New York.

Bertot, J.C., 2016. Building digitally inclusive communities: the roles of public libraries in digital inclusion and development. In: ACM International Conference Proceeding Series, pp. 95–102.

Blank, G., Groselj, D., 2014. Dimensions of Internet use: amount, variety and types. Inf. Commun. Soc. 17 (4), 417–435.

Carlsson, H., 2013. Den nya stadens bibliotek: Om teknik, förnuft och känsla i gestaltningen av kunskaps-och upplevelsestadens folkbibliotek. Lunds Universitet, Lund.

Carlsson, H., 2015. Researching public libraries and the social web, 2006-2012. J. Doc. 71 (4), 632–649.

Choi, N., Harper, L., 2019. Public libraries and the social web: a review and analysis of the existing literature. J. Doc. 76 (1), 197–211.

Eriksson, C., Michnik, K., 2018. Biblioteket på samhälleberget. In: Andersson, U., Carlander, A., Lindgren, E., Oskarson, M. (Eds.), Sprickor i fasaden. SOM-undersökningen 2017. SOM-Institutet, Göteborg, pp. 233–247 (SOM-rapport nr 72).

Eriksson, C., Michnik, K., 2019. Allas bibliotek? In: Andersson, U., Rönnerstrand, B., Öhberg, P., Bergström, A. (Eds.), Storm & Stiltje. SOM-undersökningen 2018. SOM-Institutet, Göteborg, pp. 301–320 (SOM-rapport nr 74).

Eriksson, C.M., Michnik, K.E., Nordeborg, Y., 2013. The public library user and the charter tourist: two travellers, one analogy. Inf. Res. 18 (3).

Griffis, M.R., Johnson, C.A., 2014. Social capital and inclusion in rural public libraries: a qualitative approach. J. Librariansh. Inf. Sci. 46 (2), 96–109.

Hansson, J., 2015. Documentality and legitimacy in future libraries—an analytical framework for initiated speculation. New Libr. World 116 (1/2), 4–14.

Hansson, J., 2019. Folkbibliotek i glesbygd: kunskapsläge och erfarenheter. Kulturrådet, Stockholm.

Höglund, L., 2017. Biblioteken fortsatt välanvända med höga betyg. In: Andersson, U., Ohlsson, J., Oscarsson, H., Oskarsson, M. (Eds.), Larmar och gör sig till. SOM-undersökningen 2016. SOM-Institutet, Göteborg, pp. 329–341 (SOM-rapport nr 70).

Jochumsen, H., Rasmussen, C.H., 2000. Gør biblioteket en forskel? Danmarks Biblioteksforening, København.

Jochumsen, H., Skot-Hansen, D., Rasmussen, C.H., 2015. Towards culture 3.0—performative space in the public library. Int. J. Cult. Policy 23 (4), 512–524.

Joo, S., Choi, N., Baek, T., 2018. Library marketing via social media: the relationships between Facebook content and user engagement in public libraries. Online Inf. Rev. 42 (6), 940–955.

Joo, S., Choi, N., Harper, L.M., 2019. Investigation of factors that influence public librarians' social media use for marketing purposes: an adoption of the technology acceptance model and theory of planned behavior. Libr. Q. 89 (2), 137–155.

Kann-Christensen, N., Andersen, J., 2009. Developing the library: between efficiency, accountability and forms of recognition. J. Doc. 65 (2), 208–222.

Kaplan, A.M., Haenlein, M., 2010. Users of the world, unite! The challenges and opportunities of social media. Bus. Horiz. 53 (1), 59–68.

Kronqvist-Berg, M., 2014. Social Media and Public Libraries: Exploring Information Activities of Library Professionals and Users. Åbo Universitet, Åbo.

Lessig, L., 2008. Remix: Making Art and Commerce Thrive in the Hybrid Economy. Penguin Press, New York.

Michnik, K., 2016. Swedish local politicians' views on public library digital services, digital information strategies. In: Baker, D., Evans, W. (Eds.), Digital Information Strategies. From Applications and Content to Libraries and People. Chandos, Oxford, pp. 131–142.

Michnik, K., 2018. Samhällets allt-i-allo?: om folkbibliotekens sociala legitimitet. Högskolan i Borås, Borås.

Muggleton, T.H., 2013. Public libraries and difficulties with targeting the homeless. Libr. Rev. 62 (1/2), 7–18.

Pallant, J., 2016. SPSS Survival Manual: A Step by Step Guide to Data Analysis Using IBM SPSS. Open University Press, Maidenhead.

Ranganathan, S.R., 2006. The Five Laws of Library Science. Ess Ess Publications, New Delhi (Original Work Published 1931).

Rasmussen, C.H., 2016. The participatory public library: the Nordic experience. New Libr. World 117 (9/10), 546–556.

Shah, C., Kitzie, V., 2012. Social Q & A and virtual reference—comparing apples and oranges with the help of experts and users. J. Am. Soc. Inf. Sci. Technol. 63 (10), 2020–2036.

Sin, S.-C.J., Kwon, N., 2017. Displacement or complementarity? Assessing the relationship between social media and public library usage in the U.S., South Korea, and Singapore. Libr. Inf. Sci. Res. 39 (3), 169–179.

SOM Institute, 2016. About the SOM Institute. https://som.gu.se/som_institute/about-som. (Accessed 01.12.19).

Tabachnick, B.G., Fidell, L.S., 2013. Using Multivariate Statistics. Pearson Education, Boston.

The Swedish Internet Foundation, 2019. Meaningful Time Online and the Pros and Cons of Digital Society. https://svenskarnaochinternet.se/rapporter/svenskarna-och-internet-2019/the-swedes-and-the-internet-2019-summary/. (Accessed 01.12.19).

Tóth, M., Audunson, R., 2012. Websites for booklovers as meeting places. Library Hi Tech 30 (4), 655–672.

Vakkari, P., 2012. Internet use increases the odds of using the public library. J. Doc. 68 (5), 618–638.

Wallin, B., 2019. Selling and Lending e-Books: Changes in the Swedish Literary Field. Högskolan i Borås, Borås.

Wallin, B., Tattersall Wallin, E., Gunnarsson Lorentzen, D., 2019. Bokläsning och den svenska bokmarknaden. In: Andersson, U., Rönnerstrand, B., Öhberg, P., Bergström, A. (Eds.), Storm & Stiltje. SOM-undersökningen 2018. SOM-institutet, Göteborg, pp. 287–300 (SOM-rapport nr 74).

Willett, P., Broadley, R., 2011. Effective public library outreach to homeless people. Libr. Rev. 60 (8), 658–670.

Williment, K., 2009. It takes a community to create a library. Partnership: Can. J. Libr. Inf. Pract. Res. 4 (1), 1–11.

# Digital culture: The dynamics of incorporation

# 7

*Stephen Akintunde*
University of Jos Library, Jos, Nigeria

## 7.1 Introduction

The Internet, millennials, digital natives, social media, and the Internet of Things are some of the words that distinguish today's culture from that of the past millennium. The migration from a traditional to a more dynamic youth social ecosystem is astonishing. The term 'ecosystem' is here defined as the holistic social situation of youths, including sociological, psychological, and technological behaviours. Youths appear to take centre stage in defining meaning and relationships. The world is in the midst of a 'volcanic eruption' of social life that places it in a state of flux. Social relationships are being redefined by uncontrollable forces through the use of technology and social media where youths, in particular, take centre stage and adults are left to 'catch up' with them. They seem to invent the process of information dissemination and the information disseminated is increasingly queried for credibility and authenticity. The present situation is aptly captured by Bauman (2019, p. 3): 'as we look at the young, we look with the gaze of liquefied persons who have inevitably altered their own boundaries: we are the product of whatever life's circumstances have made us'.

The globalizing effect of this phenomenon continues to impact societies, changing lifestyles and affecting belief systems. In the global South, especially in Africa, the effect is more significant as traditional systems are being impacted. Social relationships are affected by new means of communication. Traditional hierarchies of kinship are flattened as millennials who never experienced the strict rural kinship model of hierarchical relationships prefer liberal and direct relationships to members of their families through instant messaging via social media. Traditional hierarchies offer a structured relationship where seniority in age defines relationships and access to each other. For instance, in traditional African settings, it is normal for the younger to defer to the older in all aspects of social interactions. Boys are not to be seen mingling with elders, while women should always be away from men in public (Achebe, 1959).

However, the two situations are no longer prevalent because of the effects of technology, which has broken down the wall of division and has prompted a rise of advocacy for gender equality. This is attributable to the growing digital culture that is modifying social relationships, changing the geographical migration from the rural to urban centres, and breaking down the rural-urban, global north versus south divide by digital communication. This also contributes to the continuing modification of the definition of the family. Digital culture is permeating all aspects of individuals' lives,

**Future Directions in Digital Information. https://doi.org/10.1016/B978-0-12-822144-0.00007-0**

groups, and societies through technology, creating new value systems and affecting social relationships, national boundaries, economies, and governments. This culture creates prospects for a new world order for digital communication (Mosco, 2017). The anonymous nature of online interactions breaks down barriers of gender inequality and releases the hitherto restricted female gender to open competition in the world of social media.

The traditional family in Africa is made up of extended relationships which comprise the nuclear and immediate family relationships on both sides of the husband and wife. Today, this extended family structure is giving way to more nuclear units in many instances. The urbanization effect and the emerging white-collar and industrial labour system also affect the nuclear unit with the experiences of single-parent families increasing because of the need for people to earn a living and sustain a family. The family, therefore, faces an assault of modernization which has turned into a cultural meltdown because of the increasing instability of the family.

The effect of this instability appears to be felt by today's children who, with little supervision by parents and the extended family, find another, and, perhaps a bigger, family in social media. Children take their parents' mobile phone at every available opportunity, especially the mobile devices of their mothers. So, children, even toddlers, value technology because of what they see can be done with it. Parents use the situation to provide academic games on mobile devices for their children so that the children can learn as they get inducted into the technological and digital culture.

On social media and in general communication, digital natives find expression in a boundless space where anonymity reigns and structure is loose. Digital natives are those born after the inception of the Internet and who have not known any other culture beyond the digital (Prensky, 2001). They are different from 'digital immigrants' who can be described as those born before the advent of the Internet. While older generations appear to be struggling to take full advantage of technology, technological innovation and new uses of technology emerge as an ongoing development. From this perspective, there appears to be a culture clash that is gradually resulting in a new understanding of the social system. This is reflected in the migration from more predictable cultural systems and values to more dynamic ones creating dysfunctions in traditional forms of social relationships. This leads to the creation and acceptance of new value systems. This new system carries with it an ongoing crystallization of digital culture and the thorough breakdown of traditional culture in terms of beliefs, values, and social relationships while defining its own (Autry, 2011; Rikhye et al., 2009). This is the sociological situation in which today's learners and researchers find themselves. It is also the problem of a new generation of learners who are developing a preference for instant answers and convenient access to information. The question to ask, then, is how do learners today adjust to the dynamics that are pervading the learning environment through the widespread adoption of technology? How do students deal with the pressure of productive learning within their own cultural context? What are the preferences of today's learners in determining access to learning? And what is the value of digital information? These are critical questions that shape this chapter as discussions focus on the present situation and the future of students and teachers in a digital age.

## 7.2 Caught in between cultures

In a dynamic global system, the need for survival appears to be the norm and digital immigrants are in the middle of the storm. They, like digital natives, are caught between two worlds and two cultures. In the process of negotiating their survival across cultures from which they cannot separate, they become marginal people who seek to establish their own identities as a form of coping mechanism (Park, 1928; Stonequist, 1935). It is obvious that trends in access to and use of technology show that today's learner is caught in between two worlds—the world of technology and the world of the teacher, who is probably not as adaptive to technology as the student. The values of these two categories of people also appear to differ increasingly as today's learners, mainly digital natives, exhibit characteristics which make them closer to their own generation than that of the teacher. Some of these characteristics are self-belief, peer belief, individual and collaborative learning. Self-belief is the trust that the learners have concerning their ability to pursue independent learning in the way that best suits them, not necessarily the orthodox rote-learning method. Peer-belief is the dependence on 'online' peers for assessment and sanction for any action taken or about to be taken. This is most visible through posts on social media where there is a quiet surrender to peers for evaluation and approval of real or intended actions. Individual learning takes place when the learner is required to engage the self in learning, grasp a subject, concept, or idea, and submit individual assignments. Collaborative learning takes place as a norm because of growing peer culture, so that every assignment, even individual assignments, are considered, first, as subject to peer review. The pedagogy of teaching also appears to favour collaboration, especially in online or electronic environments. The social space for today's learning also encourages liberalized as opposed to stoic learning spaces, as experienced by the older generation.

In Africa, particularly sub-Saharan Africa, traditional culture is still pervasive and there is a tendency to confuse the transition through which the younger learner is passing with rebellion or lack of interest because of not following the orthodox or traditional rote-learning approach. The younger learner seeks more flexibility and collaboration in the learning process. Whereas the learner sees a global environment as their community, the classroom and learning space in the locality is usually not as advanced as that in the global North and that which is visible online. Most of the technology that is available locally is developed and passed down from the global North to the South. The student in the South is, therefore, a user of technology and, generally, a codeveloper of learning applications. This status implies that the student continues to seek improvement online and uses every opportunity to acquire, adopt, and adapt in order to be abreast of peers in the online community. And, because the young learner is more sensitive to peers than the natural cultural environment, there is a dysfunction in the operation of emerging technologies.

This dysfunction arises in the 'unrealistic' attachment to an 'outer' online world while still living in a technologically less-adaptive locality. This results in friction and dissatisfaction with both the learning process and the local environment, which affect concentration and assimilation of concepts. It also creates gaps in the world views of the learner and teacher as they both see their worlds from different perspectives, and especially the teacher, who is not as comfortable with technology as the learner.

Furthermore, classrooms in most African and particularly Nigerian institutions of learning are not as adaptive to technology as in the North. Neither are most teachers. Yet this is the environment in which today's learner is expected to operate, and from which people need to learn in order to excel.

The situation exposes a technological distance which defines learning in the global South. Technological distance is the observable difference in the use and adoption of technology between two individuals or groups. The wider the distance between the teacher and the learner, for example, the more there is a conflict in expectations of the two groups. In the case of Nigerian students, it is assumed that more of them use technology than their teachers because of the propensity of students, who are digital natives, to easily imbibe the technological culture. Their existence, learning, and subsistence revolve entirely around digital technology.

It is imperative to consider how the learner can properly exploit technology for learning and development in this context. There are several categories of learners, and the one that is the focus of this paper is the tertiary or higher education student, most of whom are 16–30 years. This age bracket is also the most innovative and adventurous group. For students, the availability of technology for learning is a further opportunity for exploration of the limits of the possibilities of that technology. This, again, may add or distract from the learning experience, depending on the use made of the available technology.

Since students are apparently a step ahead of teachers in the use of technology, they are left to drive the integration of technology in learning, which should not be so. Students need to be guided by their teachers, who should be so competent that the students have confidence in their leadership, even in the use of technology. Inappropriate uses of technology, therefore, result when they are not properly instructed. For example, instances of students downloading, copying, and pasting texts electronically without appropriate acknowledgement are common. Where detected, sanctions are applied. The use of plagiarism software is only just growing in Nigerian universities. However, there are copyright desks in Nigerian federal universities such as the Universities of Ibadan, Jos and Nigeria, Nsukka, which enforce the proper assignment of rights to intellectual or patented works. It is apparent that some students see the use of online electronic resources as normal and do not feel a sense of obligation to recognize ownership because it is in the 'public domain'. In an attempt to enhance easy migration to the digital environment, the regulatory body for universities in Nigeria, the National Universities Commission (NUC), has designed a curriculum that includes the teaching of Information and Communications Technology (ICT) as a core module in the General Studies courses for freshers in all Nigerian universities. However, the depth of teaching and availability of ICT infrastructure varies from one institution to another.

## 7.3 Practice, evidence, and impact

In determining the trend in, and the future use of technology in Nigerian HE, a questionnaire survey was carried out, together with focus group interviews. The questionnaire was designed and administered to students in 27 Nigerian higher education institutions, comprising 24 universities and 3 polytechnics. The institutions represent both public and private institutions and range from the general to the specialized. The public institutions include federal and state-funded institutions. In all, 325 responses were received from students in 12 faculties, using a purposive sampling approach, providing a good spread of responses, as seen in Table 7.1.

The age group of the students ranged from 15 to 55, as represented in Fig. 7.1. The age cluster, as discovered, is a normal age range of undergraduate students in most higher education institutions (HEIs) in Nigeria and corroborates with a global trend. The students are therefore able to supply adequate data as evidence in understanding

**Table 7.1** Faculty of respondents.

| Faculty | Frequency | Percent |
|---|---|---|
| Social Sciences | 68 | 20.9 |
| Natural Sciences | 67 | 20.6 |
| Engineering | 54 | 16.6 |
| Arts | 30 | 9.2 |
| Environmental Sciences | 28 | 8.6 |
| College of Health Sciences | 24 | 7.4 |
| Education | 20 | 6.2 |
| Management Sciences | 17 | 5.2 |
| Law | 9 | 2.8 |
| Pharmaceutical Sciences | 4 | 1.2 |
| Agriculture | 3 | 0.9 |
| Veterinary Medicine | 1 | 0.3 |
| **Total** | **325** | **100** |

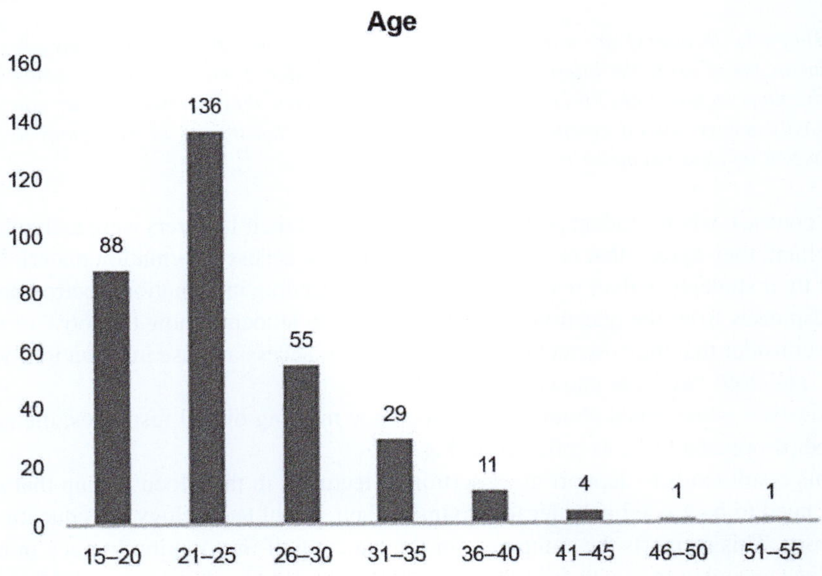


**Fig. 7.1** Age of respondents.

the true trend in the engagement of technology for information among university students in Nigeria.

In addition to the questionnaire, focus group interviews were held for students and lecturers, respectively. The interviews provided an insight into the causative factors that make digital natives behave the way they do, their expectations, and the position of lecturers in a dynamic digital environment. Among lecturers, the focus group interview was solely used to solicit information. It comprised seven lecturers from three different universities from three different regions—North Central (4), North West (1), and South West (2). Their disciplines were Education, Engineering, Environmental Sciences, and Social Sciences. The age range of the lecturers was from 26 to 57 years, with an average of 36 years, resulting in a group that is closer to digital natives than the higher age cluster which prevails in most Nigerian universities.

Among lecturers, digital information is a necessary and growing need which every lecturer must embrace or be left behind because today's learner is more of a digital native who must nevertheless be guided in exploring and using information appropriately for learning. When this is not done, students spend more time using their digital devices for social media than for academic pursuits. According to one of the participants:

> *The students have skill sets for social media but not for academics, and they need to be coached to use their gadgets for academic purposes.*

However, in the focus group for students, made up of eight students from three higher education institutions, with an average age of 21–25, most of the participants agree that they are more competent than their lecturers in the use of online sources for learning, almost without exception. One of the student participants had this to say:

> *They [the lecturers] are not technologically inclined. They are just old. They are incapable of using the Internet to update their knowledge. Some of them keep using the same lecture notes for decades and have yet to review these, even when they can easily access new information online. They even think that the use of technology to access information makes the student lazy.*

In contrast, where student participants affirmed that their lecturers were technology compliant, they agreed that they use the technology to access information materials to guide their students in their research projects and in finding information electronically.

Responses from the questionnaire administered to students show that 66% of students consider that they use technological devices to access and use information 'very well', and 26% 'well', as shown in Fig. 7.2.

However, when asked about their competency in using digital resources, the apex number dropped a little, as reflected in Fig. 7.3.

This result tends to support the assertion of lecturers in their focus group that students need to be guided in order to maximize their use of technology for educational purposes. This supports the campaign for the teaching of information literacy in universities, a campaign in which librarians would do well to lead. Whereas all Nigerian

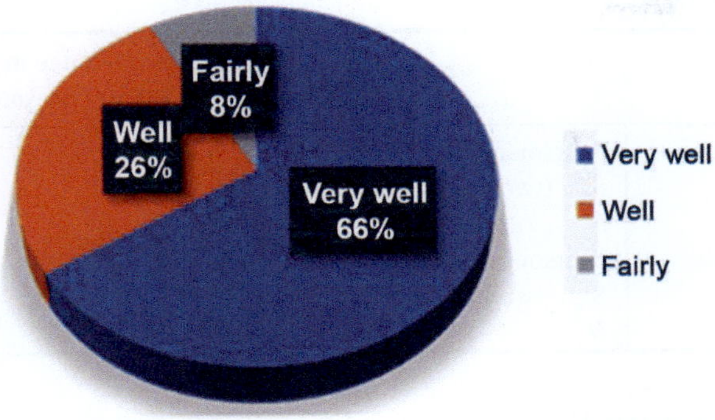


**Fig. 7.2** How well digital gadgets are used for accessing information.

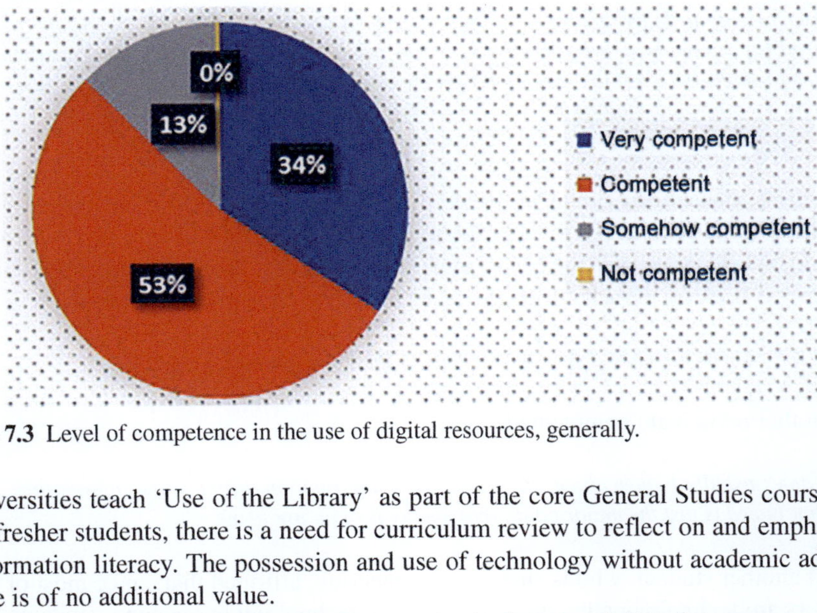


**Fig. 7.3** Level of competence in the use of digital resources, generally.

universities teach 'Use of the Library' as part of the core General Studies course for all fresher students, there is a need for curriculum review to reflect on and emphasize information literacy. The possession and use of technology without academic advantage is of no additional value.

When age was interacted with competence in the use of digital resources, using the Pearson correlation coefficient, an inverse relationship was established; implying that the higher the age, the lower the level of competence and vice versa. Furthermore, results indicate a weak relationship, with $R = -0.082$ which is also not significant with $P = 0.135 > 0.05$, as demonstrated in Table 7.2.

This is a noteworthy finding, confirming the effect of age on the use of digital devices in accessing electronic resources for learning but not necessarily affirming that the age group that best uses technological devices make the most use of learning resources for academic purposes.

Among lecturers, it was generally observed by all participants in the focus group that while there is a need to adopt digital processes in learning, the infrastructural

**Table 7.2** Pearson correlation of age and competence.

| | | Age | Competence in the use of electronic resources |
|---|---|---|---|
| Age | Pearson correlation | 1 | −.082 |
| | Sig. (two-tailed) | | .138 |
| | *N* | 325 | 325 |
| Competence in the use of electronic resources | Pearson correlation | −.082 | 1 |
| | Sig. (two-tailed) | .138 | |
| | *N* | 325 | 325 |

development in Nigerian HEIs is not generally supportive of technology. According to another lecturer participant:

> *...even ICT courses are taught manually in some of our institutions, making it difficult for students to learn appropriate uses of technology for learning...there is also a need for curriculum review, because, if it is on the use of technology, students are comfortable, but if it is for educational and research purposes, students need guidance, how to reference materials, etc., because even those who use it for educational purposes, merely lift online materials verbatim, without acknowledgement.*

Students, in their focus group, inadvertently confirmed the observation of lecturers when they answered a question put to them about whether or not they feel obligated to identify and acknowledge sources in the course of electronic research. Most of them said that they had never considered the acknowledgement of sources as critical. One of them said:

> *When I am busy online, I do not have time to jot down sources.*

Another participant commented:

> *I don't usually bother about the source of an information, because the information that I need is just the major point, referencing is of no use to me.*

But another student, who is studying Engineering, affirmed that, since most of his lecturers are technologically competent and use technology in teaching, students are made to acknowledge sources as a matter of routine.

It is interesting to note the discussion among students when asked who they would rather share information with or approach for information sharing. They agreed that they would rather chat with their peers on general and academic matters than approach lecturers, most of whom tend to regard chatting online with students as burdensome.

> *I would rather chat with my peers...they break down difficult concepts for you and lecturers do not seem to have that time because of their busy schedules...my peers have more time than the lecturers to acquire more knowledge because they are in a world where they are free to acquire as much as they can, compared to the lecturers who are constrained by their work; my peers serve as motivation in the same struggle for academic excellence...*

**Table 7.3** Use of mobile devices to access learning resources.

| Use of mobile device to access learning materials | Frequency | Percent |
|---|---|---|
| Yes | 317 | 97.5 |
| No | 8 | 2.5 |
| **Total** | **325** | **100** |

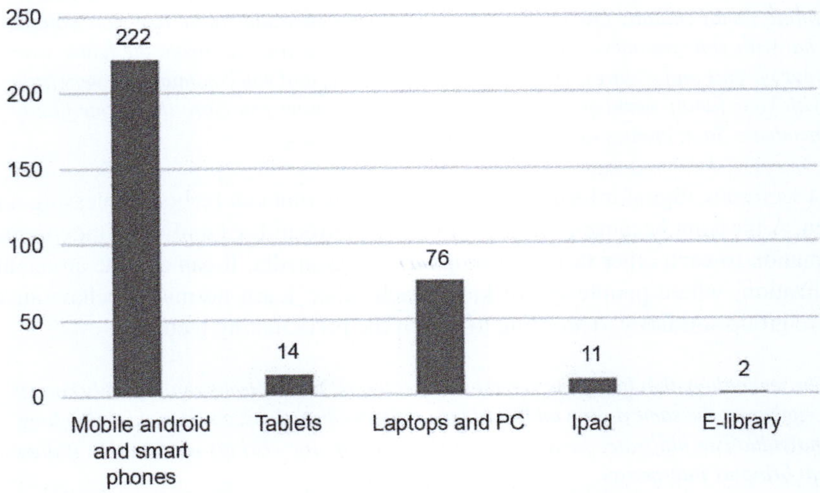


**Fig. 7.4** Devices used the most for accessing digital information.

When asked about access to learning resources in the questionnaire, 98% of students said that they use mobile devices, as shown in Table 7.3.

The mobile devices used are mobile android and smartphones, followed by laptops and personal computers (PCs), as displayed in Fig. 7.4.

This is of interest because it shows that digital natives prefer to be 'on the go' with technology. It is observable that most android and smart mobile telephones now have the capacity and features to perform services that laptops and desktops performed previously. Android and smartphones also enable digital natives to navigate social media at will, which may have consequences for their academic performance and general use of information for learning.

## 7.4 Digital information and family relationships

Since African society is so culturally conscious, an attempt was made in the two focus groups to find out how digital information affects family relationships. Both students and lecturers agreed that there are positive and negative consequences of using technology and digital information. On the positive side, for students, digital information and the way it is used by young people keep family members in touch even at a distance. On the negative side, it creates a fault line in family relationships. According to one of the participants, affirmed by two other participants:

> *When I and my siblings are far away, we do WhatsApp video chat, and distance is no longer a barrier as we do communicate and see each other.*

Another student participant said:

> *To me I feel the negative impact is more, because, most times there is a distance… online social chatting creates a distance between family and youth, like, you want to chat with your friend(s), know what's happening, and you are inside the house with your parents and siblings, yet, your mind is not there, and you communicate very little with your family members. Your friends may even know you more than your family members. So, it creates distance, so to say.*

For lecturers, digital information through the Internet can be both a blessing and a burden. A blessing because it can be a rallying platform for families as they transmit information to each other through groups on social media. It can also be an agent of socialization, where people get to know each other, learn norms of behaviour and achieve group solidarity. According to one of the participating lecturers:

> *The technology that brings us together separates us. It is an irony that a family can sit together on the same dining table and face different directions, courtesy of technology. Individualism infiltrates family relationships. Technology brings us data, but it does not bring us interaction.*

In effect, digital information has a general effect of negative impact on the family because it affects social interaction, which is a necessary socialization factor in families. Though there are positive impacts of digital information, the dominant age group that uses technology never experienced the traditional 'moonlight story hours' of African families, a major rallying point for them before the advent of technology, and, as a result, that group has little or no obligation to tradition.

The impact of this trend is the uncertain future of the family in Nigeria, and, indeed Africa, disrupting cohesion. Since families are the basic unit of socialization, this has ripple effects on society, resulting in the dysfunction, leading to deviant behaviours and a redefinition of values and a modification of belief systems. Lecturers expressed fear that digital information, as presently used by students, does not prepare them for in-depth thinking nor does it inspire the rigour that scholars are known for because the information is now so easily accessible and plentiful, but students fail to take adequate advantage of it.

## 7.5 Projections

Since the advent of digital information, and the ubiquity of technology, in particular, it is imperative to find out about its future from the present. In answer to one of the questions on the questionnaire, students preferred digital information processes to the

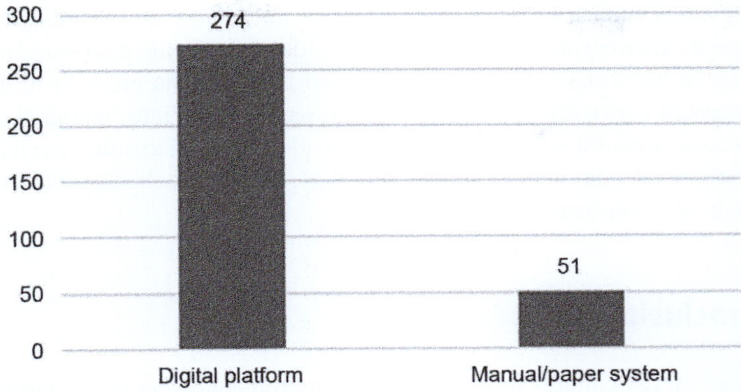


**Fig. 7.5** Platform most preferred for learning and research.

manual, for reasons ranging from 'ease of use', 'diversity and wide range of content', to 'unlimited space for data storage, speed in accessing information, and ability to back up information for future use' (see Fig. 7.5).

Among lecturers, one of the participants said that using the digital platform:

> *...is very flexible for me, because I gain electronic access to learning resources by getting online permissions and exploring links to many academic sites.*

Another lecturer mentioned that digital information helps the teacher to prepare well for lectures by providing wide virtual space and numerous resources for learning. It also makes it possible for students to access learning resources at the same time—multiple uses of a single document, which might not be feasible in the physical or manual system.

However, the future of digital information is also interesting. From the responses of lecturers, digital information is here to stay, and the world needs to recognize this. In the words of one of the lecturers:

> *...with technology today, the future moves to us, and not us going to the future.*

Another lecturer explained that:

> *[The] Library becomes a virtual space where mortar is used only as a necessary shade, because the walls of learning resources are broken down digitally.*

Another said that the future of digital information will result in:

> *More <u>isolation</u> because people will become more intrinsic, communicating more with persons at a distance than those in their physical space.*

According to these comments, digital information becomes a silent revolutionary tool of social transformation from cohesion to a new social order with more likely cases of self-centredness, marginalization, and anomie. The uses of information for anonymous social interaction become prevalent over academic uses, leading to a wide range of social experiences. With the growing digitization of education—and teaching and learning in particular—a future is envisaged in which the pressure to digitally meet the needs of native learners will turn immigrant teachers into 'marginal people'. This arises from a confluence of two different worlds meeting together to change the roles of immigrants, who must negotiate with digital natives technologically for their own (immigrants') survival.

## 7.6 Conclusion

Incorporating digital cultures into the learning environment is an inevitable pathway because the possession and use of digital devices have become a cultural symbol for digital natives. But there is a huge gap between digital natives and digital immigrants. Whereas digital natives have the technology, not much of it is used to access digital resources for learning. Lecturers, who are largely digital immigrants, appreciate the need to be digitally current but are yet to provide the leadership for their students in exploring and using digital learning resources. The traditional family which is the basic unit of socialization is also impacted by the emerging digital culture. The use of technology causes disruptions in family cohesion as family members see each other, but hardly have deep conversations and interactions because the bigger and more easily accessible virtual family provides an irresistible appeal to digital natives.

Lecturers and parents, who are mainly digital immigrants, have many adjustments to make and must understand the situation of digital natives, their access to and those uses of information which define their world. Since digital natives have only one world, the digital world, it is the digital immigrant that has the burden of coping (Cut, 2017). The situation presents opportunities for innovation, by creating space for natives to take leadership in the design and appropriate uses of digital information. They are involved already in the design of applications and platforms for sharing information. But they must also be conscious of the need to be sensitive to other 'natives' who are not digital. That way, the looming cultural clash will be less intensive and more progressive; productive migration and acculturation can take place. Otherwise, with the present trend, as discussed in this paper, a state of anomie is imminent in many countries of the global South, and especially African countries. Yet digital information, when properly understood and applied, can lead to social and national development. Indeed, for Nigeria and Africa, the rightful appropriation of digital information could be the key to national transformation amid the social and economic crises ravaging the continent.

## References

Achebe, C., 1959. Things Fall Apart. Doubleday, New York.

Autry, A., 2011. Digital natives and digital immigrants: getting to know each other. Ind. Commer. Train., 460–466.

Bauman, Z., 2019. Born Liquid. Polity, Cambridge.

Cut, M., 2017. Digital natives and digital immigrants—how are they different. Retrieved from Digital Reflections: https://medium.com/digital-reflections/digital-natives-and-digital-immigrants-how-are-they-different-e849b0a8a1d3.

Mosco, V., 2017. Becoming Digital: Toward a Post-Internet Society. Emerald, Bingley.

Park, R.E., 1928. Human migration and the marginal man. Am. J. Sociol., 881–893.

Prensky, M., 2001. Digital natives digital immigrants. On the Horizon 9 (5), 1–6.

Rikhye, R., Cook, S., Berge, Z.L., 2009. Digital natives vs. digital immigrants: myth or reality? Int. J. Instr. Technol. Distance Learn., 3–10.

Stonequist, E.V., 1935. The problem of the marginal man. Am. J. Sociol., 1–12.

# Information behaviour in an online university

8

*Eva Ortoll*[a], *Josep Cobarsí*[a], *Agustí Canals*[a], *and Lynn Silipigni Connaway*[b]
[a]Catalonia Open University, Barcelona, Spain, [b]Director, Library Trends and User Research, OCLC Research, Dublin, OH, United States

## 8.1 Introduction

In recent years, research into learners in the digital era has become increasingly interesting for two reasons: to improve the digital competences needed to face the digital environment, and to provide useful digital services supported by the Internet and related technologies (Gallardo Echenique et al., 2015).

Online technologies have been identified as a disruptive feature in higher education (Christensen and Eyring, 2011). As technologies and digital information become more and more embedded in university activities, there is more need to understand practices and expectations involving the use of digital technologies to access information in higher education (Henderson et al., 2017; Jones et al., 2016). These questions acquire even more importance in a distance-learning environment that is mediated by technologies (Christensen and Eyring, 2011); as such, and as Tury et al. (2015) point out, students' and teachers' information environment is more complex in distance learning than in a physical setting.

One of the main features of distance learning is the intensive use of technologies and digital information. Both students and faculty in a distance learning environment depend mainly on technology and digital information resources to carry out their daily academic life. So, understanding how students and faculty deal with their digital environment is important to provide better information services and digital content to enhance academic processes. Some authors argue (Spezi, 2016; Tury et al., 2015; Vighnarajah et al., 2016) that more research analyzing information behaviour in distance learning is needed.

The motivation for our study is to understand the information behaviours of faculty and students in an online university to gain further knowledge of users' attitudes and expectations in relation to information and technology engagement.

After reviewing recent literature about information behaviour in the university context, we briefly explain the Digital Visitors and Residents theoretical framework; we then describe our objectives and methodology and present the results of our investigation. The results are organized into three sections, which are followed by a discussion of the results and our conclusions.

**Future Directions in Digital Information. https://doi.org/10.1016/B978-0-12-822144-0.00008-2**

# 8.2 Related work and theoretical framework

## *8.2.1 Information behaviour in the university context*

Digital skills and competences are very important for effective information seeking (Catalano, 2013). In turn, and according to Gkorezis et al. (2017), exploration or curiosity aimed at gaining knowledge and new information result in an information-seeking activity that has a positive effect on academic performance.

A significant number of studies have been carried out on the information behaviour of university students and faculty, and recent literature reviews (Catalano, 2013; Spezi, 2016) and case studies (Borrego and Anglada, 2016; Cerretani et al., 2016; Falciani-White, 2017; Faletar et al., 2017; Komissarov and Murray, 2016) have reported similar results. Amongst the main results, we can see that the initial starting point for looking for information is the Google search engine. Faculty and researchers sometimes also use library resources and databases (Borrego and Anglada, 2016). In general, research indicates that the complexity of library search tools, the language (most digital resources are in English), accessibility (or how easy it is to get access to the resources), and information overload are the main barriers to accessing relevant information. Important factors in choosing a resource are convenience and ease of use (Connaway et al., 2011). Other research indicates that faculty and library staff may have significant influence over a student's information behaviour (Komissarov and Murray, 2016).

## *8.2.2 Information behaviour and distance learning*

Most current models of distance learning are based on digital platforms, called virtual learning environments (VLE). Therefore, one of the first elements that characterize information behaviour in distance education is the interaction that takes place in the VLE, that is, where students and teachers have access to and engage with learning materials; evaluation activities; scientific literature; books and videos; communication tools and spaces; other didactic resources and information, as well as administrative resources (Oladokum, 2014; Prior et al., 2016; Vighnarajah et al., 2016). Prior et al. (2016) put special emphasis on the importance of communication in this context. The authors argue that email and social media networks can play a significant role in the learning and information-seeking process. But as Larson and Owusu (2016) and Chawinga and Zozie (2016) point out, a lack of digital skills in distance learning is an important barrier for effective information use.

Other aspects specific to information behaviour in distance learning include individual online reading patterns and motivations (Qayyum and Smith, 2015; Yi-Li and Tsai, 2017) and their impact on academic performance. In this sense, and in accordance with Qayyum and Smith (2015) study, digital reading techniques and information-seeking strategies are considered superficial in distance learning environments and have a negative impact on the time dedicated to evaluating the relevance or authority of the information found.

Despite the existence of VLEs and the tools for accessing digital information, the presence of physical sites such as libraries is still relevant in some distance learning contexts (Larson and Owusu, 2016). Similarly, the cultural and geographic contexts (Chawinga and Zozie, 2016) also influence the way students and teachers use technologies and the Internet to access information. In the studies cited, the Internet is one of the most used resources but physical libraries also are frequently used.

The didactic materials provided by the faculty and the course instructional design have an important impact on students' information behaviour (Oladokum, 2014; Chawinga and Zozie, 2016), as these materials can promote or hinder the use of some information-seeking strategies. Similarly, how faculty and teachers behave, for example, if they use spaces like social media networks or forums, has an effect on students' information behaviour (Qayyum and Smith, 2015).

Prior et al. (2016) argue that digital capabilities positively affect one's ability to organize and execute the necessary course of action to attain designated types of performance. This idea is supported by Ting (2015), who also associates digital capabilities with autonomous learning and academic performance. However, the literature indicates that distance teachers' and students' information skills need to be improved (Chawinga and Zozie, 2016; Larson and Owusu, 2016; Oladokum, 2014; Qayyum and Smith, 2015; Vighnarajah et al., 2016). Some authors, including literature reviews, argue specifically (Spezi, 2016; Tury et al., 2015; Vighnarajah et al., 2016) that more investigation is needed to analyze the information behaviour in distance learning.

## 8.3 Digital Visitors and Residents framework

The Digital Visitors and Residents conceptual framework is a way to explain how people deal with technologies and the digital environment and why. The framework, proposed by White and Le Cornu (2011), argues that the factors that explain how people engage with technology are related, amongst others, to individual motivations and the situation and context of the digital interaction (Connaway et al., 2013b). As White and Le Cornu (2011, 2017) point out, neither a person's age nor their digital capabilities are enough to explain how people interact with technology, the Internet, and digital information. According to this framework, digital behaviour can take place in a resident or a visitor mode. Individuals with a visitor mode of engagement use technology and information in a functional way, as a tool, to solve a problem without leaving a trace of their actions. In contrast, individuals with a Resident mode of engagement see technology, the Internet and digital information as a way of life. They see the Internet as a place to communicate and build social relations, they are proactive in social networks and their digital environment is a way of life. Based on this framework, since 2011, OCLC, and Oxford University, with the participation of the University of North Carolina, Charlotte, and funding from JISC, have worked to identify factors that shape how students and faculty choose to engage with digital information. The project has been extended to different countries and universities around the world. In this setting, the Universitat Oberta de Catalunya (UOC), an online university with headquarters in

Catalonia (Spain), was selected by the Digital Visitors and Residents project team to replicate the study in an online university for the first time. The data were collected in 2015–16. This study was the first study to apply the Digital Visitors and Residents framework in a completely online university context.

The Digital Visitors and Residents framework has been applied previously to explain the use of e-books in a library context (Engelsmann et al., 2014); the use of technologies in the academic environment (Connaway et al., 2013b; Jones et al., 2016); social media network use by university students (Wright et al., 2015); the technological engagement of distance and nondistance learners (White and Le Cornu, 2017); and the use of digital resources in an online education course for health professionals (Druce and Howden, 2017).

## 8.4 Objectives and research questions

As discussed in the introduction and literature review, researching into information behaviour in distance learning allows us to better design instructional practices and digital information services. Therefore, the purpose of this study is to gain further knowledge of this issue. To achieve this general objective, we proposed two research questions:

RQ1: How and why do students and faculty in an online university make decisions to seek and use digital information?

RQ2: How do students and faculty in an online university prefer to get digital information and why?

RQ1 refers to how people really seek information, and RQ2 refers to how people would like to seek information.

## 8.5 Methodology

Our approach was based on in-depth semistructured interviews, as qualitative research data collection and analysis tools such as these enable researchers to probe and question participants as they explain their behaviours and preferences. For this project, we replicated the interview questions of the original Digital Visitors and Residents study (Connaway et al., 2013a) (see Appendix, Interview format for visitors and residents). We asked for personal and academic behaviours in order to better understand people's contexts and situations.

### *8.5.1 Research design*

The original Digital Visitors and Residents study identifies four educational stages (Connaway et al., 2013a), which are used to select the research sample and to describe an individual's engagement with digital technologies and information:

Emerging: students in the first year of undergraduate study.
Establishing: upper-level undergraduate students.
Embedding: graduate/postgraduate students.
Experiencing: faculty, research and scholars.

For this study, we tried to build a sample that was as representative as possible of all the knowledge areas offered at the University during the research period. We selected 34 participants from the University's seven main schools in the following disciplines: Arts and Humanities, Business and Economics, Computer Science and Telecommunications Engineering, Health Sciences, Information and Communication Sciences, Law and Political Science and Psychology and Education. We included at least one member from each of the educational stages for each University school discipline except for Health Sciences, as this school does not have an undergraduate curriculum.

Because of the UOC's particular structure (Cobarsí, 2008), we divided the 'experiencing' stage into two categories: Faculty-Internal and Faculty-External. The UOC's pedagogical model is handled by its internal faculty members, who design the content and pedagogical approach for each course in the curriculum, and its external faculty members, experts in each course's subject area who act as instructors and interact with the students. Internal faculty are faculty members, researchers and scholars who work full-time as permanent UOC staff, whilst external faculty are part-time or temporary. The latter are experts in their subject whose primary positions are at other universities or institutions and who collaborate with the UOC's internal faculty, imparting courses during an academic semester.

The ages of the participants ranged from 19 to 54 years old, but only four participants were between the ages of 19 and 25. All other participants were older than 26. The demographic data corresponds with the demographic characteristics of UOC students; as it is an online, distance education university, students tend to be older adults.

### 8.5.2 Data collection

Two members of the research team were present during the semistructured interviews for data collection. Although one of the researchers conducted the interview using the interview protocol, the other member of the team also intervened whenever he or she thought it was necessary for additional clarification. When something relevant or interesting was conveyed, both interviewers took notes, but only to remember it in the analysis phase or to formulate related questions later. The interviews always were recorded and transcribed by the researchers, and this transcription was the data source for analysis. The interviewees signed a confidentiality consent form prior to the interview.

### 8.5.3 Data analysis

Once the interviews were transcribed, they were entered using NVIVO qualitative analysis software, where the transcripts were coded using the Digital Visitors &

Residents codebook. To ensure intercoder reliability (ICR), we selected two interviews that were coded independently by all three members of the research team. Any instances of disagreement in the coding were identified and discussed amongst the researchers. These discussions often led to an improved agreement about how to interpret the codebook, and the coding was revised accordingly. Our ICR calculation was approximately 70%.

## 8.6 Results

### 8.6.1 *Motivations for, and barriers to, using different information sources*

During the interviews, the main information sources discussed by participants were Google and Wikipedia; human information sources; and social networking sites. In the following section, we discuss the interviewees' responses and their reasons for using or not using certain sources. At the end of the section, we draw a Digital Visitors and Residents map to illustrate the overall digital engagement pattern.

### 8.6.2 *Institutional resources beyond Google and Wikipedia*

In general, the students indicated that the VLE provides them with almost all the information they need, mainly in each subject's online classroom:

> *The didactic material provided by the UOC is enough, I don't need to find more information, just to clarify some ideas.*
>
> *(U12, establishing student, 22, female, Law and Political Sciences)*

The institutional library itself provides access to resources such as e-books, full-text papers, videos. However, students rarely consult the library website and some do not even know of its existence. This could be attributed to the fact that the library is embedded in the online classroom, which is part of the VLE. When students consult the library's website, they find it confusing. Faculty members, meanwhile, often use the library merely to access the full-text papers, although half of them indicated that they use the scientific databases provided by the library quite regularly:

> *I use the library databases a lot… You enter the databases, you say I want this or that, you click a button and in a second you have everything… But then you need the time to read it.*
>
> *(FE3, experiencing external faculty, 48, female, Health Sciences)*

Faculty members generally stated that they use Google or Google Scholar frequently because they find them easier to use than the library:

> *You spend many hours with Saint Google. We entrust ourselves to Saint Google and that solves things for us.*
>
> *(FI6, experiencing internal faculty, 48, male, Arts and Humanities)*

*In fact, I don't know how the library works, but I think that Google must do it better.*
*(G3, embedding student, 28, male, Information and Communication Sciences)*

Overall, neither students nor faculty uses the library website as their primary search tool or for general discovery. However, even though the library website is not their primary source of information, both faculty and students perceive it as being very important:

*I go to Google, and once I have a clear idea, then I go to the library databases with the detailed keywords.*
*(G3, embedding student, 28, male, Information and Communication Sciences)*

Wikipedia was mentioned frequently by last-semester undergraduate students and faculty but not so much by doctoral students. In most cases, Wikipedia is used to define a concept or to gain insight into a subject that is new to the individual:

*I use Wikipedia as a guide, to introduce myself to a concept... but then I browse the references.*
*(U5, emerging student, 30, female, Psychology and Education)*

Whilst this is the general perception of Wikipedia, some students, especially undergraduate students, have a different opinion. They believe that Wikipedia lacks credibility and neither do nor would cite it in an academic work.

The literature indicates the importance of searching for and discovering new or additional information. Amongst UOC students this is done only when they need information for their assignments, and frequently they wind up not doing this at all because they do not have time. In general, if they need to look for additional information, their first option is Google or Wikipedia, instead of the institutional library. In relation to the balance between the use of institutional resources and Internet resources, we can observe a predominant 'visitor' mode in information activities.

### 8.6.3 Social media

In general, it seems that people are reluctant to post or share on social media sites or to use social media sites to get their information:

*It's not useful for me to post on a social media site; in fact, I don't have important things to comment to the rest of the world.*
*(FI4, experiencing internal faculty, 52, male, Business and Economics)*

The interviewees gave privacy and personal issues as their main arguments against resident behaviour in terms of social media use. In general, participants are very cautious with the information they provide on social media and self-regulation is a common practice when posting:

*It worries me that people don't respect my personal moments; you're getting a coffee and you receive a Facebook notification; I don't like it.*
*(U10, establishing student, 28, female, Psychology and Education)*

*You know what kind of things you can post on social media, and who will see them.*
*(U12, establishing student, 22 years, female, Law and Political Sciences)*

In general, no students from any of the educational stages use social media platforms for academic purposes. They use them to resend a piece of interesting news, or for other personal affairs, and they stated that they are quite bored with Facebook and Twitter. Some undergraduate students (from the emerging educational stage) use social media sites to communicate with other students and to help each other with their assignments:

*Between colleagues, I send the arrangements, or whatever, by Facebook.*
*(U11, emerging student, 51, female, Arts and Humanities)*

Doctoral students (embedding educational stage) mentioned they use Twitter to follow the publication of academic papers. Some of these students also use Twitter to contact researchers outside of their institution.

Faculty (experiencing educational stage) use social media sites to diffuse and disseminate their academic work. In general, faculty said they do not feel comfortable posting on social media sites, but when they do post, they post according to institutional requirements.

The credibility of information published on social media is controversial. We observed that some faculty members feel uncomfortable about this type of information:

*Twitter is not useful for communication. For me, it is very difficult to write something in such a tiny 'space' and to be sure that the other person has understood your message. It's not a good way to communicate.*
*(FI5, experiencing internal faculty, 44, male, Law and Political Sciences)*

But in contrast, other faculty argued:

*One thing is the information a teacher or an institution puts on its personal webpage. But the information they publish on Twitter is more spontaneous and helps you to get a better feel for how the person thinks, it allows you to enter their mind.*
*(FE2, experiencing external faculty, 44, female, Business and Economics)*

The personal and professional identities shared on social media are an important issue for faculty. In general, they prefer to distinguish between their academic and personal lives. However, a few faculty members adopt the opposite mode of engagement, as indicated by the following comment:

*I don't make a distinction between my professional opinion on social media and in my private life.*
*(FI7, experiencing internal faculty, 49, female, Health Sciences)*

Out of all the faculty or students from any of the educational stages, only a few stated that they have a resident behaviour on social media sites and indicated that they generally do not use social media as an academic information source.

### 8.6.4 Humans as information sources

Another way students and faculty get access to information is to consult with other people, who act as information sources. The idea of having a 'person' or an 'expert' who can provide information is very common, as one student points out:

> *I like books and technology, but people are better.*
> *(U1, emerging student, 22, female, Information and Communication Sciences)*

In general, the interviewees saw humans as important information sources because they believe that expert advice is the surest way to access the best information. However, individuals use humans as information sources for different reasons and in different ways, as seen through these statements:

> *I only use a person to seek information if I'm very lost.*
> *(G5, embedding student, 36, female, Business and Economics)*

> *I try to seek information on my own, and when I have a knowledge base, I look to an expert to obtain more information.*
> *(U8, emerging student, 27, male, Business and Economics)*

> *You always want to contact people; even if you're reading a text, you're looking for human advice.*
> *(G1, embedding student, 35, male, Information and Communication Sciences)*

Classmates and teachers are a useful resource for students, but some of the interviewees said that they only use other people as information sources when there is no other way to access the information. Librarians are used primarily as information sources by faculty, whilst students from all educational stages use them far less. Even though students and faculty think other people are one of the best sources for obtaining information, it is not clear whether they use humans as information sources on a regular basis.

Table 8.1 shows the motivations and barriers for using different information sources.

### 8.6.5 Strategies to cope with information overload

One important concept that emerged during the interviews was information overload. The strategies individuals use to cope with the amount of information they come across is critical when it comes to accessing relevant information. The quantity of available information has two effects: on the one hand, users say they can find everything they want, but on the other, they notice it is difficult to manage the amount of information they find. Most of the participants feel that they cannot cope with information overload. This is exemplified in the following statement from a faculty member:

> *My capacity to process information is overloaded. I'm just accumulating information like on a wheel.*
> *(FE1, experiencing external faculty, 43, male, Information and Communication Sciences)*

**Table 8.1** Motivations and barriers for using information resources.

| Information source | Motivations | Barriers |
|---|---|---|
| Google | Exhaustive<br>Better search algorithms than the library<br>Fast<br>Can always find information | Do not always have access to the full text |
| Wikipedia | To learn about or become acquainted with a new concept | Credibility |
| Institutional library and scientific databases | Access to full-text articles<br>Authority<br>Good for learning materials | Lack of contextual searches<br>Lack of knowledge of their existence<br>Confusing interface<br>Few incentives to use them<br>Little human contact<br>Previous knowledge about the subject is required to search efficiently<br>Weak visualization |
| Human information sources | Timesaving<br>Better way to get access to specialized knowledge<br>Better understanding of personal information needs | Difficult to articulate the information needed, intimidating |
| Forums and other knowledge-sharing places | Useful for confirmation and to solve doubts | Difficult to go deep into a subject<br>Low level of reliability/credibility<br>Low level of emotional ties |
| Social media sites | To communicate with other students<br>To find papers and research contacts<br>Research and institutional diffusion and dissemination | Privacy<br>Lack of credibility |

Some participants, like this undergraduate student, indicated that they rely on their intuition to control information overload syndrome:

> *There's so much information, but I only incorporate it into my own affairs if I perceive it as being necessary when I receive it.*
>
> *(U12, establishing student, 22, female, Law and Political Sciences)*

The topic of information overload led to the discussion of exhaustivity. The opinions about this varied. Only five of the 20 interviewed students (establishing and embedding educational stage) thought that they need to be exhaustive with their information searches. Faculty members also had diverse opinions:

> *The information is unlimited, we don't need to feel guilty for not being exhaustive in our information searches. You must learn to say to yourself: this is the best solution right now.*
> *(FI2, experiencing internal faculty, 48, male, Psychology and Education)*

The problems related to this syndrome are twofold: when to stop looking for information, and how to choose the best information.

Table 8.2 summarizes the main strategies identified for coping with information overload.

It is interesting to note that some faculty members, aware of the effects of information overload, are proactive and try to reduce 'students' information overload', as can be seen in the following faculty member's comment:

> *Students really appreciate when they've received information... but you need to control the information flow and not send more information than they can handle and process.*
> *(FI1, experiencing internal faculty, 43, male, Computer Sciences)*

The information overload problem highlights how imperative it is that there be a commitment to developing an institutional strategy and tools for information filters and selection. This statement leads us to the second research question, which is related to individuals' expectations in regard to digital information services.

## 8.6.6 Expectations in regard to digital information services

When asked to explain their 'ideal way' of accessing information, several common themes emerged from amongst the participants. The first round of responses related to information filtering and information visualization, whilst the second related to the human aspects of digital technology.

**Table 8.2** Strategies for coping with information overload.

| Stop looking for information | Information selection and filter |
|---|---|
| When you've built an idea about the concept you are searching for<br>Results begin to repeat<br>Time pressure regarding the deadline of an assignment/journal paper<br>When the feeling of being lost is intense<br>When you've met the word count for an assignment according to teacher requirements<br>When you consider you've achieved the academic journal's requirement<br>You are aware of your own capacity to process information | Authority and reliability of the web page<br>Web page's aesthetic appearance and information visualization<br>Personal intuition and expertise<br>Reading formats (for example .pdf)<br>Social media presence of authors<br>First results |

In the previous section, we discussed information overload. Both students and faculty members from all educational stages indicated that they would like an information system that helps them filter the correct information. Most indicated that they would like an information system with a better algorithm for tagging the resources and filtering the results, and that enables them to interpret the information so they can generate their own knowledge base and theories:

> *A small range of results that saves time when selecting them, the concrete answers don't allow you to attain in-depth knowledge.*
>
> *(U6, establishing student, 22, male, Computer Science)*

> *I would like all the exact results... just ready to meet my needs... but if you don't carry out the information search process... perhaps you wouldn't learn enough.*
>
> *(U12, establishing student, 22, female, Law and Political Sciences)*

> *If everything is so easy... you ask yourself if you have already generated new knowledge, if you have created something.... yes, an ideal system would not only let you filter the results but also help you gain more criteria for selecting information and ideas.*
>
> *(FI2, experiencing internal faculty, 48, male, Psychology and Education)*

Obtaining a better visualization of the search results was also a recurrent theme for most of the participants. In this sense, several undergraduate students pointed out that they would like a more interactive search results visualization where they could select and combine different formats:

> *I imagine the search results being like a conceptual map, with text, videos, etc.... with a voice that tells you how to move from one result to another.*
>
> *(U3, emerging student, 19, female, Psychology and Education)*

The topic of student-teacher interaction and the user-information provider also emerged during the interviews. As discussed in the first section of our findings, the interviewees thought that a human is one of the best ways to access information:

> *The ideal way to access information would be a big digital library with lots of experts from whom you get advice.*
>
> *(U5, emerging student, 30, female, Psychology and Education)*

> *A wise person*
>
> *(U1, emerging student, 22, female, Information and Communication Sciences)*

> *Probably an expert would identify something that you don't know because he knows something intrinsic in your mind and you are not aware of this.*
>
> *(G3, embedding student, 28, male, Information and Communication Sciences)*

Students from all educational stages said they would like to have a person help them identify and better understand their information needs.

Both faculty and students from all educational stages pointed out other human factors that would improve the information and technology experience. They not only wished for subject and information system expertise but also nonverbal communication or empathy:

> *You need some kind of empathy to connect with someone else's knowledge.*
> *(U6, establishing student, 22, male, Computer Science)*

> *Sometimes for information to be clear and significant for the user you need emotional contact with the information provider and with information itself.*
> *(G4, embedded student, 41, male, Health Sciences)*

In a context where interaction with people takes place only through digital devices, the need for human contact and interaction appears to be relevant, not only for getting advice and information but also in order to feel less isolated.

## 8.7 Discussion

In this study, we examined undergraduate and graduate students and faculty motivations and expectations regarding the use of digital information resources in an online university using the Digital Visitors and Residents framework. The results of our study suggest that both faculty and students at the UOC adopt a more resident behaviour in the online classroom, where they interact with others and share information about themselves but adopt visitor behaviour outside the online classroom. This result is in line with the study by Druce and Howden (2017), who found that students in an online health science course had a dominant visitor behaviour in their professional and personal lives, but a more resident behaviour when engaged in the activities associated with the online course.

When students need to seek information outside of the online classroom, the search usually begins with Google, which they use in a visitor mode. This finding is similar to the findings of Catalano (2013), who argues that students at different levels of study consult the Internet as their initial search point, and Spezi (2016), who also found that doctoral students are inclined to begin their searches with Google and Google Scholar. However, this is in contrast with other studies (Borrego and Anglada, 2016) that report academics often rely on bibliographic databases as a starting point for their information search. This behaviour also was demonstrated by the faculty members interviewed, who indicated they use the institutional scientific databases. The university library was also useful for accessing full-text sources. Other studies using the Digital Visitors and Residents framework (Connaway et al., 2013b) report that Wikipedia is mainly used in the visitor mode and is perceived by students as a useful tool for their studies. However, most of the individuals in our study did not state that they contribute to Wikipedia content.

The students' and faculty's main motivations for choosing a resource are dependent upon: the potential of the search algorithms; speed and exhaustivity (Google); the context and the information needed, i.e. to become acquainted with a subject (Wikipedia);

access to the full text (library); access to specialized knowledge (peers and experts); and problem-solving in collaboration (forums in the online classroom). The convenience of use is one of the main factors when choosing a resource, but convenience is dependent upon the context and situation around the information needed, as previous research has pointed out (Catalano, 2013; Connaway et al., 2011; Spezi, 2016).

The barriers to using a resource include not having full-text access, lack of information credibility, an unfriendly or confusing interface and insufficient skill in formulating the correct information query in the system (Prior et al., 2016).

Social media network sites are mainly used in visitor mode and the interviewees stated that they are very aware of privacy issues. In general, the faculty that use social media in a more resident manner do it as an institutional requirement to promote their academic profiles and work.

The impact of information overload on the interviewees is high. As indicated by the findings of Falciani-White (2017), faculty find it hard to stay current given the amount of information produced and the limited time with which to cope with all the information. The faculty interviewees stated that they do not want to contribute to students' information overload and are cautious about the amount of information they provide in the online classroom.

Research in human-computer interaction has identified different emotions during the information-seeking process. Our findings are in line with the research identifying the need for user support and motivation (Savolainen, 2015a,b). Besides that, for our participants, increasing reliance on digitization and the online environment itself makes the need for human contact and interaction with information providers more and more necessary. This is not only because humans can provide good advice, information, and support, but also because humans can provide context for the information in question and create a more comfortable link with the information service.

Another new and important finding relates to the desire for the creation of one's own knowledge. Individuals would like a more streamlined experience and more filters when selecting information; in general, they want to feel that they are able to construct their own meaning and knowledge from the information inputs they receive.

As White and Le Cornu (2017) point out, a more 'digital resident' behaviour creates more solid relationships and fosters collaboration, and Gkorezis et al. (2017) reports that information-seeking activity increases academic performance. With this in mind perhaps motivating a more resident behaviour could help reduce users' emotional weak points and increase their explorative activities. More research is needed to determine whether more resident behaviour is more effective for online learning.

## 8.8 Conclusions

Our results indicate that distance-learning undergraduate and graduate students and faculty demonstrate a predominant visitor information behaviour, that the institutional library is used because it is conveniently embedded in the online classroom, and that social media networks are not exploited for academic purposes.

On the other hand, both students and faculty are affected by information overload and this has an important effect on their information behaviour. It is important to note that faculty feel it is important to not contribute to this overload, so we suggest that library services consider this idea when providing personalization services.

Finally, human interaction, support, and emotional factors gain importance in distance learning, not only in terms of access to information but also in helping users feel more comfortable with their overall interaction with the digital landscape. Personal coaching by information providers could be one way of improving a distance learning university's digital information service.

Future research could investigate whether more digital resident behaviour enhances academic performance and learning engagement. Research into the role of human and emotional factors in the Digital Visitors and Residents framework also could enhance the model.

# Appendix

## *Interview format for visitors and residents*

### *Background research questions:*

What are the most significant factors for novice and experienced learners in choosing their modes of engagement with the information environment?

- Do individuals develop personal engagement strategies which evolve over time and for specific needs and goals, or are the educational contexts (or, in the context of this study, 'educational stages') the primary influence on their engagement strategies?
- Are modes of engagement shifting over the course of time (influenced by emergent web culture and the availability of 'new' ways to engage), or are the underlying trends and motivations relatively static within particular educational stages?
- What is the relationship (if any) between digital and information literacy? (Suggested by DML)

REMEMBER: Before the interview commences please record the student's name on tape and fill out the attached sheet.

#### Introduction

Thank you for coming to chat with me, I really appreciate your help. My name is XXX and I am working on a research project with UOC and OCLC, a nonprofit that provides systems and services to libraries and museums. The project is looking at how learners use different digital technologies. We will be interviewing a range of learners who are at university or who are thinking of going. I would just like to ask you a few questions if you don't mind. It won't take much longer than an hour. There are no right or wrong answers. It is not a test. I just want you to be as honest as you can to find out what you think.

I also will be taping the interview so that I do not have to write everything as you speak. I will be using this later so that I can remember what you have said. I may take a few notes so please don't think I'm not listening to you. Everything you say is private and will not be discussed with anyone outside of the team. I will be changing your name to keep you anonymous and will destroy the sound recording and any information you give when it is no longer needed. Is this all okay? Do you have any questions before we start? Let's get started.

Student interview questions:
Interviewee code name:
Interviewer:
Note taker:
Date of interview:
Place of interview:

**1.** Describe the things you enjoy doing with technology and the web each week.

This is a conversational start in order to put the interviewees at their ease. We are trying to get a sense of their overall digital literacy so that we can set their information-seeking behaviours within a broader context. Do they socialize online? (See probe.) Do they 'contribute' online in the form of pictures, video, blogs, etc.?

[PROBES: How important is the web for your social life, do you use it to keep in touch with your friends? What gadgets/devices/things do you use the most, is there anything you 'couldn't live without'? How much time on average do you spend online each week? Is there anything that bothers you about being online?]

**2.** Think of the ways you have used technology and the web for your studies. Describe a typical week.

We are looking at interviewees' use of educational technologies more specifically for the study. We hope they will start to introduce informal learning, self-directed study, peer to peer learning, etc. We anticipate they will (or may not) mention Facebook, MySpace, etc.

[PROBES: How do you keep track of things? What systems for learning online do you have? Can you give us any examples of when you've asked your friends for help on assignments/homework online? What kind of online resources have you found that help you with your studies? How did you find them? What other gadgets or devices do you use for your studies?]

**3.** What did you think university studies would be like when you were in high school? How is your experience different from what you thought it would be? Describe what you think the next stage of your education will be. Tell me what you think this will be like.

This will hopefully encourage them to reflect on what they envisage their role will be in the next stage. What they imagine the next educational-stage to be like will be something we can cross-check as we follow them through the project.

[PROBES: How do you think you will use technology in the next part of your education? If you think you will need to adapt the way you use technology, what sort of changes do you think you'll make?]

**4.** Think of a time when you had a situation where you needed answers or solutions and you did a quick search and made do with it. You knew there were other sources but you decided not to use them. Please include sources such as friends, family, professors, TAs, tutors, coaches, etc. Prompt for both academic and informal (domestic or personal, for instance) examples.

[PROBES: Did you simply take the first answer/solution you were able to find? What was the situation? What sources did you use? What led you to use them, and not others? Did they help? How? What sources did you decide not to use? What led to this/these decision/s? What did source A give you that you thought source B could not? Are there situations where source B would 'be a better choice for you? How did you decide when it was time to stop looking? How did you assess what was good enough?]

**5.** Have there been times when you were told to use a library or virtual learning environment (or learning platform), and used other source(s) instead?

[PROBE: What made you decide not to use what you were asked to use? What kinds of things do your instructors want you to do when you're looking for information? Does what you do look like that, and if not, what does it look like?]

**6.** If you had a magic wand, what would your ideal way of getting information be? How would you go about using the systems and services? When? Where? How?

**7.** What comments or questions do you have for me? Is there anything you would like me to explain? What would you like to tell me that you've thought about during this interview?

# References

Borrego, A., Anglada, L., 2016. Faculty information behavior in the electronic environment: attitudes towards searching, publishing and libraries. New Libr. World 117 (3/4), 173–186.

Catalano, A., 2013. Patterns of graduate students' information seeking behaviour: a metasynthesis of the literature. J. Doc. 69 (2), 243–274.

Cerretani, P.I., Iturrrioz, E.B., Garay, P.B., 2016. Use of information and communications technology, academic performance and psychosocial distress in university students. Comput. Hum. Behav. 56, 119–126.

Chawinga, W.D., Zozie, P., 2016. Information needs and barriers to information sources by open and distance learners: a case study of Mzuzu University, Malawi. S. Afr. J. Inf. Manag. 18 (1), a692.

Christensen, C.M., Eyring, H., 2011. The Innovative University. Jossey-Bass, San Francisco, CA.

Cobarsí, J., 2008. The Open University of Catalonia as a virtual university. In: Putnik, G.D., Cunha, M.M. (Eds.), Encyclopedia of Virtual and Networked Organizations. Information Science Reference, New York, pp. 1145–1150.

Connaway, L.S., Dickey, T.J., Radford, M.L., 2011. "If it is too inconvenient, I'm not going after it": convenience as a critical factor in information-seeking behaviors. Libr. Inf. Sci. Res. 33, 179–190.

Connaway, L.S., Lanclos, D., White, D., Le Cornu, A., Hood, E.M., 2013a. User-centered decision making: a new model for developing academic library services and systems. IFLA J 39 (1), 30–36. http://www.ifla.org/files/assets/hq/publications/ifla-journal/ifla-journal-39-1_2013.pdf. (Accessed 18.06.20).

Connaway, L.S., White, D., Lanclos, D., Le Cornu, A., 2013b. Visitors and residents: what motivates engagement with the digital information environment? Inf. Res. 18 (1). paper 556 http://InformationR.net/ir/18-1/paper556.html. (Accessed 04.05.20).

Druce, M., Howden, S., 2017. New perspectives on health professions students' eLearning: looking through the lens of the "visitor and resident" model. Med. Teach. 39 (7), 704–709.

Engelsmann, H.C., Greifeneder, E., Lauridsen, N.D., Nielsen, A.G., 2014. Validation of the visitor and resident framework in an e-book setting. Inf. Res. 19 (2). paper 623.

Falciani-White, N., 2017. Information behaviors of elite scholars in the context of academic practice. J. Doc. 73 (5), 953–973.

Faletar, T., Ivanovic, M., Cupar, D., 2017. Scholarly electronic databases and library & information science students in Croatia: motivations, uses and barriers. In: Proceedings of ISIC, the Information Behaviour Conference, Zadar: Part 2. Information Research, 22 (1), Croatia, 20-23 September 2016. paper isic1625.

Gallardo Echenique, E., Marqués Molías, L., Bullen, M., Strijbos, J.W., 2015. Let's talk about digital learners in the digital era. Int. Rev. Res. Open Dist. Learn. 16 (3), 156–187.

Gkorezis, P., Kostagiolas, P., Kiakas, D., 2017. Linking exploration to academic performance: the role of information seeking and academic self-efficacy. Libr. Manag. 38 (8/9), 404–414.

Henderson, M., Selwyn, N., Aston, R., 2017. What works and why? Student perceptions of 'useful' digital technology in university teaching and learning. Stud. High. Educ. 42 (8), 1567–1579.

Jones, D., Albion, P.R., Hefferman, A., 2016. Mapping the Digital Practices of Teacher Educators: Implications for Teacher Education in Changing Digital Landscapes. SITE, Savannah, GA, UE. March 21–26.

Komissarov, S., Murray, J., 2016. Factors that influence undergraduate information-seeking behavior and opportunities for student success. J. Acad. Librariansh. 42, 423–429.

Larson, A., Owusu, M., 2016. Information Needs of Distance Learners: A Case of Winneba Study Center. University of Education, Winneba, Ghana, pp. 62–75. Turkish Online Journal of Distance Education 17(3).

Oladokum, O., 2014. The information environment of distance learners: a literature review. Creat. Educ. 5, 303–317.

Prior, D., Mazanov, J., Meacheam, D., Heaslip, G., Hanson, J., 2016. Attitude, digital literacy and self-efficacy: flow-on effects for online learning behavior. Internet High. Educ. 29, 91–97.

Qayyum, M.A., Smith, D., 2015. Learning from student experiences for online assessment task. Inf. Res. 20 (2). paper 674.

Savolainen, R., 2015a. The interplay of affective and cognitive factors in information seeking and use: comparing Kuhlthau's and Nahl's models. J. Doc. 71 (1), 157–197.

Savolainen, R., 2015b. Approaching the affective factors of information seeking: the viewpoint of the information search process model. In: Proceedings of the ISIC, the Information Behaviour Conference, Leeds 2-5 September 2014: Part 2, (paper isic28). http://InformationR.net/ir/20-1/isic2/isic28.html. (Accessed 04.05.20).

Spezi, V., 2016. Is information seeking behaviour of doctoral students changing? A review of the literature (2010-2015). New Rev. Acad. Librariansh. 2 (1), 78–106.

Ting, Y.L., 2015. Tapping into students' digital literacy and designing negotiated learning to promote learning autonomy. Internet High. Educ. 26, 25–32.

Tury, S., Robinson, L., Bawden, D., 2015. The information seeking behaviour of distance learners: a case study of the University of London International Programmes. J. Acad. Librariansh. 41, 312–321.

Vighnarajah, F., Hassan, F.A., Aziz, N.A., Lee, O.S., 2016. Profiling information-seeking behavior of distance learning students in Wawasan Open University. Asian Assoc. Open. Univ. J. 11 (2), 122–135.

White, D.S., Le Cornu, A., 2011. Visitors and residents: a new typology for online engagement. First Monday 16 (9).

White, D.S., Le Cornu, A., 2017. Using "visitors and residents" to visualize digital practices. First Monday 22 (8).

Wright, F., White, D., Hirst, T., Cann, A., 2015. Visitors and residents: mapping students' attitudes to academic use of social networks. Learn. Media Technol. 39 (1), 126–141.

Yi-Li, L., Tsai, C., 2017. Accessing online learning material: quantitative behavior patterns and their effects on motivation and learning performance. Comput. Educ. 114, 286–297.

# Part Three

# Where formal meets informal

# Mobile technology and use of educational games in HE

9

*Evgenia Vasilakaki*[a] *and Valentini Moniarou-Papaconstantinou*[b]
[a]National Library of Greece, Athens, Greece, [b]University of West Attica, Athens, Greece

## 9.1 Introduction

Mobile technology and consequently the development of mobile devices have grown at an unprecedented pace in the last few years. Mobile technology overcomes geographical, physical, and time restrictions, enabling services anytime, anywhere, and on any device. Thus, it has affected and informed the behaviour of all sectors of citizen activity. In education, it provides more freedom to learners and at the same time puts the control in their hands (Vassilakaki et al., 2016).

The implementation and effective use of mobile learning in education is a complex technical and cultural challenge requiring the adoption of changes by students, educators, and institutions. The adoption of mobile technology in education provides among other things further independence for students; facilitation of student-educator interaction, communication, and collaboration which leads to greater effectiveness and efficiency in the teaching and learning process; assistance with connections in learning in formal, informal, and personalized learning environments; and provides more opportunities for personal development (Kim et al., 2006; Pimmer et al., 2016).

It is evident that over the last few years, the use of mobile technology to support learning at all levels of education has been continuously increasing, and it is considered as one of the main challenges in education (Avramidou, 2013; Koutromanos and Avramidou, 2014); while the number of HEIs that employ mobile technology to complement the learning process is constantly growing (Yeap et al., 2016). In secondary education, teachers use mobile technology not only for educational purposes but for carrying out administrative activities, such as to manage their plans, review students' marks, assess school data, check attendance, and provide educational material (Naismith et al., 2005). Similarly, teachers in HEIs use mobile technology for managing learning activities, or for carrying out administrative tasks such as checking attendance and learning progress (Cheon et al., 2012; Su and Cheng, 2015).

In this context, the objectives of this chapter are as follows:

- to outline the incorporation of mobile learning in higher education (HE)
- to explore the benefits and challenges of mobile games in HE
- to suggest possible areas where mobile games could enhance the learning environment in LIS education.

**Future Directions in Digital Information. https://doi.org/10.1016/B978-0-12-822144-0.00009-4**

## 9.2 Mobile learning in education

Learning can take many forms (structured, semistructured or self-regulated), in many different settings ranging from classrooms, library, and museum workshop spaces to coffee shops and public transportation, solely by taking advantage of the characteristics of mobile technology (Luckin, 2010). There is growing research interest in mobile learning, judging by the various projects implemented in schools, workplaces, museums, cities, and rural areas worldwide. These showcase the opportunities for moving the learning process outside the classroom and into those different contexts that mobile technology can facilitate (Sharples et al., 2009).

The use of mobile technology in the education of all levels has gained increasing attention in recent years and thus some argue that its use in the learning environment has transformational potential in the traditional learning paradigms (Crompton et al., 2016; Pimmer et al., 2016; Su and Cheng, 2015). With the development of mobile technology and the advancement of mobile devices, a number of definitions have been formulated. Most of these definitions emphasize the absence of spatial and temporal restrictions as well as the learning opportunities provided by mobile technology. Mobile learning, in general, refers to the learning that happens through interaction with mobile devices (Demirbilek, 2010; Koutromanos and Avramidou, 2014). However, mobile learning is not only about the learning process that is facilitated by the use of mobile devices. One of the most accepted definitions of mobile learning is given by Sharples et al. (2007), who define it as 'the processes of coming to know through conversations across multiple contexts amongst people and personal interactive technologies'. This places the enabling of learning across various contexts at the centre of mobile learning and considers the conversation as the driving process of learning.

Mobile devices provide unique opportunities in formal and informal education. The characteristics of mobile devices include portability since they can be used in any location; direct connectivity, as mobile devices can be used to access information without time and place restrictions; and context-sensitivity, given that mobile devices, can collect real or simulated data (Churchill and Churchill, 2008). In addition, mobile devices: enable learning across different contexts (Pimmer et al., 2016); affect human-computer interaction, facilitate collaboration and communication; and control the learning process (Aharony, 2014). They offer active learning experiences, intensify learning experiences, enhance student engagement in learning, stimulate their learning process, improve student achievement, motivation, and student-academic interaction (Parsons et al., 2012). Based on these characteristics, the learning approaches supported by mobile devices include: (a) *individualized learning*, as students can learn at their own pace; (b) *situated learning*, since they can use mobile devices to learn within a real context; and (c) *collaborative learning*, as interaction and communication is facilitated among students and their teachers (Cheon et al., 2012).

Constant advances in mobile technology have resulted in a reduction in technical limitations related to the use of mobile devices. Specifically, more capabilities in mobile devices are offered; wireless connectivity is strengthened; storage capacity is increased; speech recognition is offered; cost is decreased and thus ownership of mobile devices is increased. As a result, mobile devices are further adopted in the learning process (Koutromanos et al., 2015; Wai et al., 2018; Whitton, 2010). Horizon reports provide a glimpse of the future and assist HE institutions to prepare in time for the relevant changes. The Horizon 2010 report estimated that future mobile devices would include functions such as mobile computing, open content, e-books, gesture-based computing, and visual data analysis which were achieved. The Horizon 2019 report further predicts in 1 year the advent of mobile learning and analytics technologies, in 2–3 years mixed reality and artificial intelligence, and in 4–5 years the adoption of blockchain and virtual assistants. It appears that the use of mobile devices in mobile learning changes as relevant technology advances (Wu et al., 2012b).

In HE, mobile learning has attracted an increasing research interest (Al-Emran et al., 2016; Pimmer et al., 2016) and is considered a suitable setting as mobile devices are more than ever-present in a university campus (Cheon et al., 2012). In a metaanalysis study, Wu et al. (2012b) reported the prevalence of HEIs regarding research on mobile learning. They found that it is more frequently used in the learning process for HE students (51.98%), followed by elementary school students (17.51%), adult learners (12.43%) and secondary school students (8.47%), confirming the results of a previous metastudy conducted by Hwang and Tsai (2011). Hwang and Tsai, investigating trends in mobile learning, found that HE students were the most often investigated research population, followed by elementary students and high school students; teachers were the least selected group as a research population. In a more recent study, Crompton et al. (2016) reported that the majority of studies in science were conducted in elementary settings.

Regardless of the educational setting, the literature on mobile learning has increased in recent years. The number of studies in the period 2005–2010 is four times higher than in the period 2001–2005 (Hwang and Tsai, 2011) and, as reported by Wu et al. (2012b), the number of studies on mobile learning in education increased significantly in 2010. Furthermore, mobile learning activities in HE have increased in the period of 2006–2010, namely from 1 study in 2006 to 50 in 2010, and in elementary schools from 2 in 2006 to 26 in 2010 (Wu et al., 2012b). A more recent study conducted by Chiang et al. (2016) indicated also the rise of mobile learning research in the period from 2005 to 2011, while the authors observe a slight decrease in relevant studies by 2012, stating that they cannot explain with certainty the reasons behind such a decrease. Further research is needed to identify trends in mobile learning publications and thus relevant research carried out from 2012 to 2019.

The majority of mobile learning studies focus on the design of mobile learning systems; the effectiveness of mobile learning; the affected domain during mobile learning (Crompton et al., 2016; Wu et al., 2012b); the distribution of content in mobile learning systems; the evaluation, strategies, and frameworks developed; learners' characteristics formulated in the mobile learning process (Wu et al., 2012b). Overall, it is argued that developments tend to focus more on the design of tools rather than on ensuring learning (Kearney et al., 2012). Issues such as different forms, practices, outcomes of mobile learning, as well as theoretical approaches, have not yet received much attention (Koohestani et al., 2018; Pimmer et al., 2016, 2016).

With reference to the research subject areas, mobile learning was examined mostly (presented here in rank order) in Language and Linguistics courses (17.05%), followed by Computer Science (13.07%), Health Sciences (10.23%), Environment (10.23%) and Physics, Mass Media (2.27%), Business (2.27%), and Library and Museum Science (1.13%) (Wu et al., 2012b, p. 824) (Fig. 9.1).

These findings partially support the findings of Hwang and Tsai (2011), who found that mobile learning was used in computers and language, separate from the learning domains of science and social science. The impact of mobile learning on the research subject area of business was also reported by Wu et al. (2012b) and Evans (2008). Similarly, Guy et al. (2010) stated that mobile learning can be applied to any discipline and reported that mobile learning could be particularly useful in research subject areas as mathematics, environment, history and geography, supporting to some extent the findings of Wu et al. (2012b).

The factors critical to ensuring mobile learning success in education include, among others, access to technology, ownership, connectivity, integration and institutional support (Naismith and Corlett, 2006). Mobile learning implementation is a complex process requiring many different perspectives to be taken into consideration (Schell, 2008). In this context, active involvement of the different stakeholders (students, academics, content producers, and HEI) is needed to create a new, enriched approach to the learning process (Cheon et al., 2012). Therefore, consideration should be given to students' readiness to accept mobile learning, as the availability and increased use of mobile devices does not necessarily promise their adoption in the learning environment (Cheon et al., 2012). Several studies indicate that HE students and academics have positive attitudes towards mobile learning (Al-Emran et al., 2016; Al-Shehhi et al., 2013; Educause Center for Analysis and Research, 2015; Koohestani et al., 2018). On the other hand, regardless of students' positive attitude towards mobile learning, a number of technical limitations on the use of mobile technology have been reported by students: fear that the technology is not working properly, mobile devices' small keyboards and devices causing distractions (Gikas and Grant, 2013). It is noticeable that despite the high level of interest in the use of mobile devices in the learning process equally by students and academics, the actual use of mobile devices in this context remains low (Educause Center for Analysis and Research, 2015). This is particularly important since academics are the ones who would promote and lead the effective use of mobile devices in the learning process (Gikas and Grant, 2013).

At this point, it is worth mentioning that nowadays students are exposed to technology from an early age; thus, they think, approach, and use technology in different ways and for various purposes (personal, educational, leisure). However, it is argued that although learners may interact with technology in many ways, people of all ages would prefer to learn in ways that are not directly associated with technological developments (IPSOS MORI, 2007; Whitton, 2010).

Overall, mobile learning provides new opportunities in education, as it expands the curriculum, enhances the learning process, and connects learning across different educational environments. Thus, the focus is placed on the creation of new and extended learning designs rather than the implementation of technology (Pimmer et al., 2016).

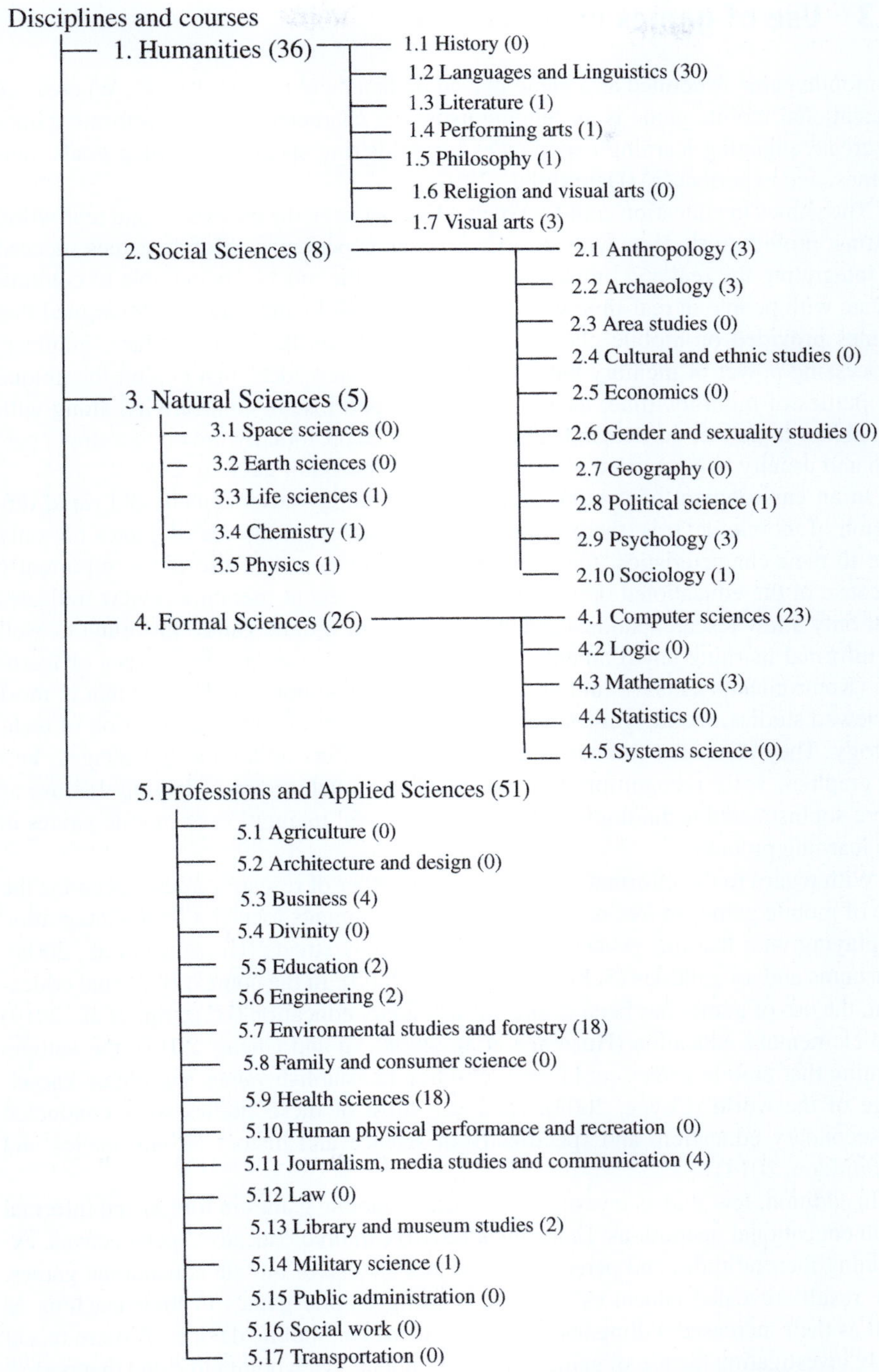


**Fig. 9.1** Distribution of disciplines and courses. As shown in Wu et al. (2012a,b, p. 824).

## 9.3 Use of games in education

A mobile game is defined as a game played on handheld mobile devices. Whereas an educational mobile game is an 'engine using the characteristics of electronic games to create engaging learning experiences for delivering specified learning goals, outcomes, and experiences' (Demirbilek, 2010).

The games in education could serve as a link between the classroom and real-world setting, providing students with real-life learning experiences. Mobile games succeed in integrating the real and online world and make the most of being able to communicate with people in real-time while on the move. Kolo and Baur (2008) argued that games provided on mobile phones cannot compete on the user interface, graphics, processing power or memory but instead work on 'new ideas that exploit the unique properties of mobility, time, location awareness and instant connectivity, along with the ability to deliver on-demand content to a device profoundly linked to a single person and usually being carried at all times' (Kolo and Baur, 2008, p. 29).

In an environment of continuing mobile technology advancement and rapid diffusion of mobile devices, there is an increasing interest in the use of games not only due to their characteristics, functionality, and enjoyment but also more importantly because of the educational opportunities offered. A recent literature review indicates that only a few research studies examined the use of mobile games in formal as well as informal learning environments, whereas no study examines both types of learning (Koutromanos and Avramidou, 2014). The same authors emphasized that in most reviewed studies, mobile games were set in the context of a prior generation of technology. They state that the advanced technology offers additional advantages: better graphics, voice recognition, Internet speed and touch screen, implying that use of more sophisticated technology will lead to successful integration of mobile games in the learning process.

With regard to the informal environment, a number of research studies examine the use of mobile games in free-activity playing environments focusing on the integration of playing with learning (Facer et al., 2004), namely streets (Huizenga et al., 2008), museums and art galleries (Schwabe and Goth, 2005). In the context of formal education, the use of games has been studied in secondary education (Huizenga et al., 2019) and elementary education (Huizenga et al., 2008; Su and Cheng, 2015), the authors arguing that mobile games could assist children to establish values and obtain knowledge of the world (Coyne, 2003). However, most of these studies were conducted in secondary education, and specifically in science and history (Koutromanos and Avramidou, 2014).

In addition, few studies investigated the use of mobile games in formal and informal adult educational institutions. Demirbilek (2010) explored educators' perspectives, examining their attitudes and perceptions towards the use of mobile educational games. The results revealed educators' interest in using mobile games in their teaching as well as their increased willingness to employ games on mobile devices. A more recent study investigating the use of games from the students' viewpoint indicated that performance expectancy is the most important factor influencing their intention to use games.

Other factors include effort expectancy, social influence, facilitating conditions, involvement, skill and control (Chung et al., 2019). It is worth mentioning that games could be employed to inform other noneducational activities such as the support of a university's orientation programme for newcomers (Schwabe and Goth, 2005).

The advantages of using mobile games in learning environments include the positive effects on students' learning, such as the possibility of capturing attention and understanding the content (Huizenga et al., 2019; Kelle et al., 2011); the interaction and the potential for collaboration (Koutromanos and Avramidou, 2014; Whitton, 2010); students' motivation enhancement and their engagement in learning activities (Ciampa, 2014; Chung et al., 2019; Demirbilek, 2010; Domínguez et al., 2013; Huizenga et al., 2019; Koutromanos and Avramidou, 2014); the opportunities they offer in a range of learning environments for the development of students; the provided skills, notably constructing arguments and debating skills; the positive effect on students' attitude towards learning (Koutromanos and Avramidou, 2014); enhanced learning promotion and the improvement of their learning performance (Chung et al., 2019; Su and Cheng, 2015).

Research subject areas that are considered suitable for the development of mobile games include language learning (Demirbilek, 2010; Holden and Sykes, 2011; Liu and Chu, 2010); business (Parsons et al., 2012; Whitton, 2010); communication, culture, computer literacy (Demirbilek, 2010); and human resources (Nunohiro et al., 2012). It should be noted here that research refers to the same possible subject areas that are suitable for promoting mobile learning and for developing mobile games. However, that does not imply that research on both mobile learning and mobile games should be limited to these specific subject areas but more like these should be seen as a starting point for further exploration in other subject areas too.

Effective content design is crucial to the success of mobile games in learning. However, the literature in educational mobile games is mainly focused on issues relevant to design and effectiveness (Kelle et al., 2011; Vogel et al., 2006). In addition, the number of studies examining the design of mobile learning systems is increasing, which can be attributed to technological advancements, in combination with researchers' readiness to examine new technologies in relation to mobile learning environments. However, the main challenge remains how to ensure a balance between playing and learning (Kelle et al., 2011) and the examination of the relationship between learners' activities during a mobile game and their learning outcomes (Huizenga et al., 2019).

## 9.4 Educational use of games in Library and Information Science

LIS education has very quickly adopted other means for delivering learning, such as distance learning environments, use of videos and social networking sites (Nicholson, 2010) and collaborative learning environments. Adopting new practices and thus advanced technological tools is not something new for LIS.

Use of mobile technology was incorporated into LIS at an early stage, considering that learning platforms such as Moodle most often provided a downloadable mobile application. Mobile devices were sometimes used by students to follow up on course material, interact with the teacher and the rest of the class, search for information resources online and share results with relevant groups on social networking sites such as Facebook. However, mobile devices were mostly employed by LIS students for entertainment purposes (Dukic et al., 2015; Vassilakaki et al., 2016). It is no surprise that mobile devices are becoming ever more integrated into the learning process, given the low, affordable cost for interested stakeholders, easy access to online information resources, quick communication, dissemination and interaction and the fact that the technology is already part of our everyday life.

There are two types of research studies that showcase the two main ways mobile games are employed in LIS. One body of research focuses on how mobile games were used in the context of a course and the way these have assisted in its successful delivery and enhanced participants' learning process. The second examines the uses of mobile games in library settings to develop and promote information literacy programmes to diverse audiences.

Becnel and O'Shea (2013) outlined the experiences LIS students acquired regarding simulation of practising professionals in charge of a library through epistemic gaming. Mobile gaming was used to simulate real experiences for students, promote communication and collaboration in an online setting, complete a task within a specific timeframe and thus acquire new knowledge and new skills of leadership. Brown (2014) reviewed relevant literature in the use of video games and gaming in LIS education. He reported on the assessment studies carried out in libraries as well as other fields. He further stressed the need for a thorough assessment and measurement of the results to define the impact these may have on mobile learning. Elkins and Hollister (2018) focused on identifying the factors behind educators' decisions on promoting or prohibiting content relevant to gaming. Encheva (2016) argued that LIS students can enhance their information literacy skills through digital educational games and the adoption of a game-based model in the curriculum. She further argued that games are an effective strategy for securing active learning and that students feel more committed and able to practise what they have learned by maintaining at the same time a high level of motivation. Finally, Mansour (2016) and Virkus (2008) explored games in the context of Web 2.0 technologies. They both found that digital native students were prone to using gaming (in the form of mobile apps on their smartphones) and new technology in the learning process. It is evident that mobile games in LIS education have been incorporated for the same reasons as in the other research subject areas. These studies also show that mobile games can be used for enhancing information literacy skills as well as imparting new knowledge.

With regard to studies that employ mobile games for promoting information literacy skills in a library setting, these also report the discussion around the suitability of offering games in libraries; the argument for promoting information literacy skills through gaming; and ways to successfully implement games in libraries (Lee Eden, 2010; Hahn, 2008; Markey et al., 2011; Smale, 2011; Smith, 2007; Wu et al., 2012a; Young, 2016). Offering mobile games in libraries provide a series of benefits, including socializing, having fun, enhancing learning experiences, and learning how to achieve goals. The activities most often related to games are bibliographic instruction, library-based classroom assignments (how to identify relevant information resources and to assess their value) (Markey et al., 2011; Smale, 2011; Young, 2016) and mobile digital library services (Hahn, 2008). Libraries in this way achieve an enhanced user experience by offering customized services tailored to students' learning styles and information-seeking behaviours (Smith, 2007; Young, 2016) and thus ensure life-long learner-citizens (Wu et al., 2012a).

Overall, it seems that in the LIS field, as well as LIS education, mobile games are integrated into the learning process and practice mainly to enhance the information literacy skills of the learners. Both soft skills (communication, collaboration, leadership, flexibility, and time management), as well as hard skills (acquire a degree, learn a foreign language or machine operation), are promoted through mobile learning. The existing literature on the research subject areas in which mobile learning was examined identified the use of educational mobile games in specific disciplines including LIS. In addition, the adoption of a technology paradigm in the development and delivery of LIS curricula further promoted mobile learning. Technology integration in LIS curricula and the business orientation of information organizations support the use of mobile learning and mobile games in areas such as technology, business, information literacy, human resource development, and the acquisition of skills such as communication. In addition, from this analysis, it is evident that further studies are needed to investigate the attitude of LIS students and educators to mobile learning and use of mobile games as well as the identification of barriers to their use.

## 9.5 Conclusions

Rapid advances in mobile technology and thus mobile devices have informed the development and adoption of mobile learning. This has been as a result of the technology being employed at all levels of the educational process while accepting the benefits and working around the challenges identified at each level. Successful mobile learning requires the involvement of all interested stakeholders—students, academics, content providers, and institutions. These all play a significant role in changing the pedagogical culture and creating the appropriate context for mobile learning (Cheon et al., 2012). No matter the benefits and/or challenges, this type of learning is here to stay, given all the technological advancements happening as well as adoption by the most important stakeholders.

In HE, games are starting to be integrated into the curriculum with the aim of exploiting the main characteristics of mobile games and thus enriching the learning experiences of the various stakeholders. No matter the benefits, there is an increased discussion around the fine line between where the fun stops and learning starts. However, relevant literature across all research subjects is constantly growing, showcasing the level of acceptance of, and preference for, this alternative and/or complementary method of teaching and learning.

In LIS education, mobile games are employed as another means of distilling new knowledge and/or making sure this knowledge is understood and thus used by learners. Most often it is also used to promote information literacy skills, teamwork, communication, and problem-solving. LIS professionals also employ mobile games to develop and offer information literacy courses and enhance relevant skills and competences.

## References

Aharony, N., 2014. Library and Information Science students' perceptions of m-learning. J. Librariansh. Inf. Sci. 46 (1), 48–61.

Al-Emran, M., Elsherif, H., Shaalan, K., 2016. Investigating attitudes towards the use of mobile learning in higher education. Comput. Hum. Behav. 56 (1), 93–102.

Al-Shehhi, M., Mohammad, M., Rajan, A.V., 2013. Smart device applications for higher level IT courses. In: 2013 International Conference on Current Trends in Information Technology (CTIT). IEEE, pp. 77–81.

Avramidou, L., 2013. The use of mobile technologies in project-based science: a case study. J. Comput. Math. Sci. Teach. 32 (1), 361–379.

Becnel, K., O'Shea, P., 2013. Teaching public library administration through epistemic gaming. J. Educ. Libr. Inf. Sci. 54 (3), 235–242.

Brown, R.T., 2014. A literature review of how videogames are assessed in Library and Information Science and beyond. J. Acad. Librariansh. 40 (1), 447–451.

Cheon, J., Lee, S., Crooks, S.J., Song, J., 2012. An investigation of mobile learning readiness in higher education based on the theory of planned behavior. Comput. Educ. 59 (1), 1054–1064.

Chiang, F.K., Zhu, G., Wang, Q., Cui, Z., Cai, S., Yu, S., 2016. Research and trends in mobile learning from 1976 to 2013: a content analysis of patents in selected databases. Br. J. Educ. Technol. 47 (6), 1006–1019.

Chung, C.H., Shen, C., Qiu, Y.Z., 2019. Students' acceptance of gamification in higher education. Int. J. Game Based Learn. 9 (2), 1–19.

Churchill, D., Churchill, N., 2008. Educational affordances of PDAs: a study of a teacher's exploration of this technology. Comput. Educ. 50 (4), 1439–1450.

Ciampa, K., 2014. Learning in a mobile age: an investigation of student motivation. J. Comput. Assist. Learn. 30 (1), 82–96.

Coyne, R., 2003. Mindless repetition: learning from computer games. Des. Stud. 24 (1), 199–212.

Crompton, H., Burke, D., Gregory, K., Grabe, C., 2016. The use of mobile learning in science: a systematic review. J. Sci. Educ. Technol. 25 (2), 149–160.

Demirbilek, M., 2010. Investigating attitudes of adult educators towards educational mobile media and games in eight European countries. J. Inf. Technol. 9 (1), 235–247.

Domínguez, A., Saenz-de-Navarrete, J., De-Marcos, L., Fernández-Sanz, L., Pagés, C., Martínez-Herráiz, J., 2013. Gamifying learning experiences: practical implications and outcomes. Comput. Educ. 63 (4), 380–392.

Dukic, Z., Chiu, D.K., Lo, P., 2015. How useful are smartphones for learning? Perceptions and practices of Library and Information Science students from Hong Kong and Japan. Library Hi Tech 33 (4), 545–561.

Educause Center for Analysis and Research, 2015. Study of Undergraduate Students and Information Technology. http://net.educause.edu/ir/library/pdf/ss15/ers1510ss.pdf. (Accessed 15.12.19).

Educause Publications, 2019. Horizon Report. Higher Education Edition. https://library.educause.edu/resources/2019/4/2019-horizon-report. (Accessed 15.12.19).

Elkins, A.J., Hollister, J.M., 2018. Power up: exploring gaming in LIS curricula. In: Poster presented at the 2018 iConference, Sheffield, UK, March 25–28, 2018.

Encheva, M., 2016. Teaching information literacy courses in the context of Library and Information Science education in Bulgaria: challenges and innovative approaches. J. Libr. Adm. 56 (5), 595–602.

Evans, C., 2008. The effectiveness of m-learning in the form of podcast revision lectures in higher education. Comput. Educ. 50, 491–498.

Facer, K., Joiner, R., Stanton, D., Reidz, J., Hullz, R., Kirk, D., 2004. Savannah: mobile gaming and learning? J. Comput. Assist. Learn. 20 (1), 399–409.

Gikas, J., Grant, M., 2013. Mobile computing devices in higher education: student perspectives on learning with cellphones, smartphones and social media. Internet High. Educ. 19 (1), 18–26.

Guy, R., Check, C., Ngesi, N., Mehigan, T.J., Pitt, I., Simbulan, I.S., Schleser, M., Williams, P.W., 2010. Mobile learning reviewed. In: Guy, R. (Ed.), Mobile Learning: Pilot Projects and Initiatives. Informing Science Press, Santa Rosa, CA, pp. 59–74.

Hahn, J., 2008. Mobile learning for the twenty-first century librarian. Ref. Serv. Rev. 36 (3), 272–288.

Holden, C., Sykes, J., 2011. Leveraging mobile games for place-based language learning. Int. J. Game Based Learn. 1 (2), 1–18.

Horizon Report, 2010. https://library.educause.edu/resources/2010/1/2010-horizon-report. (Accessed 15.12.19).

Huizenga, J., Admiraal, W., Akkerman, S., ten Dam, G., 2008. Cognitive and affective effects of learning history by playing a mobile game. In: Connolly, T., Stansfield, M. (Eds.), Proceedings of the 2nd European Conference on Game-Based Learning. Academic Conferences Ltd., Reading.

Huizenga, J., Admiraal, W., Ten Dam, G., Voogt, J., 2019. Mobile game-based learning in secondary education: students' immersion, game activities, team performance and learning outcomes. Comput. Hum. Behav. 99 (1), 137–143.

Hwang, G.J., Tsai, C.C., 2011. Research trends in mobile and ubiquitous learning: a review of publications in selected journals from 2001 to 2010. Br. J. Educ. Technol. 42 (4), 65–70.

IPSOS MORI, 2007. Student Expectations Study. JISC, Bristol.

Kearney, M., Schuck, S., Burden, K., Aubusson, P., 2012. Viewing mobile learning from a pedagogical perspective. Res. Learn. Technol. 20 (1), 1–17.

Kelle, S., Klemke, R., Specht, M., 2011. Design patterns for learning games. Int. J. Technol. Enhanc. Learn. 6 (1), 555–569.

Kim, S.H., Mims, C., Holmes, K., 2006. An introduction to current trends and benefits of mobile wireless technology use in higher education. Am. Assoc. Clin. Endocrinol. J. 14 (1), 77–100.

Kolo, C., Baur, T., 2008. Homo Ludens going mobile? Perspectives on mobile gaming. In: Proceedings of Gaming 2008: Designing for Engaging Experience and Social Interaction, Amsterdam, July 22–27. IADIS Press.

Koohestani, H.R., Soltani-Arabshahi, S.K., Fata, L., Ahmadi, F., 2018. The educational effects of mobile learning on students of medical sciences: a systematic review in experimental studies. J. Adv. Med. Educ. Prof. 6 (2), 58–69.

Koutromanos, G., Avramidou, L., 2014. The use of mobile games in formal and informal learning environments: a review of the literature. Educ. Media Int. 51 (1), 49–65.

Koutromanos, G., Sofos, A., Avramidou, L., 2015. The use of augmented reality games in education: a review of the literature. Educ. Media Int. 52 (4), 253–271.

Lee Eden, B., 2010. Game on! Gaming at the library. Collect. Build. 29 (3), 120.
Liu, T.Y., Chu, Y.L., 2010. Using ubiquitous games in an english listening and speaking course: impact on learning outcomes and motivation. Comput. Educ. 55 (1), 630–643.
Luckin, R., 2010. Re-Designing Learning Contexts. Routledge, London.
Mansour, E., 2016. Use of smartphone apps among Library and Information Science students at South Valley University, Egypt. Electron. Libr. 34 (3), 371–404.
Markey, K., Leeder, C., Jean, B., 2011. Students' behaviour playing an online information literacy game. J. Inf. Lit. 5 (2), 46–65.
Naismith, L., Corlett, D., 2006. Reflections on success: a retrospective of the mLearn conference series 2002-2005. In: Proceedings of MLEARN 2006 Conference, October 22–25, 2006, Banff, Canada.
Naismith, L., Lonsdale, P., Vavoula, G., Sharples, M., 2005. Literature Review in Mobile Technologies and Learning. A Report for NESTA Futurelab. (Report No. 11).
Nicholson, S., 2010. Inviting the world into the online classroom: teaching a gaming in libraries course via YouTube. J. Educ. Libr. Inf. Sci. 51 (4), 233–240.
Nunohiro, E., Matsushita, K., Mackin, K.J., Ohshiro, M., 2012. Development of game-based learning features in programming learning support system. Artif. Life Robot. 17 (3–4), 373–377.
Parsons, D., Petrova, K., Ryu, H., 2012. Mobile gaming—a serious business! In: March 2012 IEEE Seventh International Conference on Wireless, Mobile and Ubiquitous Technology in Education. IEEE, pp. 17–24.
Pimmer, C., Mateescu, M., Grohbiel, U., 2016. Mobile and ubiquitous learning in higher education settings. A systematic review of empirical studies. Comput. Hum. Behav. 63 (1), 490–501.
Schell, J., 2008. The Art of Game Design: A Book of Lenses. Morgan Kaufmann, Waltham, MA.
Schwabe, G., Goth, C., 2005. Mobile learning with a mobile game: design and motivational effects. J. Comput. Assist. Learn. 21 (1), 204–216.
Sharples, M., Taylor, J., Vavoula, G., 2007. A theory of learning for the mobile age. In: Andrews, R., Haythornthwaite, C. (Eds.), The Sage Handbook of E learning Research. Sage, London, pp. 221–247.
Sharples, M., Arnedillo-Sánchez, I.A., Milrad, M., Vavoula, G., 2009. Mobile learning: small devices, big issues. In: Ludvigsen, S., Balacheff, N., De Jong, T., Lazonder, A., Barnes, S. (Eds.), Technology-Enhanced Learning: Principles and Products. Springer Netherlands, pp. 233–249.
Smale, M.A., 2011. Learning through quests and contests: games in information literacy instruction. J. Libr. Innov. 2 (2), 36.
Smith, F.A., 2007. Games for teaching information literacy skills. Libr. Philos. Pract. 9 (2), 12.
Su, C.H., Cheng, C.H., 2015. A mobile gamification learning system for improving the learning motivation and achievements. J. Comput. Assist. Learn. 31 (3), 268–286.
Vassilakaki, E., Moniarou-Papaconstantinou, V., Garoufallou, E., 2016. Identifying the uses of mobile technology among Library and Information Science undergraduate students. Program 50 (4), 417–430.
Virkus, S., 2008. Use of Web 2.0 technologies in LIS education: experiences at Tallinn University, Estonia. Program: Electr. Libr. Inf. Syst. 42 (3), 262–274.
Vogel, J.J., Vogel, D.S., Canon-Bowers, J., Bowers, C.A., Muse, K., Wright, M., 2006. Computer gaming and interactive simulation for learning: a meta-analysis. Educ. Comput. Res. 34 (1), 229–243.
Wai, I.S.H., Ng, S.S.Y., Chiu, D.K.W., Ho, K.K.W., Lo, P., 2018. Exploring undergraduate students' usage pattern of mobile apps for education. J. Librariansh. Inf. Sci. 50 (1), 34–47.

Whitton, N., 2010. Learning with Digital Games: A Practical Guide to Engaging Students in Higher Education. Routledge, New York.

Wu, J., Yang, H., He, X., 2012a. A preliminary study on developing computer games for information literacy education. In: Proceedings of the 4th International Conference on Internet Multimedia Computing and Service (ICIMCS'12). ACM, New York, NY, pp. 223–226, https://doi.org/10.1145/2382336.2382399.

Wu, W., Wu, Y.J., Chen, C., Kao, H., Lin, C., Huang, S., 2012b. Review of trends from mobile learning studies: a meta-analysis. Comput. Educ. 59 (2), 817–827.

Yeap, J., Ramayah, T., Soto-Acosta, P., 2016. Factors propelling the adoption of m-learning among students in higher education. Electron. Mark. 26 (1), 323–338.

Young, J., 2016. Can library research be fun? Using games for information literacy instruction in higher education. Ga. Libr. Q. 53 (3). Article 7.

# The evolving role of library collections in the broader information ecosystem

10

*Mark Dahl*
Aubrey R. Watzek Library, Lewis & Clark College, Portland, OR, United States

## 10.1 Introduction

Over a quarter century since the advent of the World Wide Web, academic libraries remain in a state of transformation. Two of the library's most fundamental roles are highly contested. The library's role as gateway to information through its discovery service, research databases, and reference tools has been disrupted by search engines for well over a decade. The library's role as provider of scholarly information through book and journal collections is being challenged by openly accessible information resources on the Internet, some fitting the traditional forms of books and journals and others not. Students and faculty can begin their research on Google Scholar and often click through to sources to complete it without ever touching their university library.

What is to be done? Scott Walter (2011) has suggested that libraries now define themselves by their services rather than their collections. Depending on the library, these services could include information literacy education, publishing, data management, and digital humanities support. These emerging service roles have great potential, but I believe that there is still good reason to invest in the library's roles in discovery and provision of information.

In this chapter, I will argue for some strategies that academic libraries should pursue as they continue to have an information discovery and provision role in the next decade. Some of these strategies will be more familiar than others. Libraries need to extract themselves from crippling Big Deals and when possible move to transformative agreements that shift publisher incentives to open access. They should still be open to large aggregations of content if the price is right, however. They should also be open to creative approaches to demand-driven content.

The discovery and context services that academic libraries provide are in need of a critical review. Many of them overlap with each other and with discovery tools available on the open web. Discovery layers will continue to be a central starting point, but libraries should strive to improve them by advocating for an experience that integrates more information sources and makes machine learning and artificial intelligence capabilities available in a transparent manner. Many abstracting and indexing databases should be cancelled and/or integrated with the discovery layer, and libraries should look for a next generation of reference resources that can be integrated in the flow of the user.

**Future Directions in Digital Information. https://doi.org/10.1016/B978-0-12-822144-0.00010-0**

College and university libraries have a major advantage over Google: they are situated in an institutional context. They should intertwine their information discovery and provision with the local needs of their institution and with related services such as research and instruction support. They should look to provide research tools and content that is highly aligned with curriculum and that offers features that cannot be found for free on the open web.

Finally, libraries bring a set of values to the broader information ecosystem that are particularly distinctive. Libraries value preservation of knowledge over the long term. They value access to information and are sometimes in a position to promote open access resources. They value a diversity of viewpoints and voices. As libraries make choices about their bought collection guided by these values, they will help to fill gaps and offset biases in the broader, more commercialized information ecosystem.

## 10.2 The current information environment

Lorcan Dempsey (2016) has described the information provision environment of today's library as the 'facilitated collection'. Libraries help their patrons access materials that have a range of associations with the library itself. Some are part of a traditional print collection owned by the library, others are electronic resources licensed for use over a given time period, others are materials acquired through interlibrary loan, still others are open access materials in repositories not associated with the home organization at all.

Many students and faculty start their research on Google Scholar, a discovery tool that is completely independent of the academic library. And often they land on resources in open access journals, academic social media sites like ResearchGate or open cultural heritage collections. Library-provided resources may only need to come into play in the case of a more exhaustive research project. Many students say they still appreciate print resources, but circulation of print books continues on a seemingly inexorable decline in academic libraries, while print journal use is all but extinguished.

Library subscriptions to electronic journal collections provide access to the most authoritative versions of scholarship. But, as of late, many academic libraries have had to cease these large subscription bundles due to exorbitant subscription prices and flat to declining budgets. Libraries advocate for the transition to open access publishing, but the role libraries would play in an open access academic publishing ecosystem remains murky. Academic libraries could become open access publishers themselves or just use their budgets to facilitate open access publishing.

Academic library reference collections used to be key resources for provision of context around a topic when starting out research. A subject encyclopaedia could give a good overview of a person or topic and provide follow-up references. Now, most patrons look to Wikipedia for the contextual information that library reference sources once provided.

The material that students need is shifting beyond academic libraries' familiar menu of books and journals. Increasingly, students and faculty need to find raw forms of evidence and apply it to the questions that they are trying to answer. This evidence can take the form of primary source materials such as images, audio files, historical documents and, increasingly, data sets.

Though the information environment today is richer than ever before, it is extremely complex. The role of the purchased academic library collection should be to reduce that complexity by providing high-quality information resources that supplement what is available on the open web. These information resources should provide unique content and context to scholars and students.

Libraries must embrace the messy, multifaceted information ecosystem in which they find themselves. There is no clear end state towards which we are inevitably headed. We are not going to have a future where all information required for higher education is open access. Though the trend is towards open access, there will always be a mix of open and commercial sources. Likewise, the transition from print to digital will never be complete. The following strategies represent some informed recommendations for navigating this very ambiguous and fluid environment.

## 10.3 Strategy 1: Transforming purchasing

Though library budgets are off their peaks, academic libraries still have centralized purchasing power and information distribution infrastructures for their institutions. Library consortia magnify that purchasing power. Even as more content on the web is either free or marketed directly to consumers, libraries will still serve as a valuable function to college and university communities as they find, evaluate, and purchase information resources. However, as we enter the third decade of the 20th century, academic libraries need to shift their strategies as they perform this function.

The Big Deal as it has become known in the library world refers to the annual licensing of a large aggregation of journal (and less commonly e-book) content. Whereas in the world of print, there were physical limitations and incremental costs for both the publisher and the library when adding on more journal holdings, in the digital world the additional costs for a publisher to bundle in an extra journal are minimal. The Big Deal typically offers a library access to a whole collection of journals for much less than the sum of the individual subscription costs to each journal in the package.

The Big Deal is good value for the library because it provides a wider swathe of content to its users than individual subscriptions. And, it works for the publishers because it creates a large single bundle of content that the library has an incentive to continue buying year after year. Analyses of Big Deals by librarians generally acknowledge that they can provide a good value per article download but present a challenge because they tend to consume more and more of a library's budget with annual inflationary increases to subscription costs (Lemley and Li, 2015).

Unsustainable price increases by journal publishers have been a concern in the academic library world for over two decades. Increasingly, libraries are jettisoning their Big Deal subscriptions and seeking other approaches for access to journal content. In February 2019, the University of California system cancelled its subscription to Elsevier journals after negotiations between the two parties collapsed. In the absence of current Elsevier content, the University of California published guidance regarding ways to access Elsevier journal articles that included finding open access copies through Google Scholar and browser plugins, using interlibrary loan, and contacting authors directly or through academic social media sites. These alternative means of providing access illustrate the reality of content 'leakage' from publisher subscription channels. Schonfeld (2019) has convincingly argued that leakage has led to an effective loss in pricing power for academic journal publishers.

The pressure is on from funders and universities to move the system towards open access. With the Plan S Initiative, a mostly European coalition of research funders have called for Open Access publication of all research funded by national, regional, and international research councils and funding bodies by 2021. Endorsed by a number of United States' academic libraries, MIT's 2019 Framework for Publisher Contracts also calls for open access publication of research, with emphasis on author rights, green open access, sustainable pricing, and preservation of knowledge.

Transformative agreements aim to shift the system from a journal or journal package subscription model to an open access, pay-for-publication model. Some large research libraries and national-level library organizations have been able to negotiate transformative agreements with large journal publishers. These agreements typically provide the organization access to the journal publisher's content and cover open access publication of all the organization's research articles with that publisher (often known as 'publish and read'). The model works well for research institutions that publish a great deal and wish to move towards open access. It also works for publishers because they usually continue to receive a revenue stream from the university involved at a similar level to their pretransformed Big Deal subscriptions.

As Levine-Clark and Lawlor (2018) and Price (2019) have discussed, publishers have less of a financially viable pathway to a transformed pay-to-publish model with more teaching-focused higher education institutions that publish less than research universities. In a system that was fully 'transformed' to a pay-to-publish model, the greater burden for paying for publication would likely fall on research universities whose scholars publish a great deal. More teaching-focused institutions could end up playing a sort of 'free rider' role, taking advantage of open access content for which they previously paid. It remains a conundrum how to switch the entire system from a subscription-based model to a pay-to-publish open access one.

Ideally, all academic journal articles would be published as gold open access so that anyone in the world could access them in their final published format on the publisher's website. Most of the open access mandates, however, still permit green open access, which means that a manuscript copy of the final article can be released in an open access repository, while the published article in its final form usually remains behind a publisher paywall. Over the next decade, there will likely continue be a significant mass of paywalled, subscription-based journal content as well as a growing body of green and gold open access journal content.

In this mixed environment, it will still make sense for libraries to subscribe to some bundles of journal and book content. The ones to purchase will provide a good value per article or book accessed and deliver the content through a compelling interface. They will package their offerings in ways that make the user experience more compelling than finding journal articles in repositories out on the open web. The difference is akin to the value provided by a streaming music service such as Spotify or Apple

Music. Much of the content on those services is available for free if one looks hard enough, but the integrated experience of a high-quality catalogue of content makes them worth the subscription price.

JSTOR is a current example of such a platform: it provides full-text searching of digital journal content and a variety of ways to limit searches, including by academic discipline. Its content is also indexed well on the open web so users will find their way into it from general web searches. E-book 'aggregator packages' such as ProQuest's Academic Complete that offer access to a large set of backlist titles for a minimal cost also offer good value and interfaces that have improved markedly over the last several years.

Alongside the trend towards open access academic content, there is an increasingly complex array of consumer web content formatted specifically for web and mobile interfaces. Take online newspapers such as the *New York Times*, *Wall Street Journal*, or *Washington Post.* These news organs provide an integrated, multimedia content environment offered as a web site and often a mobile app. Libraries often provide backfile access to the content in these publications but without the wrapper of the website or app and sometimes without some of the multimedia add-ons included in the live site.

A similar situation exists with consumer video services like Netflix, which may have content that libraries want to provide their patrons but are unable to because of consumer-focused licensing. Libraries need to look for ways to get this consumer web content to their patrons when needed through site licences or access to back files that preserve multimedia-rich features.

Major news organs often offer a campus-wide licence to their native platforms and though these can be costly, they can be an opportunity to expose students to high-quality journalism that promotes news literacy. Furthermore, many college courses now ask students to convey arguments with digital stories and having access to high-quality news sources where such stories are published supports these efforts.

The converse approach to the Big Deal is demand-driven acquisitions (DDA). Unlike the Big Deal's 'all you can eat' approach, DDA is based on broad discoverability of material with targeted purchases of only the content that library users want. With DDA, library patrons typically come across a journal article or e-book that interests them in the library's discovery tool and as they access the resource, a purchase by the library is initiated in the background. Ideally, the patron experiences access to DDA content instantly in much the same way as content that the library already owns or leases. The library can, however, elect to mediate DDA purchases through librarian review and approval of requests, though this sacrifices seamless, instant access to content.

According to MacDonald (2017), DDA for journal articles often works well to fill in collection gaps after journal package (Big Deal) cancellations. It can also provide valuable usage data to determine when it is most economical to subscribe to high-demand journals.

In the last decade, academic libraries and academic publishers experimented with DDA for books. Some of the models incorporating short-term loans before purchase proved to be unsustainable for the publishers. However, basic DDA, in which a book is purchased once a patron accesses it for a certain amount of time, is still broadly available as are new variations on DDA such as evidence-base acquisitions, where libraries get access to a whole publisher catalogue of e-book content for a period of time in exchange for purchasing a certain block of that content. DDA e-books should play a growing role in academic library collections in the coming decade. The book format is transitioning to open access at a slower rate than journals and a well-designed e-book platform provides an extra added value. DDA allows the library to only pay for what the patron uses, and it is not tied to a subscription price that can go up by unsustainable percentages each year.

Price and Savova (2015) recommend an e-book purchasing strategy that combines large, broad spectrum, low-cost-per-title aggregator packages with the flexibility of demand-driven acquisitions for newer high-demand titles not included in the aggregator packages. Their pragmatic approach, which calls for evaluating each e-book purchasing deal for its advantages and drawbacks, fits today's fluid environment very well. Libraries should look hard at areas of their curriculum that can benefit from DDA. They should continue to work with publishers on the best models for patron discovery of DDA content including further enrichment of records and prominence in discovery and search tools.

In some ways, DDA reflects a general trend towards the use of data to manage collections. As Dempsey et al. (2014) put it:

> *To increase operational efficiencies, library workflows will need to be more intelligent and data-aware, using demand-side usage data to trigger acquisitions, collection balancing between institutions, triage for digitization, consolidation in shared print environments, transfer or withdrawal decisions, and so on.*
>
> *(p. 38)*

As libraries develop complex, data-driven strategies for acquiring materials, they should share the burden of developing and administering these strategies with consortial partners if possible. Besides helpings libraries negotiate better deals, consortia can also be a way to share the staff time required to find, select, purchase, and administer resources. The Orbis Cascade Alliance's long-standing shared e-book purchasing programme is an example of such an endeavour. It provides member libraries a mix of aggregator package, DDA, and evidenced-based e-book content through central negotiation, purchasing, and access provision.

Today, researchers often miss out on 'paywalled' content that their library has purchased because they come across it on the open web rather than through their university library's website. In the next decade, libraries should strive to make paid library content more fully integrated into research and learner workflows by adopting technology that allows library users to access it as they encounter it on the open web. The Seamless Access initiative offers a pathway to do this, but it remains in an early state and likely will have some significant costs for institutions that implement it.

## 10.4 Strategy 2: Reevaluating and improving discovery and context tools

Academic libraries have a number of tools that provide discovery and context to their patrons. That is, they help their patrons find and understand information sources. Some of these tools are bundled with the content itself. They usually include a discovery layer, abstracting and indexing databases, indexed full-text sources like Nexis Uni and JSTOR, online reference tools, and specialized nonbook/journal sources like Social Explorer (a data mapping application) and ARTstor (digital images). Given changes in the broader information ecosystem, academic libraries need to critically rethink the discovery and context tools that they are providing their patrons.

Libraries provide a discovery layer to patrons as a single starting point for research. The idea is to mimic the simplified experience of a search engine and provide patrons a searching experience over the widest possible body of library-provided resources (and often open resources on the web as well). In the coming decade, libraries should advocate for several improvements to their discovery services.

The discovery layer needs to become a more comprehensive discovery and context tool. Ideally, it should seamlessly integrate the wide variety of content and functionality provided through various search tools and reference sources currently found on library research guides (for example, LibGuides). For instance, it should not be necessary for patrons to switch between the discovery layer and a subject-focused indexing and abstracting database. Rather, the indexed content should be seamlessly built into the discovery layer. If a patron wants to home in on economics journals, they should be able to do that by focusing their search on economics in the discovery layer instead of having to go to a separate economics research database.

Breeding (2018) notes that 'competitive tensions' between discovery vendors (who are also often the vendors of the abstracting and indexing tools) prevent the broad sharing of abstracting and indexing metadata in discovery tools. Likewise, Akeroyd (2017) highlights the importance of strong metadata to effective discovery and acknowledges that metadata is a publisher and systems problem rather than a library problem. Libraries will need to continue to advocate for more comprehensive metadata and integrated subject indexes with discovery and content vendors in the years ahead.

Reference content such as term definitions and biographies from dictionaries, encyclopaedias, and statistical sources should be foregrounded in the discovery layer similar to Google knowledge panels. Discovery layers should also do a better job of highlighting authoritative content such as widely cited books and articles. They should point users to open access copies of material on the wider web, something that the Unpaywall service has recently facilitated.

Discovery layers and search tools are a natural place for the implementation of machine learning and artificial intelligence technology to enhance the relevance of results and provide new innovative features. JSTOR Labs' Text Analyzer tool (Text Analyzer Beta, From JSTOR Labs, n.d.) takes a user-uploaded textual document and searches for articles based on the content of the text within JSTOR. The tool, currently in beta, comes with an extensive discussion of how it works. Ideally, artificial intelligence tools that become part of library discovery layers will be configured in ways that illuminate their users' understanding of how algorithms work rather than the 'black box' style that is common in web search engines and social media sites.

A recent white paper from ITHAKA S+R and OhioLink calls for the next generation of library systems to be user-centred rather than collection-centred. While this paper takes aim at the entire integrated library system, it has some specific recommendations for the discovery layer. It calls for:

> *Discovery experiences that are differentiated and to some degree mediated by user type and/or entry point and have the ability to be optionally personalized. This includes intuitive information about other services that may be sought by the user.*
>
> *Evans and Schonfeld (2020)*

While personalization could provide advantages in discovery, one could also argue that a more generic discovery interface (such as Google Scholar) is more effective than the hundreds of institutionally customized discovery layers currently in service in academic libraries.

It could be that if libraries want more advanced discovery with things like integrated reference content, libraries need to accept a more generic, less customizable discovery layer that searches a standard body of content that is optimally organized and indexed. That every library's discovery layer is different according to their collections will be less relevant in an environment with more open access/open web content. Of course, the fact that some discovery metadata and reference content is proprietary presents challenges to the realization of this goal.

Dempsey et al. (2014) have made the point that library resources like books and journal articles are 'social objects' that have a value that comes from the conversations that develop around them. Academic social media sites like ResearchGate link together researchers and scholarship via a social graph and probably represent the most successful example of social activity around scholarly content in the current academic information environment.

Libraries have never had much luck adding social elements such as reviews and comment boxes to their discovery tools. A better strategy would be for the discovery layers to incorporate and link to ResearchGate and other social resources but stick to their strengths by organizing published discussion around scholarly content. For example, discovery tools should recognize book reviews and array them around the books reviewed. They should make use of review articles and bibliographies as they rank and present results.

Discipline-specific abstracting and indexing tools are a staple of academic libraries. Common names include Historical Abstracts, EconLit, and SocIndex. With discovery layers, academic search engines like Google Scholar, and multidisciplinary full-text resources like JSTOR to compete with, these resources are becoming less and less important. According to the 2018 ITHAKA S+R faculty survey, faculty were about 40% less likely to start a search for scholarly literature in a 'specific scholarly database' in 2018 as they were in 2012 (Blankstein and Wolff-Eisenberg, 2019).

Academic libraries should critically evaluate the added value that these resources provide. For example, APA PsychNet provides a platform to search across the PsychINFO, PsychARTICLES, and PsychTHERAPY databases and includes resources such as the APA Thesaurus. This bundled feature set might make this resource a compelling portal for psychology researchers. Other abstracting and indexing databases are simply a flat collection of citations with subject headings and may make sense to give up if the metadata and search functionality is similar to what is available in the discovery layer.

Studies that compare the coverage of subscription-based research databases such as Web of Science and Scopus with free research tools on the web such as Google Scholar and Microsoft Academic are an excellent prompt for libraries to evaluate overlapping discovery offerings. A recent comparison of Google Scholar, Scopus, and Web of Science for the social sciences found that Google Scholar had more comprehensive coverage than Scopus and Web of Science, though at the price of some quality control and technical issues (Martín-Martín et al., 2019).

In one sense, traditional reference resources such as subject encyclopaedias, dictionaries, and bibliographies are less relevant in the era of ready reference provided by Google and Wikipedia. On the other hand, in an age of information abundance, the context that certain kinds of reference sources can provide can be especially valuable when developing understanding of a new topic. For example, Oxford Bibliographies provide expert-edited guides to the key literature of many disciplines and topic areas. This is the kind of context that cannot readily be found in a discovery layer or Google Scholar search.

Summarizing recent research on students and information literacy, Conrad (2017) contends that students 'reach critical developmental milestones and learning thresholds that demand support from materials that define topics and connect the dots at key stages of the learning process. However, providing the right contextual material at the right time is a logistical challenge for publishers and librarians alike'. She makes the case that reference resources are a category of library content that is 'ripe for innovation' especially in ways that get the content to the user at the point of need.

In the next decade, libraries should seek out, support, and promote excellent reference sources, whether they are open access ones like *The Stanford Encyclopedia of Philosophy* or commercial ones like *Oxford Bibliographies*. They should also advocate for ways to get good reference content in the flow of the user through technological innovation in the discovery layer and other means.

## 10.5 Strategy 3: Deeper integration with the curriculum

Academic libraries operate in the context of a college or university. They work closely with academic departments and sometimes act as a bridge between departments and programmes. This embeddedness puts libraries in a unique position to identify services and resources that can have a broad benefit to their institutions. Through close relationships with faculty and students, librarians can really understand the curriculum that is being taught and the kinds of resources that are of optimal benefit.

Academic libraries exist to support the teaching and research needs of their parent institutions, with most academic libraries at smaller institutions having a curricular focus. According to Linden et al. (2018), even Yale's well-endowed research library has redirected its collection development strategy away from comprehensive collecting towards support for institutional research and teaching needs. Aligning library acquisitions with institutional and particularly curricular needs is more important than ever today with constrained funding and vast amounts of open resources available on the web.

In recent years, there has been an uptick in interest in academic library support for instructional resources such as textbooks and other required course material. Many libraries promote open educational resources to their faculty and some offer assistance in the creation of such resources. In addition, some libraries provide access to textbooks through reserves programmes and links to online content. Working with faculty to build materials to support the curriculum is a departure from an academic library's typical focus on support for faculty and student research projects. According to Steven J. Bell:

> *As we shift priorities to support student academic success, I envision fewer faculty seeking librarian collaboration for one-on-one research support. Delivering course assigned content requires academic librarians to deeply engage with faculty in identifying and providing access to instructional resources.*
>
> *Parker (2019)*

In the coming decade, academic libraries will devote an increasing share of their energies to facilitating the selection and creation of curricular resources that meet learning objectives and contribute to affordability.

While there continues to be a general downward trend in the use of print resources, interest in printed books has proven more durable than predicted a decade ago. Academic libraries should develop print collections strategically for those topics whose students and scholars have a continued interest in print. Literature and the history of art come to mind. They should also continue to maintain and build out regional resource sharing networks for print materials so that space and resources for print are used as efficiently as possible.

*The Future of the Library Print Collection* report from the University of Arizona (Arizona State University Library, 2017) highlights a number of ideas for the development of curricular-focused print collections. It recommends the creation of curriculum-specific collections related to first-year seminars, senior capstones, and other courses (p. 19). The report also highlights the complementary relationship between print and electronic sources. E-books can sometimes be used for an initial scan of a subject with the print copy being used for more intensive reading. Purchasing both the print and electronic copy of a book is expensive, but, in some cases, it may be the best way to satisfy patron needs.

According to Miller and Pressley (2015), collection development is still a significant aspect of most departmental liaison librarian roles at research libraries, though some of the more automated collection development activities have shifted to centralized roles (pp. 14, 18). The Oklahoma State University explains the transition in library liaison activities as: 'shifting collection development duties from buying resources to reach a specific dollar amount to analyzing statistics and communicating with departments' (Ippoliti, 2017).

In the facilitated collection environment, subject and collections librarians need to be aware of the changing mix of resources that serve their academic programmes. This includes the usefulness of search tools and open access resources that fall outside the scope of library-purchased resources. They should understand how to read and analyze usage statistics and perform overlap analyses on both journal and book collections. They should have a sense of how faculty and students actually navigate the information environment in the discipline including library and nonlibrary-provided resources. To optimize resources for the curriculum, they should use this knowledge to select subscription resources and to profile demand-driven acquisition strategies.

With more journal (and to some extent book) content going open access, academic libraries should provide information resources that fall outside of the journal and book categories as a larger share of their purchased collections in the coming years. These additional source types include familiar ones such as digital primary sources for historical research and digital images of art and culture. Increasingly, they should include a variety of data sources.

While much of the literature on library data services points to the curation of research data, library support for teaching data discovery, analysis, and presentation has the potential for much broader impact. Furthermore, undergraduate programs are adapting to a more data-driven society and increasingly include data science and data literacy components (Burress et al., 2020; Dahl, 2014).

While there are many raw data sets available on the open web, they are often difficult to use and interpret, especially for undergraduates. A 2019 ITHAKA S+R study focusing on the needs of business education highlighted access to data providers as a potential area of need in business education programmes (Tanaka and Cooper, 2019).

A library that purchases data sets tailored for curricular needs and provides expertise to clean, analyze, and present that data can become an essential part of a data-intensive curriculum. For example, a sociology librarian could give workshops on how to select data in the Inter-University Consortium for Political and Social Research (ICPSR) data set and then bring it into the R statistical application for manipulation and analysis. In a similar vein, a political science librarian could help students create digital maps that illustrate the relationship between socio-economic factors and voting patterns using geographic information systems software and data purchased and prepared by the library.

The combination of library-provided content and library expertise to apply that content is a powerful one. It can enable a richer, more complex curriculum for students, one in which they can learn valuable skills and answer more interesting questions in their studies.

## 10.6 Conclusion: Balancing the bought library collection

The purchased library collection serves to complement and balance the wider information ecosystem. Much of this chapter has discussed ways that library content and search tools can supplement what is available openly on the web to support the academic curriculum. At a higher level, the purchased academic library search and collection infrastructure should help to offset biases in the wider information ecosystem. It should be implemented as part of a larger strategy that supports library values such as access, preservation, privacy, and a diversity of perspectives and viewpoints.

As discussed above, algorithms drive much of our information experience on search engines, social media, and modern news sources. Libraries should strive to provide search and discovery tools that are more transparent than their commercial counterparts in the ways that they use algorithms to rank and personalize search results. They should also demand patron privacy as a part of the increasingly data-driven architecture of library collections and access.

As libraries select books and journals through more aggregated and automated strategies, they should be mindful of biases that can enter the selection process. As they develop print and electronic collections through demand-driven profiling and other automated means, librarians should work consciously to counteract mainstream narratives and expose work from lesser known publishers and authors. Ideally, librarians should work with teaching and research faculty partners as they make these decisions.

As Dempsey et al. (2014) have observed, the presence of the network has reshaped where certain library activities take place. The best means of supporting library principles around preservation and access to information happen through initiatives not at the level of local purchasing, but through system-wide solutions. Though this chapter has focused on mostly on digital content that libraries lease or purchase for their own community, libraries also have a responsibility to preserve information over the long term for the wider community.

To preserve published content, libraries should support network-level preservation solutions such as shared print agreements and long-term digital repositories like JSTOR, Portico, and CLOCKSS. Making a financial contribution to these efforts can be a strain on library collections budgets, but they are essential infrastructure going forward, and they permit libraries to take a less preservation-focused approach as they provision digital resources.

Broad access to information is a central library value and transcends the need of any particular institution. Libraries should advocate for liberal resource sharing rights when they lease and purchase article and book collections. They should support the transition to open access through transformative agreements and by advocating for open access with scholars at their own institutions.

Furthermore, libraries have an increasing role to play in their direct contributions to the open information ecosystem through so-called 'inside-out' collections. Ideally, these collections align with local priorities and also support wider information needs. Digital cultural heritage collections can support the humanities curriculum and contribute to the wider body of scholarly resources. Libraries may also act as publishers for open access books, journals, and open educational resources.

The information ecosystem will continue to shift in directions that are difficult to predict. With change as the only constant, an academic library should develop medium-term strategies and then continuously monitor the situation. This will lead to mission-driven, pragmatic choices that support institutional needs and align with long-term library values.

## References

Akeroyd, J., 2017. Discovery systems: are they now the library? Learn. Publ. 30 (1), 87–89. https://doi.org/10.1002/leap.1085.

Arizona State University Library, 2017. The Future of the Academic Library Print Collection: A Space for Engagement. ASU Whitepaper—Which Books. https://lib.asu.edu/sites/default/files/marketing/ASU%20Whitepaper%20-%20Which%20Books.pdf. (Accessed 30.04.20).

Blankstein, M., Wolff-Eisenberg, C., 2019. Ithaka S + R US Faculty Survey 2018. https://sr.ithaka.org/publications/2018-us-faculty-survey/ (Accessed 24.01.20).

Breeding, M., 2018. Current phase of discovery. Libr. Technol. Rep. 54 (8), 28–30.

Burress, T., Mann, E., Neville, T., 2020. Exploring data literacy via a librarian-faculty learning community: a case study. J. Acad. Librariansh. 46 (1), 102076. https://doi.org/10.1016/j.acalib.2019.102076.

Conrad, L.Y., 2017. Tracking the evolution of reference resources. In: The Scholarly Kitchen. https://scholarlykitchen.sspnet.org/2017/07/17/tracking-evolution-reference-resources/. (Accessed 30.04.20).

Dahl, M., 2014. Data-driven liberal arts: the library role. In: The Academic Commons. http://www.academiccommons.org/2014/07/24/data-driven-liberal-arts-the-library-role/. (Accessed 30.04.20).

Dempsey, L., 2016 January 31. The facilitated collection. In: Lorcan Dempsey's Weblog. http://orweblog.oclc.org/towards-the-facilitated-collection/. (Accessed 30.04.20).

Dempsey, L., Malpas, C., Lavoie, B., 2014. Collection directions: the evolution of library collections and collecting. Portal: Libr. Acad. 14 (3), 393–423. https://doi.org/10.1353/pla.2014.0013.

Evans, G., Schonfeld, R., 2020. It's Not What Libraries Hold; It's Who Libraries Serve (Issue Brief). ITHAKA S+R. https://sr.ithaka.org/publications/its-not-what-libraries-hold-its-who-libraries-serve/. (Accessed 23.01.20).

Ippoliti, C., 2017. Extreme Makeover: A Blueprint for Redefining the Role of the Liaison Librarian in the Academic Library. https://shareok.org/bitstream/handle/11244/52430/oksd_Ippoliti_2017-02.pdf;jsessionid=F4D3FC4ABA494C19D05E899AD8D34FF0?sequence=1. (Accessed 30.04.20).

Lemley, T., Li, J., 2015. 'Big Deal' journal subscription packages: are they worth the cost? J. Electron. Resour. Med. Libr. 12 (1), 1–10. https://doi.org/10.1080/15424065.2015.1001959.

Levine-Clark, M., Lawlor, B., 2018. Open access and its impact on access and subscriptions. Inf. Serv. Use 38 (1/2), 41–43. https://doi.org/10.3233/ISU-180008.

Linden, J., Tudesco, S., Dollar, D., 2018. Collections as a service: a research library's perspective. C&RL 79 (1), 86–99. https://doi.org/10.5860/crl.79.1.86.

MacDonald, H., 2017. 'Just-In-Time' unmediated document delivery service provides fast delivery, helps identify collection gaps, but incurs extra costs. Evid. Based Libr. Inf. Pract. 12 (2), 175–177. https://doi.org/10.18438/B8P07M.

Martín-Martín, A., Orduna-Malea, E., Thelwall, M., Delgado-López-Cózar, E., 2019. Google Scholar, Web of Science, and Scopus: Which is Best for Me? Taster. https://blogs.lse.ac.uk/impactofsocialsciences/2019/12/03/google-scholar-web-of-science-and-scopus-which-is-best-for-me/. (Accessed 30.04.20).

Miller, R.K., Pressley, L., 2015. Evolution of Library Liaisons (SPEC Kit 349). Association of Research Libraries, https://doi.org/10.29242/spec.349.

Parker, D., 2019. Blurring lines—open educational resources: the rise of the library and navigating the 'spectrum of affordability'. Against the Grain 31 (2), 44–47.

Price, J., 2019. A Collaborative Imperative? The Read to Publish Funding Gap. Charleston Conference, Charleston, South Carolina. https://static.sched.com/hosted_files/2019charlestonlibraryconference/30/Part%203%20Price%20Collaborative%20Imperative%20Funding%20Gap%20CHS%202019%20plenary.pdf. (Accessed 30.04.20).

Price, J., Savova, M., 2015. DDA in context: defining a comprehensive ebook acquisition strategy in an access-driven world. Against the Grain 27 (5). https://doi.org/10.7771/2380-176X.7177.

Schonfeld, R., 2019. Isn't Leakage Good for Libraries? The Scholarly Kitchen. https://scholarlykitchen.sspnet.org/2019/03/21/leakage-good-libraries/. (Accessed 30.04.20).

Tanaka, K., Cooper, D., 2019. Teaching Business, Looking at The Support Needs of Instructors (ITHAKA S+R). https://sr.ithaka.org/publications/teaching-business/. (Accessed 30.04.20).
Text Analyzer Beta, From JSTOR Labs, n.d. JSTOR Labs. https://www.jstor.org/analyze (Accessed 31.01.20).
Walter, S., 2011. Guest editorial: 'distinctive signifiers of excellence': library services and the future of the academic library. Coll. Res. Libr., 6–8.

# Social media as a professional development tool for academic librarians

# 11

*Daniella LaShaun Smith*
University of North Texas, Denton, TX, United States

## 11.1 Introduction

Approximately 45% of the global population uses social media (Clement, 2019, para. 1). Though social media (SM) usage around the world is different according to the part of the world one lives in, the United States exceeds the norm with a 79% consumption rate. In 2018, the United States boasted 244 million users. It is predicted that this statistic will increase to 257 million in 2023 (Clement, 2019).

Just as SM has become a staple in the personal lives of US citizens, it is now influential in other facets, such as work experiences. Prospective employers now search SM accounts to screen job applicants (Smith, 2018), and some industries hire individuals for managing SM accounts and campaigns. Because of the prevalence of SM, studies have been conducted to determine how SM can be used as a training tool (Breunig, 2016; Bruguera et al., 2019; Ranieri, 2019). More specific to this chapter, the value, purpose, and usage of SM in libraries have been questioned (Young and Rossmann, 2015, p. 20).

There is little doubt that the younger generations who are present on college campuses are enthusiastic users of SM. Hence, academic librarians need to understand SM and how it can be used to research the populations who are served in higher education (HE). Moreover, academic librarians must have the skills necessary to adopt SM to help them to fulfil their job duties (Chawner and Oliver, 2013).

Therefore, this chapter begins with a brief review of professional literature and research on how SM is used for professional development, its association with demographic variables, its impact on the workplace, and how academic libraries use SM. Next, it describes a study that was implemented to explore the perceptions, which academic librarians have of SM and how these perceptions relate to their demographic variables. The study methods and results are discussed. An overview of the findings and an analysis of their meaning are presented. The chapter concludes with the study limitations and a discussion of future research.

## 11.2 SM and academic libraries

Librarians were once apprehensive about embracing SM (Brookbank, 2015). SM has become central to the outreach and promotion activities of academic libraries (Harrison et al., 2017). Books have been written about how librarians should

**Future Directions in Digital Information. https://doi.org/10.1016/B978-0-12-822144-0.00011-2**

use SM for marketing library services (Koontz and Mon, 2014; Solomon, 2013). Even though SM use is common now, Brookbank (2015) cautions that librarians must monitor their feeds to understand the platforms, which are used the most amongst a university's population. At Brookbank's institution, students were differentiating between the information that was expected on different platforms. On that campus, students accessed Facebook for information about activities, library opening and closings, and announcements. Students were connected to Twitter to receive the latest news about what was happening in the campus library. Therefore, Brookbank resolved that an academic library cannot rely on one platform to deliver its content.

In studying six libraries in the United States, Harrison et al. (2017) deduced that the libraries used SM networking to make community connections, create a welcoming environment, and to provide content to students. SM posts about events were more common than posts about collections, services, the library community, and the university community. Similarly, King (2012) noted that the process of marketing with posts should be accompanied by listening for trends, communicating after posts are made, and being active in SM accounts.

In addition to marketing, SM is being used to train new librarians about how to interact with patrons. Hagman and Carleton (2014) explained that interacting via SM requires a significant investment from libraries in terms of time and labour. As a result, Ohio State embraces the idea of using student interns to create content for SM accounts. The library benefits from SM accounts that engage students, being able to monitor trends on SM and blogs and having SM accounts that are up to date. Conversely, the interns develop curation and research skills and showcase their work in a way that is personally rewarding to them.

## 11.3 How SM is used for professional development

Similar to viewing the use of SM as a way to teach interns research and curation skills (Hagman and Carleton, 2014), literature and research suggest that SM can be used as a tool for professional development and lifelong learning (Lampe and Ellison, 2016; Ranieri, 2019; Smith, 2018). SM is pertinent to professional development because of the timely updates and discussions of best practices (Bruguera et al., 2019). Professionals can share evidence of the materials, which they have collected. SM is also helpful for counteracting barriers such as finances for paying for professional development, travelling, and time constraints. For example, instead of paying to travel to another city for professional development, an individual can sit in their living room and participate in an online class offered with a Google Hangout. An online session can be more cost effective than going to another city because it does not involve paying for a hotel and travel expenses such as an airplane ticket or fuel.

Singer (2015) observed that there are a variety of pros and cons with using Twitter for professional development in addition to counteracting financial and travel restrictions. The list of benefits includes:

- Ideas: When one needs ideas for a topic, a message can be sent through Twitter with a hashtag, or one can participate in a chat.
- Inspiration: Twitter posts are full of inspiring posts about other educators who find solutions for complicated issues.
- Curiosity: Twitter encourages the exploration of new topics through spontaneous posts and links to resources.
- Courage: Twitter gives users a platform to express their opinions in an open forum and to find support for their ideas.
- Connections: Twitter micro-bloggers become part of a global society when they exchange ideas and form connections beyond the platform.

Using Twitter is not without drawbacks. Singer's list of Twitter shortcomings includes:

- Sustain focus: Twitter is a micro-blogging platform, which does not offer intensive, sustained (30–40 h) professional development on a specific topic.
- Depth: Chats are like high-speed brainstorming sessions instead of immersive discussions.
- Cognitive dissonance: Twitter does not encourage deep thinking about convictions, which can change how one thinks about subjects.
- Application: Twitter is limited to being a discussion platform which discourages the implementation and the practice of the ideas discovered.
- Impact on student learning: Educators can collaborate to have a Twitter chat, but Twitter is not tested to see if interaction between educators and students has a positive effect.

There are many articles about SM as a professional development tool. Bruguera et al. (2019) conducted a systematic review of research articles about professional development and SM. The results indicated that surveys are the primary method for investigating SM as a professional development strategy. The study results suggested that Twitter is the preferred SM platform for delivering professional development. Bruguera et al. further assert that research on SM professional development often concentrates on it as an informal method of learning. Studies about how SM can be used in a formal context are an emerging area of emphasis. It is also recommended that more research should be undertaken outside of the health sciences and education disciplines. Whilst academic librarianship is within the field of education, it also addresses librarianship as a separate field.

Ranieri (2019) provided an overview of findings of how SM is used for professional development purposes between 2009 and 2010. The review noted that there are several benefits and constraints present when using SM for professional development. Ranieri (2019, p. 186) found the benefits of SM are: the facilitation of knowledge exchange by connecting communities of practice, keeping up to date, building a support network, sharing resources and ideas, and facilitating knowledge translation and postpublication peer review. The challenges included: the propagation of inaccurate or inappropriate information, threats to professionalism, threats to privacy, the lack of a strategy to evaluate learning results, threats to productivity, slow adoption, a lack or low level of assistance, and the lack of representation in participation.

In addition to listing benefits and challenges, Ranieri (2019) further clarified that SM is a way of seeking mentorship and feedback. However, this mentorship comes with the risk of being exposed to information that is unprofessional and harmful.

SM is often filled with hate speech and misinformation. Privacy for the people that participate and the companies they represent is also a concern. A research gap is evident because research is needed in the arts and humanities, natural science, social sciences, and business and management. This finding is aligned with Bruguera et al.'s (2019) suggestion that research on SM for training should be conducted in fields beyond education and health sciences as well. Another finding was that most of the research which is conducted on SM is qualitative. Finally, there is a need for rigorous quantitative studies that measure the impact of learning with SM.

Part of the reason rigorous research is difficult lies within the complex nature of SM, the relationships that are developed on it, and how SM has the potential to blend personal and work relationships. 'A central characteristic of community building through SM is that the "online" experience is so connected and interwoven with the "offline" experience as to create a single seamless experience' (Young and Rossmann, 2015, p. 22).

## 11.4 SM in the workplace

Perhaps the interwoven and connected behaviour of SM described by Young and Rossmann (2015) is a part of the reason why it has reached beyond the personal lives of millions of users. For instance, Lampe and Ellison (2016) observed that SM is embedded in the American workplace. Most (75%) workers use SM for a job-related purpose. During the day, people that use SM for job-related purposes use it for several reasons. These reasons include

- Networking or finding new jobs (78%).
- Staying in touch with other people in their field (71%).
- Connecting with experts (56%).
- Getting to know co-workers personally (51%).
- Finding information for the job (46%).

Whilst SM can be mined for useful information related to work, Lampe and Ellison's (2016) results indicated that younger individuals are more likely to find information on SM that changes their perceptions about a co-worker. Moreover, if the workplace has a SM policy, the workers are less likely to use SM on the job for reasons unrelated to work. This finding supports Jeske and Shultz's (2016) assertion that clear SM policies subvert poor behaviours on SM. Employees purposely stay within SM parameters. Although Twitter has been cited as a popular on-demand SM platform for professional development (Singer, 2015), Lampe and Ellison (2016) also found that several networks were used for work-related purposes: Facebook (19%), LinkedIn (14%), Twitter (3%), SM provided by the employer (9%), and other platforms which were not listed on their survey (5%).

A wiki is a type of SM that can be provided by an employer. Breunig (2016, p. 249) conducted research on how a wiki could be used to support learning in a 'globally dispersed project environment'. Breunig (2016) surmised that wikis could be developed to foster workplace learning when employees cannot participate in face-to-face interactions. Breunig concluded that four determinants make SM tools valuable for practitioners who need to use them for virtual collaboration. Tools should meet the following criteria:

- Be relevant to the work carried out for the project. It must be interactive and contain helpful information to complete the project.
- Increase the desire for employees to use SM for documenting their work by linking SM to their job, thus increasing the visibility and recognition of worker expertise.
- Facilitate transparency concerning individual expertise.
- Ensure quality assurance through the monitoring of data that is posted.

Baxter and Connolly (2014) conducted a literature review on the topic of how Web 2.0 tools are implemented in organizations and included social networking sites (SNS), blogs, and wikis in their analysis. In their conclusion, they noted that managerial support is a key component for implementation. Support from management can shape the views of staff and cultivate a shared vision for using tools. Baxter and Connolly (2014) further asserted that organizations could take a systematic approach to implement new tools.

The interrelated phases of their implementation model were planning, support, development, and implementation. The planning stage includes assessing the organization's culture, communication, and knowledge management structures to support the technology. The support stage involves inspiring member buy-in because adopting new tools is a change in an organization's culture. The development stage applies to selecting platforms that are compatible with the organization's current system, policies, and guides. The organization pilots the tool to determine how it can be streamlined for daily use. Finally, the implementation phase involves standardizing the use of technology as a formal resource for the organization.

## 11.5 Gender differences in SM usage

Regardless of how SM may be applied by professionals and how it is used in organizations, it is worth acknowledging that males and females do not use SM in the same way. For instance, in the past, women have been more likely than males to participate in online communities (Anderson, 2015; Kimbrough et al., 2013; Muscanell and Guadagno, 2012). The difference in SM habits is present in adolescents, with girls reporting an average daily use of SM higher than boys (Twenge et al., 2019). However, the gap between usage is diminishing. Despite the usage gap being smaller, there are differences in the platforms that males and females use. Anderson (2015) reported that males are more likely to use Reddit, Digg, and Slashdot. Males also use Facebook, Pinterest, and Instagram to attract females.

Another study examined how gender and personality influences how individuals use SM (Muscanell and Guadagno, 2012). Results showed that men use SM more for developing new relationships. On the contrary, females use it to maintain the relationships that are already in place. Women may seek to maintain relationships because they are acting in accordance with gender role expectations (Kimbrough et al., 2013).

Related to building and maintaining connections, trust and privacy are other factors that differentiate male and female use of SM. It is possible that there is a difference in how genders use SM for professional development. These differences may be related to how genders view privacy on SM. For example, a metaanalysis of gender differences in privacy on Social Networking Sites (SNS) found that females had more privacy concerns and behaviours than males (Tifferet, 2019). Women are also more likely to utilize privacy settings and remove tags from photos. It was concluded that one of the reasons women have higher privacy settings is that they use more SM, post more, and upload more images.

The impact of privacy and gender on decisions about SM is illustrated by the findings of Lin et al. (2017) regarding the variables impacting the continued use of SNS:

> *For female groups, satisfaction is based on perceived usefulness and privacy risk, and continuance intention is based on perceived enjoyment, perceived reputation, community identification, and satisfaction. For male groups, satisfaction is based on perceived usefulness and privacy risk, and continuance intention is based on perceived value, perceived enjoyment, and satisfaction.*
>
> *(Lin et al., 2017, p. 392)*

## 11.6 Age and SM usage

According to Wilder (2017, p. 1), 'Librarian professionals have never been older'. The population is older because people born between 1946 and 1964 were not retiring as expected. Age is another demographic variable, which relates to internet use. The Pew Research Center (Anderson and Perrin, 2017) studied how age related to Internet use. The Center produced a report on technology adoption in the United States. The main findings of the report are based on the telephone interviews that took place September 29-November 6, 2016. The participants answered survey questions. A total of 3015 adults participated.

Overall, it is predicted that 90% of the US population has access to the Internet (Anderson and Perrin, 2017). It is not a surprise that 100% of young adults age 18–29 have access to the Internet. About 97% of people age 30–49, 88% of people age 50–64, and 73% of people age 65 years or older use the Internet. Although older adults are less likely to use the Internet, they are beginning to use SM more (Anderson and Perrin, 2017). Anderson and Perrin (2017) observed that two-thirds of adults 65 years or older go online and share information.

The Pew Research Center (Perrin and Anderson, 2019) studied age group usage of SM platforms. YouTube is a popular platform, with 73% of adults in the United States using it. Conversely, Instagram and Snapchat are more popular amongst young adults. Individuals who use Instagram and Snapchat visit them at least once a day (77%) and multiple times a day (68%). Facebook has a more consistent following. Seven out of 10 (69%) of adults in the United States are on Facebook. About 68% of adults 50–64, and almost half of adults 65 and older use Facebook. LinkedIn is used the most by college graduates (27%). Adults age 25–29 have the biggest percentage (44%) of LinkedIn users. They are followed by 30–49 (37%), 50–64 (24%), 18–24 (17%), and 65 or older (11%).

## 11.7 Research questions

As the literature review indicates, SM is an integral part of society in terms of continuing education and the workplace. SM has been a mainstay in academic libraries for years. As such, this study was implemented because of the need to understand how academic librarians use SM. It examines academic librarian perceptions of using SM for professional development. The relationship between these perceptions and socio-demographic variables is explored. Socio-demographic variables include age, gender, and years of experience. The following questions guided the investigation:

1. Do academic librarians feel they have the knowledge necessary to use SM for work and professional development?
2. Do academic librarians feel they have the resources necessary to use SM for work and professional development?
3. Do academic librarians feel using SM for professional purposes is a good idea?
4. Do academic librarians feel SM is compatible with their professional development needs?
5. Do academic librarians use SM to build online personal learning networks?
6. How do socio-demographic variables such as the years of librarianship experience, age, and gender relate to perceptions that academic librarians have of SM?
7. What SM platforms do academic librarians use?

## 11.8 The participants

In all, 173 academic librarians provided responses for this study. They had a wide range of experience as librarians. For example, 25.4% had 6–10 years of experience. Responses indicated that the remaining participants had 1–5 years (23.1%), 21 or more years (22.5%), 11–15 years (13.9%), 16–20 years (11.6%), and a year or less of experience (3.5%). Many of the participants were female (76.9%) and had a Librarianship degree (95.4%). The ages of the participants varied. The largest percentage of the participants was 35–44 years old. The rest were 25–34 years old (28.9%), 45–54 years old (22.0%), 55–64 years old (11.0%), and 65–74 years old (4.6%).

## 11.9 Data collection and analysis

The results presented in this chapter are a subset of data that was collected to learn about how librarians use SM for professional development. Responses for academic librarians were used to complete this study. After Institutional Review Board permission was granted, the survey was announced via librarian listservs. Also, the researcher purchased the service of Schooldata.com to email the survey to potential participants. The survey was posted online using the survey service Qualtrics. The quantitative responses were analyzed using the Statistical Package for the Social Sciences (SPSS). Except for the participant's gender and types of SM used, all questions were asked using a five-point Likert scale with options for strongly agree, agree, neutral, disagree, and strongly disagree. An open-ended question was asked to ascertain the types of SM. Research Questions 1, 2, 3, 4, and 5 were analyzed using descriptive statistics. Research Question 6 was analyzed using the Pearson product-moment, the chi-square test for association, and the Fisher's exact test. The frequency of responses was counted to answer Research Question 7.

## 11.10 Results

**Research Question 1:** Do academic librarians feel they have the resources necessary to use SM for work and professional development?

Participants were asked how much they agreed with the statement 'I have the resources necessary to use SM for work and professional development'. Most (54.9%) participants agreed, 31.8% strongly agreed, 8.1% were neutral, and 5.2% strongly disagreed.

**Research Question 2:** Do academic librarians feel they have the knowledge necessary to use SM for work and professional development?

Participants were asked how much they agreed with the statement 'I have the knowledge necessary to use SM for work and professional development'. None of the participants strongly disagree. The participants selected agree (54.9%), strongly agree (31.8%), neutral (8.1%), and disagree (5.2%).

**Research Question 3:** Do academic librarians feel using SM for professional purposes is a good idea?

Participants were asked if they agreed with the statement 'Using SM for professional purposes is a good idea'. The participants had a range of responses with 48.0% agreeing, 23.1% strongly agreeing, 22.0% selecting neutral, 5.8% disagreeing, and 1.2% strongly disagreeing.

**Research Question 4:** Do academic librarians feel SM is compatible with their professional development needs?

Participants were asked how much they agreed with the statement 'Social media is compatible with my professional development needs'. Most of the participants agreed (41.0%). In addition, 20.2% strongly agreed, 27.2% were neutral, 9.2% disagreed, and 2.3% strongly disagreed.

**Research Question 5:** Do academic librarians use SM to build online personal learning networks?

The participants were asked 'Do you have an online personal learning network?' The survey stated an online personal learning network could include people known personally and people and organizations that are followed online to enhance professional development. Most (68.8%) participants stated that they had an online personal learning network.

**Research Question 6:** How do demographic variables such as the years of librarianship experience, age, and gender relate to the perceptions that academic librarians have of SM?

Each demographic variable was analyzed separately. The results are listed under the corresponding demographic variable.

**Years of librarianship experience**

A Pearson product-moment correlation was carried out to determine the relationship between librarianship experience and the belief that SM is compatible with professional development needs. There was a positive correlation between librarianship experience and the belief that SM is compatible with professional development needs, which was statistically significant ($r = .191$, $n = 173$, $P = .012$). The participants' belief that SM was compatible with their professional development needs decreased as their years of librarianship experience increased. A chi-square test was conducted to determine if there was an association between the participants' years of librarianship experience and if they have an online personal learning network. There was a significant association found ($X^2(1) = 7.064$, $P < .008$). The librarians with more experience were less likely to state that they had an online personal learning network.

After conducting a Pearson product-moment correlation test, it was determined that there was no significant relationship between the participants' librarianship experience and (i) the belief that they have the resources necessary to use SM for work and professional development, (ii) the belief that they have the knowledge necessary to use SM for work and professional development, and (iii) the belief that using SM for professional development is a good idea.

### Age

A chi-square test was conducted to determine if there was an association between the participants' age and if they have an online personal learning network. There was a significant association found ($X^2(1) = 5.169$, $P < .023$). Younger participants were more likely to state that they had an online personal learning network.

After conducting a Pearson product-moment correlation test, it was determined that there was no significant relationship between the participants' age and the belief that they have the resources necessary to use SM for work and professional development, the belief that they have the knowledge needed to use SM for work and professional development, the belief that SM is compatible with professional development needs, and the belief that using SM for professional development is a good idea.

### Gender

The results of a chi-square test signified that there is a significant association between the participants' gender and the belief that SM is compatible with professional development needs ($X^2(1) = 5.107$, $P < .024$). Females were more likely to believe that SM is consistent with their professional development needs. Statistical analysis (two-sided Fisher's exact test) confirmed that females are significantly more likely to believe that they had the resources necessary to use SM for work and professional development ($P = .043$, Fisher's exact test). A more significant percentage of females (91.7%) than males (79.5%) felt they had the needed resources.

There was not a significant association found between the participants' gender and if they have a personal online learning network or the belief that using SM for professional development is a good idea. Likewise, there was no association between the participants' gender and their belief that they know how to use SM for work and professional development. The males and females had similar responses to each of the questions.

**Research Question 7:** What SM platforms do academic librarians use?

Participants responded to a question that asked them about the SM tools that they used for professional development. Many (87.9%) of the participants responded. The participants preferred Twitter, Facebook, LinkedIn, Instagram, listservs, and blogs. See Fig. 11.1 for a list of tools and the frequency of times they were mentioned. Although far less mentioned than the other networks, Instagram and YouTube were the last two SM tools that were listed.

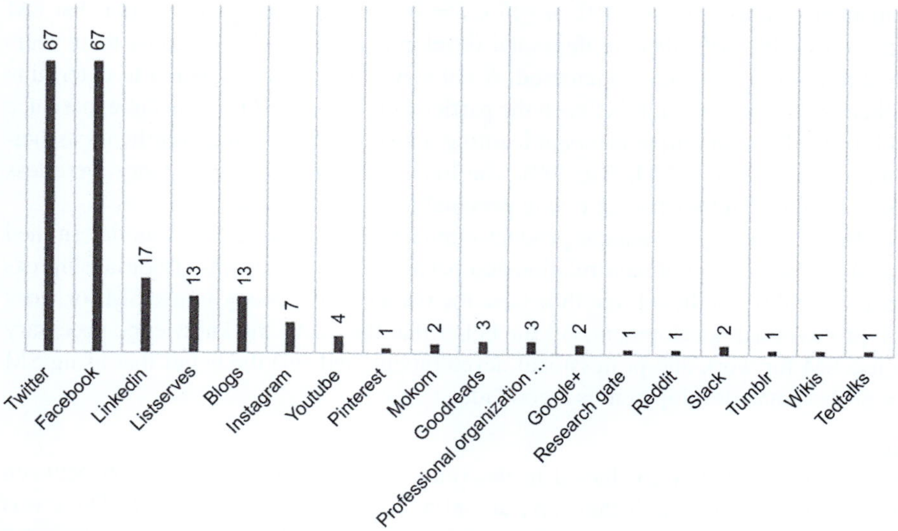


**Fig. 11.1** Frequency of reported social media platforms.

## 11.11 Discussion

### *11.11.1 SM associations with demographic variables*

Several demographic variables had relationships with the participants' perceptions of SM. Participants with more years of experience did not find SM to be as compatible with their professional development needs and were less likely to state that they have an online personal learning network (PLN). Moreover, older participants were less likely to say they have a PLN than their younger counterparts. The researcher is assuming that the librarians in their study with the most experience are also older.

Older librarians may not have grown up with computers and may not find the use of SM intuitive. SM is also an innovation that continues to evolve. Using SM to share information that may be deemed private may be implausible when one has learned that some aspects of life should always be private. The results of this study are consistent with Perrin and Anderson's (2019) finding that older adults use SM less.

The results did reveal some differences in opinions between the genders. Females were more likely to believe that SM is a good fit for their continuing education. A look at the research reveals that, historically, females are more likely to use SM than males (Anderson, 2015). Whilst the gap between SM between males and females has dropped in the general population, it seems that the participants of this study are still functioning along the lines of older research results. Anderson (2015) provides one reason that can assist with explaining this study's findings. Females are the most significant users of Facebook. Twitter has similar patterns for males and females. Twitter and Facebook were the platforms identified the most by the participants of this study for professional development. The difference in the genders might not have existed for this study if the participants were asked if SM is a good fit for their personal lives.

Females are also more likely to agree that they have the resources available to use SM for professional development and work. One explanation could be that females use SM more (Anderson, 2015). They may desire less assistance to navigate it professionally. Alternatively, males might be more interested in completing traditional work duties and prefer support from students to manage accounts, as suggested by Hagman and Carleton (2014).

Notably, there are no differences between the male and female use of PLNs and the belief that SM is a good idea for professional development. Whilst males differ in their view that they have the resources to use SM for work, they are similar in their opinion that they have the knowledge necessary to use SM. So, for males, it seems the primary drawback for them using SM in the workplace to enhance their learning is related to the ability to get the resources to support their desired learning outcomes.

### 11.11.2 Participant perceptions of SM for professional development

When asked about their belief that SM is compatible with professional development needs, 61.2% of the respondents agreed to some extent. About 71.1% agreed to some extent that using SM for professional development is a good idea. Similarly, only 68.8% of the participants had a PLN. The difference in the perceptions of compatibility and the belief that it is a good idea is reflected in a dramatic difference in the percentages. The difference signifies that academic librarians feel it is a good idea. Yet, some of them struggle with visualizing how it can be compatible with their needs.

Professional organizations frequently share updates about standards, events, and research using SM. Subscribing to their pages on SM and reading their posts is not hard to do. Reviewing posts from professional organizations, in some cases, only requires individuals to sign up for SM. Alternatively, it is possible to use tools like 'If This Then That' (IFTTT) to collect data without 'liking' a lot of people on SM. But setting up these services does require some time to learn how to use the tools. Therefore, according to the definition of PLN presented for the participants, it is possible to have a PLN without posting online. One can just monitor conversations.

Yet, the fear of SM is real. Recent activities online with deepfakes, impersonations of people who look real in video recordings, are an occurrence that adds a new layer of fear for SM users (Culliford, 2019). People are often sceptical of SM because of privacy concerns. For some, realizing that SM can be used for surveillance made them more cautious about the content that they posted online (Smith, 2018).

Then, there are issues with inaccurate information that is purposefully placed online to influence the public (Freedom House, 2017). As such, Perrin (2018) reported that concerns about social networking had led many adults in the United States who use Facebook to adjust their privacy settings (54%), take a break from the website (42%), and delete the app from their phone (26%).

Sometimes the line between using SM for work and personal reasons can be subtle. Amongst the participants, most agreed to some extent that using SM for work is a good idea. SM is an economical way to review the latest trends. Many people decide to separate the SM accounts that they use for work from their personal accounts

(Pinola, 2019; Smith, 2018). However, individuals who use SM accounts for work risk sharing their personal information if they do not switch accounts. In addition, accounts that are used for work may still be tracked even when an app is not turned on in mobile devices. This puts an individual's privacy at risk. Therefore, it is understandable that over 20% of the participants cannot reconcile the need for using SM to supplement professional development.

### 11.11.3 Knowledge of SM and access to resources

It is not a surprise that most academic librarians feel they have the knowledge to use SM for work and professional development. Academic librarians have a history of using SM to reach students to advertise services. Since SM has become an integral part of academic library services, academic librarians frequently develop the skills to use SM for work on the job. Furthermore, the personal use of SM is prevalent in the United States. Experiencing SM for private use requires similar skills.

A few participants said they did not feel like their jobs offered the proper resources to use SM for work. The meaning of proper resources can vary. For example, cameras and microphones are needed to produce videos. Approval for SM activities and computers and tablets are essential. Also, keeping up to date with SM can be time consuming (Hagman and Carleton, 2014). Regardless of the meaning of resources, it may be beneficial for librarians who want to use SM as a part of their organizational culture to collaborate with management to implement Baxter and Connolly's (2014) phases for the systematic implementation of Web 2.0 tools.

### 11.11.4 SM platforms

When categorized by site visits, Facebook (53.61%) was the most popular SM site in the United States (StatCounter, 2019). It is further noted that popular SM networks include Pinterest (34.56%), Twitter (7.11%), Instagram (1.42%), YouTube (1.33%), Tumblr (0.92%), Reddit (0.7%), and LinkedIn (0.22%). In common with the general population of the United States, the librarians in this study preferred Facebook. Twitter was also a top choice. It must be noted that although LinkedIn is not as popular amongst the general population, LinkedIn's purpose is professional networking, and it is listed by the participants. These results coincide with Perrin and Anderson's (2019) observation that LinkedIn is usually used by people who have been to college. The results indicate that whilst they are convenient, not all SM tools are suitable for providing professional development.

## 11.12 Limitations

This study has limitations. Most of the survey questions for the survey resulted in quantitative data. The survey was anonymous to increase the participants' likelihood of responding to the questions truthfully. Therefore, the researcher did not follow up on the responses submitted in the survey. Moreover, it would be good to know how librarians' perspectives about SM as a professional development tool have changed over time. However, to the researcher's knowledge, there is no specific academic librarianship study with which to compare this study. The number of librarians who participated in the study is small and is not generalizable to all academic librarians that are currently working. Finally, the survey was sent to listservs in the United States. It is assumed that the responses originated from the librarians within the country.

## 11.13 Future research

Several opportunities for future research are presented. Bruguera et al. (2019, p. 2) suggest, 'due to the constant developments of social media platforms and the increasing use made by society and its professionals, it is worth considering how research in social media and professional development has evolved…'. Academic librarianship needs a systematic review of literature that narrows down the methods of SM professional development and its results. Moreover, since this study focused on quantitative responses, there is a need to follow up with interviews or a focus group. Alternatively, another survey with additional open-ended questions should be developed. Examples of questions include the following: What professional development topics do you search for on SM? What strategies do you use for acquiring professional development on SM? How do you identify quality professional development on SM?

Two aspects of using SM for professional development were addressed by Singer (2015). These aspects were the impact of SM professional development on student learning and the application of techniques that are learned on SM. This study did not ask the participants about the results of their professional development. Nor did the study address how strategies that are discovered on SM are implemented. Whilst librarians may decide to organize and have chats or create posts about topics, there is no way to understand if the training is successful.

Studies like this one look at attitudes towards using SM for professional development. However, experimental research is needed to determine if professional development implemented via SM for academic librarians is effective (Ranieri, 2019). For example, is there a difference in the pre and posttest results of professional development implemented face-to-face and online via SM? Is there a difference between the professional efficacy of academic librarians before and after receiving sustained professional development via SM?

According to these results, males feel a need for more resources for using SM for professional development. One question that emerges is, what kind of resources are needed? What will be the impact of these resources? Why do some librarians feel that they need more support? Chawner and Oliver (2013) note that using SM is a skill that librarians need. As such, researchers and educators need to understand the type of education that current librarians recommend for new librarians to utilize SM in the workplace. Another question worth studying is what educational initiatives can be implemented to help academic librarians with more experience feel comfortable using SM for professional development. It is possible that providing some interventions can assist librarians with finding economical ways to supplement their lifelong learning through online learning.

## 11.14 Conclusion

In conclusion, the purpose of this study was to examine academic librarian perceptions towards using SM for professional development and the relationships between these perceptions and demographic variables. Understanding these perceptions and their relationship to variables can assist with designing educational interventions that help academic librarians to feel more prepared as professionals. Because of the nature of their work, educating society's future, and providing access to information, it is optimal for academic librarians to know how to have access to the most up-to-date and accurate information. SM can provide an economical way for librarians to set trends and to understand them. However, the key to moving forward with acclimating more academic librarians to SM for professional development purposes is understanding their beliefs and needs. Then, educational interventions can be designed to help them to acquire skills and information for safely maintaining their professional identities.

## References


Anderson, M., 2015. Men catch up with women on overall social media use. https://www.pewresearch.org/fact-tank/2015/08/28/men-catch-up-with-women-on-overall-social-media-use/. (Accessed 29 December 2019).

Anderson, M., Perrin, A., 2017. Tech adoption climbs among older adults. https://www.pewresearch.org/internet/2017/05/17/tech-adoption-climbs-among-older-adults/. (Accessed 29 December 2019).

Baxter, G.J., Connolly, T., 2014. Implementing web 2.0 tools in organisations: feasibility of a systematic approach. Learn. Organ. 21 (1), 6–25.

Breunig, K.J., 2016. Limitless learning: assessing social media use for global workplace learning. Learn. Organ. 23 (4), 249–270.

Brookbank, E., 2015. So much social media, so little time: using student feedback to guide academic library social media strategy. J. Electron. Resour. Librariansh. 27 (4), 232–247.

Bruguera, C., Guitert, M., Romeu, T., 2019. Social media and professional development: a systematic review. Res. Learn. Technol. 27, 1–18.

Chawner, B., Oliver, G., 2013. A survey of New Zealand academic reference librarians: current and future skills and competencies. Aust. Acad. Res. Libr. 44 (1), 29–39.

Clement, J., 2019. Social media usage in the United States—statistics & facts. https://www.statista.com/topics/3196/social-media-usage-in-the-united-states/. (Accessed 29 December 2019).

Culliford, E., 2019. Facebook, Microsoft launch contest to detect deepfake videos. Reuters. https://www.reuters.com/article/us-facebook-microsoft-deepfakes/facebook-microsoft-launch-contest-to-detect-deepfake-videos-idUSKCN1VQ2T5. (Accessed 29 December 2019).

Freedom House, 2017. Manipulating social media to undermine democracy: freedom on the net 2017. https://freedomhouse.org/article/new-report-freedom-net-2017-manipulating-social-media-undermine-democracy. (Accessed 29 March 2020).

Hagman, J., Carleton, J., 2014. Better together: collaborating with students on library social media. Public Serv. Q. 10 (3), 238–244.

Harrison, A., Burress, R., Velasquez, S., Schreiner, L., 2017. Social media use in academic libraries: a phenomenological study. J. Acad. Librariansh. 43 (3), 248–256.

Jeske, D., Shultz, K.S., 2016. Using social media content for screening in recruitment and selection: pros and cons. Work Employ. Soc. 30 (3), 535–546.

Kimbrough, A.M., Guadagno, R.E., Muscanell, N.L., Dill, J., 2013. Gender differences in mediated communication: women connect more than do men. Comput. Hum. Behav. 29 (3), 896–900.

King, D.L., 2012. Social media. Libr. Technol. Rep. 48 (6), 23–27.

Koontz, C., Mon, L., 2014. Marketing and Social Media: A Guide for Libraries, Archives, and Museums. Rowman & Littlefield, Lanham, MD.

Lampe, C., Ellison, N., 2016. Social media and the workplace. https://www.pewresearch.org/internet/2016/06/22/social-media-and-the-workplace/. (Accessed 29 December 2019).

Lin, X., Featherman, M., Sarker, S., 2017. Understanding factors affecting users' social networking site continuance: a gender difference perspective. Inf. Manag. 54 (3), 383–395.

Muscanell, N.L., Guadagno, R.E., 2012. Make new friends or keep the old: gender and personality differences in social networking use. Comput. Hum. Behav. 28 (1), 107–112.

Perrin, A., 2018. Americans are changing their relationship with Facebook. https://www.pewresearch.org/fact-tank/2018/09/05/americans-are-changing-their-relationship-with-facebook/. (Accessed 29 December 2019).

Perrin, A., Anderson, M., 2019. Share of U.S. adults using social media, including Facebook, is mostly unchanged since 2018. https://www.pewresearch.org/fact-tank/2019/04/10/share-of-u-s-adults-using-social-media-including-facebook-is-mostly-unchanged-since-2018/. (Accessed 29 December 2019).

Pinola, M., 2019. Managing your personal and professional online profiles. Lifewire. https://www.lifewire.com/social-networking-strategies-for-personal-and-professional-use-2378017. (Accessed 29 December 2019).

Ranieri, M., 2019. Professional development in the digital age. Benefits and constraints of social media for lifelong learning. Form@re 19 (2), 178–192. https://doi.org/10.13128/formare-25353.

Singer, T.W., 2015. The pros and cons of Twitter for professional development. Sage Connection. https://connection.sagepub.com/blog/sage-connection/2015/07/22/the-pros-and-cons-of-twitter-for-professional-learning/. (Accessed 29 December 2019).

Smith, D.L., 2018. Growing Your Library Career With Social Media. Chandos Publishing, Cambridge, MA.

Solomon, L. (Ed.), 2013. The Librarian's Nitty-Gritty Guide to Social Media. American Library Association, Chicago, IL.

StatCounter, 2019. Most popular social network websites in the United States in August 2019, based on share of visits. Statista. https://www.statista.com/statistics/265773/market-share-of-the-most-popular-social-media-websites-in-the-us/. (Accessed 29 December 2019).

Tifferet, S., 2019. Gender differences in privacy tendencies on social network sites: a meta-analysis. Comput. Hum. Behav. 93, 1–12.

Twenge, J.M., Martin, G.N., Spitzberg, B.H., 2019. Trends in US adolescents' media use, 1976–2016: the rise of digital media, the decline of TV, and the (near) demise of print. Psychol. Pop. Media Cult. 8 (4), 329–345.

Wilder, S., 2017. Delayed retirements and the youth movement among ARL library professionals. Association of Research Libraries. https://www.arl.org/wp-content/uploads/2017/03/rli-2017-stanley-wilder-article1.pdf. (Accessed 29 March 2020).

Young, S.W.H., Rossmann, D., 2015. Building library community through social media. Inf. Technol. Libr. 34 (1), 20–37.

# Part Four

# Applications and delivery

# Closing the digital skills gap: Working with business to address local labour market policy

**12**

*Catherine O'Connor*
Leeds Trinity University, Leeds, United Kingdom

## 12.1 Mapping the landscape

In the United Kingdom, higher education (HE) policy and the associated discourse puts a sharp focus on graduate outcomes. There is an emphasis on graduates being economically productive and also earning salaries at a certain level. Their achievement is measured through the Graduate Outcomes Survey (from 2018; previously measured by the Destination of Leavers of Higher Education Survey) and Longitudinal Education Outcomes (LEO) data and these metrics feed into the overall measure of institutional quality defined through the Teaching Excellence Framework (TEF). As policy has developed, so has the volume and range of literature which considers how graduate employability is framed, shaped, and developed within higher education. Policy is frequently countered by pushback from within HE about the negative impact on university education broadly, and on subject disciplines specifically, of such a transactional, or input-output, focus (Olssen and Peters, 2005). This case study focuses on the work being carried out at one Leeds-based university to address both policy and labour market issues. It opens by considering some of the key drivers in both national and local policy which have helped to shape the work being carried out at Leeds Trinity University (LTU), as well as the issues in responding to the graduate employability agenda. It outlines a specific labour market issue in the Leeds City Region with regard to a digital skills gap and a number of initiatives being carried out at LTU to address this. Finally, it considers the opportunities and challenges which have arisen in taking an ambitious approach to respond to policy and how they inform further developments going forward.

## 12.2 HE policy

Discussions, alerts, and concerns about a growing digital skills gap can be tracked back through numerous local and national policy documents, dating back to the Dearing Report (1997), where the link between HE and the need for skills required by employers was clearly made. In the last decade, there is a clear pattern identifying the

**Future Directions in Digital Information. https://doi.org/10.1016/B978-0-12-822144-0.00012-4**

issues being caused by technological change and increased use of digital technology, with the following particularly noteworthy:

- **Higher Ambitions: The Future of Universities in a Knowledge Economy** (BIS, 2009) focused on universities making significant contributions to the economy and identified the need for employers and universities to work together to address skills gaps.
- In the same year, **Digital Britain** (BIS and DCMS, 2009) discussed digital innovation and infrastructure broadly but also identified the need to develop digital skills at all levels.
- **The Digital Economy** (BIS, 2016) outlined the need for a clear understanding of the digital economy to inform strategy. This report was clear that the pace of innovation would always be a skills gap but a workforce with a clear grasp of fundamental skills would be best placed to tackle this.
- **Digital Skills Crisis** (Science and Technology Committee, 2016) recognized the need for the business and education sectors to work together to address the digital skills gap.

In viewing the local policy context in the Leeds City Region, this relates to the city itself, the wider region, which covers all of West Yorkshire, York, three districts in North Yorkshire and Barnsley in South Yorkshire, and the broader concept of the Northern Powerhouse. At the nucleus of this, *The Leeds Inclusive Growth Strategy 2017–2023* (Leeds City Council, 2018) is the local government blueprint to support plans for economic growth and this identifies sectors and locations for growth alongside regeneration, housing, skills, transport, and infrastructure opportunities. It identifies the creative and digital sectors as offering significant opportunities. The strategy is based around '12 big ideas', one of which is 'Leeds as a digital city'. Two policy documents address skills and the labour market specifically. New Skills for the New Economy: *The Leeds Talent and Skills Plan 2017–2023* (Leeds City Council, 2017) sets out how collective action can be taken to improve the supply of skills to the labour market. Additionally, the *Leeds Digital Skills Action Plan* (Leeds Digital Board, 2017), which was developed at the instigation of the Council working with a group of employers and education providers, outlines actions designed to create entry points to the sector and improve connections between employers and education. The second policy layer includes *The Leeds City Region Strategic Economic Plan 2016–2036* (Leeds City Region Enterprise Partnership and West Yorkshire Combined Authority, 2017) This identifies four strategic priorities, one of which is 'Skilled People, Better Jobs', which includes delivering a 'More Jobs, Better Jobs' programme to widen skills and progression opportunities and devising and delivering a programme of action to increase high-level skills. And, at the outer policy layer, *The Northern Powerhouse Independent Economic Review* (2016) identified four sectors where the north has 'prime capabilities' and the greatest potential for growth. Digital is included in this. Education is identified as a sector with important 'supporting capabilities'.

New Skills for the New Economy: The *Leeds Talent and Skills Plan* (Leeds City Council, 2017) can be seen as the document most directly relevant to the graduate community as a whole in that it sets out labour market requirements, the city's ambitions, and potential solutions to skills-related issues. The plan is positive in that it identifies Leeds as a city with significant economic growth and as a key driver of growth and development in the broader Leeds City Region, but it also identifies the risk associated with this economic success. It particularly highlights the potential impact of demand for skills outstripping supply and the lag this could cause in terms of productivity, inadequate skill levels, and worklessness.

Within the plan, universities are identified as key stakeholders with collective responsibility to address issues, including making 'firm commitments…to offer support to our city' (p. 5) and are urged 'to do more to ensure the supply of labour is adequate and appropriately skilled' (p. 12) and 'to work more closely together with business involvement directly in the classroom and the lecture theatre…' (p. 26). However, there is no assumption that the traditional HE model of undergraduate education is the answer to labour market issues. Indeed, comments within the plan are consistent with the Government's approach to furthering competition in the sector to drive performance. In this regard, the plan makes clear that the benefits of apprenticeships 'rather than prioritizing traditional academic paths' (p. 24) will be promoted and that skills are often held in higher regard than academic qualifications by employers. Such an approach makes it apparent that local policy brings its own nuances to the pressures universities are working under.

## 12.3 Evidencing the skills gap

In the Leeds City Region, there is a dual dialogue around digital and its influence—on the one hand focusing on the number of jobs which could disappear over the next 20 years as a result of automation and, on the other, highlighting the struggles of employers to find recruits with the right skills for job opportunities in the digital and tech sector. The Leeds City Region Enterprise Partnership and West Yorkshire Combined Authority *2019 Labour Market Report* projects that 34% of jobs are at high risk of automation (Leeds City Region Enterprise Partnership and West Yorkshire Combined Authority, 2019). This risk is potentially balanced by growth in digital roles. As of August 2018, 102,000 people were employed in digital roles in the region and the number of digital roles is expected to grow 10 times faster than other job opportunities (West Yorkshire Combined Authority, 2018). Whilst the *2019 Labour Market Report* identifies the strong recruitment need for specialist digital workers, it particularly shines a light on the 'misalignment' (p. 62) between the subject range offered by further education (FE) and HE and the profile of demand in the local labour market. It notes: 'the main determinant of the profile of take-up of FE and HE is individual demand which suggests that an important mechanism for addressing the misalignment is a stronger focus on careers support in order to improve learners' understanding of the relative employment and pay prospects associated with different occupational pathways' (p. 62).

In considering this statement in the context of HE, there are two points to note. Firstly, HE is about much more than careers advice so any action HE might take to address the digital skills gap must surely consider the issues and potential solutions at a deeper level than career advice. Secondly, the level of technological change in the jobs market would suggest that there is a need to consider that digital skills will cut across every occupation open to graduates. So how do universities embed digital skills across their curriculum and ignite interest, as well as advising about opportunities? This is a sphere in which universities find themselves in conflict between their role as organizations which society looks to as problem-solvers and perceptions that they are shackled by the performance agenda which government policy has imposed on the sector (Avis, 2011; Ball, 2003, 2012; Olssen and Peters, 2005). Not only that, but also some scholars take the view that universities have become less about 'enlightening, informing and engaging' (Boden and Nedeva, 2010, p. 50) and more about delivering the material which focuses on 'a narrow range of skills and competencies' (p. 50) with employers able to 'order "oven-ready" graduates' (p. 46) rather than take responsibility for training them. In such a context, given that the Fourth Industrial Revolution is set to 'disrupt nearly every industry in every country, creating new opportunities and challenges for people, places and businesses' (Department for Business, Energy and Industrial Strategy, 2019), this puts the emphasis very much on HE's role as problem-solver and innovator in the face of change. As noted by Harvey (2000), the knowledge, skills, and attributes which students acquire are part of HE's contribution to enhancing students and empowering them as 'lifelong critical and reflective learners' (p. 3). The focus, he therefore suggested, should not be about how to accommodate employability but how to shift the balance of power around this to learners. Gwata (2019) argued that the digitalization central to the Fourth Industrial Revolution brings challenges to traditional employment and education. Rather than a mono-disciplinary and increasingly narrow approach which sees a broad base of subjects early in education usually narrow to a single subject for degree study, there should be a shift to an interdisciplinary approach, with a focus on 'T'-shaped employees. Such employees have in-depth knowledge in a specialist area but broad knowledge outside of this. The challenge for HE is to find a way to develop students to see their future this broadly and beyond specific discipline and economic output boundaries.

## 12.4 Reacting to the labour market

The project being outlined here was shaped around working with employers to address a labour market issue and potentially develop opportunities for students by adding to their experience. It is therefore useful to consider the views of Aoun (2018) around the value of experiential learning as a 'two-way street between the application of classroom learning in the context of life and the application of real-world knowledge in the classroom' (p. 81). Purposeful experiential learning helps learners 'see their abilities, their present skills and knowledge, their predilections and their room for growth…as they better understand the world, they better understand their own minds' (p. 81). Harnessing this approach requires institutions to face outwards and work with the market to identify external expertise and develop existing and new industry partnerships to work collaboratively to address labour market issues.

It is worth a moment to view this approach in the context of the graduate employability literature. A significant amount of work has been built around graduate attributes and their definition and these are summarized in systematic reviews by

Artess et al. (2017) and Williams et al. (2016). Attributes can be seen as static, too fixed, and too generic but, if they are defined and developed based on the understanding drawn from both the proximal university environment and the distal labour market environment, then they can be viewed as more flexible. Such development then results from connections to both environments and a range of interventions that are either part of the curriculum, part of the wider university experience, or both. Shifting away from what might be viewed as a splintered, acquisitional, or tick list view of employability, other concepts take a 'whole person' approach through the notions of graduate identity, graduate capital, and career management. Broader views of the development and management of employability emerge when graduates and their attributes are looked at in a more holistic way and in the parameters of communities that graduates are/have been/could be part of (Holmes, 2015; Jackson, 2016; Tomlinson, 2017).

In the context of a skills gap it could be said that universities have to bridge these different views of, and approaches to, graduate employability in the form of intervention(s) to address specific needs. These interventions will be informed by specific labour market issues rather than being one-size fits all. Such interventions could be seen in the context of Harvey's (2000) work, to empower students through a variety of mechanisms, including choice in the curriculum and critical and transformative approaches to learning. His notion of the responsiveness of HE is directly relevant to interventions in the labour market to address skills gaps.

## 12.5 Institutional context and initiatives

LTU is a small institution with around 3500 students on campus, a strong focus on graduate employability and a course portfolio which includes Teacher Training, Psychology, Criminology, Sport, Law, Business, Media, and Journalism, together with the recent addition of Computer Science. The graduate employability focus is characterized through the provision of two mandatory and credit-bearing placements in every undergraduate degree. Through its emphasis on placements, the institution works with a network of more than 3000 employers and takes extensive feedback on the skills and attributes they require, how well students are equipped to address these needs, and how we might further develop this key area of work. This feedback is gathered at the subject level, meaning that course teams can respond directly to it through the inclusion of content and in the way they assess and support students. They are also encouraged to further consult and collaborate with employers through subject-specific Employer Advisory Boards. This means that employers are integral to the way LTU works and conversations with them are embedded throughout approaches to learning and teaching. It is against this backdrop that the institution has responded to employer concerns regarding the digital skills gap. There were two specific triggers for the work outlined in this case study. The first was a presentation by the Leeds City Region Enterprise Partnership on labour market data and the scale of the skills gap; the second was frustration aired by employers about the need for more robust responses to the issue.

LTU's starting point was to host an employer symposium in summer 2017. This, in itself, might not seem like a significant action given the institutional context. However, the event reached out to a group of specialist employers in the digital sector and started a conversation which resulted in a change to the profile of the portfolio and prompted further steps into Science, Technology, Engineering, and Medicine (STEM), beyond existing content in this area in Psychology and Sport. It was an event that resulted in the following actions:

- The development of a new Computer Science degree, which launched in 2018.
- The development and piloting of digital skills pathways across a range of programmes as part of the Level 5 Professional Development and Placement module (O'Connor and Sewter, 2020).
- The introduction of digital employer challenges as part of Level 4 placement preparation.

There were two clear messages from the summit which informed the overarching approach and in particular the second and third actions: firstly, employers took the view that 'everything is/will be digital', and, secondly, that they were discipline agnostic and therefore open to recruiting students from any degree. They were keen to promote that they had the expertise and infrastructure to train graduates as long as they could access candidates who were open minded and willing to learn. Whilst each of these three developments at LTU could be viewed in isolation, it is useful to take a thematic approach across them. For this evaluation, it is worth considering the opportunities and challenges of co-design; how to foster engagement with digital developments; and contextualizing digital applications. It is noteworthy that the approach taken in developments two and three was not about skills per se; rather, the intention was to work to support student awareness of broader opportunities, how to engage them with digital developments in the workplace and how we might develop their confidence in taking on new skills generally by introducing a new aspect to professional development content in their degree. As Wenger-Trayner and Wenger-Trayner (2015) note, 'professional occupations … are constituted by a complex landscape of different communities of practice' (p. 15) and, in the case of most jobs, there is now a digital community of practice present or looming. Except for the Computer Science degree, the developments were not necessarily seen as inputs which would allow students to break through 'boundaries of practice' (Wenger-Trayner and Wenger-Trayner, 2015, p. 17). However, the developments would potentially allow them to negotiate boundaries by increasing the range of practices they have engaged in and form the basis of reflection on a student journey that would 'provide material for directions, aspirations and projected images' (Wenger-Trayner and Wenger-Trayner, 2015, p. 19) of themselves. For example, arts and cultural organizations are potential work or placement destinations for Humanities students, providing a means for them to work in areas linked to their subject interest. By engaging such students with basic web design, it was considered that they would develop an understanding of a skill which would support them in disseminating work and understanding how to connect with different communities through online presence. All arts and cultural organizations have an online presence; by helping students understand how this online presence is created and populated, there is the potential to broaden the type of roles in such organizations which they can connect with and feel confident putting themselves forward for it. This approach was further informed by Tomlinson's (2017) concept of graduate capitals, including the importance of being able to access experience and then present the value of it. The work had particular regard to social capital (by potentially providing a means of 'bridging' (p. 343) across to the workplace), cultural capital (by supporting the potential for broader 'horizon scanning' for graduate employment opportunities), and identity capital (encouraging investment in self-development to impact on future employment opportunities).

## 12.6 Opportunities and challenges in co-designing interventions with employers

Programme, module, and content development in HE has traditionally been undertaken in-house, although a variety of practice around industry consultation, guest lecturing, and involvement in approval events has been increasingly used across the sector. The work undertaken at LTU in designing the new Computer Science degree and developing the digital skills pathways can be seen as ambitious and innovative for many reasons. The design process for the Computer Science degree and the digital pathways was turned over to industry from the start, allowing them to lead the process, a more radical approach than simply integrating their views during the design process. This approach was new ground for the university and the development was seen as significant given the local labour market skills gap and concerns that employers were unable to get the sort of graduates they wanted, even from specialist degrees. In the case of the digital pathways, it was considered paramount that students were able to connect directly with industry requirements, but with content contextualized to their programme of study, as a means of developing their understanding, rather than the development of content which was set in an industry context. The digital skills pathways project was also ambitious in the number of students it involved in the pilot—around 500.

In looking at the design of the Computer Science degree in detail, three key stages can be identified and these are illustrated in Fig. 12.1.

The first stage involved pulling together a group of employers and sharing with them how a degree is constructed, with the number of credits per level, the acceptable module sizes, and the LTU requirement to reserve 20 credits at Level 4 and 20 credits at Level 5 for Professional Development and Placement modules. We then asked them to consider how they would approach skills development at each level—what they considered as the foundation for Level 4, how they would develop in Level 5, and what they would see as the final building blocks in Level 6. In approaching this task, the employer group of 13 opted to sort themselves into three groups—software developers, software testers, and a mixed group of 'other' skills. After working up extensive lists of skills for each level, the groups were then asked how they would cluster the skills into potential modules and invited to 'name' the modules. This process resulted in a significant volume of information which was sifted by LTU staff and a consultant

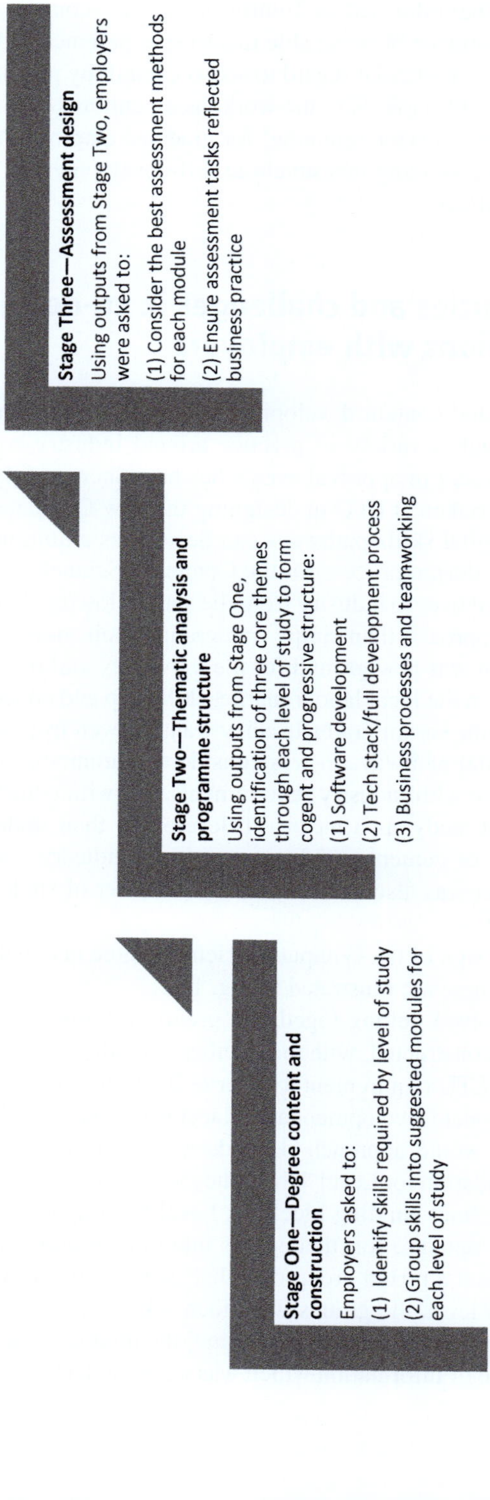


**Fig. 12.1** Computer science degree design process.

employed to support the degree development. This second-stage sift led to the clear identification of core themes: software development, understanding of 'tech stack' (full development process from client-side to server-side and tools required), understanding of business processes, and teamwork.

These themes were used to develop a cogent and progressive structure at each level which was shared (via the collaboration app Slack, which allowed the organization of information into key channels and the facility for comments from the group, and in one face-to-face discussion) to check for coherence, comprehensiveness, and applicability to labour market requirements. Many minor changes were made at this stage and then employers were invited to a further meeting—the third stage—to discuss how best to assess each module. This led to a collaborative and thorough discussion of the best way to introduce real-world and authentic tasks and assessments into the modules and, importantly, how to ensure that students integrated the learning from different modules. The integration driven by employers was not just in between modules at a particular level but also between levels, in order to reinforce the need for reflection and learning from looking back at tasks rather than just 'parking' them and moving on. One unexpected outcome of the richness of this discussion was that it essentially defined all of the learning outcomes for each module.

Once the results of this discussion were written up, the information was again shared via Slack and in one face-to-face discussion to ensure the group was happy with the outcomes before final paperwork was prepared for a course approval event. One of the employers involved in the design also joined the university team for the programme approval event. The level of employability and business-facing content within the programme was seen as both positive and negative by the approval panel. In the case of the latter, external academic panel members were concerned that it might undermine the essence of the Computer Science discipline. Through a process of negotiation and clarification, some minor changes were made to the programme but it has retained its strength as a business-facing approach, and the employers involved in the original design are still engaged as 'consultants' for feedback, as hosts for industry visits and as guest lecturers. The employer view of the design process was that it was significant in bridging the gap between industry and HE and that it allowed 'input' (initial, one-off but allows lasting impact to permeate through the programme) and 'steerage' (the opportunity for 'ongoing and light-touch nudges'). Whilst it was recognized that course design was not an everyday activity, the coming together of employers with the university was viewed by one employer as a form of knowledge exchange and something which should happen more frequently.

The framework for developing digital content pathways in web design, online communities, digital marketing, and basic programming was similar and was carried out as part of a pilot project funded by a Higher Education Funding Council (HEFCE) Catalyst grant. Each pathway was designed to introduce students to a new skill in a way that could be connected to their programme of study. The initial work involved bringing groups of employers together to develop outlines for the four pathways, which were based on a steady stream of feedback LTU received through placement feedback and involvement in other business events around key skills needs. Once the outlines had been discussed and developed, industry consultants were commissioned to work up detailed content in line with this framework. The content was reviewed by staff and by a group of student testers who gave largely positive feedback with some pointers for amendments prior to the content going live. Running in parallel with the content development process, placement module tutors were asked to consider how best to engage their students with the content, identify the pathway which worked best for their students, and how best to contextualize this content to their programme. The pathways were embedded in Level 5 Professional Development and Placement modules as it was considered that students would be open to the opportunity for enhanced development having already undertaking one 5-week block work placement at Level 4. Expert tutors, some of them with extensive industry experience, were engaged to deliver the content. In total, almost 500 students had access to the pathways as follows: Journalism, Media, Accounting, and Business—introduction to programming; Sport and Business and Marketing—digital marketing; Psychology and Criminology, Business and Management—online communities; Humanities—web design. Most groups had the content delivered in 2-h sessions over 10 weeks. Due to student numbers and constraints over when the project had to be completed, Psychology and Criminology students had the input delivered in a condensed format in a 5-h workshop. The project could have been run on a smaller scale and that would certainly have allowed more depth of preparation and individual responsiveness to student reactions. However, the project would likely have raised some of the same issues when scaled-up as it did when it ran at scale in the first place.

A piece of assessment linked to the pathways was included in the placement module portfolio but a deliberate decision was taken not to test competence in the skills themselves, rather to include a learning diary and personal reflection on the learning journey. The reason for this was that the most important outcome was viewed as enhanced confidence around new skills and, therefore, future openness to new skills. A decision was also taken not to introduce any feedback mechanism on the project over and above the standard module feedback (done through informal post-it notes and formal module evaluation questionnaires) as students have previously commented negatively on the number of evaluations they are required to complete. In the end, the best data gathered came via informal post-it note feedback from students and follow-up reflections from the tutors teaching the pathways. In summary, student views tended to be polarized at extremes but did not always remain consistent across the lifespan of the pathway. At one end of the scale, students considered the content as irrelevant, and as an input they had not asked for; at the other, they were excited by the opportunity to engage with the new subject matter and consider what it might mean for them and their future development. Some were able to see the potential applications of the content either in the context of their university work or external work or projects from very early in their experience of the pathway content; others took much longer to reach this point. It is this issue which came across most strongly in the feedback from tutors teaching the pathways, who reported that the key to engagement was through helping students find their ‘lightbulb’ moment. This was not a ‘one-size’ fits all moment and it was not a moment that occurred at the same time for all students who could be said to have ‘self-contextualized’ to a range of things, including previous work placement, outside work experience, links to the family business, links to assessment or having a strong connection to a particular task or piece of work as part of the pathway.

Reflecting on the project, it resonates with the notion of 'partnership pedagogy' outlined by Barrie and Pizzica (2019), an approach that covers curriculum co-design, co-development of curriculum resources, co-delivering of the curriculum and co-assessment with a range of partners (as appropriate for each stage) including 'community, industry…commercial providers…research institutes and students' (p. 148). Barrie and Pizzica identify the rapid development of technology as a key driver of disruption in the workplace and see partnerships as a way to 'keep us connected to external changes' and as providing 'an opportunity for the university to shape the future work context and create the jobs of the future' (p. 151).

## 12.7 Contextualization and engagement

The experience at LTU of introducing digital pathways or additional digital content across degrees has given some clear pointers for taking this work forward.

One focus needs to be on how students connect with new and broader content and how these connections are built meaningfully into their journey. A range of scholars have produced work which supports the case for further developing professionally-relevant skills and awareness but the justification for such developments is not the same as the meaningful and long-term integration of them into the student journey in a way which allows students to make connections. Jackson (2016) viewed the encouragement of interaction with a range of communities throughout the undergraduate experience as a means to fuel 'reflection, reconciliation and imagination' (p. 934) and help individuals construct a preprofessional identity. There is also a resonance with the work of Collet et al. (2015), who articulated the notion of 'interprofessionalism', signified by teamwork with an emphasis on 'highly collaborative problem solving where different professions learn with, from and about each other to improve outcomes' (p. 550). They argued that employability discourse needed to shift so the key focus is on how to enable graduates to perform in a diversity of workplace contexts and meet a range of workplace expectations.

The work of Fugate et al. (2004) also supports approaches which encourage openness to new ideas. Their dimensions of employability covered career identity; personal adaptability; social (networks and relationships) and human (knowledge and experience) capital. Their study considered employability in the context of job loss and job search and they viewed personal adaptability as the 'conceptual glue' (p. 18) that pulls the three dimensions together to result in employability, so the more adaptable an individual is, the more likely they are to develop social and human capital. The prominence given to adaptability is a key point to pull through into work which broadens student horizons and encourages engagement with the digital sector as it continues to evolve. In most cases employers are discipline agnostic, recruiting graduates from any degree background. Social and human capital are key aspects of Tomlinson's (2017) graduate capital, along with cultural, identity, and psychological capital. He viewed capitals as being acquired through graduates' lived experiences' (p. 340) and stressed the importance of accessing experience and presenting the value of it. In the context of the digital skills gap, it would be easy to consider human capital, which is focused around knowledge and skills, as being of greatest significance in closing the gap. However, such an approach would undervalue the role of social capital, networks, and human relationships, in giving graduates an insight into opportunities and the gatekeepers of those opportunities, and the place for identity capital in supporting the personal investment of graduates in their own development.

Any attempt to encourage students to develop their skillset and take a broad and flexible view on how and where they might enter the labour market can be seen as significant when viewed in the context of graduate capitals. However, the LTU experience suggests that the way this was embedded and introduced as part of the undergraduate journey is key. Trying to take what might be termed a 'light touch' to contextualization through examples of graduate pathways and an alumni case study did not prove sufficient to robustly engage students in content which, in various instances, was deemed as not relevant, seen as more akin to training than education, not required or not requested. Tutors teaching the content concluded that taking a problem-solving approach, starting with a case or issue, and building new skills development around this, would potentially help to create much earlier 'lightbulb' moments as to its relevance. Whilst some students were open minded and willing to engage in the unknown, for others the 'skills first, application second' approach was frustrating. Labour market responsiveness may be seen as desirable in policy terms and in a climate where graduate outcomes are a key performance indicator for the HE sector but students need to connect with the response and it needs to be embedded meaningfully in their undergraduate journey.

## 12.8 Visioning the future

In taking a view as to how student engagement with digital opportunities might be further shaped in the future, it is worth considering Jackson's (2016) notion of 'preprofessional identity' (p. 926) and the key role of 'relevant and interacting communities' (p. 926) as a major component of enhancing student learning. Students form their preprofessional identities through their 'membership, engagement, nonengagement and boundary and peripheral interactions with different communities' (p. 926). The key issue, however, when it comes to engaging students with the continuing impact of technology on the world of work and in virtually every workplace, is to convince them of the relevance to their development and career prospects.

In further considering this and how students and graduates might navigate communities of practice successfully, it is useful to draw on the work of Jackson and Wilton (2016) with regard to the need to develop career management competencies, including the forming of career goals, understanding the labour market, establishing job search skills, identifying useful and relevant learning opportunities and professional networking. Their ideas have resonance with Williams et al. (2016), who also identified career management—an individual's ability to navigate the labour market to achieve personal goals—as an increasingly important dimension of employability.

Bennett (2012) critiqued the way learning, identity, and work are discussed in academia and considered the development of self-identity amongst university students. She outlined that student motivation and interest will be high when they consider an activity to be meaningful and important, reinforcing the need for students to position their learning in 'relation to creatively exploring their future' (p. 27). She outlined that students need a future vision of self, motivation, and self-esteem in order to develop their identities. In the context of digitization, globalization, and deregulation, she asserted that there was a growing demand for graduates who can manage change, have an entrepreneurial outlook, who can contribute creatively, who are engaged in learning as a lifelong activity, and who can 'transform information and content into strategies and tools, and transform themselves from receivers of knowledge into participatory learners' (p. 36).

Reflection on the projects run to address the skills gap, framed by the notion of supporting students to visualize their future, resulted in a focus on many key lessons drawn from this case study. In terms of an undergraduate degree, employer involvement is a powerful tool for course currency, supporting students in growing their professional network and connecting them directly to communities of practice external to the university, as well as engaging them in the real-world and authentic assessment. This package informs core marketing messages for the Computer Science programme, meaning that students engage with this specific professional focus prior to their arrival at the university. For all LTU programmes, the embedded and credit-bearing placements are central to the messages prospective students receive about their programme of study. However, careful consideration needs to be given to how to achieve breadth, flexibility, and openness in the approach to development towards placement and transition to graduate employment. The notion of professional development is, of course, important but it would seem that it is personal development which is fundamental in approaches to encouraging students to take on board new skills and to be open to the wealth of opportunities which changes in technology are bringing to the workplace generally and to most graduate employment opportunities. Personal development cannot be imposed in isolation; it needs to be an integral part of the student journey. Bringing the three stakeholders in the graduate employability agenda—students, university, and employers—into the design, implementation, and reflection process, engaging all collaboratively in the way content is shaped and introduced around employability—is essential but not without challenges. Our learning from this project has illustrated the power of strong employer relationships in responding swiftly to labour market issues and what scale can be achieved by taking an agile approach. But the speed of reaction does not necessarily go hand-in-hand with being able to embed enhancements at the heart of the student journey. With that in mind, LTU is now working to develop interventions which make students part of that response. The institution is also looking at how it frames personal and professional development through our placement modules and, specifically, how we empower and engage students in shaping their journey. This means looking at how we embed engagement with digital capabilities and workplace developments as a central part of their student journey and allow them to take ownership of their development in this area. This is a longer-term project, but it is viewed as pivotal.

## 12.9 Conclusion

It is useful to summarize the projects discussed from the perspective of the different stakeholders in the work. From the employers' viewpoint, a range of organizations was able to be involved in two major projects aimed at introducing a programme and specific content designed to address a defined labour market issue. By involving them in all aspects of the work, from the initial discussion, the different stages of the design process, the approval process, and the launch, the partnership evolved, and strengthened. This provides a solid foundation for ongoing and future work. For the institution, the process has extended how it works with employers and provided a platform to reflect on how to enhance its professional development and placement offer in partnership with both students and employers, particularly focusing on problem-based learning solutions to introduce labour market issues and the associated skills and capabilities required. It has offered insight into how students engage with labour market issues and content designed to address them and the opportunity to consider how to embed flexibility and responsiveness into the student journey.

The work at LTU does not resolve the education versus workforce training conflict which continues to concern HE scholars but it may give shape to how the role of HE in 'enlightening, informing and engaging' (Boden and Nedeva, 2010, p. 50) can and should evolve in a labour market which requires a broad and multidisciplinary approach to support the pace of technological-driven change (Gwata, 2019). For the students involved, there are two angles. Those on our new Computer Science degree are benefitting from a programme which embeds employer involvement and which will continue to evolve in partnership with industry. For those who undertook one of the digital skills pathways as part of their second-year placement module, we are aware that the experience was more mixed. Those who achieved the 'eureka' moment as to the relevance of the content should benefit from being able to apply what they learned going forward and will hopefully be confident in the future about trying new things. Understanding how tutors worked to support students in achieving their 'eureka' moment will also inform how we work with students as we develop other projects. For those students who struggled to grasp the relevance of the content, their reflection on the experience may inform future thinking and prompt a different reaction when they are in the world of work. Of course, it may not have any impact. Knowing that does not deter us from future efforts at LTU; rather it informs reflection, further stakeholder involvement, and an even sharper focus on involving students in shaping their journey.

## References

Aoun, J.E., 2018. Robot-Proof: Higher Education in the Age of Artificial Intelligence. The MIT Press, Cambridge, MA.

Artess, J., Hooley, T., Mellors-Bourne, R., 2017. Employability: A Review of the Literature 2012–2016. Higher Education Academy, York.

Avis, J., 2011. More of the same? New labour, the coalition and education: markets, localism and social justice. Educ. Rev. 63 (4), 421–438.

Ball, S.J., 2003. The teacher's soul and the terrors of performativity. J. Educ. Policy 18 (2), 215–228.

Ball, S.J., 2012. Performativity, commodification and commitment: an I-spy guide to the neoliberal university. Br. J. Educ. Stud. 60 (1), 17–28.

Barrie, S., Pizzica, J., 2019. Reimagining university curriculum for a disrupted future of work: partnership pedagogy. In: Higgs, J., Letts, W., Crisp, G. (Eds.), Education for Employability. vol. 2. Brill, Leiden, pp. 143–152.

Bennett, D., 2012. A creative approach to exploring student identity. Int. J. Creat. Probl. Solv. 22 (1), 27–41.

Boden, R., Nedeva, M., 2010. Employing discourse: universities and graduate 'employability'. J. Educ. Policy 25 (1), 37–54.

Business, Innovation and Skills Committee, 2016. The Digital Economy. HC87. https://publications.parliament.uk/pa/cm201617/cmselect/cmbis/87/87.pdf. (Accessed 17 December 2019).

Collet, C., Hine, D., Du Plessis, K., 2015. Employability skills: perspectives from a knowledge-intensive industry. Educ. Train. 57 (5), 532–559.

Dearing Report, 1997. National Committee of Inquiry Into Higher Education. http://www.educationengland.org.uk/documents/dearing1997/dearing1997.html. (Accessed 13 December 2019).

Department for Business, Energy and Industrial Strategy, 2019. Regulation for the Fourth Industrial Revolution. https://www.gov.uk/government/publications/regulation-for-the-fourth-industrial-revolution/regulation-for-the-fourth-industrial-revolution. (Accessed 13 December 2019).

Department for Business, Innovation & Skills and Department for Culture, Media and Sport, 2009. Digital Britain. https://assets.publishing.service.gov.uk/government/uploads/system/uploads/attachment_data/file/228844/7650.pdf. (Accessed 17 December 2019).

Department for Business, Innovation and Skills, 2009. Higher Ambitions: The Future of Universities in a Knowledge Economy. http://webarchive.nationalarchives.gov.uk/+/http:/www.bis.gov.uk/wp-content/uploads/publications/Higher-Ambitions.pdf. (Accessed 17 December 2019).

Fugate, M., Kinicki, A., Ashforth, B., 2004. Employability: a psycho-social construct, its dimensions, and applications. J. Vocat. Behav. 65 (1), 14–38.

Gwata, M., 2019. To Flourish in the Fourth Industrial Revolution, We Need to Rethink These 3 Things. https://www.weforum.org/agenda/2019/08/fourth-industrial-revolution-education/. (Accessed 13 December 2019).

Harvey, L., 2000. New realities: the relationship between higher education and employment. Tert. Educ. Manag. 6 (1), 3–17.

Holmes, L.M., 2015. Becoming a graduate: the warranting of an emergent identity. Educ. Train. 57 (2), 219–238.

Jackson, D., 2016. Re-conceptualising graduate employability: the importance of pre-professional identity. High. Educ. Res. Dev. 35 (5), 925–939.

Jackson, D., Wilton, N., 2016. Developing career management competencies among undergraduates and the role of work-integrated learning. Teach. High. Educ. 21 (3), 266–286.

Leeds City Council, 2017. New Skills for the New Economy: The Leeds Talent and Skills Plan 2017–2023. https://democracy.leeds.gov.uk/documents/s165032/Talent%20Skills%20Plan%20Report%20Appendix%201%20-%20Plan%20V2%20110917.pdf. (Accessed 17 December 2019).

Leeds City Council, 2018. Leeds Inclusive Growth Strategy 2018–2023. http://www.leedsgrowthstrategy.co.uk. (Accessed 17 December 2019).

Leeds City Region Enterprise Partnership and West Yorkshire Combined Authority, 2017. Leeds City Region Strategic Economic Plan 2016–2036. https://www.lepnetwork.net/media/1119/leeds-city-region-sep.pdf. (Accessed 17 December 2019).

Leeds City Region Enterprise Partnership and West Yorkshire Combined Authority, 2019. Labour Market Report. https://www.the-lep.com/media/3311/labour-market-report-2019-final.pdf. (Accessed 17 December 2019).

Leeds Digital Board, 2017. Leeds Digital Skills Action Plan. http://www.leedsgrowthstrategy.co.uk/wp-content/uploads/2016/11/Leeds-Digital-Skill-Action-Plan.pdf. (Accessed 17 December 2019).

Anon., 2016. Northern Powerhouse Independent Economic Review. https://www.n8research.org.uk/media/Overview-NP-Independent-Economic-Review.pdf. (Accessed 17 December 2019).

O'Connor, C., Sewter, J., 2020. Closing the digital skills gap. In: Enhancing Graduate Employability, a Case Study Compendium. Advance HE, York.

Olssen, M., Peters, M.A., 2005. Neoliberalism, higher education and the knowledge economy: from the free market to knowledge capitalism. J. Educ. Policy 20 (3), 313–345.

Science and Technology Committee, 2016. Digital Skills Crisis. HC270. https://publications.parliament.uk/pa/cm201617/cmselect/cmsctech/270/270.pdf. (Accessed 17 December 2019).

Tomlinson, M., 2017. Forms of graduate capital and their relationship to graduate employability. Educ. Train. 59 (4), 338–352.

Wenger-Trayner, E., Wenger-Trayner, B., 2015. Learning in a landscape of practice. In: Wenger-Trayner, E., Fenton-O'Creevy, M., Hutchinson, S., Kubiak, C., Wenger-Trayner, B. (Eds.), Learning in Landscapes of Practice: Boundaries, Identity, and Knowledgeability in Practice-Based Learning. Routledge, Abingdon, pp. 13–29.

West Yorkshire Combined Authority, 2018. Campaign to Help People Get into Digital Jobs Launched. https://www.westyorks-ca.gov.uk/all-news-and-blogs/news-archive/campaign-to-help-people-get-into-digital-jobs-launched/. (Accessed 17 December 2019).

Williams, S., Dodd, L.J., Steele, C., Randall, R., 2016. A systematic review of current understandings of employability. J. Educ. Work. 29 (8), 877–901.

# 'It's all online!' Creating digital study resources for orchestral musicians

13a

*Matthew Naughtin*
San Francisco Ballet, San Francisco, CA, United States

## 13a.1 Orchestral beginnings

When Claudio Monteverdi created the precursor of the modern orchestra for his 1607 opera *L'Orfeo*, he probably had a skilled music copyist to create the instrumental parts for the 41 musicians and hand them out. Life was simpler then. But along came Bach, Haydn, Mozart, Beethoven, Berlioz, Wagner, Strauss, Mahler, Stravinsky, and Messiaen. Over the four centuries after Monteverdi, composers kept demanding continual increases in the size and complexity of instrumental forces available for their music. The ultimate result is that colossus of the musical world, the modern symphony orchestra, which can weigh in at over 120 players. The author has been intimately involved with that magnificent machine for over 50 years as a player, composer, and music librarian, and so has a significant interest in the complicated infrastructure that enables it to operate at full capacity.

Inevitably, as orchestras evolved in size and complexity, the task of copying, editing, and distributing instrumental materials to the players has become vitally important. In the days of Haydn and Mozart, music printing was in its infancy in Austria. A completed autograph score had to be entrusted to that humble packhorse, the music copyist, whose responsibility was to prepare a hand-copied part for each individual player and then distribute those parts to the musicians in time for the planned performance. One such copyist in Vienna, Johann Traeg (1747–1805), not only made copies for composers' use, but also made duplicates on the side to add to his own private catalogue of music for hire. Haydn and Mozart were aware of his pirated (and, due to Austria's lack of copyright laws, completely legal) editions, but necessity forced them to do occasional business with him. Mozart was especially upset by music copyists' habit of selling copies on the side and wrote to his father in 1784 (Anderson, 1938): 'I do ask you to have the four concertos copied at home, for the Salzburg copyists are as little to be trusted as the Viennese. I know for a positive fact that Hofstetter made two copies of Haydn's music. I myself have everything copied in my room and in my presence'.

By the 19th century, music printing and publishing had become industrialized and efficient to the point that composers could send their manuscript scores directly to a publisher, where in-house copyists would quickly create engraved scores and instrumental parts for sale to orchestras. By this time, each orchestra had some sort of library where music could be stored, and a librarian (usually a player in the orchestra)

**Future Directions in Digital Information. https://doi.org/10.1016/B978-0-12-822144-0.00034-3**

who would organize and distribute the parts. The author can only imagine the excitement (or dread) those librarians felt when a package with freshly printed parts for a new Beethoven or Brahms symphony arrived from Simrock or Breitkopf & Härtel, two well-known music publishers. It is not clear whether musicians would have had advance access to the music, but the parts would be passed out at the first rehearsal and it is assumed the players took them home to practise if they wanted. Then, as now, a well-prepared performance was the paramount goal.

The organizational structure of orchestras evolved as their size and cultural importance increased and by the 20th century, most orchestras had accumulated a robust support staff that included a full-time music librarian. Rehearsal time is a limited and expensive commodity in modern orchestras, and the last thing a conductor wants to do is waste precious moments running through a difficult passage several times so musicians can master the notes. So among the librarian's many tasks, one of the most important is to provide the musicians of the orchestra access to music for upcoming programmes, which they can study in advance to gain technical mastery of the material they will be rehearsing. When a conductor steps in front of an orchestra to begin the first rehearsal of an upcoming concert, he or she assumes that the musicians of the orchestra have already studied their individual parts and 'learned the notes'.

## 13a.2 Advances in technology

Until the advent of modern multifunction digital photocopiers capable of scanning and digitizing music, musicians had two options for studying their music in advance. They could (a) personally visit the music library and check out the actual sheet music or (b) request that the music librarian mail the music to them before the upcoming rehearsals. These options involved the inconvenience of accessing the music during business hours at the music library or making arrangements with the librarian for mailing it. There was also the very real danger of the music being lost in the mail or the musician failing to bring it to the rehearsal, leaving a void in the instrumentation, and forcing the librarian to somehow find a replacement part. By the mid-1980s, improvements in photocopier technology made it possible to easily scan and print copies of orchestral parts, allowing musicians to take home (or have mailed) disposable practice copies, while the original parts remained in the library. While this created more time-consuming work for the music librarian, the librarian's greatly improved peace of mind made it well worth the effort.

The next great advancement in technology to become available was the Portable Document Format (PDF), a file format developed by Adobe Systems in 1993 to present documents, including text formatting and images, independently of application software and computer operating systems. Based on the PostScript language, each PDF file encapsulates a complete description of a document, including the text, fonts, images, and other information needed to display it. This was a terrific boon for librarians, who could now scan PDF files of printed music at up to 600 dpi (dots per inch) resolution and transmit them from their digital copiers to their computers. Once the PDF files were stored on the librarians' computers, they could be sent via email to conductors, musicians, and other music librarians.

As a further advance, publishers could quickly send librarians PDFs to replace missing or damaged rental music, and in 2006 a whole new world of downloadable PDFs of public domain music became available online from the International Music Score Library Project (IMSLP), also known as the Petrucci Music Library after Renaissance printer Ottaviano Petrucci. The IMSLP website currently has scores and parts available for over 150,000 works and has become an invaluable and much-used resource for musicians and librarians.

## 13a.3 The website

So, life is good for the modern digitally savvy music librarian. Aside from the development of a viable, completely digital system for use in live performance (which may not be too far in the future) what more can we do to make orchestral musician's lives easier? The answer became apparent when the author served for 2 years as the interim orchestra music librarian for the San Francisco Conservatory of Music, which had recently moved to a new facility near the Opera House and Symphony Hall in the Civic Center district of San Francisco. At the time, the Conservatory had no dedicated library space for their orchestral collection and I worked out of a converted janitor's closet in the basement of the building. Since my hours were limited to music preparation, there was no easy way for students in the Conservatory Orchestra to obtain physical practice copies. The Conservatory addressed this issue by establishing a secure online file-sharing service using Google Drive. The author was able to upload PDF scans of orchestra parts to the Google Drive site and students who had established Google accounts through the Conservatory could view and download them on their mobile devices and computers.

While a bit unwieldy, this system appeared to have tremendous potential. The author quickly approached the Web Administrator in the Ballet Information Technology department, to explore the possibility of setting up a secure website for the musicians in the Ballet orchestra. The Web Administrator created a multilayer site using SharePoint, a web-based document management, and storage system that integrates with Microsoft Office and stores all its data on the Cloud. The clean appearance and intuitive formatting of the pages in the website is ideal for providing access to files and information for musicians who have widely variable skills in web navigation. Musicians obtain login privileges to access the site by contacting the Ballet Personnel Manager and receiving an invitation to establish a Microsoft Outlook.com account and password. Once the account is established, they have access to information on the season's repertoire, the rehearsal and performance schedule, employee benefits, scanned PDFs of individual parts for all the music in the season, and mp3 audio recordings of the repertoire. The site is also easy to manage. Uploading, editing, moving, and deleting PDF and audio MP3 files are quick and intuitive.

Fig. 13a.1 shows the home page of the musicians' website.

Fig. 13a.2 shows the second level with access to PDF practice parts for each program.

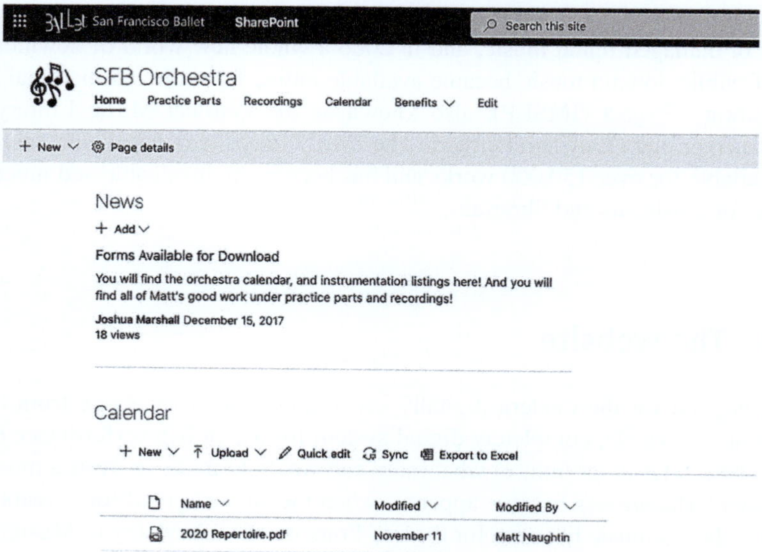


**Fig. 13a.1** Home page of the musicians' website.

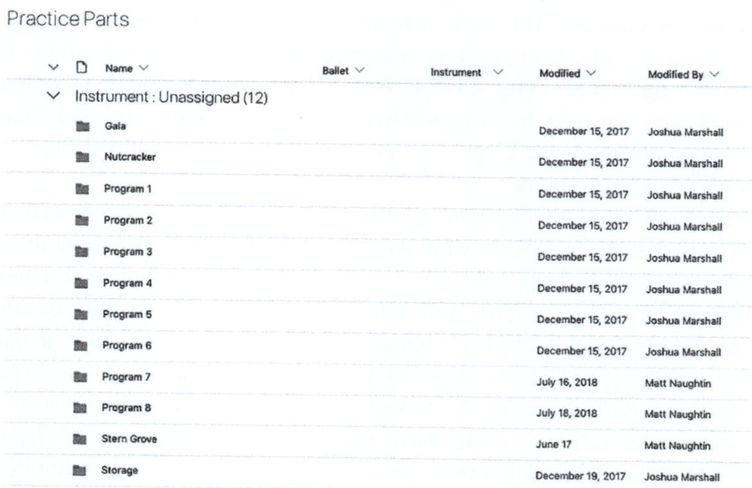


**Fig. 13a.2** Second level with access to PDF practice parts for each program.

Fig. 13a.3 shows the third level, where players can find their individual parts and view or download them to their computers, iPads, or other digital readers.

On this level, musicians can access reference recordings of the repertoire for each program to aid in their practice (see Fig. 13a.4).

Fig. 13a.5 shows access to the program folder; musicians can listen to and download mp3 recordings of previous performances of repertoire to help them determine the correct tempos and style.

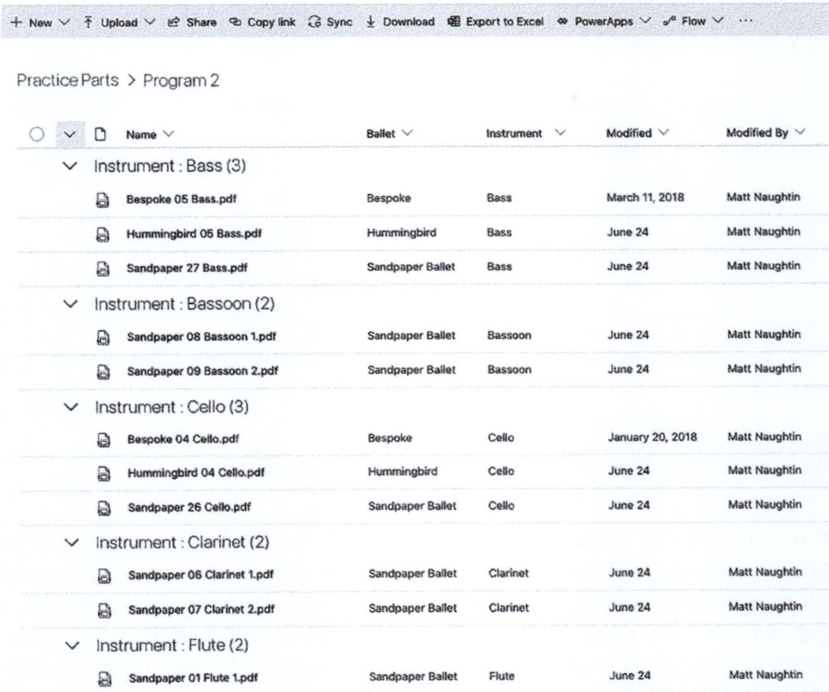


**Fig. 13a.3** Third level with access to individual parts.

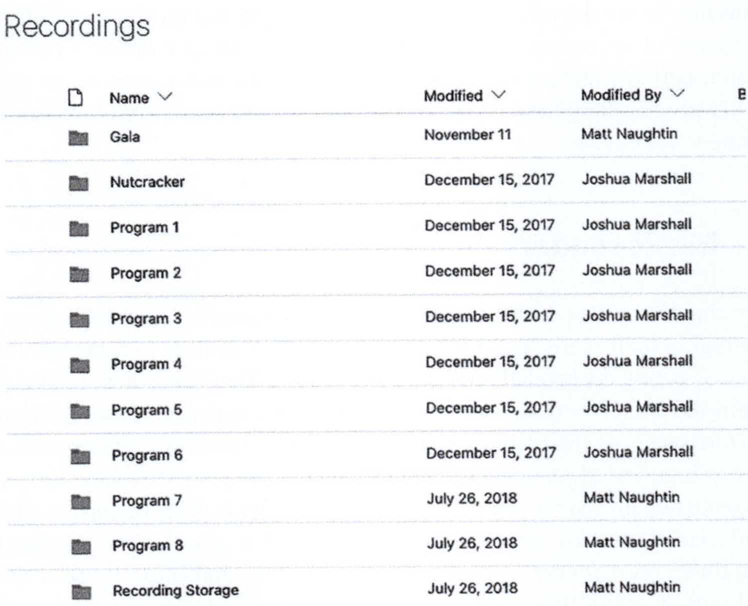


**Fig. 13a.4** Access to reference recordings of the repertoire for each program.

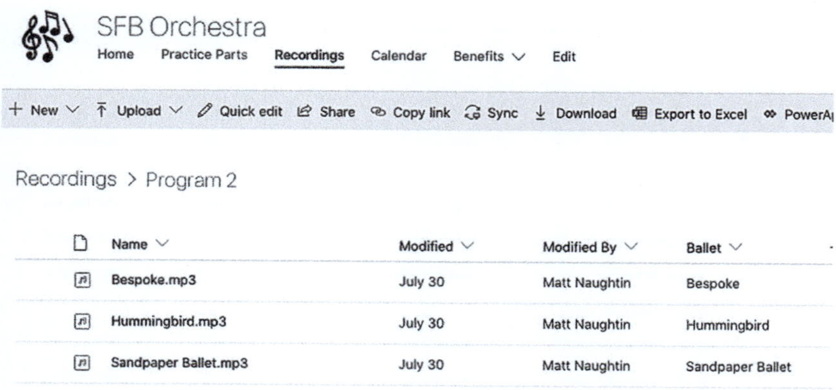


**Fig. 13a.5** Access to program folder containing mp3 recordings.

Having created this wonderful new web resource, the author's next task has been to get (sometimes digitally challenged) musicians to use it, encouraging them to set up their own Microsoft accounts, and log in to the site. Perhaps unsurprisingly, the younger players have taken to the system, enthusiastically downloading scans of their parts to their phones and tablets rather than making the trek to the library to get printed copies. But there is resistance among the older musicians who prefer to browse through the printed copies on library shelves and take music home to practise in its old analogue format. Puzzlingly, every one of them has their cellphone out the instant they leave the rehearsal hall or orchestra pit, but they are still intimidated by the process of accessing music online. While encouragement is given in trying the website, perhaps human nature will dictate that the older generation will retain the familiar process they have grown accustomed to and leave high-tech advances to their younger colleagues.

## 13a.4 Music readers

An interesting side effect of the digital revolution in music is the phenomenon of musicians bringing their iPads, e-readers, and other tablet devices to rehearsals and performances, ignoring the printed music on their stands. They have downloaded practice PDFs from the Ballet website and found it easier and quicker to use electronic foot pedals to turn pages on their tablets than wrestling with unwieldy paper scores, and the size and resolution of digital tablets has improved to the point that they are quite easy to read from when placed on a music stand. There is a wide array of apps available that allow musicians to access, edit, and perform from PDF scans of music on their tablets, including forScore, piaScore, Symphony Pro, Forzando, and MusicReader. These can be paired with wireless Bluetooth foot pedals that enable hands-free 'turning' of the PDF pages during performance. Beside the ubiquitous iPad, there are also now several touch-screen tablets available designed specifically for reading music. These include the GVIDO system, Padmu Pad 2, and the standalone MusicOne Digital Music Stand. All allow users to record edits in the digital files and include some form of foot pedal to facilitate turning pages.

This has raised interesting (and vexing) issues for orchestras and music librarians, the first being the necessary formulation of a Digital Music Readers Policy to ensure the devices are used correctly. Several orchestras have official policies banning the use of cellphones and other electronic devices on stage. These will have to be amended to enable musicians' use of their tablets during rehearsals and concerts. The musicians will also have to agree not to use their devices during services for anything but reading the music (movies, games, Twitter feeds, and online chats are prohibited). Since most librarians do not routinely produce a pdf version of every part they process, both due to time considerations and legal issues, the library will undoubtedly resist being obligated to digitize parts for players' devices. There is also the issue of making sure the editings (bowings, cuts, conductor's directions) in the digital PDFs match those in the paper copies on the stands. Should the musicians be required to mark changes made in rehearsal in both their digital copies and the sheet music on the stand? What about the brightness of the LCD screens? Will it have to be reduced when it would interfere with the lighting of staged productions?

## 13a.5 Legal issues

An important issue when posting copyrighted material online is the question of licensing restrictions publishers have placed on their music. A rental contract from a music publisher usually contains language similar to this: 'no portion of the materials may be copied or reproduced in any form or by any means whatsoever without express written permission'. The publishers' concerns are quite understandable; the advent of the photocopier led to a proliferation of 'pirate' editions among small community orchestras and choirs without room in their budgets for buying or renting music. But the Internet has now made it relatively easy for publishers to keep track of public performances of their prized assets, and small orchestras have come to realize they must 'toe the line' and have their performances legally licensed.

Librarians at larger, more established orchestras are a principled, law-abiding group who are scrupulous about maintaining good relations with music publishers. But the vexing dilemma they deal with for every concert is the fact that giving performances of copyrighted music *without* making at least a few photocopies or scans is virtually impossible. For instance, the percussion section needs an extra part, a stand of violins is added, a substitute player from out of town wants a look at the music before driving in—innumerable situations arise that require making both hard copies and digital scans of the music for the performance to happen. Publishers understand this, and, as one representative told the author when asked about the issue: 'you just do what you need to do to give a good performance. As long as our fees are paid, we'll trust you to do the right thing with our music'. So, the upshot of this is that in carrying out our duty to make sure that musicians can be well prepared and give fine performances, music librarians may occasionally break the letter of the law but they will always obey its spirit.

## 13a.6 Conclusion

The digital evolution of music production proceeds apace, affecting composers, music librarians, and performers in fundamental ways. As a composer, the author is already using synthesized sound libraries in conjunction with a digital audio workstation (DAW) sequencer to create realistic audio demos of my music rather than go to the prohibitive expense of hiring a live orchestra. The author is not alone in this—*all* of the advance recordings he receives from composers for rehearsing commissioned ballet scores are now digitally produced. As a music librarian, the salutary effects digitized music scores have had on work flow and effective use of time have been rhapsodized. The author still recalls a Major Orchestra Librarians' Association (MOLA) conference in 2005, where the idea that composers and publishers sending PDFs of orchestra scores and parts to be printed out could be a great time saver was introduced. The general reaction of the librarians was one of outrage at the idea that they could ever agree to become de facto 'music publishers', adding one more task to already heavy workloads. Now, 14 years later, some of the most popular break-out sessions at the conferences are those dealing with producing, editing, and printing digital scores and parts. And finally, for the performers, easy online access to practice copies and the increasing use of digital devices for reading music at rehearsals and performances has streamlined both the preparation and performance of their parts in the orchestra.

## Reference

Anderson, E., 1938. The Letters of Mozart and His Family, Vol. III, Translated by Emily Anderson. MacMillan, London.

# Library acquisition, delivery, and discovery for a creative university

13b

*Karen Carden*
University of the Arts London, London, United Kingdom

## 13b.1 Introduction

University of the Arts London (UAL) is Europe's largest specialist arts and design university and has around 20,000 students from more than 100 countries. UAL has six constituent colleges: Camberwell College of Arts, Central Saint Martins, Chelsea College of Arts, London College of Communication, London College of Fashion, and Wimbledon College of Arts. Together, and operating as a single university, these colleges have international reputations in art, design, fashion, communication, and the performing arts (UAL, Website, 2020).

Within our colleges, we have six libraries, three learning zones, and an archive and special collections centre. In our college libraries and catalogue, we have about half a million print books and approximately 1100 print journal titles (UAL, Library Services, 2020) along with numerous special collections (UAL, Special Collections and Archives, 2020) housed across the service, in libraries as well as in our specialist facilities. Our students have access to almost 50,000 e-journals and more than 17,000 e-books along with around 190 databases and many other resources including those in our (Green) open access repository (UAL Research Online, 2020). Our archives are of national importance (including the Stanley Kubrick Archive) and the archive is increasingly collecting born-digital materials and creating digitized content.

## 13b.2 The printed book at UAL

In a previous piece (Carden, 2017) where mine was the only chapter about print, I argued that declaring the death of the printed book—generally but particularly in a specialist art and design library context—was premature. I argued that the printed book is still a very persistent thing generally and especially in the creative sector. It seems determined to evade outmodedness and survive and thrive, despite the continual predictions of its imminent passing. This was illustrated by looking at the things that make our subject area and our students a little different. This time, I want to review our specific library collection—particularly the formats we are holding—in more detail and ask if this is changing, or at least beginning to change.

**Future Directions in Digital Information. https://doi.org/10.1016/B978-0-12-822144-0.00035-5**

When considering library users at UAL, differences include: the art school tradition; the browsing behaviour of our practice-based students; their nature and learning preferences; a lesser reliance on reading lists alone to guide their learning; and their seeming continuing preference for print where it is available. Last time I also looked at the resurgence of individually created novel print forms like artists' books and (fan) zines where the value of the book for its materiality was as relevant, or possibly more relevant, to our users as the content it might contain. I noted overall that the pace of change, such as the general move from print to e-resources, was slower for institutions like this than for many other kinds of academic library.

Reading lists are still not the primary means by which material is chosen for our libraries and there is still a great deal of professional selection and collection building by librarians at UAL, although this does vary across subject areas as some colleges teach subjects like Business and Marketing alongside the subject specialisms (for example, Fashion Marketing) and we also have teaching and research in other mainstream areas. But in terms of what we buy even for our general (rather than 'special') teaching collections, we acquire fewer textbook-like materials than most, and more subject-specific items like exhibition catalogues, film scripts, and older (but still highly relevant) material which may be in or out of print, or might arrive in the collection as donated items or in some other way. We buy items from small (often very small) and specialist publishers, and sometimes directly from individual content creators. Not all of this material can be sourced easily (or at all) from the usual library suppliers.

## 13b.3 Acquisitions and bibliographic activity

This difference leads to considerable acquisitions and bibliographic activity at UAL, and high levels of original cataloguing as we are often the first institution to catalogue a title or there isn't a suitable record to bring in from elsewhere. It also means that we are less able to benefit from the technological efficiencies, which come with purchasing a higher level of stock from big suppliers, such as catalogue records, processed shelf-ready materials, and backend utilities like electronic data interchange (EDI) and web services which allow target and supplier systems to exchange automated messages effectively and with less human intervention. Obviously, we do take advantage of these services from suppliers where we can and have put work into operating as smartly as possible for supply chain effectiveness, but the proportion of stock coming in this way is probably lower than in other higher education libraries, consistently hovering at about 60% over time.

Artists' books (one-off or very small edition works of art in a book or book-like form) and zines (self-published print items produced by individuals or groups) continue to thrive and we have growing collections of these in our college libraries. And of course, with many of the things that we need, because we have six colleges, we are often acquiring, cataloguing, and processing multiple copies of physical items—as although we allow intersite reservations between colleges for most things, they often require a copy on-site for local students and staff.

## 13b.4 Trends in e-content

Librarians talk mostly in terms of 'content' these days, rather than about books, journals, and other formats we now think of as analogue, such as audio-visual materials. But while, as noted, some of those formats are still important at UAL, since the previous survey in 2016/2017 we might finally be seeing more of a shift to e-content, quite a lot of it selected by students themselves. It is too early to be absolutely sure that we have reached any kind of true tipping point, but there is some evidence in the data we collect (mostly for SCONUL, but internal data as well) that things are beginning to change.

In Fig. 13b.1, for example, we can see that for the last SCONUL year the amount of cataloguing has reduced, and that this follows a similar decrease the previous year. However, it is still a lot of records that are being created in comparison to our size, and of those a significant and similar proportion over time (in Fig. 13b.2) is original cataloguing.

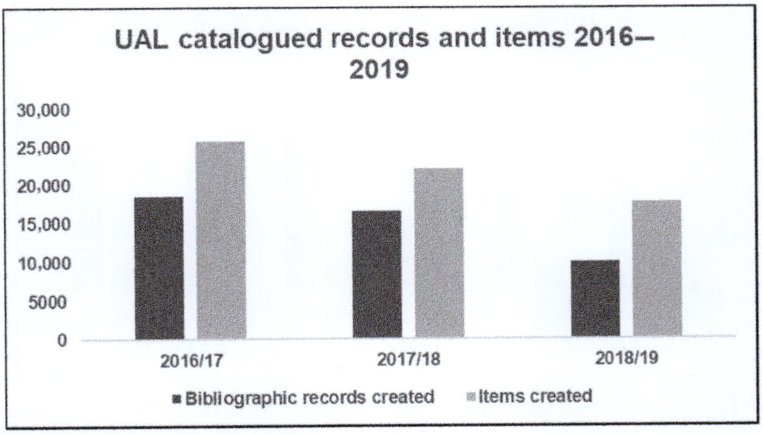


**Fig. 13b.1** UAL catalogued records and items 2016–19.

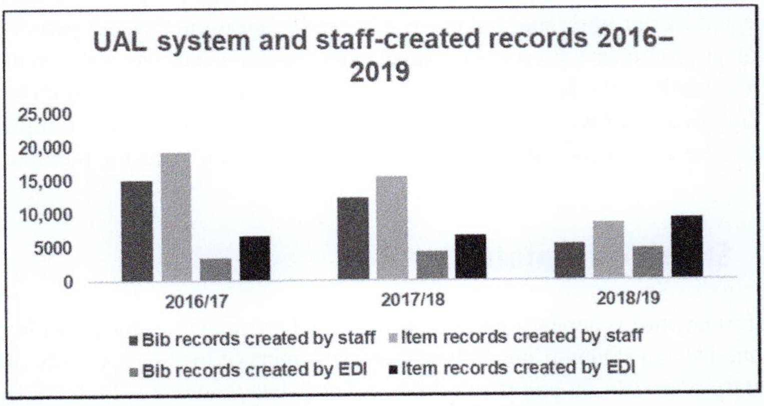


**Fig. 13b.2** UAL system and staff-created records and items 2016–19.

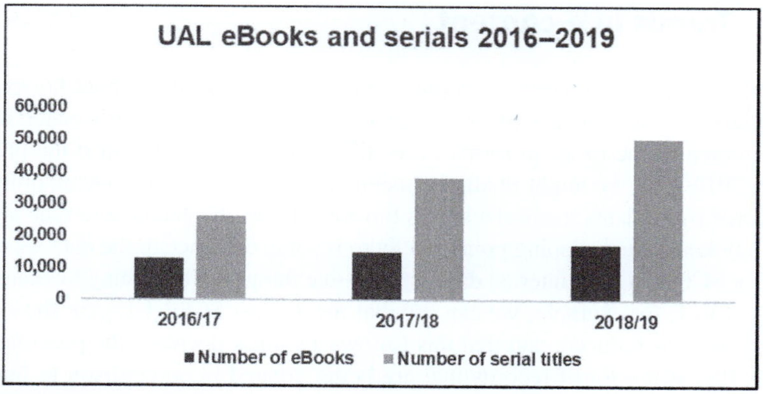


**Fig. 13b.3** UAL purchased e-books and serials 2016–19.

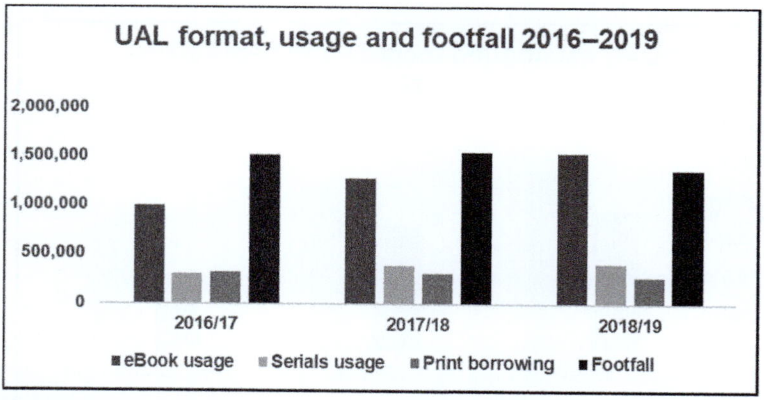


**Fig. 13b.4** E-book and serials usage, print borrowing, footfall 2016–19.

Over the same period, and illustrated in Figs. 13b.3 and 13b.4, we have seen other interesting changes. These include an increased number of purchased e-books (both those selected by our librarians and those selected by our users through patron-driven acquisition programmes with suppliers) and an increase in the usage of that material—especially e-books. This has happened alongside a fall in print borrowing (which is the first significant fall we have seen in this particular area) and a lower footfall, with 1.3 million visits to our libraries in 2018/19 from 1.5 million visits the previous year.

## 13b.5 Shifting formats

Another format shift is appearing in the audio-visual arena. All students, but in particular Art and Design students, are enthusiastic consumers of media especially film and documentary materials. In common with anecdotal data from other higher education institutions, the number of DVDs we purchase (and the use of those purchases) has fallen, as the number and amount we spend on streaming media services has risen. There will be a number of reasons for this particular change of course. These include a general user preference for streaming media of all kinds, as this is the way our current students are used to consuming moving images from services such as Amazon and Netflix. But another reason is because users simply no longer have the technology to play some formats at home. New laptops often have no inbuilt facility to play physical DVDs and require external drives as the only way to facilitate this, and some large retailers. One example is from the retailer John Lewis (BBC News Online, 2018) who has announced in recent years that they are no longer selling the equipment to play DVDs, although for now it is still possible to purchase Blu-ray players. This format shift has meant that we have had to maintain equipment in our libraries so that users can view the DVDs already in the collection, and this in turn will have an impact on their usage over time.

This format shifting has an impact on our physical and digital spaces, on our costs, and on the way our collections are discovered. In general, e-resources and streaming media are more expensive on a cost per item basis than analogue materials. They also attract both VAT and platform costs, and often have complex business models and arrangements for access and ownership. They need to be looked at differently in terms of a curated library collection in relation to preservation, as they are less likely to persist in our collections over time. There are complications for technology and rights issues, off campus services, partnerships, visitors, and overseas students. All of these things have to be managed, have influence on our human and budgetary resources and mean that we need to continually ensure that we are getting value for money in terms of usage.

In terms of discovery, shifting formats mean that this is not always as neat and tidy as we would like it to be. We started off by thinking our students needed everything to be discoverable in our catalogue. This can be time consuming with demand-driven acquisitions as it means loading records for users to find and trigger, and then bringing them out of the catalogue when the demand-driven period ends (or we run out of budget). We increasingly feel that this is no longer necessary, as students know the platforms to go to when searching for film or for e-books. For film and documentary material, they know to search on our major supplier's platform for these and we no longer list this material on our catalogue for them to find. But because we have a library management system (LMS) and discovery system running side by side at UAL (although they look like a single system) this means that some of this streaming/e-book content appears in our catalogue while other content is only hosted on the supplier platforms. Currently, this doesn't seem to be an issue for our users, but it is something to keep in mind.

At the same time, although formats do finally seem to be shifting, in our subject areas at least, print is still valued and we have to continue to resource it properly. Sometimes—especially in our curriculum areas—print is the only option or there are good reasons (materiality, image, and colour reproduction, even just 'look and feel') where it is preferred over e-content.

## 13b.6 Conclusion

Some of the changes that come out of shifting formats—like freeing up room on shelves—are positive as they liberate physical spaces for new material or other activities. Focusing on cost per use rather than acquisition cost can be helpful (but not always if the resource is vital to a limited cohort who feel it must be provided), as can committing to a philosophy where at least some patron/demand-driven acquisition is business as usual, as this fills gaps in collections that we may not even know we have, may diversify what we buy, and provides material almost immediately at the point of need. On the other hand, it does lead to uncertainty. Some of the business models (especially in streaming media where we are often purchasing licenses for access over a contracted period rather than perpetual content) require a shift in thinking from a managed library to a less demarcated collection. And there is a loss of control for librarians over what the collection of the future will look like in terms of format, as it is continually shifting. This is for us to come to terms with as a profession.

## References

BBC News Online, 2018. https://www.bbc.co.uk/news/business-45950477. (Accessed 01.02.2020).

Carden, K., 2017. Not only but also. In: Baker, D., Evans, W. (Eds.), The End of Wisdom: The Future of Libraries in a Digital Age. Chandos Advances in Information. Chandos Publishing, Oxford, pp. 191–196.

UAL Library Services, 2020. https://libsearch.arts.ac.uk/. (Accessed 01.02.2020).

UAL Library Special Collections and Archives, 2020. https://www.arts.ac.uk/students/library-services/special-collections-and-archives. (Accessed 01.02.2020).

UAL Research Online, 2020. https://ualresearchonline.arts.ac.uk/. (Accessed 01.02.2020).

UAL Website, 2020. https://www.arts.ac.uk/about-ual. (Accessed 01.02.20).

# Digital transformation trends in education

# 13c

*Sayeda Zain*
Mont Rose College, London, United Kingdom

## 13c.1 Introduction

In the 21st century, education is one of the vital elements of global competition, economic power, and political influence. The digital economy is rapidly evolving but the workforce often lacks the required digital skills to work in this new environment. Though higher education institutions (HEIs) are using digital transformation to provide educational services for various forms of learning, much work is still required in this area. The variable cost of business is also increasing because of the regular updating and replacement of technologies and the need to improve digital literacy on an ongoing basis.

According to Khitskov et al. (2017), digital literacy is the knowledge and skill required for the effective use of technologies and Internet resources. It involves digital processing, analysis, and storage of data and documentation. van Deursen and van Dijk (2011), citing Correa (2015), categorized 'four types of skills: operational, which is the ability to operate hardware and software; information, which refers to the capacity to search, select and process information on a computer; strategic, which is the ability to use the computer and the Internet to attain particular goals; and formal skills which refer to the capacity to navigate in a hypermedia context'.

To meet the demand of the 21st century digital economy, students need to develop independent learning, critical thinking, and effective use of information technology. Student expectations include finding skilled jobs in their relevant fields and earning a reasonable income after studying. They require access to the latest digital resources and best practice use of technology to be a part of the curriculum, which could help them to develop digital literacy skills. This is only possible if HEIs make the digital training of teaching staff a strategic priority.

## 13c.2 Student and staff digital experience

A survey was conducted by Knight et al. (2019) in which 23,500 students from 43 UK universities participated. This survey provided data on how students and staff use existing technology. The survey was divided into seven categories:

1. Digital infrastructure and provision: over 90% of HE students use their own laptops or computers for their studies and eight in 10 students use their smartphones. Around seven in 10

**Future Directions in Digital Information. https://doi.org/10.1016/B978-0-12-822144-0.00036-7**

use their university's own digital resources. One in 10 students need assistive technologies to study.

In response to these findings, universities have offered up-to-date computers, software, wi-fi, charge points, and assistive technologies.

2. Systems and devices: students want the latest systems offered. Half of them are not aware how the university is protecting their data, and only four in 10 think it is taking care of their online safety. About 16% of teaching staff and one-third of students mentioned they are involved in decisions about digital services.

   Universities now provide clearer guidance on data security, signposting support for all students in order to address issues concerning cyberbullying. More involvement of students and teaching staff is required concerning decisions about the teaching environment.
3. Physical and virtual learning environment: half of students and 27% of teaching staff think that classrooms are well equipped for digital ways of working. Half of the students and one-third of the teaching staff agreed that software is up to industry standards.

   So, universities are now moving towards providing well-equipped digital teaching and learning environments and up-to-date standards-based software.
4. Digital learning, teaching, and assessment: 75% of the students use virtual learning environments (VLEs) to do their coursework but less than half the teaching staff surveyed are of the view that VLEs make course materials easy to design and organize.

   About 95% of students access their teaching material through digital media. Teaching staff rarely use online environments fully while teaching, but two-thirds of them like to use digital technology more while teaching. Universities conduct regular workshops for staff to improve their use of VLEs. They offer teaching staff opportunities to use a wide range of technologies in their teaching according to their local requirements.
5. Digital learning skills: only four in 10 students think that their course is preparing them to develop the digital skills required in their chosen career. About a third of students have an awareness of what digital skills they need for their course. Students and staff both have to check with colleagues or online resources to develop their digital skills required for their courses.

   Universities are embedding digital resources and have started providing digital training as an integral part of professional development. Students are made aware at induction how digital skills will support their studies. 24/7 access is available to staff and students to an online video skill services in most of the universities.
6. Digital teaching skills: 44% of teaching staff have never searched for online teaching resources, 38% have never discussed teaching online, and 14% have never developed their digital teaching skills. A majority of staff mentioned that they need more time and support to learn and innovate their digital teaching skills. Only 15% receive guidance concerning their responsibilities regarding assistive technologies and 16% regarding student safety.

   Universities are allocating time for digital continuous professional development of staff. They have also introduced awards, secondments, and career pathways for excellent digital teachers. Training is available on demand regarding assistive technologies.

These survey results show that there is still much work to be done by HEIs. Students want to develop digital skills to be successful in their careers, so HEIs must provide them with training, guidance, and facilities. Teaching staff are also required to be more highly trained and digital continuous professional development should be mandatory for them.

Mishra and Koeller (2006) developed the Technological Pedagogical Content Knowledge (TPACK) framework. This comprises three components: technology, pedagogy, and content knowledge. These influence each other to create an effective learning environment. The development of this framework could be critical in supporting effective teaching with technology.

In essence, the TPACK framework works in the following way: while planning a lesson, first choose a learning outcome, which will then be the content. Then develop an activity to teach that learning outcome, which will be the pedagogy. Lastly, choose technology in support of developing that activity and this will help in students in their learning.

Benedek and Molnar (2015) aimed to develop content, methodologies, and structural changes to meet the challenges of knowledge-based economies. Digital curricula were developed using visual content. Students accessed competitive learning content, used flexible learning pathways, and became familiar with independent learning.

## 13c.3 Traditional vs technological learning

Some academics think that technology cannot replace the human factor in HE. The essence of teaching comes from the human dimension, which motivates students, understands their strengths and weaknesses, and accordingly provides them with help and guidance. Without the presence of the human factor, there will be a lack of interaction between the teacher and student. The lack of teacher input into the learning process has been shown to have detrimental effects on some distance learners. It has been observed that, as time passes by, anxiety or psychological discomfort resulting from learning at a distance can increase rather than decrease (Friedman and Deek, 2003).

> *The Internet has taken over. According to a 2015 UN report, over 3.2 billion people are plugged into the World Wide Web. Assuming a minimum purchasing power for anyone who can afford broadband Internet, that's over 50% of the world's consumers with healthy disposable incomes on a common, global platform.*
>
> *Monnappa (2019)*

Keeping in view the cost effectiveness and the reach of the Internet, educational providers have started offering large numbers of courses online. But there is still a debate about which medium holds more value for the employer and the student. There was a time when the employer rarely accepted online degrees and preferred those from a reputable bricks-and-mortar university. But now, as technology has transformed businesses, employers' views have changed. Now they require sophisticated and current skills from employees (Monnappa, 2019).

Online learning provides flexibility for people with personal and professional commitments. Courses can be accessed from anywhere and from any smart device. Learners choose ways to learn more effectively. Previously, the biggest drawback of online learning was that it does not allow interaction between students and between teacher and student. This issue has been resolved with the introduction of social media in education. Courses have become more interactive with the help of webinars and social media, which allow students to interact with other students around the world (Monnappa, 2019).

## 13c.4 Value for money

The Office for Students (OfS), a public body which acts as the regulator of HE in England, issued a Value for Money Strategy in October 2019. Value for money can only be ensured by improving the student's participation, experience, and study outcomes. In a digital economy, understanding of, and proficiency in, digital technologies is vital to a good career (OfS, 2019).

The role of HE is not job training but job enablement. HEIs must play a key role in ensuring digital literacy. Digitization creates more opportunities for choosing learning content and provides more possibilities for creating personalized learning pathways. There is still a huge skills gap in the labour market. To redress this imbalance, to provide students with value for money, and to satisfy regulators such as the OfS, HEIs must engage in long-term strategic planning to develop digital skills among students and teaching staff.

## 13c.5 Emergence of new technologies and pedagogies

Technologies used in designing online courses should be compatible with students' diverse needs. Students should be able to familiarize themselves with the online features of courses by using chat rooms, discussion forums, video lectures, presentation slides, and other facilities. The teacher's involvement is substantial while offering online courses, not least in developing a rapport with the students. They should use both synchronous and asynchronous methods while facilitating discussions. Studies show that students prefer synchronous communication methods as compared to asynchronous ones, but they need to be trained in the use of web cameras and microphones to have synchronous online discussions (Cranford-Ferre and Wiest, 2014).

Digital transformation in HE is not only about transforming existing products into digital ones such as creating video lectures or digital texts, but also about digitizing the operations of the educational institution such as student admissions, registration for courses and examinations, teacher allocation, and class scheduling. Many educational institutions now have digital strategies for both traditional and nontraditional students. Online learning helps to reach remote areas, providing educational opportunities to all categories of students.

The emergence of new technologies has provided flexibility in developing innovative pedagogies through online learning. With the introduction of Massive Online Open Courses (MOOCs), different social media platforms, augmented reality, and open educational resources (OER), HEIs have developed new ways of teaching and students have learned new ways of learning, including:

i. Blended learning: it is the combination of classroom time and online learning; a lecture is recorded, and students receive access to it so they can work through the material prior to coming to the classroom. The classroom time is used for discussions, case studies, practical exercises, and so on (UB, 2019).

ii. Multimedia and open educational resources (OER): OER are in the public domain and anyone can use them legally and can reshape them according to need. OER also appeal to people who are interested in becoming familiar with a topic but do not want to enrol in a course.
iii. Communities of practice: through social media, communities of practice are developed for students to discuss and share theories, challenges, and experiences and learn from each other. In this scenario, the role of the teacher is more of a facilitator and assessor.
iv. Student control and independence: through e-learning, students are responsible for their own learning. They can access course material from anywhere and at any time through smartphones, tablets, or any other smart devices.
v. Online assessment: students can be assessed through e-portfolios, computerized marking of quizzes, online formative and summative feedback, and peer assessment, which involves students reviewing each other's work (TEACHONLINE, 2018).

Pedagogical changes are continuously happening with rapidly changing technology. Innovative teaching methodologies continue to transform the educational experience:

i. Gamification: a set of activities designed to solve problems by using game elements to motivate students (Learning Theories, 2019).
ii. Cloud computing: cloud-based applications reduce infrastructure and IT costs, increase accessibility, enable collaboration, and allow organizations more flexibility in customizing their products both for their brand and for their audience (NetApp, 2019).
iii. Adaptive learning: this uses technology to provide customized learning experience to students. The digital tools used for this purpose are designed adaptively and algorithmically (Smart Sparrow, 2018).
iv. Artificial intelligence (AI): this can help in developing learning tools, which can provide guidance and explanation to students. The approach increases student efficiency. Some educational institutions use AI to provide students with information about admissions, financial aid, campus life, and similar activities (Fedirko, 2019).
v. Learning analytics: learning analytics use can improve learning and teaching through the measurement, collection, analysis, and reporting of data about the progress of learners and the contexts in which learning takes place.
vi. Microlearning: this deals with small learning units and short-term learning activities, as, for example, text, images, videos, audio, and games (Andriotis, 2018).
vii. Critical digital literacy: this is a set of skills, competencies, and analytical viewpoints that allows a person to use, understand, and create digital media and tools (Hinrichsen and Coombs, 2013).
viii. Teaching through audio-visual media: these media can be effective tools in enhancing teaching and in disseminating knowledge. They offer a reality of experience, which can stimulate self-activity on the part of the student (Rasul et al., 2011).
ix. Block chain: this is a technology which institutions can use to store, track, and use students' data. This technology can also be used to do authenticity checks, which can help to reduce cheating (Fedirko, 2019).
x. Virtual and augmented reality: this technology can be beneficial in student learning and development, though the cost can be higher. It is an accessible technology requiring mobile phone only and can be useful in medical, engineering, and science disciplines (Fedirko, 2019).
xi. Big Data: With big data management, it is possible to analyze and use each student learning experience to develop digital pedagogies further (Fedirko, 2019).

**xii.** Increased accessibility: HEIs are using digital tools to provide equal and accessible education to all students and especially students with disabilities. They are using speech recognition, audio, and video recording of lectures, while dyslexia friendly font is used (Fedirko, 2019).

**xiii.** Chatbot: through this technology, students can get rapid answers to their simpler, most frequent questions. This has reduced the load on phone lines and provided quick customer service to students (Fedirko, 2019).

Technology can help to develop new opportunities for teaching and learning. According to a report developed by the Open University and Norway's Centre for the Science of Learning & Technology (SLATE) 2019, the digital pedagogies that might transform education in the future are:

**i.** Playful learning: this strategy is suitable for both children and adults. It helps in developing critical thinking, problem solving, and analytical skills. This form of learning can take many forms like pretend learning, mobile learning, digital games, and developing playful values.

Minecraft is one example that enhances creativity, teamwork, problem solving, critical thinking, reading, writing, and history learning. It also develops business principles, and knowledge of science, technology, engineering and mathematics as well as global perspectives through different creative activities as a part of the game (Aurora, 2016).

**ii.** Learning with robots: working with robots is no longer a science fiction and using them for educational purpose is not new. Humanoid robots are teaching programming skills to students, because students desire to teach the robot how to do things without initially knowing how to do so.

A robot can take different roles in the learning process. It can be used as learning tool/ teaching aid or it can be a co-learner or a mentor. But a clear mapping is required to connect different activities with these roles (Mubin et al., 2013).

**iii.** Decolonizing learning: digital decolonization transfers decisions about how to use technology to the people. It helps, for example, by sharing history and empowering indigenous cultures.

**iv.** Drone-based learning: drones are proving to be useful in areas such as land surveying, farming, construction, and film making.

**v.** Virtual studios: digital technologies have changed the creative industries by the introduction of new tools. Virtual studios provide a digital complement to the physical studio. They provide an online exchange of ideas, feedback, and collaboration.

**vi.** Making things visible: digital tools offer a wide range of opportunities for students to express themselves and collaborate with each other. Augmented reality can be used to create holograms and computer-generated sound, text, and effects to enhance the student's real-world experience. Social media like YouTube, Twitter, Facebook, Google docs, and Padlet can be used to support collaboration in learning.

## 13c.6 Google and education

Google is the world's largest and most used search engine since its inception in 1998. It has played a vital role in transforming technology to impart education and knowledge, making it accessible to everyone. Google has contributed by helping educational institutions to become paperless organizations, to develop staff, and to initiate innovative ways of student collaboration. Google provides students with limitless possibilities by making available a wide range of information, learning material, and tools for their education. It offers a wide range of choices to teachers as well as students concerning reading and educational devices. It also provides hundreds of educational apps, many of which are either free or low cost and are widely used by students all over the world irrespective of their socioeconomic background (Brishti Technologies, 2018). Google products can be customized and are user friendly. They enhance productivity, efficiency, and effectiveness among students and teachers (Google, 2019).

## 13c.7 Google Scholar

Google has launched a free web search engine, which covers scholarly literature in many disciplines (Google Scholar, 2019).

## 13c.8 Google and digital literacy

Google has introduced many education applications, which work with Google Classroom. A few of them are as follows:

- **i.** Squigl: this helps develop effective learning.
- **ii.** Writable: this app helps students to become proficient writers. It contains hundreds of assignment templates. It works alongside Google Docs and Google Classroom to deliver timely and structured teacher and peer feedback.
- **iii.** PBS LearningMedia: this helps in enhancing curriculum goals by aligning classroom resources to state and national standards.
- **iv.** ASSISTments: this gives feedback to teachers and students once the students complete the assignment.
- **v.** Actively Learn: this helps in building students' literacy skills.
- **vi.** Additio App: this assists in managing day-to-day classroom activities and track student progress with digital gradebooks.
- **vii.** Aladdin: this can maintain electronic attendance records and simplify school administration.
- **viii.** Alma: this can help in tracking student attendance and performance.
- **ix.** BookWidgets: this can help in developing interactive quizzes and work sheets.
- **x.** Brain POP: this can engage students through animated movies, interactive activities, and playful games.
  Google (2019)

There are many apps in different categories such as:

- **i.** Coding and computer science
- **ii.** Creativity tools

iii. Digital literacy
iv. Family engagement
v. Instructional tools
vi. Language, art, and culture
vii. Schoolwide tools
viii. STEM (Science, Technology, Engineering and Medicine)

Google Classroom is a free web-based service, its aim being to improve teachers' productivity by creating, distributing, and grading assignments in a paperless environment.

## 13c.9 Role of social media in education

New technologies have changed the ways in which organizations and individuals engage with, communicate, and share information. Use of social media through smartphones, tablets, and computers has increased considerably. Social media tools are useful in enriching teaching material. Social media can be used as an effective teaching tool in HE because of their ease of use, availability, and affordability. Facebook is used by educational institutions to facilitate teacher/student discussion, and wikis and blogs have been used to collaborate on projects and receive rapid feedback. YouTube is used as a platform for students to create and share videos for their courses. Students also use Twitter to discuss course topics, with tweets being displayed on a large screen to encourage cross-group communication (Devi, 2019).

## 13c.10 Web 2.0

Technology has made it easier to communicate information to a selected or wider audience. Web 2.0 is a term used to describe various websites and applications that enable the creation and sharing of information. The most popular Web 2.0 applications currently in use for teaching and learning purpose are:

Twitter (microblog tool)
YouTube (video share)
Google Documents (administrative teamwork tool)
Delicious (social bookmarking site)
SlideShare (presentation storage)
Skype (instant messaging/VoIP)
Google Reader (RSS/feed reader)
WordPress (blog tool)
Facebook (social network)
Moodle (LMS system)
Prezi (presentation software)
Google (search tool)

In addition to Web 2.0, now there is Web 3.0, which means content, commerce, community, and context are all personalized and combined with vertical search (Molnar, 2014).

## 13c.11 Use of technology in special education

Everyone has a right to be educated. Students with disabilities or other special needs should have an equal opportunity to realize their full potential just like any other student without any disability. Online education made education more easily accessible to disabled students. For example, students on the autism spectrum, who may have difficulty concentrating amid the normal distractions of a classroom, or have emotional challenges that prevent them from maintaining appropriate classroom behaviours, can have an environment in which their ability to focus will not be compromised (Pinantoan, 2012).

The continuous transformation of technology is playing a vital role in providing all sorts of opportunities for these students. As there are diverse types of disabilities, so there is no single solution for all of them. Custom-made solutions are required to satisfy each group of students to enhance their learning experience (Dikusar, 2018). There are many ways technology can help students with special needs:

**Human speech recognition and synthesizing**: this technology helps those students who either cannot process visual information correctly or their disability does not allow them to use handwritten text.

Augmentative communication: this technology helps students with speech issues to overcome communication barriers (Dikusar, 2018).

**Text-to-speech software**: this software helps students with visual impairments by allowing them to listen to the text that appears on a computer screen. This programme can read anything on the screen irrespective of the format. Through this facility, the students can participate in online activities. They can use email, text, and can have immediate access to course materials. There are many free versions of this software available online, such as Natural Readers (Pinantoan, 2012).

**Visual aids**: this assistive technology includes screen magnification software that enlarges portions of the screen, where the reader directs the mouse; screen reader software that translates screen text to Braille; text-to-speech programs; and audio texts. These programs can be used by students of different kinds of visual disabilities (Pinantoan, 2012).

**Audio aids**: this assistive technology is helpful for students with hearing difficulties. The software includes sound amplification tools; alerting devices that use flashing lights or icons on the computer screen rather than sounds to signal users; close captioning for videos; and TTY (TDD) also known as Telecommunication for the Deaf (Pinantoan, 2012).

**Physical aids**: different technologies are available for students with physical mobility issues. These technologies assist them in completing their schoolwork, as, for example, including audio books for students who cannot physically handle books;

keyboard adapters such as key guards to prevent mistyping from tremors or loss of control (Pinantoan, 2012).

## 13c.12 Conclusion

There is a strong relationship between education, technology, and economy. Technology has completely changed the educational environment. It can improve literacy and the learner's ability to analyze and evaluate knowledge and the information they receive. Policy makers, strategists, leaders, administrators, teachers, students, business, and education entrepreneurs: everyone understands the importance of technology in education.

Technology is playing a significant role in providing education to people in developing countries. Though in the developing countries availability is still limited, some countries are trying to develop an infrastructure where people will be able to access education through e-learning. Adaptive technology is helping students to learn different skills according to their needs. It is making education accessible for students with special needs.

Educational institutions are designing flexible and customized courses to meet the needs of their students. 'What we see emerging is a perception that virtual education is part of the broader e-commerce revolution' (Farrell, cited in Friedman and Deek, 2003). In this era of the digital economy, a majority of the jobs advertised require some sort of digital literacy. HEIs are bound to change their curriculum and must include digital literacy. They need to train the teaching staff and should initiate digital continuing professional development programmes. This is important for the successful delivery of courses. Once graduated, a student will only be able to find a skilled job in the relevant field if he/she is properly trained according to the needs of the job market (Twining et al., 2013).

Digital technologies have made self-employment an attractive option because they provide entrepreneurial opportunities characterized by low start-up and marketing costs as the digital economy of microentrepreneurs, contract-based workers, and freelancers continues to expand. There is a need to promote the development of entrepreneurial capabilities in order to increase workers' understanding of how their skills might be applied to start a business.

HEIs are developing different electronic pedagogies such as MOOCs, OER, social media platforms, augmented, and virtual reality to impart knowledge. Google and other companies have developed hundreds of applications to be used in the classroom to teach, to assess, and to develop analytical skills among the students. These applications and social media more broadly are helping in developing students' interactions with each other. The students are not only learning while interacting as they sit in a classroom but also through these platforms they can learn from people around the world. The Internet has changed the world into a global village. HEIs have to evolve continuously to keep pace with the rapid changes in technology. Digital transformation has already revolutionized the society and the economy. Higher education has to embrace this change for further advancement.

## References

Andriotis, N., 2018. What is Microlearning: A Complete Guide for Beginners. eLearning Industry. https://elearningindustry.com/what-is-microlearning-benefits-best-practices. (Accessed 22.12.19).

Aurora, 2016. The Educational Benefits of Minecraft. iD Tech. https://www.idtech.com/blog/educational-benefits-minecraft. (Accessed 24.12.19).

Benedek, A., Molnar, G., 2015. Changing Teaching and Learning Environment by the Digital Transformation. ResearchGate. https://www.researchgate.net/publication/285056765. (Accessed 25.12.19).

Brishti Technologies, 2018. The Role of Google in Education. Brishti Technologies. https://www.brishtitechnologies.com/uploads/products/14884516500The_Role_of_Google_in_Education.pdf. (Accessed 25.12.19).

Correa, T., 2015. Digital skills and social media use: How internet skills are related to different types of Facebook use among 'digital natives'. Inf. Commun. Soc. https://doi.org/10.1080/1369118X.2015.1084023 (Accessed 02.05.20).

Cranford-Ferre, H.G., Wiest, L.R., 2014. Effective Online Instruction in Higher Education. ResearchGate. https://www.researchgate.net/publication/263620466. (Accessed 25.12.20).

Devi, K.S., 2019. Role of Social Media in Teaching-Learning Process. ResearchGate. https://www.researchgate.net/publication/330497773. (Accessed 22.12.19).

Dikusar, A., 2018. The Use of Technology in Special Education. eLearning Industry. https://elearningindustry.com/use-of-technology-in-special-education. (Accessed 21.12.19).

Fedirko, D., 2019. 8 Top Trends of Digital Transformation in Higher Education. eLearning Industry. https://elearningindustry.com/digital-transformation-in-higher-education-8-top-trends. (Accessed 22.12.19).

Friedman, R.S., Deek, F.P., 2003. Innovation and Education in the Digital Age: Reconciling the Roles of Pedagogy, Technology, and the Business of Learning. ResearchGate. https://www.researchgate.net/publication/3076800. (Accessed 25.12.19).

Google, 2019. Apps That Work #withClassroom. Google. https://edu.google.com/intl/en_uk/products/classroom/apps/. (Accessed 24.12.19).

Google Scholar, 2019. Stand on the Shoulders of Giants. Google Scholar. https://scholar.google.com/intl/en/scholar/about.html. (Accessed 30.12.19).

Hinrichsen, J., Coombs, A., 2013. The five resources of critical digital literacy: a framework for curriculum integration. Res. Learn. Technol. 21. https://doi.org/10.3402/rlt.v21.21334 (Accessed 26.12.19).

Khitskov, A.E., et al., 2017. Digital transformation of society: problems entering in the digital economy. Eurasian J. Anal. Chem. 12 (5b), 12973.

Knight, S., et al., 2019. Digital experience insights survey 2019: findings from students in UK further and higher education [online]. Jisc. Available from: https://www.jisc.ac.uk/reports/digital-experience-insights-survey-2019-students-uk. (Accessed 24.12.19).

Learning Theories, 2019. Gamification in Education. https://www.learning-theories.com/gamification-in-education.html. (Accessed 22.12.19).

Mishra, P., Koeller, M.J., 2006. Technological pedagogical content knowledge: a framework for teacher knowledge. Teach. Coll. Rec. 108, 1017–1054.

Molnar, G., 2014. Modern ICT Based Teaching and Learning Support Systems and Solutions in Higher Education Practice. ResearchGate. https://www.researchgate.net/publication/288826739. (Accessed 25.12.19).

Monnappa, A., 2019. Digital v/s Traditional Learning—Why Online Education Is Here to Stay. Simplilearn. https://www.simplilearn.com/digital-vs-traditional-learning-why-online-education-is-here-to-stay-article. (Accessed 24.12.19).

Mubin, O., Stevens, C.J., Shahid, S., Al Mahmud, A., Dong, J., 2013. A review of the applicability of robots in education. Technol. Educ. Learn. https://doi.org/10.2316/Journal.20902013.1.209-0015 (Accessed 22.12.19).

NetApp, 2019. Cloud Computing in Education With Cloud Volumes ONTAP. NetApp. https://cloud.netapp.com/blog/cloud-computing-in-education-trends-and-challenges. (Accessed 22.12.19).

Office for Students, 2019. Office for Students' Value for Money Strategy 2019 to 2021. https://www.officeforstudents.org.uk/media/336c258b-d94c-4f15-af0a-42e1be8f66a1/ofs-vfm-strategy.pdf. (Accessed 24.12.19).

Open University, 2019. Innovating Pedagogy 2019. Open University Innovation Report 7. https://iet.open.ac.uk/file/innovating-pedagogy-2019.pdf. (Accessed 02.05.19).

Pinantoan, A., 2012. Learning Difficulties: What Can Technology Do for Disabled Learners? informED. https://www.opencolleges.edu.au/informed/features/what-can-technology-do-for-disabled-learners/. (Accessed 21.12.19).

Rasul, S., Bukhsh, Q., Batool, S., 2011. A study to analyse the effectiveness of audio visual aids in teaching learning process at university level. Procedia. Soc. Behav. Sci. 28, 78–81. https://doi.org/10.1016/j.sbspro.2011.11.016 (Accessed 02.05.20).

Smart Sparrow, 2018. Let's Talk About Adaptive Learning. Smart Sparrow. https://www.smartsparrow.com/what-is-adaptive-learning/. (Accessed 22.12.19).

TEACHONLINE.CA, 2018. A New Pedagogy is Emerging… and Online Learning is a Key Contributing Factor. TEACHONLINE.CA. https://teachonline.ca/tools-trends/how-teach-online-student-success/new-pedagogy-emerging-and-online-learning-key-contributing-factor. (Accessed 25.12.19).

Twining, P., Raffaghelli, J., Albion, P., Knezek, D., 2013. Moving education into the digital age: the contribution of teacher's professional development. J. Comput. Assist. Learn., 246–437. https://doi.org/10.1111/jcal.1203 (Accessed 23.12.19).

UB, 2019. New Learning Models in Higher Education—Pedagogical Trends. University Business. https://universitybusiness.co.uk/Article/machine-teaching/. (Accessed 26.12.19).

van Deursen, A., van Dijk, J., 2011. Internet skills and the digital divide. New Media and Society 13 (6), 893–911. https://doi.org/10.1177/1461444810386774.

# Transforming reference work into teaching: From a librarian to an information literacy-oriented university professor

14

*Juan D. Machin-Mastromatteo*
Autonomous University of Chihuahua, Chihuahua, Mexico

## 14.1 Introduction

In this chapter, I examine different aspects of my career regarding my work in the development of information literacy (IL) initiatives. The first section of this chapter deals with the current dynamics of change affecting librarians. These are bringing forth an increasing number of opportunities that we librarians can harness to position ourselves in current learning institutions and environments, characterized by an all-pervasive, all-encompassing—presence of digital technologies. Next, I present a review of the issues around career changes and what can motivate librarians to change careers, as it is a change that I experienced myself. The second section of the chapter is about the practice of IL, with analysis and practical examples of the instruments that we can use to assess the success of our IL initiatives, together with advice on how and where to use them. Then, I present the instruments that I designed and used myself as a librarian and university professor still focusing attention on IL in my classes; I also provide a summary of the results gathered. In conclusion, I reflect upon the lessons learned from both perspectives: working with IL as a librarian and then as a professor. Given the practical instrument design and results gathered through their implementation, as well as the discussion and reflection of the lessons learned throughout my career as an IL specialist, this chapter will be particularly useful for IL practitioners wanting to enhance their own initiatives.

The chapter includes the presentation of data systematically obtained from the application of formal research instruments, personal experiences, and observations derived from my own experiences. Such personal narratives and reflections are framed in a self-study action research approach, which, according to Feldman et al. (2004) encapsulates the subject, their educational experiences and practices, as well as their roles as resources for research. Similar approaches, although not explicitly recognized by their authors as neither self-study nor action research, are evident in the reviewed literature as personal and professional journeys and reflections on professional library careers (Bagnall, 1993; Dougherty, 2001; Edwards, 2002; Fontenot, 2008; Johnson, 2002; Zemon, 2002). Although not always specified, action research is essentially connected to most IL research and practice (Machin-Mastromatteo, 2017).

**Future Directions in Digital Information. https://doi.org/10.1016/B978-0-12-822144-0.00014-8**

## 14.2 Dynamics of change for librarians

Networked information ecosystems and information and communication technologies (ICTs) have been acknowledged as amongst the most important factors driving library innovations. They create new dynamics, which give rise to diverse work challenges and opportunities that library and information science (LIS) professionals may be exposed to, transcending the traditional functions of our profession (Corrall, 2010; Kong and Goodfellow, 1988; Lancaster, 1982; Noh, 2010; Walter, 2008). This affects librarians' teaching roles, exercised through IL and research support activities (Bewick and Corrall, 2010; Corrall, 2010; Davis, 2007; Fowell and Levy, 1995; Sanches, 2019; Walter, 2008; Wheeler and McKinney, 2015), aimed at students, teachers, researchers, and citizens in general, depending on the type of library or information service in which they are based.

Designations for librarians have emerged, depending on their working domains and identities, such as para-academic, hybrid, blended, or embedded librarian (Corrall, 2010). Hybrid librarians are related to hybrid libraries, which work with both print and digital resources (Rusbridge, 1998); librarians' para-academic roles include resource-based instruction, learning, and supervision (Fowell and Levy, 1995). Blended librarians apply skills from librarianship, ICTs, and education (Bell and Shank, 2004) and thus require a combination of the skills from these three areas (Allen, 2005) in order to fulfil three functions: administrator, teacher, and member of support staff. Librarians must, therefore, develop a triple identity in order to perform such functions, particularly in university libraries.

Corrall (2010) clarifies that a hybrid usually refers to a combination of two elements, whilst blended refers to a combination of three or more. Embedded librarians are those who actively participate in instruction processes either as a partner of the teaching staff or by providing support to teachers and students (Association of College and Research Libraries, 2016). Shumaker (2012) highlights that embedded librarians' value-added contributions and activities, which take place in the same course environments (digital or otherwise), can include co-teaching, which is considered the most important aspect, as well as retrieving and reviewing the literature, participating in the curriculum of a given programme or course and even in its development, providing research and support to faculty and students. He also stresses that embedded librarianship does not imply repeating traditional library activities in other places; what it involves is offering librarians' skills for the purposes of educational activities.

LIS education tends to provide very good research and management skills, including research management (Corrall, 2010; Lambert and Newman, 2012), which are useful for librarians to fulfil their many tasks, including those that are related to their new roles in education. IL, an area of growing importance for the LIS field, is at the centre of this steadily growing teaching role for the librarian; hence, LIS curricula need to address these considerations or be updated accordingly, as it must comply with the state-of-the-art research in the field, national and international standards, as well as the realities of librarians' work (Corrall, 2010).

From her experience at the Sheffield Information School, Corrall (2010) recommends working with the LIS curriculum by questioning the nature of our profession, competencies, identity, evolving roles and career paths. Not all LIS schools worldwide offer courses about teaching or developing IL and perhaps fewer schools include courses related to teaching, learning, and education. Hence, many LIS professionals are not professionally prepared in their studies to assume a teaching role (Walter, 2008) and librarians highlight the importance of addressing this weakness in future LIS curricula including courses on IL instruction (Bewick and Corrall, 2010). It is also interesting to note the scarcity of specialized research addressing topics such as (a) how librarians learn how to teach; (b) ascertaining their actual knowledge of IL; and (c) how they apply such knowledge in their teaching practices (Bewick and Corrall, 2010). Although the previous statements may define the general global situation, LIS programmes in the United Kingdom that are accredited by the Chartered Institute of Library and Information Professionals (CILIP) include teaching and training courses (CILIP, 2013, cited by Wheeler and McKinney, 2015). Something similar happens in the United States since the 1990s, as most of the LIS programmes accredited by the American Library Association have courses related to teaching (Walter, 2008).

Houtman (2010) states that library professionals may not be prepared to teach. From her study in which she interviewed eight Canadian librarians, we can summarize some of the challenges related to our limited training in education and the dynamics of our work within a library. It was found that library professionals:

**(a)** provide too much information and too many demonstrations in teaching activities, which is hard for users to assimilate and presents challenges in structuring sessions
**(b)** are required to deliver large amounts of information in short sessions, or even in a unique session
**(c)** have difficulties in developing instructional designs, lesson plans, and classes
**(d)** lack strategies for working with different group sizes
**(e)** are required to show various software tools, websites and applications, so it is challenging to prevent sessions from being merely a demonstration with some educational value appended
**(f)** are not necessarily prepared for teaching given their experience in guiding users
**(g)** effectively reveal the importance of the teaching content to our users in their endeavours, in order to maintain their attention, engaging them, and enabling meaningful learning
**(h)** may not be trained to teach and educate, but techniques and theories learned are significant assets which aid learning 'as we go' although librarians are usually very good self-learners
**(i)** should find enjoyment in teaching others, presenting and speaking in public, especially because in previous roles and before working in libraries (particularly academic ones), these were not considered traditional functions

Some librarians may exhibit issues of anxiety when teaching, related to speaking in public, preparing for lecturing, handling difficult questions, having to manage large groups, lack of teaching training, and also because of the additional work and demands that teaching-related activities may exert on top of their other more 'librarian-like' duties (Davis, 2007; Walter, 2008). Wheeler and McKinney (2015) established that some of them might not be so confident about their teaching and do not see themselves as teachers, nor might they think of themselves as teaching, even if they do. Librarians can be successful teachers, as Bewick and Corrall (2010) found, when they surveyed 82 UK academic librarians, most were confident with their teaching and their knowledge about it, which they mainly gained from development programmes at their jobs, trial and error in their practice, peer interaction, conferences, as well as from short or extended courses although they highlight that the ideal would be that librarians get access to teacher education content within their professional training. According to Davis (2007), librarians who do not enjoy teaching cited issues of anxiety as the reason for this, but she found out that about three quarters of the librarians she surveyed enjoy it.

Nevertheless, we should accept that our lines of work are currently closely tied to teaching, as we help others and we strive to train our users to become independent, so they can solve information problems by themselves in the future; which is a value of our work philosophy that is closely related to lifelong learning. Thus, we have to reflect deeply upon our practice and on how we can teach information skills and about information, research management, and production to others. Apart from this, it is necessary to find out more about which educational content librarians should learn more about to enhance their teaching practices. Although such inquiry can be part of further research, the librarians surveyed by Bewick and Corrall (2010), provide us with a nonexhaustive list of content we should learn about to improve our teaching: (a) learning styles and abilities; (b) teaching theories, techniques, and methods; (c) educational planning; (d) curriculum work; (e) making our teaching dynamic, engaging, and interesting; (f) developing support materials and learning activities; and (g) learning to evaluate, assess, provide feedback, and enable reflection. The authors highlighted that the main weaknesses they found were on teaching and learning theories as well as in developing learning activities and few librarians conduct an assessment.

The challenges faced by librarians who teach are problematic and are not easy to overcome, but we need to do so, as society and educational institutions are demanding us to assume teaching roles. According to Walter (2008), during the past 40 years, curricular advances, university demographics and the role of ICTs in education have led us to this requirement and having teaching skills is a current advantage in the job market, especially in libraries. The development of such skills could provide librarians with opportunities for changing their career to full-time teaching although this requires both developing professional skills and committing to a professional teaching identity.

## 14.3 Career change

Given the need for librarians and their new roles, why would a librarian want to change their career? According to Lambert and Newman (2012), it was previously common for people to have a single career throughout their lives, but nowadays, we are more used to individuals changing career paths during their lives, even more than once. The factors motivating other professionals to change their careers to librarianship include common elements common to other careers, such as better opportunities, burnout, and the search for better working conditions (Lambert and Newman, 2012).

There are models that divide a person's career into different phases or stages. Hall (1976) divides careers into four stages: the exploring, establishment, maintenance, and declining phases. It is relevant to note that in the establishment phase, the individual shapes a sense of belonging if they are at an acceptable job and they have a wish to settle down.

Feldman (1988) developed this model to include (a) in the exploring phase, individuals evaluate their fields of interest and capacities; (b) during the trial and establishment phases, individuals find a job and adapt to the organization they are working for, although some anxiety may arise from facing new challenges and assessing the effort they must put into their work; (c) in a mid-career phase, the individual assumes upon more responsibilities and the role of mentor, but may enter a competing position with their staff; (d) in the late career phase, which includes maintaining and declining periods, strategic decision-making, and organizational problem-solving are key, whilst tension between the development of their organization and maintaining their values takes place. Zemon (2002) states that burnout is amongst the factors that affect career decisions towards the mid-career stage.

Phillips et al. (1994) state that librarians are more satisfied with their line of work and develop a stronger career identity as time goes by, as individuals invest in their careers and they will have fewer alternatives as they mature, although they found that career identity tends to be weakest for early (lowest) and late career librarians. Changing careers tend to be increasingly difficult with age, particularly because individuals make several investments (time, personal sacrifices, psychological, and financial) in their current career (Carson et al., 1996), so the possibilities for a career change decrease.

In reviewing the literature, I was surprised that one of my initial assumptions was completely disproven, as there are no sources dealing with librarians changing their career from a library position to a teaching one. Fontenot (2008) observed that the specialized literature dealing with librarians changing careers is scarce; and years later, this is still the case. Noh (2010) found that amongst the professionals he surveyed, there were some university teachers that changed their career to libraries, but not vice versa, and the majority moved from one kind of library to another. The trend of professionals from many different fields changing careers to librarianship might be very common in countries where LIS professional degrees are granted exclusively in graduate studies, as it happens in the United Kingdom and the United States (de la Peña, 2009), but this tendency is lower in countries where there are undergraduate LIS studies, such as in Latin America in general.

Some of the reviewed sources report career changes from various professions into professional librarianship (Deeming and Chelin, 2001; Nicholson, 2016); a library director position to organizational development work (Dougherty, 2001); from historian to librarian and then to programmer and entrepreneur (Zemon, 2002); from academic to public librarianship (Edwards, 2002); from librarians to archivists (Johnson, 2002); from a law librarian to a general academic librarian and then to outreach services (Fontenot, 2008); from teachers to librarians, which is a common change (Lambert and Newman, 2012); and from librarian to counsellor and therapist, but interestingly retaining her librarian's traits to motivate counselees' return to education (Bagnall, 1993). However, I could not find any source discussing a change such as the one I want to discuss in this chapter: from academic librarian to university professor; but there is a wealth of literature on topics such as career changes into librarianship, the motivation to become librarians, and change careers within the profession, and about librarians as teachers, which are mostly related to IL. Although I could not find other studies about librarians changing careers from working in a library to a higher-education teaching position, this change is not so extravagant because both are service professions that are about collaborating and helping others (Lambert and Newman, 2012); in both careers, teaching and education are amongst the most important processes or results from our work.

According to Noh (2010), there are many studies about what motivates people's decision to become a librarian (e.g. Bello, 1996; Deeming and Chelin, 2001; Lambert and Newman, 2012) and their career development within libraries and about librarians' satisfaction with their profession and employment; but claims that studies about career paths are rare in the information field. Bello (1996) states that the choice of librarianship as a career is not necessarily the first a person makes and, hence, librarians are led through this path because of experiences, the influence of others, or because there is no other choice available. Large groups of librarians claim to be satisfied with their jobs (St. Lifer, 1994), even studies with second career librarians have found high levels of satisfaction with their career change to librarianship (Deeming and Chelin, 2001).

Noh (2010) studied Korean librarians' career changes and determined certain patterns that influenced such movements, particularly that many of the librarians who participated this study came from different backgrounds, but they moved from one type of librarian position to another (e.g. from the public to academic librarian), then, amongst the most important reasons for career change include compensations, job conditions, and organizational culture. Interestingly, he pointed out that in Korea it is not common for professional librarians to get jobs outside of libraries, whilst there are library staff working without professional education in the field (18% of the librarians and 44% of the chief librarians he surveyed did not have studies in information science); both issues might not be so present in countries such as the United States and the United Kingdom, but they are in Latin American countries; where it is not uncommon to see library staff and even library directors without higher education studies or coming from very different professional backgrounds.

Edem (1999) studied career advancement obstacles for librarians in Nigeria, determining that professional requirements, institutional requirement of publishing in journals, the difficulties in climbing the organizational ladder, and librarians' educational gaps were amongst the main obstacles. Professional achievement has been important for academic librarians, as they produce satisfaction with their career, but there are few opportunities for promotions to advanced positions within libraries; particularly within libraries, because they are typically flat organizations with very few management positions and levels (Holder and Lannon, 2018). The issue of stagnation in the library can be frustrating; it can hamper work achievements and individual well-being and can cause dissatisfaction (Carson et al., 1996; Kong and Goodfellow, 1988; Phillips et al., 1994), which may move librarians to change careers. Particularly in the United States, some librarians have been granted faculty status after many debates in universities (Kong and Goodfellow, 1988), although this is rarely the case in the developing world.

Ball (1997) examines the growing issue of flat organizations that do not offer as many job security or promotion opportunities to employees as in the past, which is something that affects staff retention and motivation. Arguably, this occurs in many libraries, even university ones and may be amongst the reasons why librarians would wish to change careers, not just change employers. Fontenot (2008) states that despite the positive aspects related to reference work, it also entails some burnout and the individual may wish to decide to do something before showing their stress to their coworkers and patrons, such decision may involve changing their career, which he states may have a positive effect on the person. Davis (2007) surveyed more than 600 academic librarians and found out that more than half would consider changing their career.

According to Newhouse and Spisak (2010), librarians point out some unfavourable issues with their experiences working in the field, such as gaps in their education and training needs, working conditions, relationships with senior staff, high volume of work, lack of appreciation and feedback, low salaries, and working in rigid organizations, which are issues that may discourage many new professionals, because they clash with our-almost universal—mantra of 'librarians as agents of change'.

I became trapped within the reference librarian position throughout my LIS career (if I count my years as a student, but also working in libraries, that would be 17 years). I spent 2 years stuck after graduating PhD. The issue of being the sole reference librarian in the libraries I worked in started to weigh heavily, as many responsibilities depended upon me; I had an increasing number of disagreements with the library management. This resulted in an increasing sense of burnout, which motivated me to seek alternatives, enhancing my research career, by entering into a publishing overdrive, in order to have more work opportunities as a university professor. I already had a decade of experiences as an IL researcher and practitioner and delivered university courses at undergraduate and graduate levels as the main lecturer. Could I turn that in my favour and commit fully to research and teaching? In the next sections, I provide some consideration that may be useful for IL practitioners, as well as lessons learned from both perspectives regarding IL instruction, as a librarian and a professor, together with recommendations about the instruments we can use to assess our work from both perspectives and results from the application of those instruments.

## 14.4 Information literacy, its practice, and instruments to assess initiatives

The importance of IL for students, teachers, researchers, educational institutions, and for society in general cannot be overstated. Its continuing relevance is highly pertinent in educational environments for enabling and enhancing the use of information resources whilst fostering critical thinking, as well as facilitating and strengthening academic and research activities (Sanches, 2019). Librarians have become more immersed and their work more embedded in learning activities and even in the curriculum through increasingly formal IL activities (McGuinness, 2009).

IL as a research and practice area for librarians began in the 1970s and 1980s as an evolution of bibliographic instruction (Davis, 2007). Its concept and limits are still very contested, particularly with the emergence of many newer terms such as digital literacy, new literacies, literacies, media, and IL. These and many other concepts have been widely discussed and many sources refer to their subtle differences (I recommend Bawden, 2001 as a starting point). It would not be useful for the purposes of this chapter to add to that discussion. Instead, given the topic of this book *Future Directions in Digital Information* and the focus of this chapter, I will be using IL as a very broad and far-reaching term, given the fact that it is the original one used within LIS and also because of the ubiquitous nature of technology. Hence, throughout the rest of the chapter, I use the term IL to refer to basic information skills that an individual requires to successfully seek, use, and evaluate information in general, as well as those involving similar tasks in digital environments, using ICTs.

Reference librarians are those who provide support, advise, and train users to access knowledge (Reference and User Services Association, 2016). Given the characteristics of the Latin American country where I have worked as a reference librarian, we redefined this role as a way of raising awareness and institutional recognition of its importance; because, as strange as it may sound, in Latin America, it is very common to find only one reference librarian per library, even in university libraries. Another challenge they face is that the community they serve, in general, does not know what a reference librarian is. So, we renamed the reference librarian positions as information and learning development librarians (ILDLs) (Machin-Mastromatteo et al., 2014; Machin-Mastromatteo, 2015).

An ILDL's profile includes information retrieval, organization, management, and dissemination; mastery of ICTs (e.g. Microsoft Office suite and software related to information and research management, as well as digitization and digital documents) and information resources, so they can easily move within physical and digital environments; ILDLs should also know about knowledge management, IL, collection development, planning and management, intermediate statistical and research methods knowledge, command of English at an advanced level. An ILDL must have a bachelor's in LIS, but a master level degree is desirable, and it helps if the individual is a researcher in LIS. It is important to note that in English-speaking countries, LIS professional education is usually offered at a graduate level, but in Latin America, there are many bachelor-level LIS programmes.

Other desirable qualities in ILDLs are basic-level use of content management systems, hypertext markup language, social media, and use of audiovisual editing software. Personal traits must include independence for making decisions, proactivity, enjoying teaching others and a commitment towards improving users' conditions. ILDLs support the learning and research activities of all the kinds of users and hence they are information experts, which involve effectively working, evaluating, researching, planning, and providing training by considering information needs, types, structures, processes, technologies, and environments.

RUSA's (2016) document about professional competencies was very important for defining ILDL and our IL initiative. Of particular importance are those competencies related to the development of an IL initiative that impacts the institution where it is implemented, such as (a) conducting collaborative work; (b) establishing alliances with other stakeholders to strengthen library services, the IL initiative, and even positioning the library in such a way that it is present within the institutions' processes and decisions; (c) ensuring that IL is integrated to all library services, including training other staff, especially those that are not professional librarians; (d) implementing communication and dissemination strategies (mainly using social media and various promotional resources such as bulletins, alerts, podcasts, and videos to reach users in different spaces) to foster learning, participation, engagement with the library and showcasing the value of the library's services; (e) continuously assess and conduct research on the initiative itself, from its various stages such as planning, piloting, implementation, and evaluation of results.

As a parenthesis, it is relevant to point out another Latin American reality in libraries, which is related to issue (c) in the list above: a significant number of the staff do not have professional degrees; this includes those in charge of circulation services, cataloguing, and it might even include management staff. A way of alleviating this is to hire reference librarians with strong profiles, but as I stated before, this is sometimes limited to just one per library. First-world LIS professionals may find it strange that reference librarians perform the most specialized tasks in the library. If so, you must keep in mind that other roles such as liaison or subject librarians are not so present in Latin American libraries, where it seems that the reference librarian has developed as the sum of all these roles.

Conducting proper planning, piloting, implementation, and especially evaluating the results from the IL initiative are particularly important processes, because they will ensure that the IL initiative is capable of: (a) being useful for all kinds of users; (b) innovating, which can impact the IL initiative or the library, for example, ILDLs can make collection development decisions and they can even enable user-driven development; (c) fulfilling its objectives (especially that the user community is improving and that we are developing independent users); and (d) growing until we can completely embed it in the parent organization.

All these implications are challenging to handle, and they involve much work, but these recommendations emerge from my experiences coordinating IL initiatives and training colleagues. The topics that colleagues wish to improve are, in no particular order: (a) strategies for searching in academic databases and their new tools; (b) knowing more about the resources that are available for each institution; (c) learning about new ICTs and resources; (d) generally improving teaching skills and learning strategies they can apply; (e) knowing more about open access (OA) databases and resources; (f) increasing the portfolio of information resources and tools; and (g) optimizing the time taken over information seeking.

The remainder of this chapter will have a practical focus on designing and using instruments for assessing and measuring IL initiatives, from the perspective of a university librarian and a university professor. In planning, it is useful to write a short document where we set the bases for our IL programme. Justification is a good place to start, as we would do for a research project: by determining and listing the main audience for, and the stakeholders, detailing what they are, how they can affect, benefit or profit from the programme. Then, we determine our users' needs from the perspectives of existing and potential users, keeping in mind the needs of both the institution and the surrounding community.

The programme must respond to the following questions: what, who, for whom, how, for what, when, in which ways, and with which resources; as we have defined our stakeholders in a previous step, a SWOT Analysis can be a very useful tool. Other instruments we can employ at the planning stage are user studies and usage statistics, analyzing frequently asked questions, and conducting formal interviews with key members of each stakeholder group. Interviewing the teaching staff has two aims: (a) determining their needs and what we can do for them (e.g. discovering the information deficiencies of their students); and (b) involve them as allies in the development of the IL programme. It is important to analyze institutional documents and plans because institutional characteristics and endeavours can assist in distinguishing and then fulfilling institutional needs; having this kind of approach helps to find ways of including an IL philosophy in future institutional documents, such as mission, strategic plans and policies, otherwise known as 'infiltrating IL'. We can also see this as incorporating the library through IL to an institution, the essence of embedded librarianship, as summarized by Shumaker (2012).

It is necessary to assess the library's IL activities in order to determine if the programme is working and fulfilling its purpose and objectives to evaluate the extent to which our users are learning and are satisfied with it. In order to measure learning and satisfaction which is arguably more difficult to do, I suggest the use of different kinds of instruments that are presented in Table 14.1. The first column shows the different instruments, the second state the corresponding type of instrument (quantitative and/or qualitative), the third establishes what each instrument measures (learning and/or satisfaction), and each instrument's application mode (individual and/or in group). In the next section, I include two examples of questionnaires used.

These instruments can be used to evaluate the IL initiative and to do so is vital, as I highlighted above, because we need to determine if our users are learning with our IL activities and if they are satisfied. Conducting such evaluation allow us to gather evidence and data from our work, which can be useful for accreditation and research purposes; it can also help in establishing or developing institutional indicators. Although I focus on evaluating learning (which can have cognitive, emotional, and social implications) and satisfaction, Table 14.1 includes other aspects that these instruments can help in evaluating. Apart from deciding the elements we wish to evaluate, before designing or adapting instruments, it is useful to question why we are going to evaluate our IL activities, by answering questions such as what to evaluate, what have students learned, how they feel about it, are they actually learning, are we really measuring what we intend to measure (validity and trustworthiness), is our way of evaluating consistent with IL standards, how challenging are the tasks we are using for the evaluation, are we considering different IL skills/levels of difficulty, will everything we are doing be useful for the workplace/lifelong learning (Lau, 2006).

**Table 14.1** Types of instruments used to evaluate IL initiatives.

| Instrument | Type | Measures and/or assesses | Application |
|---|---|---|---|
| Questionnaire or survey applied before starting the workshop (diagnostic pretest) | Quantitative/ qualitative | Learning and satisfaction | Individual |
| Follow-up questionnaire or survey after finishing the workshop (posttest) | Quantitative/ qualitative | Learning and satisfaction | Individual |
| Unique questionnaire or survey after finishing the workshop (posttest) | Quantitative/ qualitative | Learning and satisfaction. It may be less tiresome for participants to fill out only one instrument. If this is the case, it is best to pick this type | Individual |
| Learning evidence or students' assignment portfolios | Mixed methods | Learning, skills, results, understanding. Evidence can consist of essays, presentations, screenshots, videos or audio | Individual |
| Interviews | Qualitative | Learning and satisfaction of students. Interviews also allow the gathering of insights into skills improvement, feelings, opinions, and perceptions of students | Individual |
| Focus group | Qualitative | Learning, satisfaction, level of improvement, feelings, opinions, and perceptions. It can be combined with a survey, questionnaire, or an activity. Focus groups are best implemented if participants have experienced several IL workshops or a full training programme | Group |
| Recording participants' computer screens during workshops | Mixed methods | Learning, steps taken to solve a problem, common errors, concentration, interest in the workshop, and understanding. The use of these recordings must be done with students' consent and adherence to ethical and privacy policies and agreements. Their analysis is time consuming | Individual |

*Continued*

**Table 14.1** Types of instruments used to evaluate IL initiatives—cont'd

| Instrument | Type | Measures and/or assesses | Application |
|---|---|---|---|
| Standardized tests | Quantitative | Learning, level of competence, steps taken to solve a problem. There are few IL standardized tests, but they are an outstanding complement to our instruments and some of them compare our results to other institutions (see Lau et al., 2016) | Individual |
| Rubric | Quantitative | Learning, problem solving and application of knowledge. This may be a more objective evaluation type, which is applied over students' work. They have to be provided with guidelines on what is expected from them, be taught how to fulfil such guidelines and then the rubric serves to measure how well they handled the relevant requirements. The issue is that it might not be possible to assess why they cannot comply with some requirements if we do not plan to ask them about it. Keep in mind that rubrics and standardized tests cover a weakness of other more subjective instruments; namely, that you have the limitation of asking students about their own level of competence and thus you will gather answers on what they think such level is. Rubrics and standardized tests allow the measuring of the level of competence more objectively | Individual |

## 14.5 Instruments employed from a librarian's perspective (2013–17)

In the last IL initiative in which I was involved in a Mexican library, we decided to establish an IL programme, called Information Culture Development (ICD), with the aim of positioning the library as one of the engines of our higher education institution (HEI). As such, ICD was developed through four main working axes, which contained different activities:

- Axis I. Curriculum and learning support through IL: providing support for the development of courses and curricula; engaging in collection development processes (digital and print)

and evaluating providers' offers; developing promotional materials, strengthening the library website, developing and implementing a communication strategy for social media, which obviously includes the production of original contents (e.g. images, text, audio, and video).

- Axis II. IL development: developing workshops, courses and other training activities and developing tutorials in video about the use of information resources.
- Axis III. Research and scientific communication support: offering digital reference and documentary provision services; providing proofreading, support, and advice for research projects and their derived products.
- Transversal axis. Evaluation and communication of results: this axis involved improving the ways in which IL data and also library usage data were collected, analyzed, and reported to university authorities for strengthening institutional indicators; new indicators were developed, and standardized tests were employed (see Lau et al., 2016); all library staff were also trained, mainly on IL and for improving their functions; we improved library processes and their manuals and provided support for national and international accreditations.

In Table 14.1, I suggested the use of seven different kinds of instrument that can be used for evaluating any IL initiative or programme to assess different elements. Table 14.2 presents three examples of such instruments, as we used them in the ICD programme that practitioners may adapt for their use: a diagnostic questionnaire, a follow-up questionnaire, and an interview intended for faculty staff. The table includes the types of questions that each of these instruments may include and what each question allows measuring, either learning, or satisfaction.

Further details about ICD's design and results are available in other publications (see Machin-Mastromatteo et al., 2014; Machin-Mastromatteo, 2015; Lau et al., 2016). However, in the following section, I summarize the results gathered with the instruments described.

**Table 14.2** Examples of instruments used as a librarian.

| ***Instrument 1. Diagnostic questionnaire, to be applied before the workshop starts (pretest)*** | |
|---|---|
| Measures learning | 1. How do you usually _______ (e.g. search, retrieve, read, research, cite)? This open question can be adapted by replacing the blank space with the verb related to the main skill or activity developed in the workshop<br>2. What can you do with _______ (e.g. APA Publication Manual [or similar, depending on each institution's choice of standard], name of database, search engine or reference manager)? Open question to adapt by using the name of the resource, service, or software that the workshop is about |
| Measures satisfaction | 3. Have you ever used _______ (e.g. APA Publication Manual, name of database, search engine or reference manager)? Binary question (Yes/No) to adapt by using the name of the resource, service or software that the workshop is about<br>4. What is your experience with _______ (e.g. APA Publication Manual, name of database, search engine or reference manager)? If the previous is answered with a yes, use this open question with the respective name of the resource, service or software that the workshop is about |

*Continued*

**Table 14.2** Examples of instruments used as a librarian.—cont'd

| | |
|---|---|
| ***Instrument 2. Follow-up questionnaire, to be applied after the workshop has ended (posttest)*** | |
| Measures learning<br>Measures satisfaction | 1. What did you learn in this workshop? Open question<br>2. How do you think you can use what you learned? Open question<br>3. Please rate from 1 to 5 the following workshop elements (1 corresponds to poor and 5 to excellent). Close-ended question with a Likert-type scale for gathering students' perceptions of the quality of variables such as the following: (a) classroom's resources and equipment; (b) workshop's content; (c) practical exercises; (d) learning strategies employed; (e) trainer's performance; (f) originality; and (g) workshop's usefulness for your endeavours. Variables can be added or removed, depending on the workshop's characteristics<br>4. Highlight at least one positive and a negative aspect of the workshop. Open question<br>5. Did this workshop meet your expectations? Please indicate why or why not. Open question |
| ***Instrument 3. Interviews with teachers*** | |
| Measures learning and satisfaction | 1. In what ways have the IL initiatives aided you in your academic endeavours?<br>2. Have you noticed improvements in the library, specifically related to services for faculty staff, digital platforms, and promotional materials?<br>3. Have you noticed any IL improvements in your students, specifically regarding their academic performance and projects?<br>4. How do you think that IL initiatives are supporting teaching, learning, and research practices in the university?<br>5. Where do you think we should make more efforts? As an academic, what actions or strategies would you like the library to offer? |

## 14.6 Results gathered as a librarian

This section includes a summary of the most relevant results gathered through three data collection stages for ICD. Although more activities were conducted and more results were obtained, these are the most relevant for the purposes of this chapter and were those in which I applied instruments such as the ones shown in the previous sections (see Tables 14.1 and 14.2). Davis (2007) questions if we, as librarians, should teach IL skills within the curriculum or in separate sections. There are clearly advantages and disadvantages in each approach. The amount of time we got for teaching such skills as highlighted at the beginning of this chapter, will determine how we do it and with which methods. If we have too little time, our sessions can turn into just quick demos or informative sessions about our resources. If we have too much time with a group, particularly with undergraduate students, we might struggle to keep their attention. Then, if we teach a full course on IL skills, the challenge is to develop a semester-long curriculum that is interesting and useful for students in all fields, which we may try to tackle by connecting the course's contents and activities to real-life information problems and needs. ICD was a driving force that helped, in a short time, to establish a mandatory course on information management for all first-semester undergraduate students, but this topic goes beyond the aims of this chapter. The three data collection stages were conducted in the context of a short course for teachers, one course for first-semester students enrolled in an undergraduate programme (both courses were part of ICD's pilot stage) and by interviewing teachers with whom a partnership based on IL efforts was established. A summary of the main results is presented next.

### 14.6.1 Course for teachers

A group of 58 teachers participated in an IL course within the ICD programme, which included academic databases (one 2-h session), the use of Mendeley (one 2-h session), a short seminar on research methods and scientific writing (8h divided into 4 sessions), and after that, 81% of the teachers presented a draft of a research project about their teaching. Results from the diagnostic questionnaire employed (see Table 14.2) showed that 44% had used academic databases before, but 9% stated that they could not find what they were looking for in them, whilst 6% found that the systems are difficult to use. From this survey group, 53% consistently and exclusively use the Internet in general for retrieving academic information, only 10% stated that they consistently used the subscribed databases, 9% use printed books, 8% use Google Scholar, only 2% claimed to have used the library catalogue. Regarding the use of Mendeley, only 2% had used reference managers before, 61% claimed to save academic and scientific documents in folders in their computer, 14% save them in a dedicated USB drive, whilst others provided answers such as in the favourites in their Internet browser, email or the cloud. By assessing their research projects, some areas of improvement that I identified were clarity and structure of their writing, use of sources, citation style and organizing sources in the body of the text and increasing the use of appropriate information sources.

In the follow-up questionnaire (see Table 14.2), teachers evaluated the course. For 40% it was their first library course, 26% stated that it was a better course than those previously offered by the library, others thought it was similar (17%) or worse (17%). The areas for improving the course that teachers highlighted were having more practical activities, having a better balance between what is optional and mandatory, making available a reading list related to the course, adding advisory sessions, revising durations and schedules, dividing the group into smaller subgroups according to competences for example proficiency using ICT; encouraging more collaborative work and active participation; improving computer equipment; and demonstrating tools' usefulness more clearly. The teachers stated that the digital tools learned throughout this course can help them improve their teaching practices (26%), conducting research (17%), and managing a personal digital library thanks to Mendeley (11%). The most highly rated elements of the course were the course's contents, the instructor's performance, and the usefulness of the contents for their endeavours; whilst the lowest-rated aspects were originality, learning strategies, and practical exercises.

### 14.6.2 Course for first-semester undergraduate students

A diagnostic and follow-up questionnaire was, applied at the beginning and the end of each stage of the course circulated to 13 groups of first-semester undergraduate students (188 students in total). The first stage of the course was about academic databases and the second was about the American Psychological Association's (APA) Publication Manual; each part consisted of a 2-h-session. The following is a summary of the results.

The diagnostic questionnaire revealed that 69% had used databases before, but 63% mainly use the Internet in general to retrieve information, 17% consistently used the databases subscribed by the library, 12% use print books, and only two students claimed to have used the library catalogue. They mostly knew that through databases they could retrieve reliable information (39%), locate specialized information (32%), and information for their classwork and for conducting research (24%). Their experiences using databases had been good (31%), but they thought that searching and navigation was complex (15%); some could not find what they needed (13%) and complained that there are very few platforms in Spanish (10%). Regarding APA, 43% had used them before, but when asked how they usually cite a document, 57% stated that they just copy documents' URLs and 19% did not know or did not answer. However, 26% recognized from the start that APA is a formal and standard way of citing and referencing sources.

The follow-up questionnaire revealed that, thanks to the course, they could learn more about writing academic papers (75%), accessing the databases (42%), searching them (39%), using APA citation style correctly (24%), retrieving and downloading valuable information (23%), creating personal accounts (14%), and refining search results (14%). Half of the students shared the opinion that knowing more about using databases and APA can help them perform better in academic work. Interestingly, students' ratings of the course's elements were similar throughout all the evaluated elements, although their ratings were much lower in the APA course. The most highly rated aspects were learning strategies used, instructor's performance, and usefulness of the contents for their endeavours; whilst the lowest-rated were originality, practical exercises, and classroom resources and equipment. The databases part of the course fulfilled the expectations of 82% of the students, whilst 77% thought that about the APA session.

### 14.6.3 Interviews with partner teachers

I interviewed a group of 16 teachers who benefited from and collaborated with ICD's initiatives. They stated that they had received adequate support regarding information seeking, complementing the bibliographies of their courses, and for their research. ICD has furthered their understanding of digital information services and the promotional materials, and in general, the communication strategies implemented through email and social media have kept them updated about new acquisitions and available information products. Most interviewees recognized that the library has gained a wider reach with faculty, that ICD's courses were more complete and better than previous courses offered by the library and have helped them access more tools for conducting research.

Teachers observed an improvement in their students' handling of information sources, particularly their use of higher-quality digital information sources; fewer students were asking them questions such as where they could seek information for doing an assignment, and they were more careful in citing information sources. They agreed that the key to improving students' use of information is for teachers to promote them in class and require them to use and cite reputable sources in their assignments. According to the teachers, ICD's roles are to find more collaboration opportunities with teaching staff and to keep providing support to students and staff. They observed that teachers tend to use the same information resources every semester in their courses because they might not know that they can contact the library for help, so promotion and outreach are very important. Moreover, there are teaching staff that use the same printed sources and such a practice is transmitted to their students who, in turn, do not search for other sources; hence, teachers and students must be encouraged to use digital documents. In general, teachers said they wanted students to develop excellent IL skills.

## 14.7 Instrument employed from a teacher's perspective (2017–19)

Between 2017 and 2019, though having changed jobs from librarian to a full-time teacher, I was still interested in developing IL skills and hence I have been including some sessions in all my courses. In the case of undergraduate courses, I teach students the basics of information seeking by using the databases to which we subscribe as well as Google Scholar and also the use of APA; as the embedding of IL-related contents was limited in these undergraduate courses and I did not apply the survey instruments that I applied at the graduate level, I will not go deeper into the undergraduate experiences as a teacher. Instead, I will focus on what I have been doing in my two main graduate programmes [Master in Educational Innovation (MIE) and Doctorate in Education, Arts and Humanities (DEAH)], which are research-centric and have two main graduation requirements: the publication of an article in an indexed journal [in Latindex, Scielo, Redalyc, Scopus and/or Web of Science (WoS)] and the preparation and defence of a thesis. The research-centric nature of these programmes provides excellent opportunities to include IL sessions. I tackle the following IL-related topics: (a) search tips; (b) indexes; (c) commercial databases; (d) OA databases; (e) APA; (f) Mendeley; (g) writing tips for word; (h) journals' quality criteria; and (i) publishing anecdotes. I include and collate these topics within the regular lectures and discussions of the course's topics and if any doubts arise during the semester, we go back and discuss or explain the IL-related topics again. In my teaching of these topics, I try to combine my librarian side with my current position as a professor (as Bagnall, 1993 did). I mix and embed in my courses my librarian skills and experiences, as well as those that I have developed as a researcher, which are very useful assets for teaching in these kinds of academic programmes in which we must help students develop research and at the same time develop them as new and independent researchers. As instructors of new researchers, we must also take into consideration the dynamics of the knowledge economy, bibliometrics—because every researcher, regardless of their field, must have at least a basic understanding of bibliometrics—and information and data overload, as well as the challenges of evaluation systems for educational institutions and researchers; because nowadays researchers' skills involve embracing high standards regarding research outputs, rankings, and their associated metrics (Sanches, 2019). The way in which I implemented IL into the courses I have been facilitating is through:

**(a)** Introducing the course's syllabus and its basic concepts. Then, I work with students to create a collaborative tag cloud to develop common concepts related to the course's topics (e.g. for the course Learning Environments that would be concepts such as learning environments, infrastructures, strategies, activities and pedagogical models; for Scientific Writing, it would be concepts such as syntax or paraphrasing).

**(b)** Searching academic databases with them with two purposes: firstly to gather the state of the art in the research field related to the course and to explain to them what the bibliometric patterns that we can retrieve in indexes such as Scopus and WoS can tell us in any given research field (e.g. who are the most cited authors, what are the most important journals in a research field, where—country and institution—is most of the research conducted); second, for them to be able to use new search tips and tricks they learned me to retrieve better material in order to enrich their theses.

**(c)** I provide a long session on APA. The students have to retrieve digital documents and make citations and references. We also check the citations and references they already have in their theses to improve them. I provide guidance on how to structure their texts and incorporate different kinds of citations. This can be very time consuming, but with dedication, they learn how to use APA and to improve their writing style.

**(d)** Then, I teach them how to instal and use Mendeley on their computers and smart devices. The choice of first teaching APA and then a reference manager is deliberate because one of the features in reference managers is getting the references of any document in a wide variety of formats. It is my belief that you first have to teach them how to build the basic references (i.e. book, book chapter, journal article, thesis, website) by themselves and then let them know that Mendeley can help them obtain the references very easily, provided that the documents' metadata in Mendeley's library is correct. Sometimes they complain about this, by asking me why I first teach them to do the references by hand. To which I reply in mathematics, I can't teach you how to add, subtract, multiply, and divide with the calculator; you must learn to do it manually. I also highlight that the correct use of a citation style is vital because if they send an article to a journal and the use of the citation style is sloppy, then they cause a bad impression with reviewers and they might suspect that the contents are also deficient. From ICD's experiences, I could see that during the years 2007–13, the use of a reference manager was not as common and although more people now know about them and use them, I still consider them a very niche software type. Most of the time, students have a moment of revelation when they see how easily they can create and manage their personal digital libraries, apart from reading, citing, and annotating documents, which is much more effective and efficient than saving those documents in computer folders and relying on their operating system's search function, which is not at all effective for retrieving the full text in documents, especially in Windows. I highlight that using reference managers implies a very steep learning curve and a drastic change of practices regarding the use of digital documents, but if we implement the use of a reference manager, we can save much time and have more efficient information practices.

**(e)** After learning more about APA and Mendeley I share some writing tips for Microsoft Word, such as using the search and replace functions, configure paragraphs and headings, create tables of contents, setting multiple paginations in a document, amongst others. I advise them against using Word's automatic citations and references, as they are rarely correctly used. It is a feature that introduces computer code within documents, and it can lead to issues. Some journals are requesting authors to refrain from using it, as it causes problems with typesetting software. Word might be amongst the most used software in the world, but most students and even teachers just use its basic features.

**(f)** I usually deliver the lectures about the last two topics (journals' quality criteria and publishing anecdotes) towards the end of the semester, as I require them to write a journal article as the final assignment for my courses, for which they have to use the publication guidelines of a real journal in the field of education to develop their article. In these sessions, I teach them about topics such as how to comply with publication guidelines, how to search for the most appropriate journal to publish their research in, the different characteristics of scientific journals and how they are evaluated and ranked, what is peer review, what are the processes involved in scientific publication, and so on. I share my experiences as a published researcher about the challenges and pitfalls, providing them with guidance on how to overcome them, particularly because they have the institutional requirement of publishing an article (apart from defending their theses) in order to graduate.

As shown in Table 14.3, I used two instruments to assess the experience with the IL content. The next sections of this chapter focus on the design and results of the survey, which was used during four consecutive semesters (2017–19) of teaching different courses at MIE and DEAH, mainly to assess the perceived usefulness of the IL content of their courses, as well as their learning and satisfaction with such content.

The first part of the survey required two personal details from students, although this did not allow identification: the graduate programme which they were studying, in order to segment them into groups; and requirement (or not) to prepare a thesis as a graduation requirement in their previous academic programme. This second question was added because there is a growing concern that students entering these programmes have serious issues and limitations regarding their information, writing, and research skills because there are many bachelor, master, and even doctoral programmes that do not require a thesis for graduation, which may harm graduates' information, writing, and research skills. It may even lower the level of the education system as well as harming society's literacy and produce a negative perception of science, research, innovation, and academia in general. Sadly, this seems to be a condition that is worsening through the popularization of euphemisms such as 'teaching-centred institutions' or 'professionalizing programmes', which are used to refer to institutions that do not produce research and programmes that do not require the development and defence of a thesis.

The second part of the survey required students to rate different IL content taught in class by using a scale from one (minimum) to five (maximum), depending on relative usefulness. The content, which had an emphasis on digital technologies, tools, and processes, was (a) Mendeley reference manager; (b) APA, which is the style officially

**Table 14.3** Examples of instruments used as a teacher.

| | |
|---|---|
| ***Instrument 1. Unique survey after finishing the workshop (posttest)*** | |
| Measures of learning | How would you describe your previous knowledge of the content taught in class? Which content do you consider was the most unfamiliar?<br>Do you still have challenges with the content? Which? What are the challenges? Please elaborate your answer<br>State two or three things you learned regarding the IL content |
| Measures of satisfaction | Rate the following contents taught in class, depending on the usefulness of these contents for your work and studies (e.g. thesis)<br>Which content do you think we should focus more on why?<br>Which aspects of the IL sessions do you think can be improved?<br>In your own experience, how important do you consider IL content for training new researchers? |
| ***Instrument 2. Rubric for evaluating an assignment consisting of the presentation of a scientific text (e.g. scientific article, thesis)*** | |
| Measures of learning, problem-solving, and application of knowledge | Formal aspects: the work is divided into thematic sections, alternating between citations from sources and authors' contributions, avoiding focusing on a sole source for long sections of text. Sentences and paragraphs are of appropriate length and the syntax employed facilitates readability. There is appropriate use of abbreviations and symbols (punctuation, parentheses, quotation marks). There are no consecutive titles; all heading subdivisions include at least a paragraph<br>Content aspects: the problem statement is explicitly declared, it specifies the knowledge gap being addressed, and how the present research is going to proceed. The justification of the research is present and its usefulness for different stakeholders is explained. There is coherence across the content, with integration of the work. A critical stance is assumed by the author and any position is grounded in available sources and data. The writing style is clear, direct and there are no spelling or grammar errors<br>Use of information sources: the work is original (antiplagiarism software will be used). The work complies with the APA Publication Manual guidelines regarding citations and references. A diverse range of information sources was used [a good proportion of international publications, most are peer-reviewed, more than half are from indexed journals (Scopus and/or WoS), and more than half should be in English and current (from the past 5–10 years)]<br>Briefly describe how useful the IL content was for developing your work and how the skills and knowledge gained contributed to your thesis and how they can support your future endeavours. Please state any challenges you may still have with any of the evaluated elements (this last part enables a space for students to provide some insights into why they could not comply with any of the requirements and, although it might not be typical to include such open-ended question in a rubric, it is important for us to gather such insights; e.g. it allows us to understand why students might still be struggling with specific IL skills or problems) |

used in our university; (c) Commercial databases, which included the use of platforms such as EBSCO, ScienceDirect, Emerald Insight and Wiley; (d) OA databases, which included Latin American resources such as Scielo and Redalyc, as well as international ones, such as SSRN and CORE; (e) writing tips for word, including how to work in word under APA's guidelines, for example, set heading levels and format, tables of contents and checking citations and references; (f) search tips; (g) indexes, particularly Scopus and WoS in order to determine the state of the art, tendencies and main journals of students' lines of research; (h) journals' quality criteria, showing examples of real journals' requirements and explaining how to follow them; and (i) Publishing anecdotes, drawn from my experiences in publishing articles.

The survey's final section included open-ended questions about students' previous knowledge on the contents, which topics were the most unknown to them, which required more time to be further explained, which represented the main difficulties, what did they learn, what could be improved, and which topics they consider are the most important for training new researchers. They also had the option of submitting an additional comment.

## 14.8 Results gathered as a teacher

The survey was applied to a total of 53 students from eight groups, two groups per semester (one group from MIE and another from DEAH for each semester) and the data was collected over four semesters (2017–19). This survey was undertaken electronically. I gave the link to students by the end of the semester and I sent out just one reminder for eliciting their participation. The survey was completely anonymous and was not mandatory, because the only personal detail asked was to which graduate programme they belonged, so it is not possible to identify individual students from the data collected. Not all students responded, but around 70%–80% of the total students per group did so. In order to simplify the presentation of results, they were grouped into four new groups, a group per semester, thus combining students from the two programmes. Basic figures about these groups are presented in the following list and summarized in Table 14.4:

- **(a)** Group 1 had 15 students, four MIE (26.7) and 11 DEAH (73.3%). Three students from this group were not required to produce a thesis in their previous academic programmes, one MIE and two DEAH.
- **(b)** Group 2 had 9 students, only from DEAH, because I did not have MIE students that semester. One student did not have the experience of writing a thesis.
- **(c)** Group 3 had 14 students, eight MIE (57.1%) and six DEAH (42.9%). Students without a thesis were two MIE and one DEAH.
- **(d)** Group 4 had 15 students, six MIE (40%) and nine DEAH (60%). Students without a thesis were two MIE.

Contrary to expectation, the number of graduate students with no experience of writing a thesis in their previous academic degree was low. The initial expectation was based on three issues: (a) the concern with the proliferation of academic programmes

**Table 14.4** Descriptives of the four groups.

| Group | Programme | Number of students | Percent | Students without thesis | Percent |
|---|---|---|---|---|---|
| 1 | MIE | 4 | 26.7 | 1 | 25 |
| | DEAH | 11 | 73.3 | 2 | 18.1 |
| | Total students | 15 | 100 | 3 | 20 |
| 2 | DEAH | 9 | 100 | 1 | 11.1 |
| 3 | MIE | 8 | 57.1 | 2 | 25 |
| | DEAH | 6 | 42.9 | 1 | 16.6 |
| | Total students | 14 | 100 | 3 | 21.4 |
| 4 | MIE | 6 | 40 | 2 | 33.3 |
| | DEAH | 9 | 60 | 0 | 0 |
| | Total students | 15 | 100 | 2 | 13.3 |

that do not require a thesis for graduation; (b) the alternatives that some academic programmes offer to students for graduating without a thesis (e.g. internship reports, academic materials, and time spent conducting social work); and (c) certain general deficiencies in students' literacy and writing skills. These issues cause academics and librarians to fear that by removing the mandatory requirement of a thesis in academic programmes, the education system is lowering the levels of literacy and research skills, which starts to be evident in the results obtained in standardized tests such as the Organization for Economic Cooperation and Development (OECD)'s Programme for International Student Assessment (PISA).

The survey asked students to rate on a scale from one (minimum) to five (maximum), the usefulness of IL-related content taught in class. Reliability analysis was conducted using Cronbach's Alpha, which resulted in a high value of $\alpha$=0.969. Table 14.5 summarizes the main results obtained regarding these items in which the groups were sorted again depending on their response to the question of whether they wrote a thesis in their previous academic programme.

Although the means from these two groups were very similar, the students without a thesis experience, compared to the other group, scored higher on publishing anecdotes, indexes, commercial databases, and APA; their lowest scored topic was journals' quality criteria and the highest was APA. The students that had thesis experience gave higher scores to journals' quality criteria, search tips, writing tips for word, OA databases, and Mendeley; their lowest scored topic was Mendeley and the highest was APA. These results allow hypothesizing that students' perceived usefulness of the topics taught may depend on how much they have identified the need to know more about a given topic during their progression through their respective academic programmes. Such a hypothesis means that students' current academic needs drive the perceived usefulness of, and interest in the various topics, reinforcing the idea that if teachers highlight the importance of topics, it can contribute to students' interest and perceived usefulness, a belief highlighted by librarians; for example, a thesis supervisor who neglects the importance of having students work within APA's guidelines will transmit such a lack of interest to their students.

**Table 14.5** Descriptives of the four groups by topic and divided by students with or without a thesis experience.

| Thesis | Topic | Min. | Max. | Sum | Mean | Std. deviation | Variance |
|---|---|---|---|---|---|---|---|
| No ($n=9$) | Mendeley | 2 | 5 | 37 | 4.11 | 1.054 | 1.111 |
| | APA Publication Manual | 3 | 5 | 43 | 4.78 | 0.667 | 0.444 |
| | Commercial databases | 3 | 5 | 40 | 4.44 | 0.882 | 0.778 |
| | OA databases | 3 | 5 | 38 | 4.22 | 0.833 | 0.694 |
| | Writing tips for word | 2 | 5 | 38 | 4.22 | 1.093 | 1.194 |
| | Search tips | 3 | 5 | 38 | 4.22 | 0.833 | 0.694 |
| | Indexes | 3 | 5 | 39 | 4.33 | 0.866 | 0.75 |
| | Journals' quality criteria | 2 | 5 | 36 | 4 | 1 | 1 |
| | Publishing anecdotes | 3 | 5 | 41 | 4.56 | 0.726 | 0.528 |
| Yes ($n=44$) | Mendeley | 1 | 5 | 184 | 4.18 | 1.018 | 1.036 |
| | APA Publication Manual | 1 | 5 | 196 | 4.45 | 0.951 | 0.905 |
| | Commercial databases | 1 | 5 | 187 | 4.25 | 1.037 | 1.076 |
| | OA databases | 1 | 5 | 188 | 4.27 | 1.02 | 1.04 |
| | Writing tips for word | 1 | 5 | 187 | 4.25 | 1.037 | 1.076 |
| | Search tips | 1 | 5 | 186 | 4.23 | 1.097 | 1.203 |
| | Indexes | 1 | 5 | 188 | 4.27 | 1.042 | 1.087 |
| | Journals' quality criteria | 1 | 5 | 187 | 4.25 | 1.081 | 1.169 |
| | Publishing anecdotes | 1 | 5 | 190 | 4.32 | 1.052 | 1.106 |

This hypothesis may explain why, for instance, regardless of their experience of writing a thesis, the highest scored topic for both groups was APA, the style manual used in the university. Conversely, many students may have not yet seen the importance of a reference manager, nor the importance of knowing about journals, as they have not yet faced the need to write an article.

Although the sample was small, a correlation analysis using the Pearson coefficient was conducted, resulting in no significant correlations between the academic programme and the thesis writing; these variables did not present any correlation between them and the course content. Students' answers were independent of their programme and thesis experience. Correlations amongst the contents were significant at the 0.01 level and the highest correlations ($r \geq 0.8$) were between: (a) Mendeley and commercial databases ($r$=0.856) and with indexes ($r$=0.818); (b) APA and OA databases ($r$=0.812); (c) commercial databases and indexes ($r$=0.924) and with publishing anecdotes ($r$=0.831); (d) OA databases and Word tips ($r$=0.822) and with search tips ($r$=0.872); (e) Word tips and search tips ($r$=0.903); (f) search tips and journals' quality criteria ($r$=0.802) and with publishing anecdotes ($r$=0.818); and (g) indexes and journals' quality criteria ($r$=0.807) and with publishing anecdotes ($r$=0.831).

We would need to conduct further research into these relationships. However, it is possible to postulate several hypotheses to explain the above correlations: (a) students having an increasing interest in publication, due to the graduation requirement of publishing an indexed article, are giving importance to the publishing ecosystem and to the processes behind writing articles, such as reference managers, commercial databases, indexes, journals' quality criteria and are also interested in hearing others' publishing experiences as they have started to see that choosing a journal and getting their articles accepted are not easy tasks; (b) students that are progressing with their theses recognize the need to improve their use of the APA guidelines and learn Word tips. They also require search tips and are interested in OA databases to retrieve more specialized literature (this corresponds to the previous hypothesis about perceived usefulness vs need). These latter relationships could be further explained because access to commercial databases is limited in our institution and because in OA databases it tends to be more difficult for students to identify a given document type. It is, therefore, more difficult for them to cite and reference OA documents, as repositories do not always offer an explicit reference of the document shown on screen, which commercial databases do.

The survey's third and final section included open-ended questions. By using such questions, IL practitioners must be aware that participants' answers will not be exhaustive and thus the data gathered depends on what was most memorable for them and on which they wished to comment; depending on participants' willingness to write answers, sometimes we might not get meaningful responses. However, with these groups of students, there were interesting answers, which were coded and then summarized in the following paragraphs.

Sixteen students said that the topics of the workshop were very new to them and had little or no prior knowledge about them, whilst eight claimed to have an average level of previous knowledge. Two stated that they had a good level of previous knowledge, and another two said that the workshop allowed them to review these resources and improve their proficiency handling them. One student remarked that 'in bachelor programmes, you do not work with APA in the same way as we did it in the graduate program'. Two students had a very general knowledge of scientific databases and Mendeley, whilst two said that in their previous academic degree they developed the belief that books were the quintessential information source, but now see the importance of journal articles and digital databases. Interestingly, one student claimed that 'there are few professors that know about or share information about the databases we have access to'.

The most novel and useful content, according to students' answers, were Mendeley (which was an answer provided by 14 students), APA (9), information seeking tips (9), journal indexes (9), databases (7), Microsoft Word tips (5), and journals' quality criteria (2). The following topics were highlighted by one student per topic: OA journals, the use of Boolean operators, antiplagiarism software: all resources that are based on digital technologies evaluate information sources and identify their trustworthiness, 'how to use the information I gather in my own texts', and the teacher's publishing experiences.

Students thought that more time should be devoted to the following topics: APA (which was an answer provided by 13 students), particularly invest more time on writing paragraphs with various citation types (2), working on the thesis' structure (2), checking citation errors (1), checking references and citations on the thesis (1), and working with different types of reference. Students also said that more time should be dedicated to Mendeley (9), how to improve thesis writing style (6), conducting specialized searches in databases (5), how to write and publish articles in journals (4), how to retrieve articles not available in our institutional subscription (2), journal quality criteria (2), research types and methods (1), indexes (1), other research tools (1), and OA repositories. According to one student, 'first-semester courses should tackle this content, so we are familiar with them from an early stage in the program'. Regarding the workshop's general duration, one student stated that 'time was too brief', but for seven students, it was adequate.

The topics that represented the main difficulties for students were: APA (according to 17 students), particularly practising, remembering, and mastering APA (8), the various citation styles (3), and referencing 'strange sources' in APA (1). One student pointed out the issue that various teachers have different interpretations of APA; Mendeley (5); the use of databases (3), specifically making the remote access to databases work (1); information seeking (4), especially finding articles in arts and humanities disciplines (2); the use of indexes (3); difficulties with scientific writing in general (3), but in particular developing an article (1), and 'using more diverse words for connecting sentences in a paragraph' (1); identify journals' quality criteria (2). Seven students claimed that they did not have difficulties with any topics, whilst one stated 'I need an advanced level workshop to master all these tools'.

During the workshop, students claimed that they learned the most about: (a) Mendeley (according to 17 students), (b) APA (14), specifically about citations (5), and references (2); (c) improving information seeking (14), evaluating information sources (3), managing information (2), retrieving useful information for research (2), using Boolean operators (2), and sharing information (1); (d) databases (10), indexes

(7), and access OA repositories (1); (e) learn more Word tricks (5), specifically how to do a table of contents (1); (f) learn about journal's quality requirements (5), specifically about the format of an article (3), the impact factor (2), selecting a journal for publishing (1), and knowing more about scientific publishers (1); and (g) improving scientific writing skills (5), especially to develop the thesis' structure (3), improving literature reviews (2), using an antiplagiarism software (2), and 'framing my own project within other social sciences' research' (1).

Ten students thought that all the aspects of the workshop were appropriate. However, others made recommendations for improvement by expanding their length (9), including more practical exercises (7), spending more time with APA (6), particularly to provide more examples (5), spending more time with Mendeley (3), working more directly with the thesis (3), increasing the emphasis on research methods (2), complementing the workshops with video tutorials available to students (2), including more Word tips (2) and databases (1), adding more content about bibliometric indicators and journals' quality criteria in different disciplines (2), and continuing the workshops during other semesters (1).

For information professionals, it is commonly accepted that information skills and ICT skills are vital for research and researchers, but I was curious to ask for insights about if and why these IL-related topics are important for training new researchers. All students agreed that they are indeed important and fundamental, whilst some of them recognized that researchers must be proficient in the use of ICTs and these topics (5), which form the basis of all research processes (4), particularly those associated with research production and evaluation (3) and topics that allow improving scientific writing skills (3). Moreover, the development of the skills in question influences the quality of their research output (3), enables researchers to be up to date in their respective fields (2), are key skills that any researcher requires (1), because their appropriate development allows spending less time in activities such as searching for information, structuring references, and revising texts. Two students claimed that the content should also be included at the undergraduate level, so they have the background to build upon later, at the graduate level, as new researchers such as them face challenges that can be resolved with these IL-related topics One student appreciated that examples and practical activities were conducted with their own research topics and theses and claimed that this resulted in meaningful learning.

## 14.9 Conclusion

Although I provided results emerging from the systematic collection of data, I also used my own experiences and observations as a librarian and university teacher. This latter evidence might be seen by some scholars as anecdotal and lacking in scientific value, but action research self-study of our own practices and experiences is a valid avenue and most of the insights deriving from personal experiences are consonant with what other researchers (including myself) have found through the use of other methods.

The issues arising from developing IL initiatives from the library and then from doing so as a teacher are closely related to the challenges highlighted by Houtman

(2010) and other sources cited. Although ICD was not my first experience developing, coordinating, and implementing an IL programme from a library, it was my strongest experience and was where I started being more systematic about planning and the application of instruments. The challenge, as highlighted by Davis (2007) and Walter (2008), is that IL activities present us with an extra workload that is difficult to cope with, particularly if we are in very small teams because we have to take care of the reference service and thus of the demands of our users at the reference desk, as well as delivering IL instruction (and its planning, design, and measurement) as well as our typical administrative behind-the-desk tasks.

During the early years of my IL experience (2006–08), I started to learn about harnessing the possibilities of (a) grounding the IL initiative in the institution's vision, values and educational model; (b) positioning the library within the institution as a dynamic engine in such a way that we start being involved in other institutional processes—developing an IL programme helps us doing this (these first two elements enables the library to gain more importance in the institution and it might then get more recognition and resources dedicated to it); (c) IL permeating and improving other library services and products, including collection development; (d) the library's IL courses becoming the main instruction-delivery method, but we must also develop others (e.g. flyers, podcasts, tutorials, videos, and social media); and (e) transcending typical library work and stereotypes by venturing into new functions, ways of working and even in media production, but requiring the best and most creative human resources to do so (Machin-Mastromatteo, 2009).

The lessons learned after developing, implementing, and analyzing ICD's results include (a) highlight the role of academic libraries as an educational partner; (b) develop partnerships with teaching staff; (c) have a wide reach for students and lecturers as not all of them visit the library; (d) have an institutional reconceptualization of the library, including all its activities, resources and possibilities, to make sure that our efforts to embed it in the institution's endeavours are successful; (e) take on the challenge of lowering resistance towards reading and help develop deep and critical approaches; (f) keep working on promoting the library; (g) some lecturers will need our support for conducting research; and (h) ensure that IL endeavours are aligned with institutional plans and work towards embedding IL and the library in them. In my experience, the most important element for starting an IL programme is to find and partner with faculty that are frequent library users, that 'get' what we do, and that like books and libraries. Amongst the effects of such collaborations, our faculty partners may improve their teaching (Mackey and Jacobson, 2005). Moreover, the learning community, in general, may conduct some of their academic and research activities more effectively. They may wish to continue expanding their IL skills and can be more mindful of aspects such as having the most recent and best information available for their work (Sanches, 2019). However, keep in mind that some academic staff can have varied perceptions of IL; some of them might not understand the skills in question and others may not see their usefulness for their students (Davis, 2007; Webber et al. 2005).

From my experiences as an academic embedding IL in my classes, I highlight that (a) if we complain as librarians that we do not have enough time for teaching IL, by increasing the hours dedicated to IL I have seen that it is still not enough and students agree, however, they mostly need support in writing, revising, and editing their texts, as well as remembering the nuances of information seeking and management; (b) students' perception of the usefulness of an IL topic may depend on how much they think they need to know more about it and that, in turn, depends on the activities they are conducting and on their level of advancement in their academic programme. This corresponds to a belief held by librarians that students will grant importance to something if they have a need for it, which is why you will be more successful if you connect IL-related content to what students need to know and highlighting such connections; (c) the greatest struggles come from using a publication manual; (d) do not expect that students and even other teachers will have knowledge of the topic: start from the beginning, if only to bring the classroom to the same level and speed, but do not overdo this as you might need to divide the larger group into smaller ones according to their level of IL competence; and (e) when embedding IL into research-oriented academic programmes you will be teaching at the highest level possible, so prepare accordingly and invest the time required by students to achieve a considerable level of improvement. As a closing statement, students usually ask me why they were not taught these IL-related contents in such a high level of detail and I candidly answer them that it is because I am the only librarian teaching in their programme.

## References


Allen, L., 2005. Hybrid librarians in the 21st century library: a collaborative service-staffing model. In: Proceedings of the 12th National Conference, Association of College & Research Libraries, April 7-10, Minneapolis, ACRL, pp. 291–301. http://www.ala.org/acrl/sites/ala.org.acrl/files/content/conferences/pdf/allen05.pdf. (Accessed 07.05.20).

Association of College and Research Libraries, 2016. Standards for Distance Learning Library Services. http://www.ala.org/acrl/standards/guidelinesdistancelearning#definitions. (Accessed 07.05.20).

Bagnall, C., 1993. On becoming an ex-librarian. Libr. Career Dev. 1 (4). https://doi.org/10.1108/09680819310048391.

Ball, B., 1997. Career management competences: the individual perspective. Career Dev. Int. 2 (2), 74–79. https://doi.org/10.1108/13620439710163653.

Bawden, D., 2001. Information and digital literacies: a review of concepts. J. Doc. 57 (2), 218–259. https://doi.org/10.1108/EUM0000000007083.

Bell, S., Shank, J., 2004. The blended librarian: a blueprint for redefining the teaching and learning role of academic librarians. Coll. Res. Libr. News 65 (7), 372–375. www.ala.org/ala/mgrps/divs/acrl/publications/crlnews/2004/jul/blendedlibrarian.cfm. (Accessed 07.05.20).

Bello, M., 1996. Choosing a career: librarian? Libr. Career Dev. 4 (4), 15–19.

Bewick, L., Corrall, S., 2010. Developing librarians as teachers: a study of their pedagogical knowledge. J. Librariansh. Inf. Sci. 42 (2), 97–110. https://doi.org/10.1177/0961000610361419.

Carson, K., Carson, P., Phillips, J., Roe, C., 1996. A career entrenchment model: theoretical development and empirical outcomes. J. Career Dev. 22 (4), 273–286. https://doi.org/10.1177/089484539602200405.

Corrall, S., 2010. Educating the academic librarian as a blended professional: a review and case study. Libr. Manag. 31 (8/9), 567–593. https://doi.org/10.1108/01435121011093360.

Davis, K., 2007. The academic librarian as instructor: a study of teacher anxiety. Coll. Undergrad. Lib. 14 (2), 77–101. https://doi.org/10.1300/J106v14n02_06.

de la Peña, K., 2009. Opportunities in Library and Information Science Careers, third ed. McGraw-Hill, New York.

Deeming, C., Chelin, J., 2001. Make your own luck: a study of people changing career into librarianship. New Libr. World 102 (1160/1161), 13–25. https://doi.org/10.1108/03074800110365453.

Dougherty, R., 2001. Being successful (nimble and agile) in the current turbulent environment. J. Acad. Librariansh. 27 (4), 263–267. https://doi.org/10.1016/S0099-1333(01)00229-4.

Edem, U., 1999. Issues in career advancement prospects among librarians in Nigerian universities. Libr. Manag. 20 (2), 76–83.

Edwards, R., 2002. Migrating to public librarianship: depart on time to ensure a smooth flight. Libr. Trends 50 (4), 631–639.

Feldman, D., 1988. Managing Careers in Organizations. Foresman, Glenview.

Feldman, A., Paugh, P., Mills, G., 2004. Self-study through action research. In: Loughran, J., Hamilton, M., LaBoskey, V., Russell, T. (Eds.), International Handbook of Self-Study of Teaching and Teacher Education Practices. vol. 12. Springer, New York, pp. 943–977. https://doi.org/10.1007/978-1-4020-6545-3_24.

Fontenot, M., 2008. The ambidextrous librarian, or 'you can teach a middle-aged dog some new tricks!'. Ref. User Serv. Q. 48 (1), 26–28. https://doi.org/10.5860/rusq.48n1.26.

Fowell, S., Levy, P., 1995. Developing a new professional practice: a model for networked learner support in higher education. J. Doc. 51 (3), 271–280. https://doi.org/10.1108/eb026951.

Hall, D., 1976. Careers in Organizations. Goodyear, California.

Holder, S., Lannon, A., 2018. Managing the Multigenerational Librarian Workforce. Elsevier/Chandos, Oxford.

Houtman, E., 2010. 'Trying to figure it out': academic librarians talk about learning to teach. Libr. Inf. Res. 34 (107), 18–40. https://doi.org/10.29173/lirg246.

Johnson, T., 2002. Making it to the major leagues: career movement between library and archival professions and from small college to large university libraries. Libr. Trends 50 (4), 614–630.

Kong, L., Goodfellow, R., 1988. Charting a career path in the information professions. Coll. Res. Libr. 49 (3), 207–216. https://doi.org/10.5860/crl_49_03_207.

Lambert, C., Newman, N., 2012. Second career librarians: teachers transitioning to librarianship. Libr. Rev. 61 (6), 428–446. https://doi.org/10.1108/00242531211284348.

Lancaster, F., 1982. Libraries and Librarians in an Age of Electronics. Information Resources, Arlington.

Lau, J., 2006. Guidelines on Information Literacy for Lifelong Learning. International Federation of Library Associations and Institutions. https://www.ifla.org/files/assets/information-literacy/publications/ifla-guidelines-en.pdf. (Accessed 08.05.20).

Lau, J., Machin-Mastromatteo, J., Gárate, A., Tagliapietra-Ovies, A., 2016. Assessing Spanish-Speaking University Students' Info-Competencies With iSkills, SAILS, and an In-House Instrument: Challenges and Benefits. Communications in Computer and Information Science, vol. 676, pp. 327–336.

Machin-Mastromatteo, J., 2009. Programa de desarrollo de competencias en el uso de la información de la Biblioteca Pedro Grases: Presente y futuro. In: Lloret, N. (Ed.), Nuevas perspectivas para la difusión y organización del conocimiento. ISKO, pp. 169–179. https://dialnet.unirioja.es/servlet/articulo?codigo=2922068. (Accessed 08.05.20).

Machin-Mastromatteo, J., 2015. Two Years of Information Culture Development for Supporting Higher Education: Initiatives, Teacher's Perceptions and Future Actions. Communications in Computer and Information Science, vol. 552, pp. 517–526.

Machin-Mastromatteo, J., 2017. The use of participatory methodologies for conducting literacy activities: a perfect but not explicit fit. Inf. Learn. Sci. 118 (9/10), 456–470. https://doi.org/10.1108/ILS-07-2017-0075.

Machin-Mastromatteo, J., Beltrán, O., Lau, J., 2014. Piloting a Holistic Information Culture Program: The Experience of CETYS Universidad System of Libraries. Communications in Computer and Information Science, vol. 492, pp. 350–360.

Mackey, T., Jacobson, T., 2005. IL: a collaborative endeavor. Coll. Teach. 53 (4), 140–144. https://doi.org/10.3200/CTCH.53.4.140-144.

McGuinness, C., 2009. Information skills training practices in Irish higher education. ASLIB Proc. 61 (3), 262–281. https://doi.org/10.1108/00012530910959817.

Newhouse, R., Spisak, A., 2010. Fixing the first job: new librarians speak out on problems in the profession. Libr. J. 129 (13), 44–46. https://www.libraryjournal.com/?detailStory=fixing-the-first-job.

Nicholson, A., 2016. Where Do We Come From? A Survey of Current Library Workers, Their Previous Careers, and Paths Into Library Work (Master's thesis). Victoria University of Wellington. https://researcharchive.vuw.ac.nz/xmlui/bitstream/handle/10063/5634/report.pdf.

Noh, Y., 2010. A study analyzing the career path of librarians. J. Acad. Librariansh. 36 (4), 329–346. https://doi.org/10.1016/j.acalib.2010.05.007.

Phillips, J., Carson, K., Carson, P., 1994. Evolution of affective career outcomes: a field study of academic librarians. Coll. Res. Libr. 55 (6), 541–549. https://doi.org/10.5860/crl_55_06_541.

Reference and User Services Association, 2016. Professional Competencies for Reference and User Services Librarians. http://www.ala.org/rusa/resources/guidelines/professional.

Rusbridge, C., 1998. Towards the hybrid library. D-Lib Mag. 4 (7/8). www.dlib.org/dlib/july98/rusbridge/07rusbridge.html.

Sanches, T., 2019. Changing Roles for Research and Information Skills Development: Librarians as Teachers, Researchers as Learners. Communications in Computer and Information Science, vol. 989, pp. 462–471.

Shumaker, D., 2012. The Embedded Librarian: Innovative Strategies for Taking Knowledge Where It's Needed. Information Today, Medford, NJ.

St. Lifer, E., 1994. Are you happy in your job? LJ's exclusive report. Libr. J. 119 (18), 44–49.

Walter, S., 2008. Librarians as teachers: a qualitative inquiry into professional identity. Coll. Res. Libr. 69 (1), 51–71. https://doi.org/10.5860/crl.69.1.51.

Webber, S., Boon, S., Johnston, B., 2005. A comparison of UK academics' conceptions of IL in two disciplines: English and marketing. Libr. Inf. Res. 29 (93), 4–15. https://doi.org/10.29173/lirg197.

Wheeler, E., McKinney, P., 2015. Are librarians teachers? Investigating academic librarians' perceptions of their own teaching roles. J. IL 9 (2), 111–128. https://doi.org/10.11645/9.2.1985.

Zemon, C., 2002. Midlife career choices: how are they different from other career choices? Libr. Trends 50 (4), 665–672. https://www.ideals.illinois.edu/handle/2142/8436. (Accessed 08.05.20).

# Part Five

# New paradigms

# Envisioning Education 4.0—A scenario planning approach to predicting the future

15

*Martin Hamilton*
Principal at martinh.net, Digital Innovation Consultancy

## 15.1 Macro trends in libraries and information science

Even as we enter the 2020s, the lay reader could be forgiven for picturing libraries as principally physical buildings full of books and journals, populated by librarians whose job is primarily to organize these assets and help patrons to find the material most relevant to them. As the Society of College, National and University Libraries (SCONUL, 2018) notes:

> *The total number of visitors entering the library during the year has been collected since the SCONUL survey began and it is an encouraging sign that the average number of visits per FTE user is currently 1.2% higher than ten years ago.*

However, there is a clear directional shift towards libraries as more fluid organizations whose role is primarily facilitation of access to knowledge and the development of information and data literacy skills, which can play a catalytic role in developing and sustaining digital capability. The Association of College and Research Libraries (ACRL, 2018) observes that

> *Librarians can assist researchers by clarifying legal aspects and negotiating licensing permissions with publishers. By creating guides on text and data mining tools and methods and providing information on library databases and data sources, librarians support training and awareness of the data resources and tools that they purchase. Librarians and library technicians also provide support in areas such as digitization, data extraction, data preparation, and even devising models for data analysis. At the end of text and data-mining projects, libraries may help preserve the data sets for reuse, assist researchers to contribute to open access data sets, and record metadata for discovery... The establishment of data science programs at numerous institutions has led to the need for librarians to adapt and integrate growing management, accessibility, and technical subject expertise to support data scientists.*

In a recent study for SCONUL, Pinfield et al. (2017) identify a nexus of five trends that are impacting academic and research libraries, and that libraries are impacting on

- Nexus 1: **'datafied' scholarship**—research increasingly underpinned by large data sets and digital artefacts, involving open, networked, algorithmically driven systems.

**Future Directions in Digital Information. https://doi.org/10.1016/B978-0-12-822144-0.00015-X**

- Nexus 2: **connected learning**—new pedagogies supported by technology-enabled flexible learning.
- Nexus 3: **service-oriented libraries**—libraries shifting their strategic emphasis from collections to services.
- Nexus 4: **blurred identities**—boundaries between professional groups and services being broken down with more collaboration and new skills development.
- Nexus 5: **intensified contextual pressures**—a myriad of political, economic and other pressures creating demands on higher education and libraries.

Dempsey (2014) introduces the concept of the inside-out library, or 'the library as an actor in research and learning environments of its users' and argues that this move towards library services built around the patron's workflow is highly significant—made possible by the now largely inevitable digital delivery of both content and discovery services. Dempsey notes that

> *No single website is the sole focus of a user's attention. Increasingly, people discover websites, or encounter content from them, in a variety of places. These may be network-level services (Google...), or personal services (my RSS aggregator or 'webtop'), or services which allow me to traverse from personal to network (Delicious, LibraryThing...). This means thinking about services in different ways. About how we disclose stuff to other discovery environments; about where our metadata is; about URL structures, RSS feeds, and so on.*

At the same time, the broader field of information science is being transformed through a new-found abundance of content and data, particularly open access publications, open data, and open-source software from research projects. Hou et al. (2018) conclude that

> *By comparing the research topics from 2009 to 2016 and from 1996 to 2008, we find substantial changes in the research topics in the IS domain. The core topics from 1996 to 2008, including information retrieval, webometrics and citation behavior, clearly turned to scientometric indicators, citation analysis (citation performance and bibliometrics), scientific collaboration, and information behavior, and particularly the scientific evaluation indicators represented by the h-index. The ranking of the h-index among core topics rose from fifth from 1996 to 2008 to the top.*

Around the h-index and other proxies for impact, Hou et al. also observe that

> *This study finds that the emerging scientific evaluation promoted by the h-index in 2005 is currently the most important research front. This research front primarily involves research on evaluation indicators for the ranking of institutions (universities and institutions), interdisciplinary scientific research measures, and academic prestige of journals. Traditional IS research topics, including bibliometrics, citation analysis, and scientific collaboration, currently remain research fronts. Science mapping and visualization pay special attention to research on visualization tools and automatic word extraction algorithms. Altmetrics, represented by research on social networks including Twitter and blogs, has already become the most promising research front at present.*

The studies we have referenced so far have been primarily concerned with academic and research libraries. Hackett (2018) considers issues around the need for greater digital and information literacy in the wider population and the role that public libraries could potentially play:

> *As information skills are frequently mentioned in the library narrative, and the [information literacy] narrative mentions the positive impact it can have on lifelong learning and social inclusion, it seems that there are natural intersections between government policy, public library capabilities and IL's benefits. These intersections are not currently being fully exploited to the advantage of public libraries at a time when they need advocacy and support to avoid further cuts and closures, nor are they being fully exploited to promote the benefits of IL to support policy goals.*

The International Federation of Library Associations and Institutions (IFLA) has a wider global perspective that also encompasses public library services. Their Trend Report Update (IFLA, 2018) notes four distinct emerging trends:

- **Scenario planning and libraries**: 'Expectations—and hopes—that the future of libraries was assured proved unfounded, due to erroneous assumptions about the context in which they operated'.
- **Libraries are under attack**: 'The shift to digital has put many core library principles and activities into question'.
- **Libraries matter**: 'Rather than falling victim to the web, libraries have the potential to make the Internet more useful, more accountable and more inclusive'.
- **Libraries and community networks, a collection of win-win opportunities**: 'Libraries can play a key role, through their existing Internet connections, as gateways between the local crowdsourced infrastructure and the global Internet, as a source of locally relevant material, and as a physical place to carry out discussions and training'.

The IFLA report is notable for its emphasis on the existential threat that many classes of library face, and the potential of techniques like scenario planning to help library leaders to envisage and adapt to the challenges the sector faces. In the report, scenario planning expert Rafael Ramirez states that

> *Scenario planning offers a powerful tool for testing assumptions, exploring the interrelation between trends, and developing strategies that put institutions and sectors in a better position to face the future. Libraries could gain from adopting such an approach.*

In this chapter, we will go on to introduce key concepts around scenario planning and look at how some in the library and information science community are using them. Before doing that, we will consider some broader geopolitical and social-technical trends that can be expected to have an impact on the sector, in particular, Education 4.0.

## 15.2 Education 4.0—The future of teaching and learning?

One of the most significant megatrends impacting humanity is undoubtedly the paradigm shift that has been brought about by pervasive Internet connectivity and the commoditization of computing power, most notably in the form of the now-ubiquitous smartphone. The Internet has already transformed many industries beyond all recognition—from travel to banking, bookshops to record stores. To date, education has tended to selectively adopt particular technologies, often referred to as education technology or 'edtech', whilst also resisting any wholesale transformation. Will this continue to be the case, or will the fourth industrial revolution lead to what Seldon and Abidoye (2018) refer to as a 'fourth education revolution'—Education 4.0?

Ravenscroft et al. (2020) consider the possible ingredients for Education 4.0, with a particular focus on pedagogical underpinnings and the importance of placing student wellbeing and mental health at the heart of what could otherwise be purely technology led developments:

> *'Since Klaus Schwab introduced the notion of the fourth industrial revolution (IR4.0) in 2016 there has been intense dialogue, and arguably a lot of hype, particularly in Higher Education, about what an implied Education 4.0 should look like and be operationalized as pedagogy. This debate is centred on the notion that the intersection of AI, Big Data, constant connectivity and robotics (Industry 4.0) means that we are fast entering the need for an Education 4.0, where teaching, assessment and learning administration could be completely transformed. There isn't a clear and consensual definition of what Education 4.0 is, it is more of an important rallying call to re-think Education, and particularly Higher Education, to map to the needs of Industry 4.0, and the rapidly evolving digital landscape in which we live and work more generally'.*

Edtech not-for-profit Jisc (2018) held a series of workshops with their members and customers to look at possible challenges and opportunities around Education 4.0. They arrived at four high-level Education 4.0 themes as a result of this work:

- **Teaching transformed**—how should human teachers focus their efforts if AI and other technologies become used to their full potential in the university experience?
- **Personalized adaptive learning**—an individualized approach that takes learner diversity, performance and behaviour into account.
- **Assessment reimagined**—can AI, digital experiential learning and micro-credentials replace high stakes summative tests?
- **Intelligent digital and physical estates**—this concept is responsive to student journeys and interactions, helping universities deliver efficiencies and a smart approach to campus design.

Ravenscroft et al. discuss the particular significance of artificial intelligence (AI) in the thinking about what might constitute Education 4.0 and how it might be used in practice. Significantly, they characterize today's AI as 'what machines do best' as opposed to 'what humans do best', as for example:

1. Solving well-defined problems regardless of their scale and complexity, usually based on concrete rules (e.g. chess and route-planning).
2. Generating knowledge and data-driven diagnosis, predictions and questions (e.g. medical diagnosis and tax compliance).
3. Language processing and communication (e.g. speech recognition and chatbots).
4. Adapting to human behaviour (e.g. recommender systems using machine learning).
5. Doing all these things (1–4) repetitively and at a scale and speed that is impossible for humans.

Ravenscroft et al. also note that whilst it may be some time before AI begins to exhibit more characteristically human behaviour, such as 'ethical, reflexive, emotional and agentive' intelligences, these are important design cues for humans and taking account of them may be crucial to the success of AI-based approaches to augmenting teaching and learning.

Mourtzis et al. (2018) examine how the teaching factory concept can be evolved to encompass fourth industrial revolution technologies like virtual reality, truly transforming teaching for the better. They state that

> *Teaching factories are an important way of practicing the technical knowledge that is included in the emerging Education 4.0 concept. Education 4.0 considers, on the one hand the exploitation of the developed technologies (e.g. advanced visualization techniques that integrate virtual reality) to facilitate the teaching process and on the other hand the methods and the workshops that will familiarize the aspiring engineers with these technologies, as will work in Industry 4.0 environments.*

But how ready are we for Education 4.0, and what is required to complete the transition? In a recent survey, Jisc (2019) heard from over a hundred practitioners at universities and colleges around the United Kingdom about their plans to use Education 4.0 immersive technologies like virtual and augmented reality (VR and AR) in teaching and learning. VR lets the user experience computer-generated virtual worlds and 360-degree photo and video captures from the real world, usually through a headset device, whereas AR superimposes virtual objects onto the real world, typically using existing mobile phones and tablets.

Key messages from the survey were that

- **Implementation of AR/VR is patchy**. Most organizations use it in only one or two departments and use AR more than VR.
- **There is an appetite for further use of AR/VR, which is seen as an important and as yet untapped technology for the future**. Health, creative arts, education, engineering, and architecture are identified as key subjects for HE, and sciences, construction, hair and beauty, agriculture, arts, and childcare for FE.
- **Responses to technology are positive. Key benefits are the immersive, engaging learning experience and the opportunity for situated/experiential learning that is not otherwise possible.** It inspires innovative approaches to teaching and improves learning outcomes.
- **The relative infancy of the technology means that there are issues with implementation, cost being the biggest barrier**. It is also difficult to scale when access to equipment is limited. Sector licences and negotiated deals would be welcomed to help with this.
- **There needs to be a better understanding of how AR/VR can be used for education and its impact**. Organizations need advice and guidance about best practices and are keen to learn from peers and to develop communities of practice in order to embed the technology more widely. Case studies, facilitation of community, and advice and guidance would help the sector with these issues.

It is clear from the survey data that there are significant challenges in terms of the digital capability of teaching staff if they are to exploit immersive technology to its full potential. In his oral evidence to policymakers in the UK's Education Select Committee (House of Commons, 2019), the author makes the point that cost aspects can be prohibitive for many education institutions. This was subsequently backed up by the survey results:

> *DCMS Local Full Fibre Network programme has been … using schools to anchor connectivity in rural communities, so that is a real success story. The problem is when you get into the building, and we see from BESA—the British Educational Suppliers Association—that does an annual survey, two thirds of secondaries and two fifths of primaries say, 'We have inadequate infrastructure'. We hear about eight-year-old PCs, I heard on social media last night from a college that is using 10year-old PCs, so there is a lot that we could do even with just a one-off capital injection to say, 'Let us get everybody on a level playing field'. Capital injection to pull cabling, to install wireless access points, to replace those—eight to 10-year-old PCs. I think that would go a long way to creating the environment that [Education 4.0] can prosper in.*

These very real difficulties around equipment costs and available funds present significant challenges when developing a business case for introducing an Industry 4.0 technology like AI, AR/VR, or robotics into our classrooms and lecture theatres. Davies et al. (2017) argue that such decisions should not be based on the perceived benefits of the technology itself, but rather on measurable benefits in terms of key indicators such as learning outcomes and learner wellbeing rather than efficiency savings and cost reduction:

> *It is essential that any changes to delivery are driven by educational considerations rather than university balance sheets. Any perception that technology is being used just to cut costs will make it harder for universities and students to benefit from future developments in educational technology.*

Practitioners and institutional leaders also need to be especially cautious about new technologies that are at the peak of the hype cycle and often presented as revolutionary and magical. For example, the author (Hamilton, 2019) notes some key considerations for those considering projects to explore the potential of blockchain:

> *Blockchain and other distributed ledger technologies are interesting and hold potential for solving wicked problems that the sector struggles with, such as provenance of research results, tracking citations and reproducibility of research results. However, as you have seen, there are many traps for the unwary, such as transaction costs, block size limitations, issues around resource consumption and the enclosure of blockchain within wholly proprietary systems.*

Looking at potential roles for AI in Education (AIED), Holmes et al. (2019) note the particular need for an ethical focus:

- What are the criteria for ethically acceptable AIED?
- How does the transient nature of student goals, interests, and emotions impact the ethics of AIED?
- What are the AIED ethical obligations of private organizations (developers of AIED products) and public authorities (schools and universities involved in AIED research)?
- How might schools, students, and teachers opt out from, or challenge, how they are represented in large data sets?
- What are the ethical implications of many ITS and other AIED approaches adopting an instructional approach to learning?

- What are the ethical implications of not being able to easily interrogate how AIED deep decisions (using multilevel neural networks) are made?

Many of these concerns about how increasingly personal data from people's 'digital exhaust' is used were addressed as part of the UK All-Party Parliamentary Group's enquiry into data ethics (APPG Data Analytics, 2019). In the report's foreword, enquiry co-chairs Darren Jones MP and Lee Rowley MP consider the impact on public service delivery:

> *For such [an ethical approach to data gathering and processing] to start, the government and those organizations providing public services to our constituents need to meet new, consistent standards. And in our mixed economy of public, private and voluntary organizations it is all the more important there should be a single set of principles for all those interacting with the citizen. We are therefore proposing that all such organizations should conform to the highest standards of transparency and engagement as their 'licence to provide public services'. We have built on the latest thinking in relation to freedom of information: that these important issues of openness and accountability to the public should apply to all those delivering services paid for by the taxpayer.*

Whilst many of our education institutions enjoy a degree of independence from government, it can be clear that policy makers will take an increasing interest in those areas that are in their locus of control and regulation—including quasipublic entities such as universities.

## 15.3 Introducing scenario planning

So how could we go about predicting what the future could hold for education institutions, libraries, and librarians—and how might that help us to understand the changes that Education 4.0 is likely to bring? We will look at scenario planning, the umbrella name for a family of techniques that have seen widespread adoption from large corporates such as Apple to policy strategy units such as the UK's Government Office for Science and innovation foundations like Nesta. Scenario planning was originally developed by Shell in the 1970s and subsequently adopted by groups as diverse as the fashion industry (Forum for the Future, 2019), the International Olympic Committee (IOC, 2020).

In their Compendium of Innovation Methods, Nesta (2019) characterize their scenario planning approach in terms of

- Gathering intelligence about the future (e.g. seven Questions and the Delphi method).
- Exploring the dynamics of change (e.g. Driver Mapping and the Axes of Uncertainty).
- Describing what the future might be like (e.g. Visioning and SWOT Analysis).
- Developing/testing policy and strategy (e.g. Backcasting and Roadmapping).

In their Futures Toolkit, the Government Office for Science (GO-Science, 2017) notes that they are working to deliver according to a five-stage policy lifecycle. This policy lifecycle could also be viewed through an organizational lens in terms of strategy and implementation:

- **Formulate policy** using consultation, research, and fit with the wider strategic or policy aims of government to establish relevant goals and targets.
- **Implement policy** by creating and funding appropriate initiatives and policy instruments.
- **Monitor events** to track progress towards goals and targets and to adjust activity if necessary.
- **Evaluate impact** against the project goals and targets and to test contribution to the overall strategy.
- **Modify the objectives** if required to increase impact or strategic relevance.

Spaniol and Rowland (2017) describe the evolution of scenario planning from Cold War scenarios devised by defence strategists through to their adoption by corporate interests—notably Royal Dutch Shell under Pierre Wack during the oil crisis of the early 1970s. They also note that the theory underpinning scenario planning has largely been retrofitted to existing practice and as such can be viewed as exhibiting 'dismal theory and methodological chaos'. Nevertheless, they find that there is significant evidence that organizations of all types and sizes have found scenario planning to be a useful technique and indeed that they continue to use it.

Oliver and Parrett (2017) describe the application of a common scenario planning approach that builds on the pioneering work of the Shell team, in the context of media experts looking at possible strategies for Google's YouTube brand as it faces increasing competition in the streaming media market from both incumbents and challengers such as Netflix. They describe a scenario planning approach that we will draw upon for this chapter—'identify the key focal issue, driving forces, and critical uncertainties before designing four plausible futures and a series of strategic options'.

According to Oliver and Perrett, the participants in the YouTube strategy workshop 'generated 49 driving forces… in a lively debate that lasted 1.5 hours, during which time the participants contested the different views presented. Following this discussion, two critical uncertainties were identified: (1) an increase in the regulation of video content and (2) the extent to which video content can be monetized'. These uncertainties acted as drivers to prompt the participants to devise four scenarios to model:

1. Low increase in the regulation of video content and the low extent to which video content can be monetized, *aka* 'Porn-riddled, cat-infested YouTube rebrands to YouCloud in last-ditch attempt to make £££'.
2. Low increase in the regulation of video content and the high extent to which video content can be monetized, *aka* 'Trillionaires prefer Laissez-Faire'.
3. High increase in the regulation of video content and the low extent to which video content can be monetized, *aka* 'No-Ella! Former online sensation gone down the (You)Tube'.
4. High increase in the regulation of video content and the high extent to which video content can be monetized, *aka* 'YouTube takes first steps towards the monetization of freedom of speech as anonymous user pays £100k for live ISIS stream'.

Whilst these scenarios may seem overblown or hyperbolic, scenario planning practitioners would say that it is important to create a compelling narrative which will encourage participants to give the exercise their full attention. This approach is often characterized using a 2×2 matrix such as the one shown in Fig. 15.1, which shows how the scenarios relate to the uncertainty areas around regulation and potential to monetize.

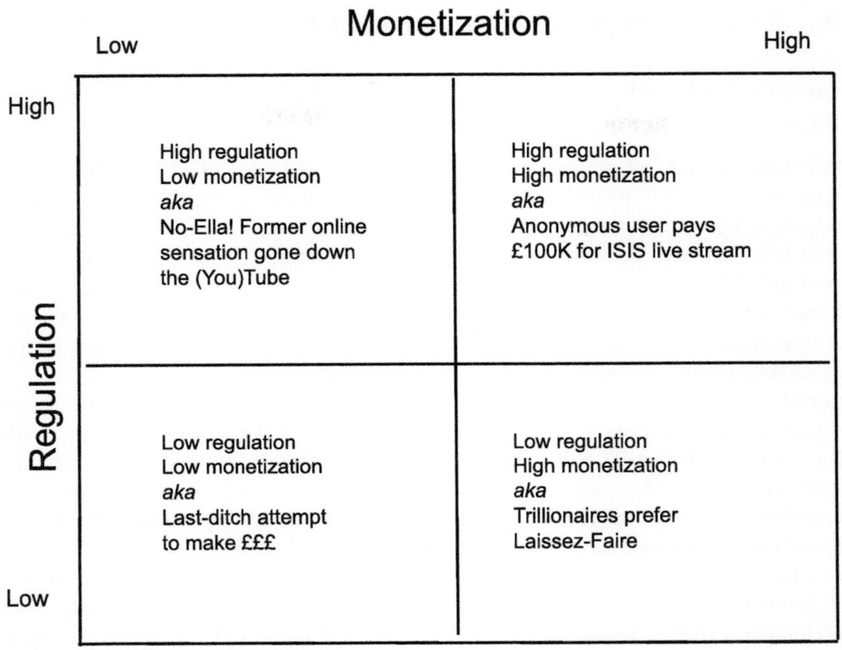


**Fig. 15.1** Example 2×2 matrix for YouTube scenario planning.

In the YouTube case, alongside each of the scenarios, the participants considered early warning signals that would help YouTube to establish the likelihood of the scenario coming to pass. They also explored potential strategic responses that would help YouTube continue to thrive in each of the scenarios. We can do something similar when we consider the transition to Education 4.0 for libraries and the institutions that they exist to support, looking at possible scenarios and potential institutional responses.

Having identified critical uncertainties and modelled potential scenarios the organization undertaking scenario planning is often left with a variant of what Clayton Christensen characterizes as the Innovator's Dilemma: How should one go about setting up a new business unit or developing a new product for a business model, technology, or approach that is the antithesis of everything that the organization stands for or the way that it works at present?

As part of an interview with Christensen, Denning (2016) observes that

> *The classic pattern of disruptive innovation ... is one in which an unobtrusive competitor eats away at the low end of an incumbent's market with a lower quality product. The incumbent is happy to concede the low-value customers and concentrates on adding more features for its base of high-value customers. Next the disruptor steadily improves quality to move up-market, and then devours the whole market of the incumbent, who often doesn't perceive the threat until it's too late.*

Somewhat ominously, Denning also notes that 'at one extreme, some incumbents were not innovating at all, such as universities'.

## 15.4 A scenario planning approach to Education 4.0

We cannot consider Education 4.0 without also looking at the broader geopolitical environment. Let us consider three key areas of critical uncertainty:

- **Digital disruption**—at present, the bulk of education still takes place using the old paradigms of classes and timetables, lectures, and examinations. Learners assemble on school, college, or university campuses, for which (particularly for higher education) they often travel long distances, relocate, or even travel internationally. Could Education 4.0 utterly transform delivery paradigms, or might our education institutions continue to resist radical change? If we accept that the opportunity exists for significant disruption, is it even possible for slow moving and often bureaucratic large organizations to embrace this, or will the future belong to agile innovators operating much more like Internet start-ups?
- **Impact of climate change**—at present, it is generally expected that learners in postcompulsory education of even modest means will be able to travel nationally if not internationally to study. Schemes such as student loans and bursaries, Erasmus+, and the European Credit Transfer and Accumulation Scheme (ECTS) exist to support these activities. With increasing awareness that punitive measures may need to be taken to mitigate the impact of climate change, reduced personal mobility for all but government operatives and the wealthiest citizens could be a consequence. Climate scientists also advise (Kellogg and Schware, 2019) that significant disruption to normal life can be expected from climate change related developments such as rising sea levels, large scale and long-lived wildfires, crop failures, and water shortages. As the author notes (Hamilton, 2020) that the COVID-19 coronavirus pandemic has given us a very stark insight into the wholesale changes to our lifestyles and ways of working that may be required if climate change is not addressed with radical action.
- **Nationalism versus globalism**—the rise of populist leaders such as Donald Trump, Jair Bolsonaro, and Viktor Orbán comes alongside and arguably arises from a crisis of personal identity in the early 21st century. Are we world citizens, with rights and responsibilities to our planet and the human race that transcend any accidents of birth, or will ties of nationhood and cultural identity prove reassuring in an age where other historically shared tribal bonds like religion and politics have fallen by the wayside? Do we need an 'other' to project our fears and concerns onto, and if so do we know who our real allies and enemies are? The UK's referendum on EU membership has thrown many of these tropes into sharp relief, with families and communities still largely divided as Hobolt et al. (2018) found

> *Brexit has given rise to new political identities. When asked whether they think of themselves as 'Leavers', 'Remainers' or 'neither', we consistently find that, since the referendum, around 35% of people identify as Leavers and around 40% as Remainers. These identities have remained largely unchanged since the referendum, and cut across existing party lines.*

How could these uncertainties play out? Let us envisage some possible scenarios in two of the uncertainty areas, focussing on postcompulsory education…

**Digital innovation and disruption scenarios:**

- D1. **Digital vegans**: Artisanal education is on the rise as a growing intake of 'digital vegans' (Hill, 2019) demand a return to traditional chalk and talk values such as the conventional lecture. This causes significant difficulties for institutions that responded to the removal of student number controls by recruiting very large numbers of learners for particular courses, as it becomes hard to ensure that students receive the contact hours they expect.

- D2. **Status quo—the worried well**: Institutions continue to take a cautious approach, thoroughly testing new technologies and pedagogies before putting them into practice—essentially rejecting rapid and potentially disruptive innovation. In doing so, they consciously gamble that their peers in the United Kingdom and internationally will not find ways of leapfrogging them and grow increasingly worried that the smallest mistake or misstep could fatally damage their reputation.
- D3. **FAANG University**: Challengers emerge that are not encumbered by the trappings of conventional education—picture a FAANG (Facebook, Apple, Amazon, Netflix, and Google) company like Netflix or Amazon decided to start a university with a radically different operating model. With little or no campus estate and permanent staff costs by comparison with conventional institutions, the challengers can offer courses at a significantly lower price point. They hire the best bought-in teaching staff for more than traditional institutions were prepared to pay, to ensure their courses are high quality and obtain validation from professional societies and associations.

## Climate change scenarios around student mobility:

- C1. **Study local**: Reduced personal mobility leads to a focus on local and regional institutions for learners who want to have a face-to-face campus-based education and might previously have been tempted to spread their wings. Courses are more heavily tailored to the needs of regional employers, with students wishing to learn about other subjects largely opting for online education instead of campus-based courses.
- C2. **Faster, better?** Institutions feared that students would be put off travelling due to measures such as carbon taxes for long haul flights and road pricing, but in practice what happens is that students spend more time on and around campus and go home less. This gives institutions the opportunity to move to shorter courses, for example, 2-year degrees, but these measures also have a drastic impact on faculty's ability to travel for research project work and to attend conferences.
- C3. **Oligarchs only**: Governments feel they have to get tough on key contributors to climate change, and long-distance travel becomes all but unaffordable except to the ultra-wealthy and those on government business. Overnight, many universities' business models become unsustainable due to their reliance on international student fees. It transpires that international students are unwilling to pay more than a fraction of their current fees for online delivery or branch campus type approaches, which they perceive as inferior options.

Fig. 15.2 illustrates these scenarios as institutions begin to plan their transition to Education 4.0.

Having considered uncertainty areas and their possible implications, we are in a position to strategize as to how institutional leaders, practitioners, and policymakers could respond to the envisaged outcomes. For example, let us consider a hypothetical 'FAANG University' operated by Amazon, who are already in the first division of digital disruption through initiatives like Amazon Marketplace and Amazon Web Services:

- Low operating costs as there are no campuses to maintain or permanent staff other than a small number of developers and administrators—allowing Amazon the opportunity to significantly undercut conventional providers.

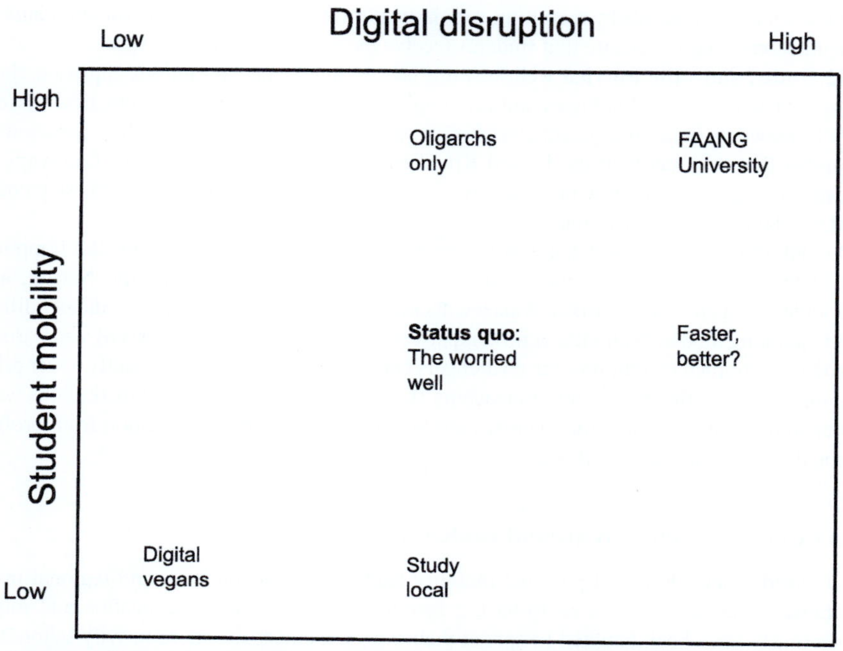


**Fig. 15.2** Student mobility and digital disruption on the path to Education 4.0.

- Can buy in physical facilities for an hourly rate as and when required, for example assessment centres operated by existing providers such as Pearson.
- High quality as Amazon can hire the same bought-in teaching staff that would be running courses at conventional institutions, securing the services of high performers by paying them significantly more.
- Good brand recognition and ability to use other products in the company's portfolio to enhance the value proposition—for example 'all of your textbooks will automatically appear in the Kindle app'.
- Can leverage marketplace capabilities to support ratings and reviews of tutors and courses, potentially splitting courses into bite-sized chunks that learners can study at their own pace.
- Can leverage marketplace capabilities such as Amazon Ignite (Holt, 2019) to put tutors in competition with one another, giving students the ability to choose between tutors based on a range of metrics including price point and perceived quality.
- Creates opportunities for new products and services that can be part of FAANG University and also sold separately, for example, 'Amazon Notary: authenticated online delivery of important documents to their intended recipient, such as evidence of eligibility and qualifications'.
- International recognition for FAANG University qualifications in countries that participate in the Bologna process.
- Students can potentially transfer credit they have earned from FAANG University to conventional courses and institutions via the European Credit Transfer Scheme—although FAANG companies might well prefer to lock students into ongoing services such as periodic revalidation of qualifications.

However, there are many areas where a challenger like Amazon would be particularly weak:

- Recognition as an awarding body—this would require the company to build a relationship with regulators such as the UK's Office for Students, and there could be significant political sensitivities around what might be perceived as a full-frontal attack on the conventional higher education system.
- Ongoing quality checks, working with the likes of the Quality Assurance Agency (QAA), which measures compliance with the Quality Code for UK Higher Education. A wholly new approach to quality assessment might be required, which could significantly delay a challenger like Amazon from bringing its product to market.
- Perception that a FAANG degree is less worthwhile than one obtained in a conventional way from a traditional institution—although this could be ameliorated via business partnerships with respected professional bodies such as the UK's royal societies.

In strategizing for a possible institutional response to the emergence of a challenger like the as-yet hypothetical FAANG University, senior leaders ultimately have to make a judgement call based on the weight of available evidence. For example, what if the government of the day showed significant animosity towards higher education institutions and the progressive values they generally espouse, as we have recently seen in countries where populist leaders have risen to power? Might this predispose some policy advisors to conclude something to the effect of 'to hell with the snowflakes, the FAANGs will eat them for breakfast!' If so, what could senior leaders do to monitor for weak signals and warning signs and affect a course correction for their institutions?

**Monitoring weak signals**: It seems likely that some institutions would be more exposed than others to this sort of competition, for example, those whose qualifications are perceived as subpar or are slow to recruit students to new growth areas such as artificial intelligence. We could view their travails as part of a process of transition to a new operating model, as Christensen says (Denning, 2016), in which case significant lessons may emerge for the rest of the sector from these institutions.

It is important to note that challengers may not be constrained by geography or prior ties to the sector and so may emerge unexpectedly from the perspective of those who are primarily looking at their own country or their peers. And whilst we have used FAANG University as an example, it is also important to consider the possibility of traditional institutions radically reinventing themselves. Let us picture MIT deciding that it was in their interests and in line with their mission to offer the next billion learners the opportunity to earn an MIT degree, leveraging the Internet and AI to make this possible. Closely monitoring initiatives like MITx MicroMasters (MIT, 2018) might help us to spot this trend emerging, for example by tracking recruitment to software engineering, business development, and marketing roles.

**Course corrections**: The particular circumstances and operating model for an institution could be expected to dictate its response to a significant extent. For example, an institution that operated by renting building space around a city could make a strategic decision to reduce its operating costs by letting leases lapse and encouraging staff to work flexibly. The past decade has already seen significant casualization of all levels of the education workforce, and there may be limits to how much further down this route institutions might be able to go before the pipeline of future academic talent is irreparably damaged (HEPI, 2019).

Efforts by incumbents to develop online education approaches have largely focussed on the corporate training market or free-open online courses that effectively act as halo products and loss leaders for the 'real' courses, for example, FutureLearn and edX. There is a very real challenge for institutional leaders about setting up new online-oriented courses that have just as much validity as traditional ones—in the process of asking your people and your organization to work in fundamentally different ways. And what if you shoot for the next billion learners, but all you manage to do is cannibalize your core student demographic—a very real Innovator's Dilemma?

## 15.5 Summary and conclusions

In much of the thinking about societal trends and library and information science trends that we have highlighted in this chapter, there is a tacit assumption that things will carry on much the same as before. We can surmise that policymakers might wake up one morning and realize that actually, they really do value public libraries and will go back to funding them accordingly; that climate change will simply make things a bit warmer and wetter, which will give the British something to complain about if nothing else. More generally, whilst most people would acknowledge that a degree of change is inevitable, our expectations are of a slow and incremental change rather than sudden step changes.

However, in the public library arena, the UK's austerity years have provided a powerful counter narrative: libraries have often been perceived as a luxury item by comparison with areas such as rubbish collections, highway maintenance, special educational needs provision, and social care. The wholesale dismantling of the public library network has of course had a knock-on effect on demand for library and information science degrees, with the result that it is becoming increasingly difficult to qualify as a librarian—and university library schools are now an endangered species.

When we come to look at trends like the potential for technological disruption, the shifting political sands, and the growing evidence of runaway climate change, the signals are far from weak. We already have libraries without books (such as Amazon's Kindle), universities with just a single lecture theatre (Armellini, 2018), and a growing number of online education providers like Udacity who aim to fill needs that conventional providers have either neglected or have simply been slow to respond too.

Universities UK (UUK, 2019) observe that tuition fee income alone for UK universities amounted to some £18.1 billion pounds in 2017–18. A challenger that managed to secure just 6% of this business would in itself be a billion-pound business. This puts higher education institutions very firmly in the sights of startups and investors that are seeking to disrupt the education market, and many of the lessons learned in a country like the United Kingdom could be directly transferable to other Anglophone countries with a high fees culture such as the United States.

It might seem like science fiction that Udacity (2019) offered a 'nanodegree' in Flying Car Engineering, but this comes at a time when the authorities in Dubai have prepared for 2020s launch of the world's first flying taxi service (WEF, 2019). And in the United Kingdom, Innovate UK's Future Flight programme is investing £125 million over the next 4 years to create the infrastructure for electric aircraft, flying taxis, and drone delivery. As the author and futurist William Gibson says, 'the future is already here, it's just not very evenly distributed' (Gibson, 2012).

However, as Lepore (2014) notes in reference to Christensen's theories, there is a risk of getting carried away by adrenaline and hyperbole: 'the University of Virginia's panicked board of trustees attempted to fire the president, charging her with jeopardizing the institution's future by failing to disruptively innovate with sufficient speed'. Institutions should probably not plan to dispose of their estates holdings just yet, or indeed to shut down libraries and other facilities that are well used and have consistently proven vital to the student experience. Perhaps the real issues as we move forward into the 2020s are how to upskill our staff to meet the information literacy and digital skills needs of tomorrow's learners and researchers, and how best to exploit the potential of Education 4.0 to educate the next billion learners.

## References

APPG Data Analytics, 2019. Trust, transparency and tech—building ethical data policies for the public good. Report of the All-Party Parliamentary Group on Data Analytics Enquiry Into Data Ethics, Policy Connect. https://www.policyconnect.org.uk/appgda/research/trust-transparency-and-technology-building-data-policies-public-good. (Accessed 29 April 2020).

Armellini, A., 2018. The Large Lecture (Theatre) Is Dead. Jisc Inform Interview https://www.jisc.ac.uk/news/the-large-lecture-theatre-is-dead-11-jan-2018. (Accessed 29 April 2020).

Association of College and Research Libraries (ACRL), 2018. 2018 top trends in academic libraries—a review of the trends and issues affecting academic libraries in higher education. Coll. Res. Libr. News 79 (6). https://crln.acrl.org/index.php/crlnews/article/view/17001/18750. (Accessed 29 April 2020).

Davies, S., Mullan, J., Feldman, P., 2017. Rebooting learning for the digital age: what next for technology enhanced higher education? Higher Education Policy Institute (HEPI) Report 93 https://www.hepi.ac.uk/wp-content/uploads/2017/02/Hepi_Rebooting-learning-for-the-digital-age-Report-93-02_02_17Web.pdf. (Accessed 29 April 2020).

Dempsey, L., 2014. The Network Reshapes the Library: Lorcan Dempsey on Libraries, Services, and Networks. Facet Publishing, London. https://www.oclc.org/content/dam/research/publications/books/dempsey-network-reshapes-library.pdf. (Accessed 29 April 2020).

Denning, S., 2016. Christensen updates disruption theory. Strateg. Leadersh. 44 (2), 10–16. https://doi.org/10.1108/sl-01-2016-0005.

Forum for the Future, 2019. Fashion Futures 2030 Scenario Planning Toolkit. https://www.forumforthefuture.org/fashion-futures-2030. (Accessed 29 April 2020).

Gibson, W., 2012. The Future Has Arrived—It's Just Not Evenly Distributed Yet. Quote Investigator Search. http://quoteinvestigator.com/2012/01/24/future-has-arrived/. (Accessed 29 April 2020).

GO-Science, 2017. The Futures Toolkit—Tools for Futures Thinking and Foresight Across UK Government. Government Office for Science. November. https://assets.publishing.service.gov.uk/government/uploads/system/uploads/attachment_data/file/674209/futures-toolkit-edition-1.pdf. (Accessed 29 April 2020).

Hackett, D., 2018. An elephant in the room? Information literacy in the narrative of UK public libraries. J. Inf. Lit. 12 (1), 4–26. https://doi.org/10.11645/12.1.2305.

Hamilton, M., 2019. Of modems and pixie dust—blockchain demystified. Insight 32 (1). https://doi.org/10.1629/uksg.447.

Hamilton, M., March 2020. Universities Need to Lead on the Responses to COVID-19. University World News. https://www.universityworldnews.com/post.php?story=20200316144641880. (Accessed 29 April 2020).

Higher Education Policy Institute (HEPI), 2019. New Data Show Complexities Around Casualisation. Higher Education Policy Institute. https://www.hepi.ac.uk/2019/01/29/new-data-shows-complexities-around-casualisation/. (Accessed 29 April 2020).

Hill, K., 2019. I Cut the 'Big Five' Tech Giants From My Life. It Was Hell. Gizmodo, February https://gizmodo.com/i-cut-the-big-five-tech-giants-from-my-life-it-was-hel-1831304194. (Accessed 29 April 2020).

Hobolt, S., Leeper, T., Tilley, J., 2018. Emerging Brexit identities. In: Menon, A. (Ed.), Brexit and Public Opinion. UK in a Changing Europe. http://ukandeu.ac.uk/wp-content/uploads/2018/01/Public-Opinion.pdf. (Accessed 29 April 2020).

Holmes, W., Bektik, D., Woolf, B., Luckin, R., 2019. Ethics in AIED: who cares? In: 20th International Conference on Artificial Intelligence in Education (AIED'19), 25–29 Jun 2019, Chicago.

Holt, K., 2019. Amazon Offers Teachers a Place to Sell Resources They Create. Engadget. December https://www.engadget.com/2019/11/12/amazon-ignite-educational-materials-store/?guccounter=1. (Accessed 29 April 2020).

Hou, J., Yang, X., Chen, C., 2018. Emerging trends and new developments in information science: a document co-citation analysis (2009–2016). Scientometrics 115 (2), 869–892. https://doi.org/10.1007/s11192-018-2695-9.

House of Commons, 2019. Education select committee oral evidence: fourth industrial revolution. Transcript of evidence session from Priya Lakhani, Martin Hamilton, Vinous Ali and David Brown. 8th January 2019 http://data.parliament.uk/writtenevidence/committeeevidence.svc/evidencedocument/education-committee/fourth-industrial-revolution/oral/94845.html. (Accessed 29 April 2020).

International Federation of Library Associations (IFLA), 2018. IFLA Trend Report 2018 Update. International Federation of Library Associations and Institutions. https://trends.ifla.org/update-2018. (Accessed 29 April 2020).

International Olympic Committee, 2020. Health and Safety Paramount as IOC Executive Board Agrees to Step Up Scenario Planning for the Olympic Games Tokyo 2020. International Olympic Committee News Release https://www.olympic.org/news/health-and-safety-paramount-as-ioc-executive-board-agrees-to-continue-scenario-planning-for-the-olympic-games-tokyo-2020. (Accessed 29 April 2020).

Jisc, 2018. Preparing for Education 4.0. Times Higher Education. December https://www.timeshighereducation.com/hub/jisc/p/preparing-education-40. (Accessed 29 April 2020).

Jisc, 2019. AR and VR in Teaching and Learning Survey Findings. https://repository.jisc.ac.uk/7555/1/ar-vr-survey-report-2019.pdf. (Accessed 29 April 2020. October.

Kellogg, W.W., Schware, R., 2019. Climate Change and Society—Consequences of Increasing Atmospheric Carbon Dioxide. Routledge, https://doi.org/10.4324/9780429048739.

Lepore, J., 2014. The disruption machine—what the gospel of innovation gets wrong. New Yorker. June https://www.newyorker.com/magazine/2014/06/23/the-disruption-machine. (Accessed 29 April 2020).

MIT, 2018. MITx MicroMasters Adds New Pathways to Access to Master's Degrees. MIT Center for Transportation and Logistics. https://medium.com/mitsupplychain/mitx-micro-masters-adds-new-pathways-to-access-to-masters-degrees-ab3ad1434d10. (Accessed 29 April 2020).

Mourtzis, D., Vlachoua, E., Dimitrakopoulosa, G., Zogopoulos, V., 2018. Cyber-physical systems and education 4.0—the teaching factory 4.0 concept. Proc. Manuf. 23, 129–134.

Nesta, 2019. A Compendium of Innovation Methods. https://media.nesta.org.uk/documents/Compendium-of-Innovation-Methods-March-2019.pdf. (Accessed 29 April 2020. March.

Oliver, J.J., Parrett, E., 2017. Managing future uncertainty: reevaluating the role of scenario planning. Bus. Horiz. 61 (2), 339–352. https://doi.org/10.1016/j.bushor.2017.11.013.

Pinfield, S., Cox, A., Rutter, S., 2017. Mapping the Future of Academic Libraries: A Report for SCONUL. Society of College, National and University Libraries (SCONUL), London. https://sconul.ac.uk/publication/mapping-the-future-of-academic-libraries. (Accessed 29 April 2020).

Ravenscroft, A., Richards, P., Bunce, M., 2020. Education 4.0: is characterising and harmonising intelligences and fostering mindfulness and positive mental health a way of thinking about a pedagogy 4.0 for HE? In: Malloch, M., Evans, K., Cairns, L., O'Connor, B. (Eds.), Learning and Work. Sage, New York.

Seldon, A., Abidoye, O., 2018. The Fourth Education Revolution: Will Artificial Intelligence Liberate or Infantilise Humanity? The University of Buckingham Press.

Society of College, National and University Libraries (SCONUL), 2018. Spotlight On: The Continuing Evolution of UK Academic Libraries. Excerpt From 2017–17 SCONUL Annual Statistics. https://www.sconul.ac.uk/sites/default/files/documents/The_continuing_evolution_of_UK_academic_libraries.pdf. (Accessed 29 April 2020).

Spaniol, M., Rowland, N.J., 2017. The scenario planning paradox. Futures. https://doi.org/10.1016/j.futures.2017.09.006. October.

Udacity, 2019. Flying Car and Autonomous Flight Engineer Nanodegree. Online Course Description. https://www.udacity.com/course/flying-car-nanodegree--nd78. (Accessed 29 April 2020).

Universities UK (UUK), 2019. Higher education in facts and figures 2019. UUK report https://www.universitiesuk.ac.uk/facts-and-stats/data-and-analysis/. (Accessed 29 April 2020).

World Economic Forum, 2019. Can Dubai Go Green With Flying Taxis and 'Rooms on Wheels'? World Economic Forum/Thomson Reuters Foundation. October https://www.weforum.org/agenda/2019/10/dubai-flying-taxis/. (Accessed 29 April 2020).

# Data-driven modelling of public library infrastructure and usage in the United Kingdom

16

*Flora Roumpani*[a], *Maja Maricevic*[b], *and Alan Wilson*[a]
[a]The Alan Turing Institute, London, United Kingdom, [b]The British Library, London, United Kingdom

## 16.1 Introduction and context

As far back as 1994, the International Federation of Libraries Association (IFLA) and UNESCO published the Public Library Manifesto, defining that the public library is 'the local centre of information, making all kinds of knowledge and information readily available to its users' (IFLA, 1994). This ensures that public libraries are understood as places that provide the population with access not only to physical books and traditional materials but also to digital content and media. Whilst public libraries' efforts to provide effective digital services remain a work in progress, many libraries have been active in embracing digital innovation; from the digitization, production, and preservation of online content, to being involved in the provision of spaces and resources for digital innovation, coding courses and clubs, and introductions on the impact of new technologies such as artificial intelligence (AI) and robotics (EBSCO, 2019).

However, when it comes to embracing the potential of data analysis, data enabled services are still far from becoming an integral part of the UK public library sector. With the exception of some individual initiatives of good practice—for example, the *Libraries Hacked* website (Rowe, 2019), there is, as yet, a lack of a national data platform for understanding how people use public libraries. One of the reasons, as per the conclusions of William Sieghart's Independent Libraries Report in 2014, is that there are still significant challenges in the provision of key digital infrastructure for public libraries in the United Kingdom, such as the lack of universal provision of free Wi-Fi, an absence of a national e-lending system, as well as a lack of a strategic framework for public libraries in England (Department for Digital, Culture, Media and Sport (DCMS), 2014).

The Data-driven Libraries Project explores how we may unlock the potential of data science methods, in particular mathematical modelling, to gain a better understanding of the UK public libraries and communities that use them. In nearly all economic sectors and across many areas of government, the explosion of data has been seen as a route to innovation, greater productivity, and efficiency, as well as a way, to better understand customers and provide a platform for new, data-driven services. The project is exploring if data science could enable public libraries to move beyond

**Future Directions in Digital Information. https://doi.org/10.1016/B978-0-12-822144-0.00016-1**

traditional data collecting and reporting that is typically used to inform public policy, such as data analysis underpinning cost-effectiveness, and economic value studies, and which is frequently described as unsuitable for capturing educational, community, and other types of value provided by public libraries (Arts Council England, 2014).

There are significant gaps in the UK public libraries' data. Data sets, if available, are fragmented across many different types of libraries, which are run by local authorities, communities, or independently run libraries, all using different methods of data collection and reporting. Therefore, the core national data set for public libraries is of poor quality and difficult to use in any meaningful way, as recognized by the government itself (DCMS, 2018).

This project sets out to integrate these fragmented data sets and suggests modelling techniques to help us better understand the demand and supply of public library resources and their multifaceted role in supporting communities. This includes their role in providing public spaces, working spaces, accessibility to technology, providing key support services for employment and skills development, delivering events for both children and adults, and so forth. Whilst it has been shown that varied functions of public libraries are understood and valued by public library users and even nonusers (Oliphant, 2014), there is no current methodology for measuring the value of public libraries for the communities, and therefore, the future of libraries is left in the hands of each current local authority. There remains an urgent need, especially in the United Kingdom, to develop new methodologies that would deepen the analysis of libraries' data and provide a much stronger basis for informing public policy and planning related to public library provision on both national and local levels.

This is especially relevant in the current context of mass closures of public libraries in the United Kingdom, which has led to vigorous public debate and several governmental reviews, but has been conducted in the absence of robust data and evidence about the public libraries' services and impact, and largely failing to stem the current decline. The annual survey of the Chartered Institute of Public Finance and Accountancy (CIPFA) is a revealing and ongoing picture of library closures as the decade's austerity pressures see local authorities continuing to apply swingeing cuts to their budgets. In 2018, spending on libraries by local authorities fell by £30 to £741 m with a net loss of 127 public libraries in England, Wales, and Scotland (CIPFA, 2018). CIPFA is revealing a similar picture each year since 2010 and for some indicators showing even earlier signs of decline. A recent briefing produced for the House of Commons, largely based on CIPFA data, reports that since 2010–11, library net expenditure, excluding capital, has declined by 36% in real terms from £1.15 billion to £741 million in 2017–18. In the same period, the number of service points that were open 10 h or more per week fell by 738 or 17% (Woodhouse and Zayed, 2019).

In the period between 2005 and 2018, the number of full-time equivalents (FTE) employees working in public libraries across England, Wales, and Scotland fell from 25,777 to 15,483, which represents a reduction of 40% (Woodhouse and Zayed, 2019). Consequently, 'community-run' library branches have become the norm in the United Kingdom: in 2010, it estimates that there were only around 10 libraries in the hands of volunteers; by 2017, the figure had risen to around 500 (Anstice, 2017; Flood, 2017). Unsurprisingly, this meant that during the period between 2009–10 and 2017–18, visitor numbers reduced by 26%, and between 2007 and 2008 and 2017–18 the total number of books issued for loan fell from approximately 302 to 183 million—a reduction of 119 million or 39% (Woodhouse and Zayed, 2019).

The impact of the closure of libraries in the last decade requires further investigation. One study that attempts to analyze the impact of library closures by using data analysis methods emerged from two British Library funded projects, looking at the impact of the previous library closures and opening hours reductions from 1986 to 1997 in England and Wales (Proctor and Simmons, 2000). The study finds that over 88% of respondents have reduced access over the period but with significant differences between individual authorities and categories of authority. The case studies demonstrated that library closures had a variety of impacts: between 8.3% and 29% of users lost access to a public library entirely, but in the case of young children, loss of access was as high as 67%. This indicates that the closures of the last decade must have had an equally significant effect, but in the absence of data, we can provide only anecdotal and case study—based impacts.

Library closure is a topic of controversy. For some researchers, the library closures and decline are primarily about the local authority funding cuts (Busby, 2019), whilst others see it as a result of bad management (Kean, 2017), or as a longer-term trend linked to society's loss of faith in objective information and decline in civic engagement (Smith, 2019). Some blame the Internet for changing habits of readers and libraries losing their relevance, whilst others see technology as a key factor that will lead to the sector's revival (Wyatt and Leorke, 2018).

All of the above claims are difficult to dispute or substantiate through data-based evidence due to a lack of good quality libraries' data. O'Bryan (2018) shows in her report, completed with the help of the Libraries Taskforce, the limitations of the CIPFA data set due to its structure, consistency, accuracy, lack of standardization, and variable selection and measurement, emphasizing that these flaws impair our ability to understand trends at the national level in a comprehensive way. The report attempts to show a different way to understand libraries' data by, for example, recognizing the existence of 'trendbuckers', the libraries that have continued to grow despite the overall decline. Whilst criticizing the CIPFA data and suggesting that the downward trend might be slowing, this report also recognizes that there is a correlation between declining expenditures and declining visits and book issues.

O'Bryan also recognizes the overall lack of data in the sector:

> *We lack good data on how libraries are used and the changes they've been undergoing. Data at the national level is often incomplete, bolstered by estimations, or missing critical variables. Until the creation of the Basic Data set by the Libraries Taskforce in 2017, there didn't even exist a definitive list of all public libraries in England.*
>
> *(O'Bryan, 2018)*

This is where the Data-driven Libraries Project fits in—trying to connect fragmented data sets to offer new insights and shows how libraries could use techniques for modelling demand and supply which are successfully being used for years to grow many other services sectors. We are hoping that this work will show new ways in which libraries could use modelling and scenario building techniques, to provide a new perspective on how data could be used by public libraries to better serve communities by understanding the demand and supply of knowledge. We hope that this might enable the sector to expand its outlook on how data can be used to improve public libraries and thus encourage more consistent data collection.

## 16.2 Objectives

The project has three interconnected sets of objectives, starting with an attempt to integrate the UK data on public libraries on the national level and presents the findings in a new and useful way. This was especially deemed important in relation to the high level of closures of public libraries across the United Kingdom, with the significant public outcry regarding the closures, including the recognition of their key role for local communities (Busby, 2019; CIPFA, 2018). Whilst the decision for each closure has been made by individual local authorities in relation to their own budgetary pressures, our objective is to show the national model of the libraries and the library closures in relation to population and its key characteristics in order to begin to present evidence regarding types of communities that have been most affected by the library closures. In this chapter, we show the progress that we have made with the national modelling and the challenges that the project has yet to address.

The project's second objective is to investigate how data could be used to model a picture of libraries beyond the traditional data on book lending, which is often reported as falling and used to underpin the narrative regarding the changing habits of readers and the changing roles of libraries (BBC, 2014). Whilst it is frequently acknowledged that public libraries have many other uses besides book lending (Oliphant, 2014), there is very little data to help us understand how public libraries serve a wider range of purposes—for example, providing study and workspace and Internet access. Whilst they remain suppliers of books, much of today's 'knowledge' is digitized, meaning that structured access to digital resources offers libraries a new role.

In other words, much of what libraries can provide is data-driven and hence our title. Ultimately, if we can collect adequate data on libraries and their use, it becomes possible to provide an analytic base to advance our understanding of their role, their impact on different types of population, as well as to underpin the future planning of libraries across the United Kingdom. The data can be used to calibrate mathematical and computer models of library systems to provide a realistic representation of the system—a digital twin—which can be used to explore future scenarios and the effectiveness of future plans. In this paper, we show how such models can be designed, calibrated, and tested, and used for these purposes.

Because data availability is poor, we build a demo model and show how it can be used to explore current library challenges in a period of cutbacks and austerity. The imperfect state of data means that our models are also likely to be imperfect in certain aspects, but it is hoped that they show potential and a methodology of what could be done if data was collected across the United Kingdom in a more standardized way.

The third objective of the project is to comment on the current state of the UK public libraries' data, to recommend more comprehensive and standardized data collection, as well as showcase some potential uses of such data for public policy and planning.

## 16.3 There are no data for libraries on a national scale

Data availability for UK public libraries is poor—the available data is fragmented and has multiple gaps. We begin with a brief review of data at the national scale. One of the richest sources for libraries' data across the United Kingdom is the *Libraries Hacked* project, an open-source project by Dave Rowe established in 2015 (Rowe, 2019), which collects, visualizes, and makes available open data for libraries from different sources around the United Kingdom. Other sources include closed data sources, such as the SCONUL data for higher education libraries, but also local data-collecting initiatives from libraries themselves, such as the Newcastle Libraries, which we consider further below. There are further local sources of data, collected by local authorities, which use their local systems for data collection, management, and organization. There is no current method to coordinate the collection of data from these sources, but DCMS is currently attempting to coordinate a collection of an open national data set for libraries (DCMS, 2019).

In addition, in order to provide the UK public library data model, it is important to take into account the differences in how different UK nations approach public libraries and data collecting, including Arts Council England that acts as a development agency for libraries in England, Scottish Library and Information Council, Northern Ireland Library Authority, and Welsh Public Library Authority. Whilst this project aims to model the public libraries system across the United Kingdom and it has already deployed some basic data sets across all four countries, at this stage, it has been mostly wrangling data from key sources for England, which is a significant challenge in its own right.

As to this date, there are only two official data sets available which contain surveyed data relating to public libraries in England. The Ordnance Survey 2011 data, which has mapped noncategorized libraries throughout the United Kingdom, and the 2016 Libraries Taskforce data. The Libraries Taskforce in 2016 (DCMS, 2016a,b), includes all the locations (postcodes) of libraries in England. This basic data set provides information on public libraries in England, validated by 151 library organizations. It shows the number and location (by postcode) of static libraries in England (statutory and nonstatutory) as of 1 July 2016. The extended basic data set also includes the type of library, the number of hours open as well as libraries that were temporarily closed, on 1 July, for example for refurbishment. It lists **3267** libraries in England. This data set includes the following fields for all public libraries in England:

- Library service
- Library name
- Address

- Postcode
- Email
- Website

Combining these data enables us to offer an initial UK picture and to calculate some crude indicators of library provision by the local authority in England. The map in Fig. 16.1 also shows the distribution of libraries by type in England—local authority run, community run, and commissioned.

Whilst the first map in Fig. 16.1 offers an expected clustering effect around the major UK urban centres, the second map in Fig. 16.2 shows the number of libraries in England per head of local authority population, which is starting to give us more comparative information about public libraries' provision in England. However, to ensure further accuracy and usefulness of this map, it will be necessary to calibrate it with additional layers of data regarding the socio-economic characteristics of the population in each area, travel access to each library, as well as key characteristics of each library, including their size and types of services on offer.

The described data sets are not collected on the national level, which means that at this stage we are not able to go any further in developing a national model for libraries. However, we were able to have a first view of the library system in the United Kingdom. In the following sections, we will attempt to explain, how a library model in combination with a comprehensive national data set could potentially be used to better inform the policy and planning of public libraries and evaluate the impact of closures.

## 16.4 What is a model?

What do we need to know about a library system? Essentially, what kinds of people use libraries, and for what purpose? If we have this information, we can calculate the indicators of effectiveness and efficiency and use these as aids in future planning. These can lead to the development of predicting models, or 'theories of systems of interest' (Wilson, 2012). Such systems can provide insights into the 'what-if', with their analytical properties for planning and policy development. In this case, what-if a library shuts down? Wilson characterized them as 'flight simulators' for planners (2016), or as Batty states:

> *Models are simplifications of reality, theoretical abstractions that represent systems in such a way that essential features crucial to the theory and its application are identified and highlighted. In this role, models act as a vehicle to enable experimentation with theory in a predictive sense, and to enhance understanding which may be prior to predictions of situations as yet unrealized, for example, in the future.*
>
> *(Batty, 2013)*

In that sense, models contribute to the development of scenarios by modelling the behaviour of their independent elements. The increasing availability of spatial data, combined with increasing computer power, has enabled the calibration of these models using observed data and modelling characteristics such as what is the demand of users

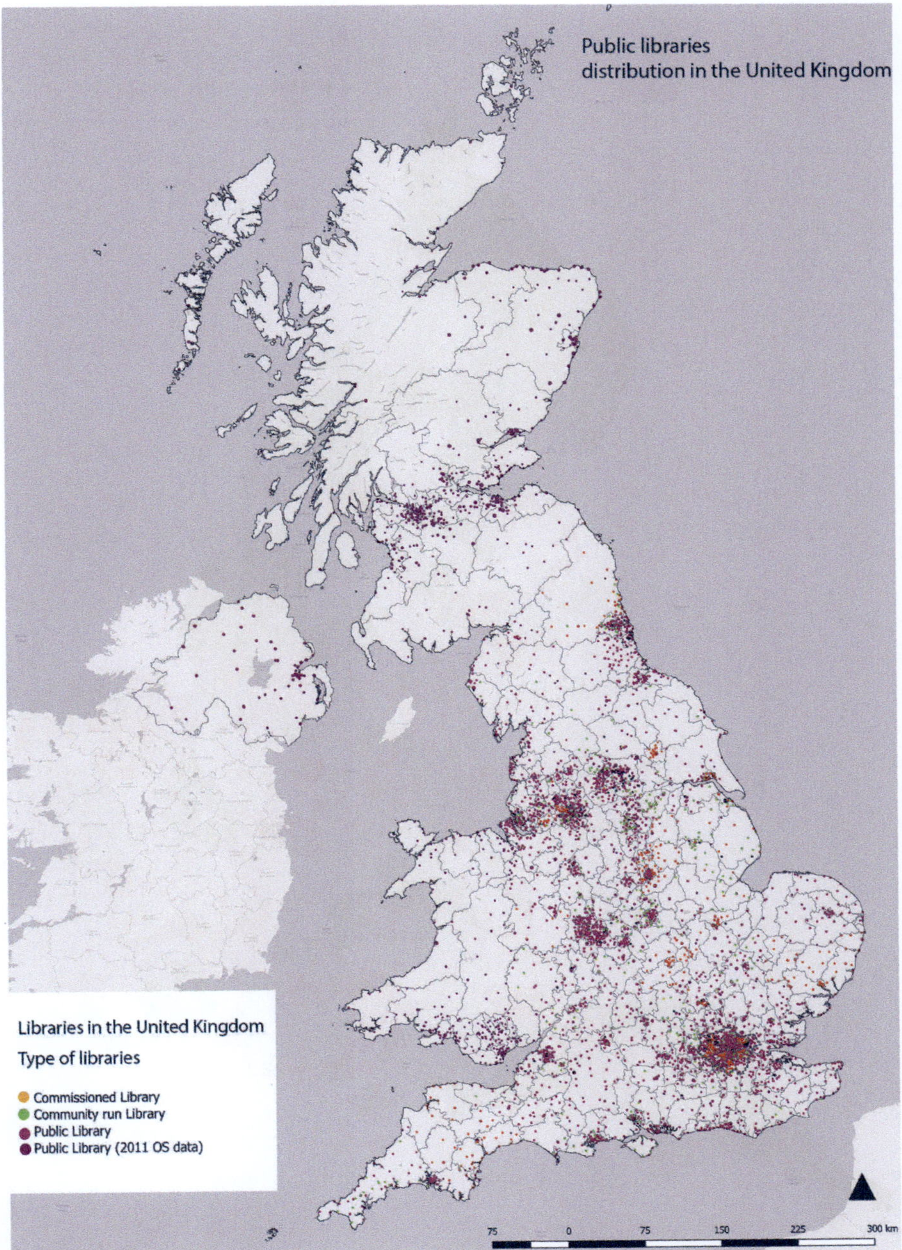


**Fig. 16.1** Distribution of public libraries in the United Kingdom, a national view. Data from Ordnance Survey Local Maps, 2011. Open Data, Important Buildings Layer, Contains Ordnance Survey data © Crown copyright and database right 2018; Ordnance Survey Ireland, 2013. Regional Geographic Placenames- from EuroGeographics 1:1m and 1:250k data; Libraries Taskforce, 2017. Basic Dataset. Downloaded from: https://data.gov.uk/dataset/782d6528-11bd-4ae0-ae47-63b456c84e76/public-libraries-in-england-basic-dataset and as mentioned in the references.

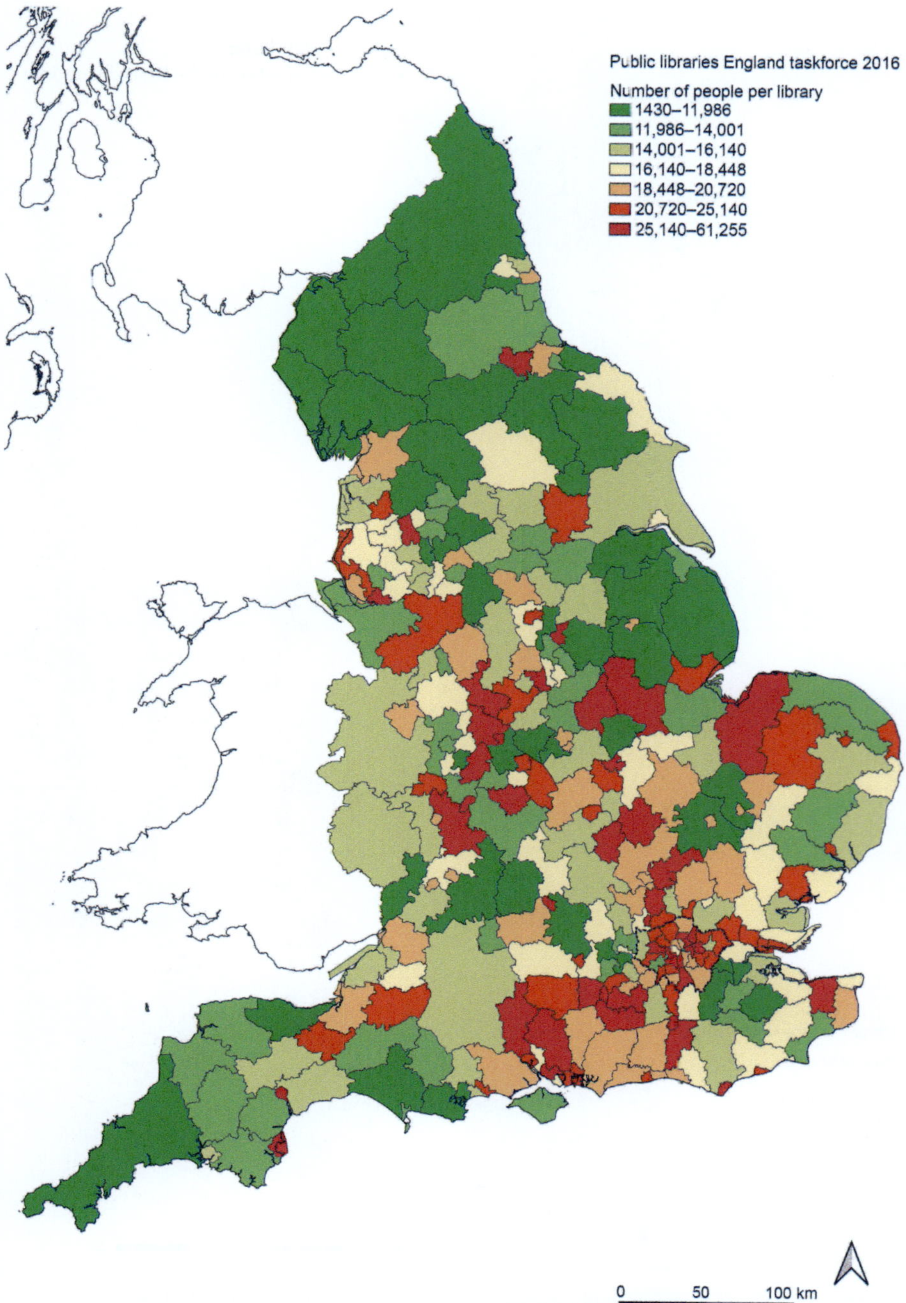


**Fig. 16.2** Public library provision in England per head of local authority (LA) population.

for a specific urban facility. Thus, such systems are now being increasingly developed and widely used for location analysis of all kinds of public services.

Specifically, the Spatial Interaction Model (SIM), or gravity model, has a long and distinguished history in the fields of urban and regional science. It is used in the retail sector to predict store revenue based on consumer demand to a high degree of accuracy (Birkin et al., 2010; Newing et al., 2015). Within the industry itself, based on a 2010 survey of location planning departments, it is estimated that around two-third of retail location planning teams make use of SIM for location planning including major grocery firms (Reynolds and Wood, 2010).

SIMs are used to forecast flows of users or consumers from an origin, usually the residents' homes to one of many accessible competing stores. Inherent in the design of the model is the concept that expenditure flows and subsequent store revenue are driven by store attractiveness and constrained by distance, with consumers exhibiting a greater likelihood to shop at stores that are geographically proximate. In short, more attractive and larger facilities, attract more population, and the more accessible these facilities are to the population, the larger the turnout is.

Accessibility in this case is usually a function of the relative 'cost' in terms of distance or travel time, calibrated using a distance decay parameter, which reflects the willingness or ability of consumers to travel to stores in the modelled region. This reflects the fact that consumers will rather not travel hours away from their home place to shop. Store attractiveness is commonly identified using variables such as store size, brand name, and range of products stocked (Birkin and Heppenstall, 2011). The production-constrained model (Wilson, 1971, 2016) is most commonly used in grocery retail applications, where expenditure estimated in origin zones is given as fixed and is distributed amongst the competing retail destinations. A basic form of the production-constrained model used to forecast the expenditure flow ($S_{ij}$) between zone ($i$) and store ($j$) is shown in the following equation:

$$S_{ij} = A_i e_i P_i W_j \exp\left(-\beta c_{ij}\right) \tag{16.1}$$

where $e_i$ is expenditure per head on retail goods, $P_i$ is the population (both in zone 1), $c_{ij}$ is a measure of the impedance between $i$ and $j$—for example increasing with distance—and here a negative exponential function is used to show that the $i-j$ flow will decrease with increasing impedance.

Birkin et al. (2010) assert that one reason why these models may have become so popular in the industry context is that the clear return on investment achieved through using these models can be quantified, and this can lead to an empirical way to study and understand the parameters that affect turnouts. Thus, this type of modelling can help in a better understanding of the sectors need in relation to their users.

## 16.5 Libraries as cultural retailers

But what do libraries have to do with retail centre modelling and stores? Libraries are one of the few remaining public services that do not require users to spend money in order to use their facilities. In fact, their purpose for serving communities is the supply of knowledge. In this case, if retail attempts to measure the flow of income coming from residences to shops to calculate a shops revenue, perhaps a library model could measure the flow of knowledge to calculate the libraries value in the community. We can then use the same equations of the retail model, by replacing revenue to knowledge factors. We can reinterpret the retail model to represent library flows, by replacing, for example, expenditure per head to propensity to use libraries in some unit time period.

The model reported here uses an appropriately disaggregated version of the retail model, which attempts to capture the demand for knowledge instead of products. In essence, we are viewing libraries as cultural retailers, in which demand and supply is the demand for knowledge and supply is the libraries ability to offer this. In our model, revenue is how much a library is used by its community and for what purpose, which reflects different types of library users (by income or social class), and different types of library facilities provision.

In this chapter, we report on the development and calibration of a SIM, disaggregated on both the demand and supply side of libraries, which has been developed using our own demand estimates and calibrated with reference to the available empirical data. A disaggregated model allows us to add more sophisticated demand terms in the model which reflect different types of library users with very different 'shopping' behaviours in terms of facilities available.

## 16.6 Analytics for libraries: Descriptors for a model

For the purposes of a demo model, we assume that users travel from home—we can add the additional flows such as via the workplace later on. Users can be characterized in a simple way—for example, by age, the level of income, or level of education. We similarly have a small defined number of 'purposes' of visit, such as borrowing books, using computers, finding a quiet workspace, and attending an event.

The next level of modelling is about determining spatial descriptors. Let us suppose that we wish to model the library system of a city where the responsibility for the library is with the local authority. We need two spatial descriptors—residential zones—usually small, defined areas of housing—and library locations, which can be taken as destination points for our model. We then need to know the number of people who travel from each residential zone to each library, and for what purpose.

The key step is to represent these descriptors as algebraic variables which will be the basis of our model. The spatial descriptors will all have 'names' but we give each of the numbers. Suppose there are r residential areas and s libraries and we number these as 1, 2, 3,…, $r$ and 1, 2, 3,…, $s$, respectively. We label a typical residential zone as $i$ and a typical library as $j$. Let $m$ be a typical person type, $m=1$, 2, or 3, for example representing, say, a low income, medium income, or well-off household; and let $n$ be a typical purpose, $n=1$, 2, 3 say, representing book borrowing, workspace, and Internet access. Then, in algebraic terms, $S_{ij}^{mn}$ is the number of type $m$ people travelling from residential zone $i$ to library $j$ for purpose $n$. If there are 100 residential zones, 10 libraries, 3 population groups, and 3 purposes, then this array has

$100 \times 10 \times 3 \times 3 = 9000$ elements. As a further exemplar, note that $S_{23,8}^{3,1}$ is the number of type 3 (high income) people travelling from residential zone 23 to library 8 for purpose 1 (book borrowing).

The general notation is a very powerful one, enabling the computer model to calculate all 9000 elements through a single equation by looping through the equation 9000 times. Of course, realistically, these arrays can be much bigger with more granular and extended classifications. The estimation of these elements is the task of building a computer model and we do this in the following section.

To fix ideas, we work first with a simplified version of the model—with only one population category and a single purpose of visit, such as students wanting to borrow books. We can then drop the superscripts and the flow variable is then simply $S_{ij}$, the number of people travelling from $i$ to $j$ in some time period for library visits. We then need to add more descriptors: let $P_i$ be the population of $i$ and $c_{ij}$ a measure of the 'cost' of travelling from $i$ to $j$. (In the simplest form of model, this might just be Euclidean distance.) We also need a measure of the relative attractiveness of a library, and we designate this as $W_j$, and in a simple model, we can take this as measured by size. Then the basic model, following the retail model in Eq. (16.1) is

$$S_{ij} = A_i e_i P_i W_j \exp\left(-\beta c_{ij}\right) \tag{16.2}$$

where

$$A_i = 1/\Sigma_j B_j D_j f\left(c_{ij}\right) \tag{16.3}$$

to ensure that

$$\Sigma_j S_{ij} = e_i P_i \tag{16.4}$$

that is, that all the potential users are accounted for.

We can then calculate

$$D_j = \Sigma_j S_{ij} \tag{16.5}$$

as the total number of library users at library $j$.

$\beta$ is a parameter that determines how far people travel on average to visit a library: low $\beta$ implies longer trips and vice versa.

This simple model is deceptively powerful. The estimated number of trips from a zone to a library is proportional to the number of people who can set out ($P_i$) and the attractiveness of the library ($W_j$), but inversely proportional (through a declining function, in this case exponential) to travel cost ($c_{ij}$). The factor $A_i$ fulfils a key role, taking into account, for the flow from $i$ to a particular library $j$, the 'competition' of other libraries, relating to both their size and their place in the spatial structure. For example, if there is another large ($W$) library 'near to' $j$, then the bulk of the flow from $i$ will go to the large library. It also turns out that $1/A_i$ is a good measure of accessibility to libraries from residential zone $i$, say $X_i$.

$$X_i = 1 / A_i = \Sigma_k W_k \exp(-\beta c_{ik}) \tag{16.6}$$

The model can be run for personality types and purposes simply by writing $S_{ij}^{mn}$ for $S_{ij}$ and making the corresponding changes in the other variables.

We will apply this model for a city, but first, we review the national data and the extent to which this allows us to calculate some simple indicators at the national scale.

## 16.7 Developing a library's model

How can we build a data-driven model which can be used, for example, to understand the effect of closures of libraries? We need to understand the demand for a library in an area, and whether that may change if a library is closed. We can then design simulation for the effects of closures in that area. We begin by explaining the process in a schematic demo model built in CityEngine. Esri's CityEngine is a 3D GIS tool which allows city models to be visualized procedurally (i.e. models are generated using a set of rules). This approach allows us to define simple conditions which govern the appearance of a library-city model. We begin the construction of the model by defining the set of blocks that represent the already existing libraries and the ones that represent residential (user) zones. In CityEngine, any discrete zone can be defined as a block, which is essentially an object that symbolizes either an actual block or a city, an output area, or a ward, for example.

For the library demo model, we are going to represent the library locations in the lower scale of the blocks, where each block is either a separate residential *i*-zone or a *j* library. Each block is allowed to obtain certain characteristics. In this example, the blocks are programmed to accept land uses, either residential or library.

Assume there is a hypothetical city neighbourhood, as shown in Fig. 16.3. For the library demo model, we are going to represent the library locations in the lower scale of the blocks, where each block is either a separate residential *i*-zone or a *j* library. Each block is allowed to obtain certain characteristics. In this example, the blocks are programmed to accept land uses, either residential or library. In this model, we can set a few libraries, using interactive controls. Let us assume that there are five libraries in this instance (Fig. 16.3A and B)—we can then develop a rule to assign resources in those libraries and extrude the volumes based on the number of resources each library has (e.g. number of titles, provision of workspaces, Wi-Fi provision, services, etc.). Our model calculates the number of borrowers/users for each library based on the population of each residential block and the 'attractiveness' of each library, which in this case is the number of resources available. We can use the measure of accessibility to then visualize the catchment area of each library (Fig. 16.3C).

If we assume a scenario where the local authority of this area decides to cut funding for libraries and close the smallest library and also cut the resources for the biggest library, our model recalculates the accessibility and then simulates the effect of closures in the population of that area (Fig. 16.3D).

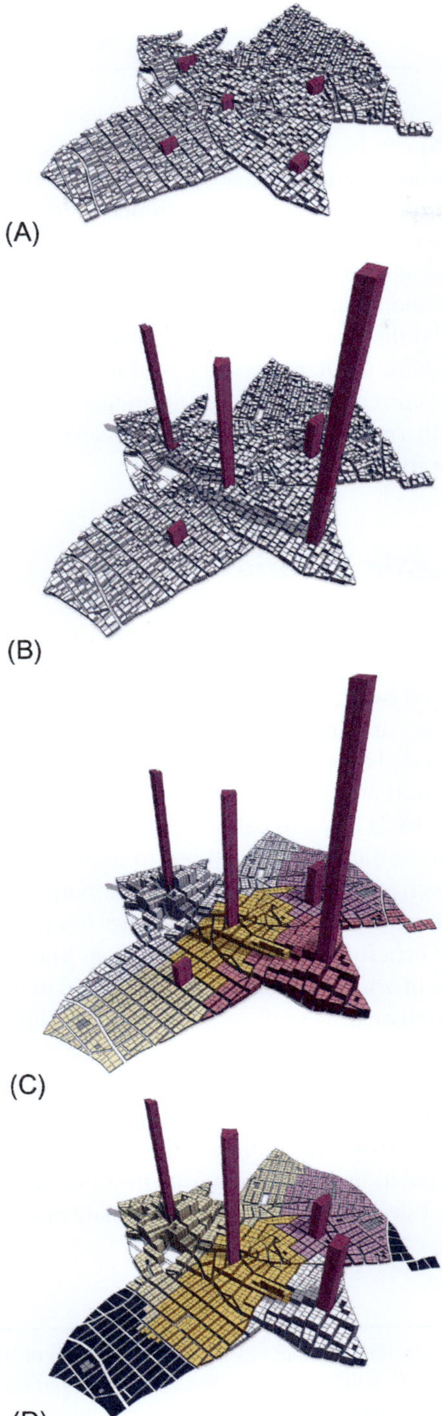

**Fig. 16.3** A demo libraries model system. (A) A hypothetical neighbourhood with five libraries. (B) We are using the building height to simulate the amount of each library's resources available for the community (e.g. no of titles, Wi-Fi provision, workspaces).

*(Continued)*

The demo model is an interactive virtual game with simplified synthetic data, demonstrating how SIM can be adjusted for the libraries sector in a comprehensive way. The parameters, which the user can adjust to produce closure scenarios, are the number and location of zones and libraries, the number of population in each residential zone, the percentage of library users per zone, and the number of resources in each library, which add to the attractiveness of the library.

To be able to model the demand for libraries on a national level, we require real data for the calibration of the model, such as the current catchment areas and number of users per area for the libraries in the United Kingdom. This can be done in principle, but since this data is not currently available on a national level, we proceed to demonstrate a real scenario with a case study which has been carried out in collaboration with the Newcastle City Library.

## 16.8 The Newcastle Libraries model

There are currently 14 Libraries managed by the Newcastle City Council as shown in Fig. 16.4.

Data has been provided by the Newcastle Libraries' management system, courtesy of Aude Charillon, Library and Information Officer at Newcastle Libraries. These include anonymized user travel data and are an indication of the postcode of each library member who had borrowed or returned an item at a particular branch library. These will provide the $S_{ij}$ (Eq. 16.2) flows to calibrate our model (Fig. 16.4). The borrower number associated with each transaction is used to remove the lines that had duplicates within the borrower number columns. Then the borrower number is removed entirely for privacy. Essentially, each line is a distinct library member. The data are anonymized transaction data for the past 12 months from May 2019. We are also provided with the numbers of computers and other seats, which provide an indicator of workspaces, as well as other uses such as services for children, or conference and meeting rooms.

For the digital use of libraries, we have an indication of the number of Wi-Fi users in libraries per month. These are data from April published on the Data Mill North (Newcastle City Council, 2019) and are updated monthly. The Newcastle data set is then augmented with population data coming from the OS census 2011 data, as well as postcode data. Table 16.1 describes the full list of the data provided for the Newcastle libraries model.

**Fig. 16.3, cont'd** (C) The simulation generates the catchment area of libraries, based on population and accessibility of each library's resources. Each colour represents a different catchment area of a library, whilst extrusion represents accessibility to that library. (D) Assuming cuts in funding, we close the smallest library and reduce the number of resources in the largest library. The model calculates the effects of closures by highlighting the areas where the remaining libraries take additional strain and also highlights that a certain population has no longer access to library provision *(blocks shaded in black)*.

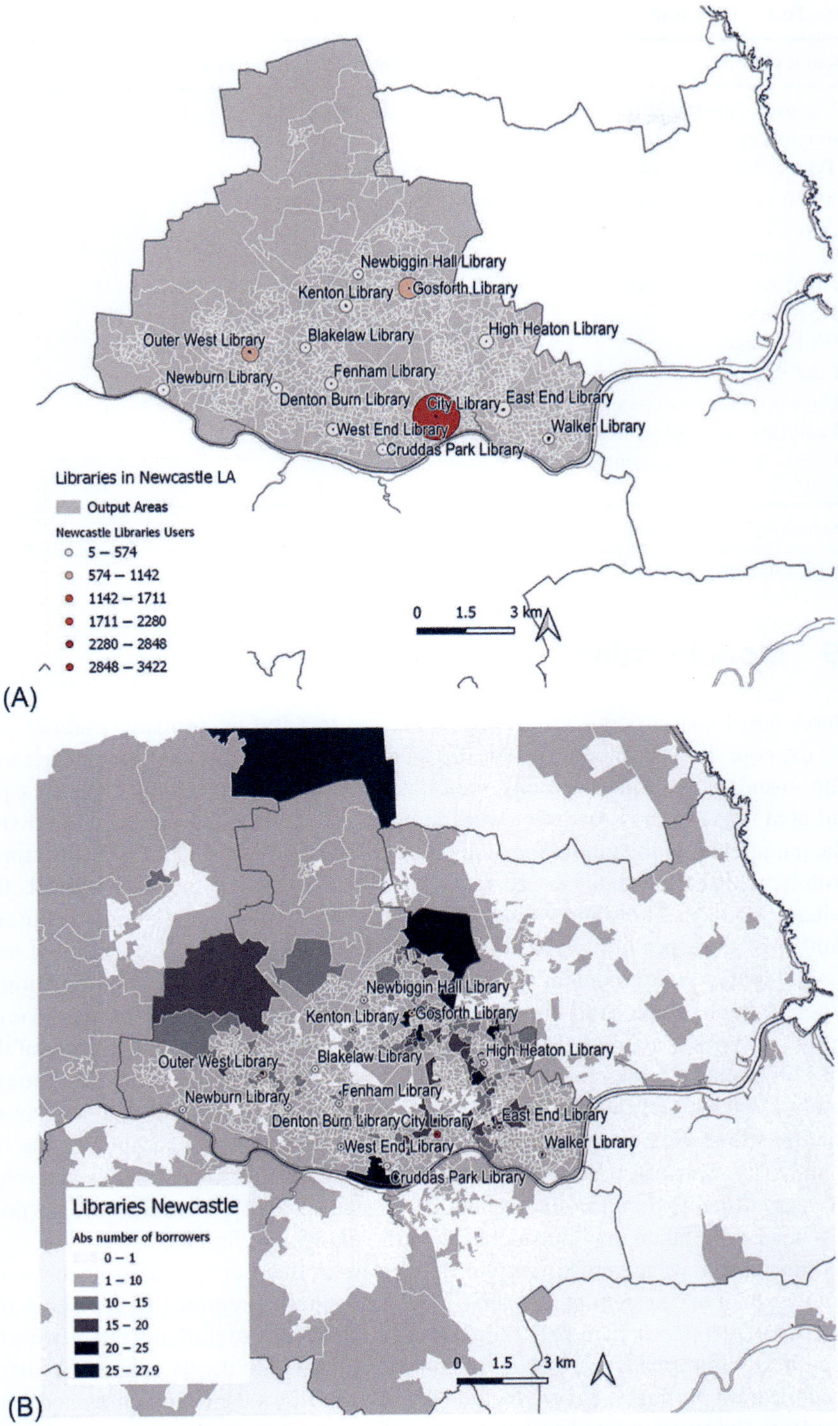


**Fig. 16.4** (A) Absolute number of library users in the local authority of Newcastle per library. (B) Absolute number of users, aggregated per output area (OA).

**Table 16.1** Indicators for the Newcastle Libraries model.

| **Libraries**[a] | **Newcastle Libraries users**[a] |
|---|---|
| • Location (postcode-footprints, latitude, longitude)<br>• Type of library (public, research)<br>• Status of library (statutory, closed, etc.)<br>• Area (floorspace)<br>• Accessibility<br>• No of workspaces (with/without PC)<br>• No of titles<br>• Wi-Fi usage<br>• Eduroam provider<br>• Days/no. of hours open per week<br>• Facilities (unemployment, storytelling)<br>• Events (no/type of events)<br>• Staff | • Location (no. of users per postcode subsection)<br>• Travel data<br>• Accessibility<br><br>• Population[b]<br><br>• Output areas (OA)<br>• Population per OA<br>• Deprivation<br>• Income-unemployment<br>• Education<br>• Age<br>• Ethnicity |

[a] Data from the Newcastle Libraries.
[b] Data from Ordnance Survey Census Data, 2011. Population per Output Area. Contains Ordnance Survey data © Crown copyright and database right 2011.

## 16.9 Model testing

We have developed a demo model for Newcastle in CityEngine using Python. The model uses our libraries model system and is calibrated using the data from Newcastle.

The visualization shows the observed data for the absolute number of users per output area (OA) in the broader Newcastle area. The controls on the right-hand side are the parameters of the model for each (*i*) zone. The flows for each library are stored separately, whilst the indicators are set on the lower right. The top 'vis' controls the visualization mode. The sliders allow change of values, such as the number of users, or number of titles per library, or closing down a library. We can then use these new values as inputs to our model and study the effects of this change on the population.

When trying to understand library demand, one important aspect is the spatial configuration of types of users. In Fig. 16.5, we are presenting an aggregated image of the use of borrowers of books for the Newcastle Libraries. We can see that even though the users cluster mostly within the area of the local authority, there is a substantial population who are using the services (mostly the City Library) residing outside the local authority. This can lead to two assumptions—firstly, borrowing books and other services are valuable for an extended population, and secondly, these flows of the population need to be taken into consideration in the model development.

For this reason, we are creating a two-tier system. A two-tier system is when we are using more than one system of zones (*i*), to include external regional flows within our system of interest (Roumpani, 2019). In our case, where we are studying the Newcastle local authority libraries, we are using the output areas within the local authority itself for visualization purposes, but we include the outside flows using an aggregated zone system from the surrounding local authorities (Fig. 16.6A).

**Fig. 16.5** System for the residential zones-OA (*i*) in CityEngine.

Fig. 16.6C and D demonstrate the results of the calibrated model. Inherent in the design of the retail model is the concept that flows are driven by store attractiveness and constrained by distance, with consumers exhibiting a greater likelihood to shop at stores that are geographically proximate.

Store attractiveness is commonly identified using variables such as store size, brand name, and range of products stocked (Birkin et al., 2002; Birkin and Heppenstall, 2011), suggesting that for grocery retailers, factors including price, product range, opening hours, and the availability of parking all have an important influence on consumers' perception of store attractiveness. In our case, the indicators of attractiveness that correlate with the increasing number of users, include the number of titles, Wi-Fi usage, floorspace, opening hours, and facilities including workspaces. From the demand side, it is important to consider the attractiveness factor from different types of population. For example, students are likely to be attracted more to libraries that have eduroam or Wi-Fi access, whilst families with children 0–5 maybe will be more attracted to libraries with storytelling events.

In the case of retail, there is the competition element which forces the separation of retailers into two categories, the independent stores and the retail centres. This however does not apply for libraries. Libraries are independent units and the closing of a library does not necessarily mean that users will find the resources or will travel to use another library. Consequently, we need to consider the accessibility of a library as a function of its population and users.

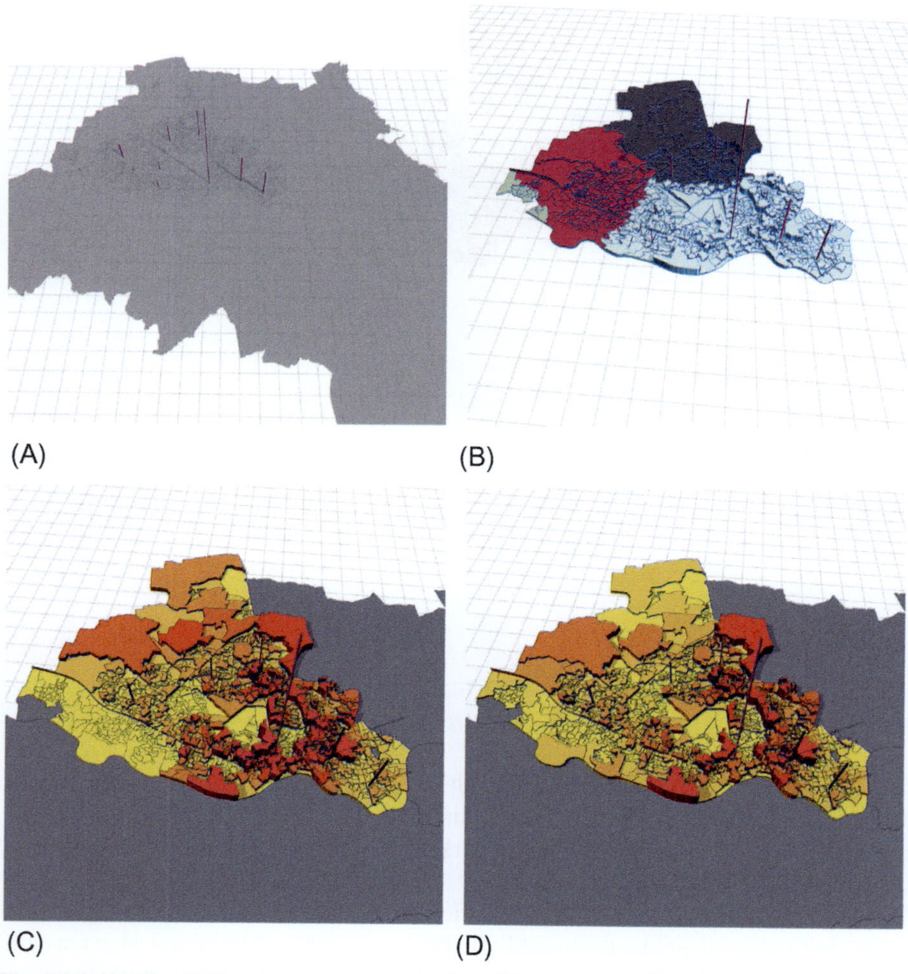


**Fig. 16.6** (A) Newcastle libraries in CityEngine with output areas (OA) and the surrounding local authorities. (B) Catchment area of libraries in Newcastle using a calibrated model. (C) Observed data for the absolute number of library users for Newcastle Libraries within the Newcastle City Council. (D) Results of a calibrated model run for the users of the Newcastle Libraries within the Newcastle City Council.

Accessibility for libraries can then be calculated as:

$$X_i^{rk} = \Sigma W_j^{Lmk} \exp\left(-\beta c_{ij}^{rLmk}\right) \tag{16.7}$$

Accessibility is the sum of how attractive a library is to a specific user, with a distance decay cost, with $X$ essentially showing how much a user wants to use a library.

For each user the model can then become singly constrained:

$$D_j W_j^{Lmk} \exp\left(-\beta c_{ij}^{rLmk}\right) \tag{16.8}$$

where

$$D_j = \Sigma W_j^{Lmk} \exp\left(-\beta c_{ij}^{rLmk}\right) \tag{16.9}$$

$c_{ij}^{rLmk}$ with $(m,j)$ a definer of model of accessibility.

The cost $c_{ij}$ of accessibility is defined by the type of user $r$, the library type, and the facilities. Example: An architect will have a low attractiveness factor for a health library near him, but a high attractiveness for a library that has architectural books or a public library. A student will have a high attractiveness factor for a public library and research libraries with appropriate resources and workspaces.

There can be another submodel for the cost of transferring supply (materials) to libraries: $V_j$.

Catchment areas of libraries ($\Pi_j$) can then be defined by

$$\Pi_j = \Sigma_i \left(S_{ij} / S_i\right) P_i \tag{16.10}$$

## 16.10 Scenario testing

Using our model, we can start testing scenarios. From the demand side, assume that there is an increase in unemployment and deprivation in Newcastle. This may lead to an inflection of the low-income population. We can then study the effect of this in the example shown in Fig. 16.7A and B. Fig. 16.7A shows the absolute number of users in the East End Library. The East End Library is located within an area of high deprivation in Newcastle. As a result, based on the data sent by the City Library, it has a PC usage per average of 50%, 700 Wi-Fi users and approximately 700 borrowers, whilst it also supports unemployment services. Fig. 16.7A shows the current users from the calibrated model. Whilst Fig. 16.7B shows the results after an increase in deprivation. In our model that translates as an increase in demand and an increase in users within the most deprived areas and a concentration of users because of the reduction in accessibility.

Assume now that we want to study the effect of cutting down funds in the main Newcastle City Library, whilst simultaneously shutting down two libraries in the west side: the Outer West library with 600 users and 700 Wi-Fi users and Kenton library with 250 users and 1370 Wi-Fi users. We are then effectively decreasing the attractiveness of the main library which has over 3500 borrowers and 161 workstations and recalculate the accessibility of the other libraries as a result of the two closures. This overall reduces the number of users to demanded facilities. Therefore, that leaves certain parts of the population deprived of resources (see Fig. 16.8).

This exercise attempts to show that with a comprehensive aggregated data set, it would be possible to provide a nuanced picture of the provision of public libraries in the United Kingdom, including the impact of their closures in different parts of the country and for different types of population. The development of a core data set for UK libraries is now becoming the focus of several library organizations and the ambition would be for this work to be a helpful addition to this effort.

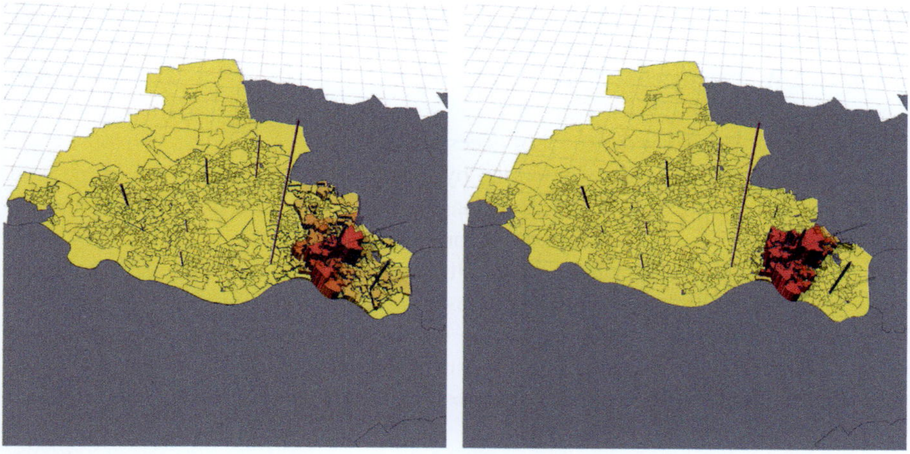

(A) (B)

**Fig. 16.7** (A) Current users for the EE library. (B) Scenario where deprivation increases in Newcastle (low-income users find the services and Wi-Fi provision of the library more attractive, whilst other accessibility decreases for the users outside the catchment area).

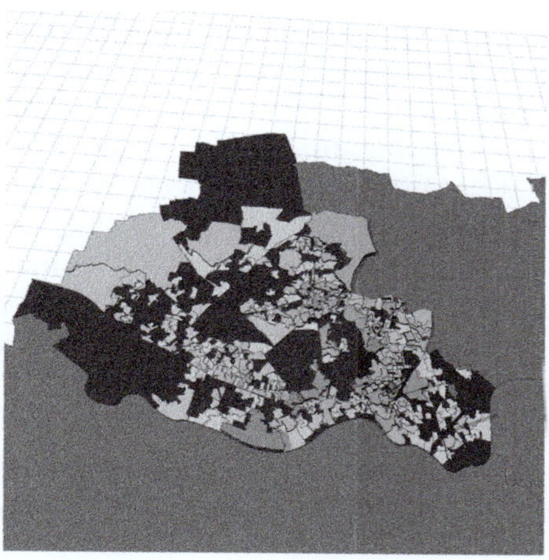

**Fig. 16.8** Scenario where the number of titles and provision of facilities is cut in half, for the main City Library, whilst two of the main libraries which serve the west side of Newcastle (Outer West library and High Heaton library) are closed completely, leaving significant segments of the population without library access (areas illustrated as *black*).

## 16.11 Performance indicators

There are currently no official performance indicators for libraries in England. The DCMS is currently in the process of creating a core data set for libraries in the United Kingdom, looking to create a transparent and automated process to gather and share public libraries' data. This appears to be an ongoing work that is scheduled to finish in 2021 (DCMS, 2016b).

With this model, we are demonstrating which data sets and how different data sets can be used as indicators to model a library system and therefore can also be used as a measure of how a library performs. For example, measures of accessibility per type of population, as defined in Eq. (16.7), can provide an indicator for the attractiveness of libraries in relation to different facilities and the type of population using libraries and their resources. This connection between users and library facilities allows the library's performance to be assessed, not just as an independent provider of resources, but also in relation to how well it serves its immediate community. The outcomes of this, depending on the effective collection of targeted data by the local authorities and also depending on the effective use of more strategic policy for libraries in the United Kingdom can be used for the definition of performance indicators.

Part of the future work necessary to enable this would be to extend the model on a regional level to define performance indicators for libraries in the United Kingdom, such as the accessibility measure, which can help identify areas that may have little or no access to libraries. It could also extend to include different types of libraries, such as research, health, or the mobile libraries, as already shown by Dave Rowe's map of Somerset mobile libraries (Somerset Libraries, 2019).

## 16.12 Planning and policy implications: Future data requirements

The current lack of standardized and comprehensive data sets covering all key activities of public libraries means that it is extremely difficult to make evidence-based policies for the sector, on the either national or local level. It also means that however keenly we might feel about the loss of libraries in our local communities, we are not able to provide evidence of the impact caused by their loss or indeed make a good argument why we might want to protect them.

This work is attempting to show how data could help us model the use of libraries in relation to different localities and population, as well as show how we can arrive at a more nuanced, comparative national picture of the sector if the relevant data was available. We are encouraged by the DCMS promise under the Libraries Deliver programme to publish a core data set for libraries (DCMS, 2019). However, as well as recommending that public libraries' data is collected in a more standardized way, it is our recommendation that such data includes a range of indicators that reflect the actual activities and roles that libraries play in the community, alongside traditional indicators such as book borrowing.

Laura Swaffield, Chair of the Library Campaign, was quoted in an article for the *New Statesman* saying the following: "Council-run [libraries] with professional staff... are the first step to almost anything. You can walk into the smallest one with a query as vague as 'I'm bored' to 'How do I find out about butterflies?' or 'I don't know how to use a computer' and they can set you on your way". A good library is 'conveniently local, with a unique level of public trust, and a noninstitutional atmosphere that encourages adults who've fared badly in [the] education system' (Dunn, 2017). All these library characteristics, as described by Laura, can be captured through collecting the right data, which would help us to model the benefits that libraries have for education, employment, and social inclusion.

Anderson and Whalley (2015), in their study of the public library Internet access in Glasgow, showed that there is a correlation between library user types and poverty, and especially the role of libraries in addressing the digital divide and how inadequate are libraries' resources for fulfilling this essential role. This is also a key premise of the report charting the way forward for the digital infrastructure of public libraries compiled by the Society of Chief Librarians et al. (2015). CILIP (2018) also asserts that 'usage figures of the public library service show that these changes are likely to have the greatest impact upon vulnerable groups in our society' and also emphasizes the issue of unequal access to new technologies in the society. With this in view, the better collection and analysis of public library data in relation to access to technologies and types of the population accessing these services is an essential ingredient for planning the future services provided in public libraries.

## 16.13 Future work

Data-driven Libraries is a project in progress, and it is our intention to add further data and calibrate both the UK national and the Newcastle models. In 2020, we are planning to present a White Paper report with the project findings, data, and detailed models, including further recommendations for future data collection and how these models can be used in policy and planning.

## References

Anderson, G., Whalley, J., 2015. Public library internet access in areas of deprivation: the case of Glasgow. Telematics Inform. 32 (3), 521–537.

Anstice, I., 2017. 500: Editorial. Public Libraries News. 18 July, https://www.publiclibrariesnews.com/2017/07/500.html. (accessed 21.12.19).

Arts Council England, 2014. Evidence Review of the Economic Contribution of Libraries. https://www.artscouncil.org.uk/sites/default/files/download-file/Evidence_review_economic_contribution_libraries_2014.pdf. (accessed 18.12.19).

Batty, M., 2013. The New Science of Cities. MIT Press, Massachusetts.

BBC, 2014. Book Borrowing Figures Show Library Habits Are Changing. https://www.bbc.co.uk/news/uk-england-35788332. (accessed 18.12.19).

Birkin, M., Heppenstall, A., 2011. Extending spatial interaction models with agents for understanding relationships in a dynamic retail market. Urban Stud. Res. 2011.

Birkin, M., Clarke, G., Clarke, M.P., 2002. Retail Geography and Intelligent Network Planning. John Wiley & Sons.

Birkin, M., Procter, R., Allan, R., Bechhofer, S., Buchan, I., Goble, C., Hudson-Smith, A., Lambert, P., De Roure, D., Sinnott, R., 2010. Elements of a computational infrastructure for social simulation. Philos. Trans. R. Soc. A Math. Phys. Eng. Sci. 368 (1925), 3797–3812.

Busby, E., 2019. Nearly 800 public libraries closed since austerity launched in 2010. Independent. 6 December, https://www.independent.co.uk/news/uk/home-news/library-closure-austerity-funding-cuts-conservative-government-a9235561.html. (accessed 18.12.19).

Chartered Institute of Library and Information Professionals (CILIP), 2018. Universal Credit. Broadband Internet Access and UK Public Libraries. Information Professional, 3 September, https://www.cilip.org.uk/page/UNSpecialRapporteur. (accessed 23.12.19).

Chartered Institute of Public Finance and Accountancy (CIPFA Research and Analytics), 2018. Public Library Statistics 2018/19 Estimates and 2017/18 Actuals Hard Copy. https://www.cipfa.org/policy-and-guidance/publications/p/public-library-statistics-201819-estimates-and-201718-actuals-hard-copy. (accessed 05.05.20).

DCMS, 2014. Independent Libraries Report for England. https://assets.publishing.service.gov.uk/government/uploads/system/uploads/attachment_data/file/388989/Independent_Library_Report-_18_December.pdf. (accessed 18.12.19).

DCMS, 2016a. Public Libraries in England: Basic Dataset. https://www.gov.uk/government/publications/public-libraries-in-england-basic-dataset. (accessed 22.12.19).

DCMS, 2016b. Libraries Deliver: Ambition for Public Libraries in England 2016 to 2021. https://www.gov.uk/government/publications/libraries-deliver-ambition-for-public-libraries-in-england-2016-to-2021. (accessed 01.05.20).

DCMS, 2018. Analysing Data: CIPFA Statistics and the Future of England's Libraries. https://www.gov.uk/government/publications/analysing-data-cipfa-statistics-and-the-future-of-englands-libraries/analysing-data-cipfa-statistics-and-the-future-of-englands-libraries. (accessed 18.12.19).

DCMS, 2019. Libraries and Open Data. Blog by Jenny Harland, 6 September, https://dcmslibraries.blog.gov.uk/2019/09/06/libraries-and-open-data/. (accessed 23.12.19).

Dunn, W., 2017. The loss of Britain's libraries could be a huge blow to the economy. New Statesman. 18 December 2018, https://www.newstatesman.com/microsites/skills/2017/11/are-libraries-worth-keeping. (accessed 23.12.19).

EBSCO, 2019. Coding in Libraries: Benefits and Tools. https://www.ebsco.com/blog/article/coding-in-libraries-benefits-and-tools. (accessed 18.12.19).

Flood, A., 2017. Save your local! Should volunteers help keep our public libraries open? The Guardian. 8 August, https://www.theguardian.com/books/2017/aug/08/public-libraries-at-the-crossroads-should-volunteers-be-keeping-them-open. (accessed 21.12.19).

IFLA, UNESCO, 1994. Public Library Manifesto. https://www.ifla.org/publications/iflaunesco-public-library-manifesto-1994. (accessed 18.12.19).

Kean, D., 2017. Major report on libraries' future slammed as over-optimistic. The Guardian. 2 May, https://www.theguardian.com/books/2017/may/02/major-report-on-libraries-future-slammed-as-over-optimistic. (accessed 21.12.19).

Newcastle City Council, 2019. Newcastle Libraries Wi-Fi Users. Data Mill North. https://datamillnorth.org/dataset/ncclibs-wifi-users. (accessed 29.12.19).

Newing, A., Clarke, G.P., Clarke, M., 2015. Developing and applying a disaggregated retail location model with extended retail demand estimations. Geogr. Anal. 47 (3), 219–239.

O'Bryan, J., 2018. Analysing data: CIPFA statistics and the future of England's libraries. Report of the Libraries Taskforce and DCMS, 12 June, https://assets.publishing.service.gov.uk/government/uploads/system/uploads/attachment_data/file/734348/Analysing_data-CIPFA_statistics.pdf. (accessed 21.12.19).

Oliphant, T., 2014. 'I'm a library hugger!': public libraries as valued community assets. Public Libr. Q. 33 (4), 348–361.

Proctor, R., Simmons, S., 2000. Public library closures: the management of hard decisions. Libr. Manag. 21 (1), 25–34.

Reynolds, J., Wood, S., 2010. Location decision making in retail firms: evolution and challenge. Int. J. Retail Distrib. Manag. 38 (11/12), 828–845.

Roumpani, F., 2019. The Role of Procedural Cities in the Future of Planning: An Integrated Method (Doctoral dissertation). UCL (University College London).

Rowe, D., 2019. Library Data and Technology. Libraries Hacked (Website). https://www.librarieshacked.org. (accessed 21.12.19).

Smith, M., 2019. Top ten challenges facing public libraries. Public Libr. Q. 38 (3), 241–247. https://doi.org/10.1080/01616846.2019.1608617.

Somerset Libraries (Website), 2019. Mobile Services. https://somersetlibraries.co.uk/redesign/mobile-services/. (accessed 31.12.19).

The Society of Chief Librarians, The Reading Agency, Arts Council England, 2015. Essential Digital Infrastructure for Public Libraries in England. BiblioCommons. 24 November, https://www.librariesconnected.org.uk/sites/default/files/Essential%20Digital%20Infrastructure%20for%20Public%20Libraries%20in%20England_0.pdf. (accessed 23.12.19).

Wilson, A.G., 1971. A family of spatial interaction models, and associated developments. Environ. Plan. A 3 (1), 1–32.

Wilson, A., 2012. The Science of Cities and Regions. Springer, Netherlands.

Wilson, A., 2016. Approaches to Geo-Mathematical Modelling: New Tools for Complexity Science. Wiley, Chichester.

Woodhouse, J., Zayed, Y., 2019. Public Libraries: Briefing. House of Commons Library. Number 5875, 20 June.

Wyatt, D., Leorke, D., 2018. Technology hasn't killed public libraries—it's inspired them to transform and stay relevant. The Conversation. 19 August, https://theconversation.com/technology-hasnt-killed-public-libraries-its-inspired-them-to-transform-and-stay-relevant-100900. (accessed 21.12.19).

# How can the specific skills of the librarian in a digital context be used in the future? 17

*Anja T. Ingwersen, Mai Aggerbeck, and Signe Nielsen*
VIA Library, VIA University College, Aarhus, Denmark

## 17.1 Introduction: the profession in its societal context

We begin by framing and placing the profession of 'librarian' in its societal context.

### *17.1.1 Technology and knowledge*

The conditions that increasingly influence society, institutions, and working life are persistent, accelerating, and unpredictable (Stegeager and Laursen, 2011, p. 21). The French philosopher Manuel Castells (Castells, 1996) postulated in the 1990s that technology *is* society, and that society can, therefore, not be understood without technology. He reasoned that systems, processes, and institutions, through information technology, are based on network logic (Castells, 1996, p. 5). This development impacts both work structures and human relations because work will primarily be carried out within networks (Castells, 1996, p. 68). When work to a greater degree takes place within networks, it becomes necessary to have a more communication-based culture in institutions and this will affect the institution's social, technological, and structural conditions (Castells, 1996, p. 68).

Gibbons et al. (1995) share this view and describe how knowledge production will change when society develops to become based on the information and communication technology, and how the focus will increasingly shift towards access to knowledge. They predicted that the boundaries between the various societal areas will dissolve, and the division of functions will be replaced by integrated knowledge processes that will interact in completely new ways. In Denmark, this is already familiar in the shape of the attention that is paid to voluntary and committed partnerships with regard to developing new and improved solutions in the educational sector and society in general. This can, for example, be seen in a project under the auspices of the Ministry of Higher Education and Science, in which interdisciplinary and intercontextual development and research networks will be established with the aim of generating knowledge about how to organize courses that aim to develop innovation skills (University College Syddanmark, 2013). At the same time, the boundary between generation and dissemination of knowledge has become more fluid than before: knowledge dissemination takes place within the framework of the actual knowledge generation process. The question is whether these developmental trends necessitate significant changes for academic librarians, if there is a need for new types of relations with the campus, students, and educational programmes, and whether there is a need for new ways of organizing the work in the academic libraries.

**Future Directions in Digital Information. https://doi.org/10.1016/B978-0-12-822144-0.00017-3**

Looking forward in time, the general picture of development indicates that it is necessary to acquire increased and improved skills in addition to a mere education, and that the demands for work skills are dynamic, in that they are constantly changing in line with a company's tasks (Holdt Christensen, 2002, p. 21). Psychologist Peter Holdt Christensen emphasizes that work processes change due to, amongst other things, international sharing of work tasks in networks. It will, therefore, not suffice for employees to be high-level specialists only, but they must also develop their specialty in interaction with society's general developmental trends (Holdt Christensen, 2002, p. 21).

Another important impact of major developments on academic libraries is that since the millennium, just about every type of institution, distributor of knowledge, and party that takes over the role of disseminators of knowledge at will, have offered free knowledge resources (Schreiber, 2018). This development is in stark contrast to the past when academic libraries almost had a monopoly on the dissemination of academic literature and existed in a more or less symbiotic relationship with publishers.

### 17.1.2 Labour market

The development outlined above provides a background to the present, where The Danish Centre for Social Science and Research (VIVE) produced a report in 2018 *Den teknologiske udvikling og kompetencer på fremtidens arbejdsmarked – en litteraturoversigt* (The technological development of skills in the future labour market – a literature review) (Albæk and VIVE, 2018). The publication reviews a range of international reports and studies to identify trends in the demand for skills, and, based on the technological developments, those that will dominate the future labour market. One of the conclusions is that the future labour market does not necessarily preclude current skills from being used in the future, but that they will be prioritized differently. Overall, most studies cite cognitive skills, social skills, and problem-solving skills as the most important (Albæk and VIVE, 2018, p. 6).

The report distinguishes between routine work functions that can be taken over or performed by machines, and nonroutine work functions, and asks whether work functions are cognitive or manual. Routine work functions have been reduced significantly in the recent years, both cognitive and manual. At the same time, there has been a large increase in cognitive nonroutine work functions, whilst the manual nonroutine work functions are placed somewhere in the middle (Albæk and VIVE, 2018, p. 36). The report argues that the movement towards fewer routine work functions and more nonroutine work functions is expected to mean that social skills, collaborative skills, and the ability to interact productively with colleagues will be important in the future labour market. It is presumed that this polarization of skills in the work market will not continue because middle skill job functions, where technical skills combined with basic intermediate skills in reading, arithmetic, adaptability, problem solving, and common sense cannot be translated into components that enable machines or technology to fully take over the work without a significant reduction in quality.

These work functions at the middle level, which are a combination of routine functions and nonroutine functions, are characterized by requiring abilities such as interpersonal interaction, flexibility, and adaptability. In the future, it will thus be important that the labour force has skills that complement new technology; skills that cannot be replaced by technology.

### 17.1.3 Librarianship in Denmark

The description of middle skill job functions matches to a certain extent what we in Denmark also describe as profession subjects. Profession subjects are characterized by a combination of technical knowledge and interpersonal skills. Profession subjects involve a wide range of skills compared to how they are described, for example, in VIVE's report. They concern specialized/abstract the knowledge on which the profession is based, how 'heavy' the knowledge is, how much authority and autonomy the profession has, and how 'important the tasks are for society at the time'. Therefore, the connotation 'semiprofession' coexists. A semiprofession often suffers the lack of recognition from the ambient society. Overall, the profession librarian is considered either one of the professions or even a semiprofession. In Denmark, as is the case in many countries, library science degrees are at master's level. As with other professions, there has been an academicization of librarianship over the years. Originally, it was a master's apprenticeship, but today it is an academic degree. In this chapter, the focus is on academic and research librarians. What characterizes the job functions in this area of librarianship is teaching and supervision of students carrying out basic education, continuing education, assistant professorships, and PhD studies. This area is also concerned with knowledge gathering, registration of research, dissemination, copyright, preparation of systematic reviews, information technology tasks, and more. Many librarians have also taken a master's degree related to learning processes, knowledge management, coaching, or similar subjects.

### 17.1.4 Knowledge as emerging, fleeting, and context dependent

An overall picture emerges that is characterized by the fact that knowledge is a crucial product in the global market. Knowledge is emerging, fleeting, and context dependent, and is created in the space between people, society, and technology. Functions that require cognitive skills are on the rise. At the same time, an intermediate group of job functions deals with technical knowledge combined with human judgement, which in all likelihood cannot be outmanoeuvred by technological solutions because its justification lies in the space between the human and the profession.

In any case, the above review bears witness to a close interaction between technology and society that affect each other mutually, and there is much to indicate that technology is strongest. By that we mean that technology has a larger impact on society than the other way around. In this context, we wish to investigate the librarian skills in a digital context today and in the future.

## 17.2 Research question

How can the specific skills of the librarian in a digital context be used in the future?

### 17.2.1 Method

This chapter is based on a literature review and two qualitative interviews. The literature review was inspired by the scoping review method (Pedersen, 2017). This was chosen because we wanted to maintain and highlight the breadth of the question, with regard both to the impact of digital developments on future librarianship, and with regard to the type of studies that are included in the selected literature. The two qualitative semistructured interviews shed light on the views of leading Danish librarians with regard to the question of research. The results from the literature review indicate that there is little Scandinavian literature that sheds light on this particular question. The aim of the two interviews was, therefore, to place the Danish educational sector librarian's (digital) future into a global context.

### 17.2.2 Scoping review

Our scoping review was carried out according to the following methodology: identification of the research question, preparation of inclusion criteria, literature search, identification of relevant studies, data extraction, and conclusion (Pedersen, 2017).

#### 17.2.2.1 Inclusion criteria

The review includes articles that describe education and research librarians and/or libraries. Even though other types of library (public libraries and school libraries) exist with the same societal environment, we believe that the context from which they originate is not transferable to an educational context. The most important factor that differentiates the two segments of the library sector is that work in a research or education library is not the core product for the institution, whilst work in a public library is the core product in itself. This could mean that the education and research librarian must constantly legitimize herself with regard to the core services: teaching and research.

We have chosen to include studies with various empirical bases. To maintain breadth in the review, we are interested in studies with various approaches. Our research question can thus reveal trends and predictions, and various approaches can precisely, therefore, be relevant. We only searched for studies and materials published 2016–20. We chose this relatively short timeframe because of accelerating technological and digital developments. In addition, we only selected studies in English from countries and states in which the educational system is constructed in a manner that is comparable to the Danish educational system. We searched the following databases during September-November 2019: Scopus, Library Information Science & Technology Abstracts, Academic Search Premier, Eric, Oria (Norwegian) and SwePub (Swedish), Bibliotek.dk, and Forskningsdatabasen (Danish). The databases were selected on the basis of search results from initial exploratory searches. The databases searched are thus a mix of national library databases, databases concerned primarily with educational research, and interdisciplinary databases. We made this choice to ensure breadth of coverage and to shed light on the research question from a sociological perspective overall rather than solely a library sector perspective.

The procedure for the search in all the databases was the same. Initially, we carried out a series of broad and transversal pilot searches. Searches were undertaken with natural language and on title/abstract, keyword, author-keyword/author-abstract levels. Wherever possible, the limit functions of the databases were also used. The aim of the initial searches was to identify relevant subject words, core journal titles, and choice of databases. We reviewed the search results and selected a number of articles on the title/abstract level. These articles are the basis of the final search matrix in the individual databases.

**Table 17.1** Search matrix for systematic search.

| Academic libraries/ librarians | Skills | Digital | Future |
|---|---|---|---|
| Academic librarianship<br>Academic librarians<br>Librarian<br>Library roles<br>Library role<br>Librarian attitudes<br>Teacher-librarian-collaboration<br>Library development<br>Academic libraries<br>University library | Competence<br>Knowledge<br>Skills | Technological<br>Technological innovation<br>Technology<br>Artificial intelligence<br>Digital? | Transformation<br>Organizational change<br>Educational change<br>Educational trends<br>New user needs<br>Future of society<br>Time perspective<br>Repurposing |

We used the following search matrix in the systematic search (Table 17.1).

The searches were carried out in blocks with the use of Boolean operators. Where possible, we used the database's controlled subject word lists. The search matrix was adjusted and adapted to the various databases. The last search was carried out on 27 November 2019. After sorting on the title level, we had 47 articles that we read through critically at abstract level. Thereafter, we selected six articles based on our inclusion and exclusion criteria and the research question. None of the articles was from Scandinavian databases. The content and conclusions from the selected articles are reviewed in the following section.

## 17.3 Summary of articles

Since the research question was *How can the specific skills of the librarian in a digital context be used in the future?* We have kept our focus, in the following summary, on the elements that deal with librarian skills in a digital future.

### *17.3.1 Article 1*

Bandyopadhyay, A., Boyd-Byrnes, M.K., 2016. Is the need for mediated reference service in academic libraries fading away in the digital environment? Ref. Serv. Rev. 44(4), 596–626. doi:https://doi.org/10.1108/RSR-02-2016-0012.

In this literature review, no answer is provided as to which skills will be in demand in a digital future; instead, the review indicates the skills that (still) cannot be taken over by digital solutions and that, therefore, are still an important part of librarianship. As the title implies, the focus is on working with references.

The article indicates that the shift from printed matter to electronic resources and the Internet's possibilities for giving access to information has had a great impact on users' search behaviour and thus on working with references. Technological developments mean that users can access materials on their own wherever and whenever they wish. This paradigm shift, in combination with declining budgets, has forced many libraries to redefine their reference services and it has been shown that there has been a change from librarians being 'information seekers' to being 'information creators'.

The article concludes that no matter how the work is organized, the digital environment will still need human intervention because it is not possible to transfer processes that take place during human communication to electronic solutions. This applies to problem solving and critical thinking as well as the ability to interpret information and user needs in various contexts. These skills can still not be translated into digital solutions.

### 17.3.2 Article 2

Ciccone, A., Hounslow, L., 2019. Re-envisioning the role of academic librarians for the digital learning environment: the case of UniSA online. J. Univ. Teach. Learn. Pract. 16(1).

The second article focuses exclusively on work in a digital environment and describes three librarians' reflections on being associated with the start of an online educational process at the University of South Australia (UniSA) and the relational, pedagogical, and digital challenges they experienced. The librarians experienced a discrepancy between the role, which they had envisioned and the role that the rest of the participants in the project envisioned for them. For example, the project partners believed that the librarians should check all the materials for copyright clearance and had expectations that they could gain access to e-books for all the students.

The librarians had to assert their value and explain where and when they could be used in the project. They made sure to highlight not only traditional librarian skills but also their abilities in developing students' digital and academic skills.

The three librarians had challenges with the software they used. There were limits in relation to developing what they wanted to develop. In addition, it did not interact optimally with the overall online platform. Digital ingenuity, a good dose of personal robustness, and the close relations they developed were a great help. According to the article, librarians in the 21st century must be good at communication, technology, supervision, teaching, and project leadership.

### 17.3.3 Article 3

Cox, A.M., Kennan, M.A., Lyon, L., Pinfield, S., Sbaffi, L., 2019. Maturing research data services and the transformation of academic libraries. J. Doc. 75(6), 1432–1462. https://doi.org/10.1108/JD-12-2018-0211.

The article investigates how research data management (RDM) in academic libraries has developed as a consequence of digital developments and, by extension, the influence these developments has had on the roots of the academic library. The background is that other studies clearly indicate how RDM develops and helps transform the role of academic libraries. The study, which is from 2018, was carried out as a web-based questionnaire survey with respondents from employees in academic libraries in many parts of the world: Australia, Canada, Germany, Ireland, the Netherlands, the United Kingdom, and the United States.

The results of the survey indicate that RDM is primarily advisory. Service development is seen mainly as an expansion of traditional librarian supportive tasks in connection with research data. However, a potential transformation can be identified when the traditional service is combined with the demands of new services, such as text and data mining, bibliometrics, and artificial intelligence (AI).

The study seems to confirm the previous studies that indicate that librarians still experience a gap between skills and abilities in relation to delivering qualified work in the area. It also contributes to a broader and promising discussion of how the fundamental approach in academic libraries is fundamentally changing as a consequence of digital developments. In sum, RDM will likely mark a potential paradigm shift in, and re-structuring of, professional relationships by opening up new types of collaboration across professions and faculties, resulting in a new concept of 'co-opetitive', a hybrid between competitive and cooperative. This transformation is also likely to impact traditional skills and professional identity, and create the potential for librarians' involvement in data analysis.

### 17.3.4 Article 4

Cox, A.M., Pinfield, S., Rutter, S., 2019. The intelligent library: thought leaders' views on the likely impact of artificial intelligence on academic libraries. Libr. Hi Tech 37(3), 418–438. doi:https://doi.org/10.1108/LHT-08-2018-0105.

The article is based on interviews with 33 library directors, library commentators, and experts within the education and publishing sectors. It investigates future expectations of the influence of artificial intelligence (AI) on academic libraries.

The expectation is that AI will optimize search machines significantly, and that text mining and research data management will become a part of librarians' work portfolio. At the same time, new ways of publishing, where traditional publishers no longer provide the only way to publish research and other knowledge, will have an influence on librarians' work and the skills and tools that will become necessary to service users. The librarian will not disappear but there will be changes in the profile. The point of the article is that the modern librarian is a software engineer with skills within procurement and licensing of e-content, software, and services; digital management and digital preservation; design of information discovery infrastructure; with an understanding of the scholarly publishing landscape.

### 17.3.5 Article 5

Koltay, T., 2019. Accepted and emerging roles of academic libraries in supporting research 2.0. J. Acad. Librariansh. 45(2), 75–80. https://doi.org/10.1016/j.acalib.2019.01.001.

Based on a nonexhaustive review of the recent literature, the article describes theoretical and practical questions, and presents results of the empirical research in the area.

The literature review identifies some of the roles and tasks that academic librarians, as a consequence of development of Research 2.0, must relate to, and which require new and supporting activities and actions. The areas in question are research data management, expert service, and data curation. The article points at new tasks and roles for data librarians. Some of them are as follows: continuous storage of data, distribution of unique identifiers, creation and management of metadata, data curation, and development of an infrastructure that supports data management throughout the research process.

Academic librarians must adapt to new conditions and new requirements in research environments. Today, librarians can, on the one hand, make use of their traditional skills when managing data. On the other hand, they need to bring a conceptual understanding of data into the process and must be able to find, extract, gather, filter, organize, analyse, and present data. Some librarians acknowledge that the library is not seen to offer RDM support because involvement in research data management happens too late. It is, therefore, important to create personal relations between researchers and librarians.

### *17.3.6 Article 6*

Poremski, M.D., 2017. Evaluating the landscape of digital humanities librarianship. Coll. Undergrad. Libr. 24(2–4), 140–154. doi:https://doi.org/10.1080/10691316.2017.1325721.

Digital humanities (DH) is not an independent area of knowledge, but a number of different practices that explore a world where printed material is no longer the exclusive or normative medium. The American Association of Research Libraries describes DH as a growing field that uses computer-based technologies to explore new areas of research in humanities. Librarians working in this field face the special challenge of finding the best ways to support this rapidly developing discipline. How do we satisfy the users' new demands? How do we adapt librarianship to this growing field of study?

The study indicates that for academic, specialized librarians, DH can potentially lead to new partnerships. DH offers new, emerging, and intellectual space and methods for using new technologies and tools. The challenge for specialized librarians is to identify and meet the needs of this new intellectual discipline. The particular challenges in the digital environment call for expertise with regard to the creation and navigation of sustainable digital solutions.

The results of the study coincide with a bigger picture: that libraries are experiencing an identity crisis and that there is a need to find out which disciplines are important in the academic environments. A DH librarian builds bridges between the current humanities research methods. Academics in the Humanities need to collaborate with librarians with regard to new methods and technological solutions on campus.

## 17.4 Interviews

We carried out two qualitative interviews. The interviewees were selected on the basis of their roles as leaders with many years of experience in the sector. They were also selected because they work at the strategic level, setting the direction for future work in research and educational libraries. The two respondents each represent their professional college. For the sake of anonymization, we will refer to the interviewees as interviewee A and interviewee B.

The focus of both semistructured interviews was to elicit answers to the question of how leaders view the future role of specialized librarians and which specific skills they feel these people either have or will need to have to ensure the continuing development of research and educational libraries in their respective contexts. Prior to both interviews, the interviewees received a guide because, as questions had a certain complexity, we felt that the quality of the answers to our questions would have improved significantly if the subjects were given an opportunity to reflect on the themes.

The questions were as follows:

1. Do you agree with the statements that, over the last 15 years, there has been a tremendous digital development and that it has had a great impact on the educational libraries?
2. What in digital development do you think has been the most crucial element for the libraries? And in which way?
3. How do you see the role of the educational library today in a world characterized by digital services and digitization at all?
4. What do you think educational librarians' core competencies are—what are we doing that others cannot?
5. Do you see any new tasks that the education library could benefit from?
6. How do these tasks differ from library tasks in the past? Why do we have to take these tasks?
7. In what areas do you think that we, as an educational library, are particularly challenged by the digital development when it comes to competencies?
8. Do educational librarians have some special strengths in relation to digital development and the competencies it demands?
9. What is unique about us? Do we have any competencies that cannot be acquired by other professional groups or put in an electronic formula or algorithm? If so, which ones?
10. When you work with library development on a strategic level, where do you look for inspiration?
11. How do you select which trends the education library should follow?

The interviews were processed on the basis of the qualitative research method with transcription, meaning condensation, and theme derivation (Kvale and Brinkmann, 2015).

### 17.4.1 Analysis of data

The interviews were performed and recorded via Skype business (audio file attached in the addenda) and were then transcribed in fragments. The analysis was performed according to Kvale's five steps (Kvale and Brinkmann, 2015) where, first, (1) an overall impression is made, (2) units of opinion are identified, (3) then thematized, (4) the units of opinion are questioned, and (5) the themes are connected in a descriptive statement (Kvale and Brinkmann, 2015, pp. 269–270).

The analysis is thus made in relation to a hermeneutical circle structure as mentioned above, where the intention is to initiate the process which through preunderstanding leads to understanding and postunderstanding (Thisted, 2014, p. 62). Postunderstanding will thereby appear as new interpretations that can enlighten the thesis, as will become evident in the conclusion.

### 17.4.2 Interview themes

#### 17.4.2.1 The asynchronous meeting

Both respondents agree that the technological changes are more than 15 years old. The most significant transformation caused by these is that the librarian must be able to relate to the asynchronous meeting with the students and other users and the fact that we no longer hold the sole access to information.

#### 17.4.2.2 Relational and collaborative skills

There has been a migration away from the physical space towards a collaboration with the educations. And, the respondents put great emphasis on the relational skills and the interdisciplinary collaboration, where the educational librarian needs to apply his/her skill set in different contexts and milieus.

#### 17.4.2.3 Critical thinking and digital formation

One respondent emphasizes the role of the educational librarian regarding digital formation in that there is a great task in teaching the students to be critically reflective, particularly because, when moving around digitally, we leave behind data which is then picked up by tech giants and used for commercial purposes. The tech giants already know far too much about us. In the digital formation lies also the understanding of how these data can be used against us. Here, we see an ethical and democratic dilemma in which the educational librarian also plays an essential role.

#### 17.4.2.4 The unique skills of the educational librarian

Both respondents agree that the educational librarian has a special task related to knowledge production and dissemination. They can qualify the research process because they can aid in qualifying the research question and in finding the pre-existing information. Moreover, when it comes to the handling of information in general, we can provide tools to all types of users, which can support the processes of finding and assessing. Within this area lies the unique skills of the educational librarian.

#### 17.4.2.5 From generalist to specialist

Technological development entails some of the traditional work areas in which the educational librarian has been taken over by technologies. They nevertheless still need to support their use. The field has grown too vast for one to have a general overview. The educational librarian must, therefore, dare to specialize within specific areas of knowledge such as, for instance, some of the aforementioned. They need to possess the more general skills within the pedagogical and didactic area, as these particular fields of knowledge define the very existence of the trade.

## 17.5 Results

Overall, as described above, the literature indicates that various societal conditions will contribute to disruption of the concept of libraries in the educational sector. In the light of technological developments, the skills that will be in demand in the future library job market will include cognitive, social and problem-solving skills, and increasing numbers of librarians will have their skills challenged and must work on them (Ciccone and Hounslow, 2019). Some studies emphasize digital literacy and data literacy as key concepts behind the digitization of library work and education in general (Ciccone and Hounslow, 2019). This concerns the content of what we need to know and be capable of with regard to new media and digital tools, and how we interact with them and each other in a digitized world. Studies as well as interviews point out the following themes for the skills of the specialized librarian in the future.

### *17.5.1 New ways of retrieval, preservation, and dissemination*

Overall, the studies and interviews show broad consensus that the transition from physical materials to electronic materials is the most important change in the work conditions and tasks of the librarian because he or she no longer has control of the indexation and search processes. This means that she can no longer predict and explain a search result with the same precision. A loss of control has occurred here. The changes have a great impact on what previously could be described as the core of the traditional work of specialized librarians (Bandyopadhyay and Boyd-Byrnes, 2016; Ciccone and Hounslow, 2019; Cox et al., 2019a,b).

Since the advent of the Internet and search machines such as Google, much knowledge can be accessed online. Users have altered their search behaviour and no longer need to go to a physical space for help (Bandyopadhyay and Boyd-Byrnes, 2016). In addition, more and more academic programmes can be taken online. The librarian must, therefore, liberate herself from the physical space and seek users and partners in various places and contexts. She must work across disciplines and relate to an asynchronous reality (Bandyopadhyay and Boyd-Byrnes, 2016; Cox et al., 2019a,b).

## 17.6 Librarian skills in a digital society

When we look across the literature and the two interviews, there is a sizeable convergence of the skills that are regarded as being important for the future librarian. They fall within a range of themes that we have chosen to mention highlighted here:

- Technological and digital skills.
- Skills within the research area, including knowledge generation and knowledge processes.
- Skills within digital humanities.
- The last theme, interpersonal skills, is clearly dominant.

The four themes are described as follows:

### 17.6.1 Technological and digital skills

A wide-ranging set of skills predominates here. First and foremost is data management in a broad sense. It is described as, amongst other things, data curation and the management of big data. Common to both is that they concern the ability to procure large amounts of data from various sources, to analyse them, and then put them to good use in a given context. Data curation is more in line with classic librarianship skills because there is an emphasis on organization, quality assurance, and dissemination of data, whilst big data, which stems from computer science, has a more commercial aim (Cox et al., 2019a; Koltay, 2019).

Another important topic within this theme is research data management: the digital processes in the research process (Cox et al., 2019a; Koltay, 2019). Other skills that emerge from both textual informant empiricism are familiar librarian skills, but that are believed to gain greater importance, such as bibliometrics, information architecture, and text mining. Roles such as web developer and programme supporter are also mentioned. There is also a new concept, co-opetitive, as described previously, which describes the librarian as a hybrid between a collaborator and a competitor (Cox et al., 2019a).

Development within AI is also mentioned as an element that will affect librarianship in the future; the question is how. One study indicates that the modern librarian is a software engineer with skills in, amongst others, procurement and licensing of e-content, software, and services; digital management and digital preservation; and design of information discovery infrastructure (Cox et al., 2019b). A final topic includes a number of transversal skills within digital humanity and digital literacy (Poremski, 2017).

### 17.6.2 Skills within the area of research

There are many indications that in the future librarians will become close collaborators with researchers in several ways as perhaps an 'extended research assistant'. Librarians need to have knowledge about or at least insight into all disciplinary landscapes and their standards for research, their norms, and their ethics. Librarians must be able to facilitate research processes and ensure access to the gathering and dissemination of the knowledge that the research generates (Cox et al., 2019a,b; Koltay, 2019). One article mentions the 'hybrid researcher' (Poremski, 2017).

### 17.6.3 Skills within digital humanities

This theme includes skills that are already required for most librarians in educational institutions (at least in Denmark). They include didactics, classroom teaching, critical reflection, source criticism, academic skills, and the ability to produce syntheses.

Topics such as entrepreneurship, innovation, and project management are mentioned repeatedly. These three topics have all been important in Danish educational policy for years as skills that are necessary for our survival. There will, therefore, be a number of librarians employed at research and educational libraries, who have worked with these skills in various ways in the past 10 years or more (Regeringen, 2006).

### 17.6.4 Interpersonal skills

This theme is clearly the biggest one. 'Relational', in particular, is a term that appears regularly (Bandyopadhyay and Boyd-Byrnes, 2016; Cox et al., 2019a,b; Koltay, 2019; Poremski, 2017) (interviewee A and interviewee B, 2020). In addition, terms such as communication, interpretation of needs, broker, interpreter, host, partner, collaboration, dissemination, and intermediary are used. Common to these terms is that they touch on the inter and intrapersonal, and that they are precisely the skills that cannot (yet) be translated into technological and digital solutions (Bandyopadhyay and Boyd-Byrnes, 2016; Poremski, 2017; Koltay, 2019). It is about using personal abilities and skills to understand people in various processes and contexts. This means that the librarian must constantly be able to relate to something dynamically emerging and analyse how her own skills can be brought into play in the context in question (Poremski, 2017; Koltay, 2019).

## 17.7 The overall picture

Rapid digital development has major implications for *what* we need to learn and *how* we need to learn. The need for new forms of interaction and collaboration, including how the librarian should enter into new knowledge generation and knowledge processes in completely new contexts are pointed out (Ciccone and Hounslow, 2019; Koltay, 2019; Poremski, 2017).

The librarian must be capable of being in what Mezirow calls a transformative learning process. According to Mezirow, learning is 'creating new or revised interpretations of the meaning of an experience that contributes to shaping subsequent understanding, assessment, and action' (Illeris, 2012, p. 157). This means that learning can have various depths or levels in the individual. Mankind seeks meaning and is reflective and must, therefore, be understood as an interpretive being. Man must be understood via what takes place on the intrapersonal level. Man seeks meaning, which is structured by setting up frames of reference and perspectives. These are created through the socialization process, where emotion exerts a strong influence on how deeply the meaning perspective is stored in mankind. Knowledge generation is perceived as a construct: the individual constructs a meaning with his or her experiences based on assumptions and experiences, and when this basis of understanding no longer gives meaning, a new understanding of meaning is constructed.

Mezirow's conceptualization of learning operates at different learning levels. Here, we would like to highlight (i) instrumental learning, a cause-effect relationship, where there is a focus on the actual action and (ii) communicative learning, where the idea is to understand meaning and create coherent understanding (Illeris, 2012, pp. 162–163). Critical reflection happens when we experience problems or dilemmas, where our current 'frames of reference' no longer give meaning. We are forced to change perspective. Changes in perspective are a critical reflection of how and why previous meaning perspectives helped us to experience and understand the world around us and how this perspective is no longer viable. Critical reflection on one's own terms can thus lead to transformative learning.

What the librarian need is to be capable of ongoing critical reflection on her way of mind and 'frames of reference'. It represents a state of constant willingness to change mindset and views to what is important in any given environment/context at any time.

## 17.8 Discussion

As mentioned above, a common feature of both the studies and the interviews is the assumption that technological development increases the need for new ways of working and new skills. These developments give rise to new trends, where society's focus shifts from products to processes. A characteristic of these processes is that we are constantly on the move, and that we as employees must constantly be able to regulate the course of, and review, the processes since new elements must be taken into account. According to the articles and the interviews, these changes exert considerable influence on what is considered the core of the academic library, which has traditionally been the procurement, creation, and dissemination of knowledge and is now about facilitating knowledge generation. The change indicates a significant need for developing the academic library of the future, where there are demands for new and even more complex and diverse skills.

The pervasive and most central skills are, according to the studies we reviewed and the statements from the interviewees, the interpersonal skills that focus on individual interaction, and their importance and role in relation to learning and learning processes. The focus could be on dialogue, practices, or ways of interacting (Säljö, 2003). There are strong indications that academic librarians and libraries worldwide face a common challenge. We believe that two central issues can be identified:

**(1)** Academic libraries need to be more visible and present in educational institutions—at different levels. The prerequisite for this is development of a new library image, where the library is perceived as a dynamic function that is deeply involved in many different processes in the educational environment. It can be postulated that the role is, therefore, no longer to view oneself as an institution within an institution, but rather as a process. This perspective is also fundamentally linked to the fact that knowledge is built up and changed in the processes. This means that:

**(2)** The academic librarian must go out to where things are happening, and establish new relations, as traditional roles are dissolved. We believe that it can be destructive if the librarian seeks to cling to old roles and tasks. The question is how academic libraries can liberate the future so they do not just end up being copies of the present. This is supported by the empiricism presented in this chapter, which emphasizes that academic librarians must balance working with new tasks in new relationships and new ways of collaborating, with the existing tasks—within organizational or structural conditions, which will not necessarily change.

In addition, it is not necessarily a process without conflict for the individual academic librarian, since learning is about questioning the validity of a meaning perspective—a meaning perspective that has perhaps always been taken for granted and that is based on an academic understanding of oneself and which may mean rejecting values that have been central to one's professional self-perception (Illeris, 2012, p. 165). As we have mentioned previously, Mezirow describes this process as transformative learning:

> *Transformative learning refers to the process by which we transform our taken-for-granted frames of reference (meaning perspective, habits of mind, mind-sets) to make them more inclusive discriminating, open, emotionally capable of change, and reflective so that they may generate beliefs and opinions that will prove more true or justified to guide action.*
>
> *(Illeris, 2012, p. 68)*

According to the Danish learning theorist Knud Illeris, transformative learning is also central to the concept of skills because it is about what the things learned can be used for in relevant contexts. In Denmark, the new generation of librarians has also received another education, because the educational programme has been reformed continuously and has been closed as an independent institution. Our Danish management interviewees, therefore, ask themselves if what they regard as the essence of academic librarians is simply on the way out. In line with this, they point out that there is an identity crisis.

## 17.9 Conclusion

In answer to our research question: *How can the specific skills of the librarian in a digital context be used in the future?* Digital development and video production have radically changed work in academic libraries. In future, academic librarians must take on roles that require cognitive, interpersonal, and pedagogical/teaching skills. The librarian must work closely and in an integrated manner with a wide range of partnerships, including with researchers and teachers, and be skilled at creating close work relationships with a range of collaborative partners. The librarian must be able to keep pace with a dynamic and emerging reality, where new tasks and skills must be introduced. We are talking about skills and tasks within areas such as RDM, artificial intelligence, and creation of digitally sustainable solutions.

In addition, the librarian must have solid insight into the knowledge, ethics, and research methods of each domain. These are skills that to a great extent build on the librarian's core skills. In future, the librarian cannot survive by being a specialist within her specific domain but must instead constantly enter into new processes and partnerships with the other actors in the institution. As such, the library goes from being a function to a process that is constantly part of a number of other processes.

## 17.10 Outlook

According to Trine Schreiber, the profession is not predetermined but is something that is created and developed by participating in various networks within and outside of the institutional framework. The actors are students, teachers, researchers, programmes, and digital technologies. The individual librarian is formed by networks and tasks (Schreiber, 2015).

The processes and the various networks will reflect the realities that will affect and shape each librarian's understanding of her own reality. Seen in that light, there are strong indications that the concept of skills in an educational environment will be in constant movement, and that it may develop variously at different educational institutions. We will leave that question open.

## References

Albæk, K., VIVE, 2018. Den teknologiske udvikling og kompetencer på fremtidens arbejdsmarked – En litteraturoversigt. Available at: https://www.vive.dk/media/pure/6911/1201096.

Bandyopadhyay, A., Boyd-Byrnes, M.K., 2016. Is the need for mediated reference service in academic libraries fading away in the digital environment? Ref. Serv. Rev. 44 (4), 596–626. https://doi.org/10.1108/RSR-02-2016-0012.

Castells, M., 1996. The Rise of the Network Society. Information Age: Economy, Society and Culture. vol. 1 Blackwell Publishers, Malden, MA. CN - 30.11.

Ciccone, A., Hounslow, L., 2019. Re-envisioning the role of academic librarians for the digital learning environment: the case of UniSA online. J. Univ. Teach. Learn. Pract. 16 (1).

Cox, A.M., Kennan, M.A., Lyon, L., Pinfield, S., Sbaffi, L., 2019a. Maturing research data services and the transformation of academic libraries. J. Doc. 75 (6), 1432–1462. https://doi.org/10.1108/JD-12-2018-0211.

Cox, A.M., Pinfield, S., Rutter, S., 2019b. The intelligent library: thought leaders' views on the likely impact of artificial intelligence on academic libraries. Libr. Hi Tech 37 (3), 418–438. https://doi.org/10.1108/LHT-08-2018-0105.

Gibbons, M., Trow, M., Scott, P., Schwartzman, S., 1995. The new production of knowledge: the dynamics of science and research in contemporary society. Contemp. Sociol. 24 (6). https://doi.org/10.2307/2076669.

Holdt Christensen, P., 2002. Om vidensledelse: perspektiver til refleksion. Samfundslitteratur, Frederiksberg.

Illeris, K., 2012. 49 tekster om læring. Samfundslitteratur, Frederiksberg.

Koltay, T., 2019. Accepted and emerging roles of academic libraries in supporting research 2.0. J. Acad. Librariansh. 45 (2), 75–80. https://doi.org/10.1016/j.acalib.2019.01.001.

Kvale, S., Brinkmann, S., 2015. Interview: det kvalitative forskningsinterview som håndværk, third ed. Hans Reitzel, Copenhagen.

Pedersen, P.U., 2017. Fra forskning til praksis. Munksgaard, Copenhagen.

Poremski, M.D., 2017. Evaluating the landscape of digital humanities librarianship. Coll. Undergrad. Libr. 24 (2–4), 140–154. https://doi.org/10.1080/10691316.2017.1325721.

Regeringen, 2006. Fremgang, fornyelse og tryghed: strategi for Danmark i den globale økonomi: de vigtigste initiativer. Regeringen, Copenhagen.

Säljö, R., 2003. Læring i praksis: et sociokulturelt perspektiv. Hans Reitzel, Copenhagen.

Schreiber, T., 2015. Fleksible koncepter for integration af det virtuelle bibliotek i uddannelsernes læringsmiljøer. University of Copenhagen, Copenhagen.

Schreiber, T., 2018. Bibliotekarerne: en profession der former og formes af et aktør-netværk. Nordisk tidsskrift for informationsvidenskab og kulturformidling online (NTIK) (Nye tider, nye udfordringer og nye kompetencer) https://tidsskrift.dk/ntik/article/download/111482/160486/. (Accessed 10.05.20).

Stegeager, N., Laursen, E., 2011. Organisationer i bevægelse: læring, udvikling, intervention. Samfundslitteratur, Frederiksberg.

Thisted, J., 2014. Forskningsmetode i praksis : projektorienteret videnskabsteori og forskningsmetodik. Munksgaard, Copenhagen.

University College Syddanmark, 2013. Innovative partnerskaber for udvikling af viden om innovativ uddannelsespraksis i velfærdsrettede uddannelser. Uddannelses- og Forskningsministeriet. https://ufm.dk/publikationer/2013/inno-det-innovative-danmark/inno/modtagede-indspil/et-kompetent-samfund-med-sammenhaengskraft/copy_of_et-kompetent-samfund-med-sammenhaengskraft/innovative-partnerskaber-for-udvikling-af-viden-om-innovativ-uddannelsesprak. (Accessed 07.03.20).

# The user as a data source: The advance of surveillance capitalism 18

*Carl Gustav Johannsen*
University of Copenhagen, Copenhagen, Denmark

## 18.1 Introduction

Reports and articles on digitization in libraries and the introduction of new library services based on digitalized technologies have typically been concerned around which kinds of benefits and advantages the user would obtain and also around the complexities and problems related to utilizing the new technological opportunities. The more problematic and negative aspects of digitization, such as the risks of users being misused, exploited, and the threats of privacy violations, on the other hand, have apparently not received corresponding attention.

In a recent book, *Users, Technology, and Library Design: From Clients to Participants and Data Sources*, I dealt with—through academic library cases—how libraries have contributed to a variety of research monitoring and research management-oriented services (Johannsen, 2019, pp. 140–148). It was pointed out that the role of the end users, who were researchers at universities, had obviously been changed. Through the use of advanced, digitized bibliometric methods academic libraries to an increasing extent had been able to identify quantitative indicators for academic productivity and quality (Åström and Hansson, 2013; Whitley and Gläser, 2007). Such sensitive data were subsequently communicated to research management departments at universities. A shift from a situation where the primary focus and goal of the academic library was to deliver services directly to students and researchers, to a different context where the needs of research administrative units were prioritized amongst the main concerns of the academic library, had apparently taken place.

The aim of this chapter is both to consider the use of bibliometric data by research management units at universities and to move one step further and investigate to what extent a new phase of digitization, linked with notions like surveillance society, surveillance state, and surveillance capitalism, has influenced public and academic libraries.

This new, surveillance business model, is, according to Zuboff (2019) based on the acquisition and consolidation of very large volumes of personal data, and its exploitation to target advertisements, and to manipulate consumer behaviour. Indeed, as admitted by the architects of the model, "users are 'bribed' and 'induced' to make their data available at minimal cost to marketers" (Clarke, 2019). As well as a presentation of the concept of surveillance capitalism, this chapter will also discuss the importance and challenges of the model in a library-oriented environment and context.

**Future Directions in Digital Information. https://doi.org/10.1016/B978-0-12-822144-0.00018-5**

## 18.2 Research questions addressed

Four main research questions will be explored. The first concerns the extended digital services provided by academic and public libraries. Extended here means library services that differ from traditional library services like information and literature searching in one or more respects. When an academic library provides access for its users to external online databases or assists in searching procedure, it represents a traditional approach to digitization. If, however, the same academic library also provides research management units at universities with research productivity data on the universities' researchers, we are dealing with an extended library service. It also makes sense to call such a library activity surveillance since the library watches over the researchers publishing activities.

The second research question is about surveillance capitalism and, in particular, the importance of surveillance capitalism in library contexts. Surveillance has, however, a different meaning in digital contexts. Instead of apparently sensitive data about a researcher's productivity as in the case of extended library services, the focus of the surveillance could also be seemingly innocent collateral data regarding user thoughts, preferences, feelings, interests, and behaviours. In the private sector, such data have been made profitable by companies like Google, Facebook, and Microsoft, enabled by digitization and the Internet.

There seem to be both important differences and also similarities between the extended services and the surveillance-based approaches. Although both models are based on digital user behaviour data, the differences are obvious.

Extended services are typically based on sensitive data of researchers such as the quantity of their work-related research outputs, the character and quality of their publications, and the professional networks of the researchers, whereas the surveillance-based model mostly feeds on collateral data on leisure time, everyday activities of ordinary users. The collateral data are first made profitable when they are collected, interpreted, and transformed through the use of artificial intelligence algorithms. Application of such algorithms can, for example, explain why the mere mentioning of a certain destination, for example, Costa Rica, by a user of a social media platform can lead to the subsequent reception by the same user of emails with special offers from diverse travel agencies of trips to Costa Rica. Indeed, it is the capture, storage, analysis, and learning from the by-products of search queries that have turned Google into the gold standard of web search (Zuboff, 2019, p. 69).

An interesting question here is whether libraries and the library sector have—or should have—learned from such applied private sector business models, or—on the contrary—whether they should resist and fight against all shapes of surveillance capitalism to ensure 'a human future at the new frontier of power' (which is also the subtitle of Shoshana Zuboff's latest 2019 book).

Another significant difference concerns the nature of the consequences to the users involved. Here, extended services targeted towards research administrative units at universities could lead to serious, career-oriented—negative or positive—outcomes, whereas the surveillance capitalistic model, typically, will lead to more innocent consequences like unwelcome offerings and marketing efforts to produce behavioural modifications.

The third main research question will deal with the more positive one of how digitization could not only lead to extended services and expropriation of critical human rights but also to more attractive future developments such as the creation of 'participatory information spaces' (Björneborn, 2011), where social media platforms both allow users to leave 'behavioural traces' of their informational activities and also to find such traces from other users, which has also been termed 'user-to-user mediation' and 'social navigation'.

The fourth research question concerns the extent to which the users themselves appear to be interested at all in pro-active, technology-based library services? The answer will draw upon data from a 2017 Danish National Library user survey.

The four research questions to be dealt with in this contribution can be summarized as:

1. What has characterized the use of extended library services through digitization?
2. Should libraries get inspired by the pioneers of surveillance capitalism to obtain desired behavioural modifications of their users or should they oppose the development?
3. To what extent are user-to-user mediation and social navigation related to the threats of surveillance capitalism?
4. To what extent are library users interested in more pro-active technology-based services?

## 18.3 The use of extended library services

I have defined and exemplified 'extended library services' as services concerning university researchers, and also as library services particularly addressing the information needs and interests of administrative-oriented staff and units at universities and other research agencies rather than addressing the information needs of the researchers themselves.

During the last few decades, significant changes in research management and policy systems have taken place. Amongst the important ones is the development by which the allocation of research funds—from the individual scholar to institutions and international programmes for academic research—has increasingly been linked to the evaluation of research outcomes (Johannsen, 2019, p. 140). The productivity and the quality of the research conducted by individual researchers as well as by different research teams has thus become a parameter of significant importance. As an important element of this change, bibliometric methods have been applied to an increasing extent in order to identify and measure key quantitative indicators for academic quality and productivity (Åström and Hansson, 2013; Whitley and Gläser, 2007).

However, research management activities and parameters do not only serve narrow managerial and administrative purposes. Indeed, they can also be seen as beneficial by the researchers themselves because they make research activities and results more visible and transparent. Thus, research management outputs can also facilitate networking, partnership finding, and research project funding cooperative activities. Furthermore, expressed in terms of a simple business model, extended library services provide responsible administrative units at universities and relevant government agencies with useful services. Since such units and agencies have a legitimate purpose to fulfil to ensure that research means are applied in accordance with laws and policies, these extended library services are usually regarded as legitimate.

In my latest book (Johannsen, 2019, p. 151), extended library services are moreover emphasized as source of a new library user metaphor, *the user as a data source*. Concerning university researchers, this application seems to be reasonable and legitimate. However, *data source* can also imply other applications and contexts, which appear to be more problematic. Indeed, when addressing the research question about 'surveillance capitalism', the question of legitimacy appears to be different and more complex.

## 18.4 Should libraries find inspiration in the methods of surveillance capitalism?

Indeed, when one tries to compare digital development in the private sector with the corresponding development in public and academic libraries, similarities, but also some significant differences, appear. An important similarity concerns the role of digital business models.

Amongst the primary differences, the nature and complexity of the applied business models should be mentioned. Shoshana Zuboff, professor emerita at the Harvard Business School, has developed—through a number of research-based studies (Zuboff, 1988, 2019)—surveillance capitalism as an almost apocalyptic vision of a future to be avoided. Also, other authors (e.g. Clarke, 2019; Cecez-Kecmanovic, 2019) have noticed the emergence and rise of the digital surveillance economy and warned against its serious threats to the interest of individuals, societies, and polities. One purpose of this contribution will be to consider to what extent Zuboff's, Clarke's, Cecez-Kecmanovic's, and others gloomy visions also would make sense in a public and academic library context.

I start with explaining the concepts of surveillance capitalism based on the theses of Clarke, Zuboff, and others. Then, I turn to how their ideas and critical assessments have been perceived and received by some members of the library world. Finally, I consider how libraries and the library world could and should offer resistance to the menaces of surveillance capitalism or rather—as pointed out by the Australian professor, Dubravka Cecez-Kecmanovic—why the rise of the digital surveillance economy has not so far been met with serious resistance (Cecez-Kecmanovic, 2019). First, however, I provide a short presentation of the conceptual framework concerning surveillance capitalism.

## 18.5 What is surveillance capitalism?

According to Zuboff's definition of 'surveillance capitalism', it represents a

> *New economic order that claims human experience as free raw material for hidden commercial practices of extraction, prediction and sales' and a 'parasitic economic logic in which the production of goods and services is subordinated to a new global architecture of behavioural modification'.*
>
> *(Zuboff, 2019, p. vii)*

Indeed, Zuboff here emphasizes the negative aspects of this new economic order by considering it to be a serious threat to 'human nature' and as a 'new instrumentarian power that asserts dominance over society and presents startling challenges to market democracy'. Moreover, surveillance capitalism represents an 'expropriation of critical human rights that is best understood as a coup from above: an overthrow of the people's sovereignty' (Zuboff, 2019, p. vii).

An earlier definition of surveillance capitalism by Zuboff refers surveillance capitalism to the aim of corporations:

> *'to predict and modify human behavior as a means to produce revenue and market control'.*
>
> *(Zuboff, 2015, p. 75)*

If we compare the concept of surveillance capitalism with the term 'extended library services' as previously mentioned, similarities and differences appear. An important similarity is that data produced by or belonging to one side—as, for example, researchers and ordinary users—are communicated and utilized by another (e.g. administrative units and commercial interests). In the extended library case, data on a researcher's work are formatted in a way to match the needs of administrative unit at universities. In surveillance capitalism, on the other hand, data on human experience are communicated and utilized by commercial companies—not by public, administrative units—to predict and modify human behaviour to achieve profit and market control.

## 18.6 The early digital dream

Surveillance capitalism historically runs contrary to the early digital dream of being 'connected' as something intrinsically pro-social, tending towards the democratization of knowledge:

> *Twenty years ago, there was a widespread enthusiasm about the World Wide Web that enabled everyone to communicate and share ideas, knowledge, views, and photos free of charge. But service providers struggled to invent a viable business model to support free usage... It turned out that only advertising revenue could provide a business model and attract venture capitalists and corporate executives. The emergence of the business model based on advertising revenue led to increasing and more invasive data capture and exploitation practices and widespread surveillance of users.*
>
> *(Cecez-Kecmanovic, 2019)*

Instead of democratization of knowledge, surveillance capitalism has transformed digital connection into a means to further others' commercial ends. Compared to industrial capitalism that feeds on labour, surveillance capitalism, according to Zuboff, feeds on every aspect of a human's experience (Zuboff, 2019, p. 9).

Of course, the mechanisms and causes which have created the present 'age of surveillance capitalism' have been analyzed and discussed both inside and outside the library world. The development has, typically, not been seen as either a necessary or an inevitable consequence of modern IT development or digitization. On the contrary, 20 years ago, there was a widespread enthusiasm about the Internet and the World Wide Web. Indeed, it was widely believed that democracy and digitization would move forward hand in hand.

## 18.7 'The fiasco of the web'

This is why early web pioneers talk about the 'fiasco' of the web as a direct, but unintentional, consequence of choosing advertising as the default model to support online content and services (Cecez-Kecmanovic, 2019), according to a long-standing aphorism in media theory: 'If you're not paying, you're the product' (Clarke, 2019, p. 62).

## 18.8 Surveillance and behavioural modification

As an example of the practices of surveillance capitalism, which many have experienced, concerns reference to a geographical unit sometimes automatically leading to travel agency commercials related to that specific destination. Zuboff points out that such occurrences show that automated machine processes not only know our behaviour but also in different ways try to modify and shape that behaviour towards profitable outcomes through techniques like nudging, coaxing, tuning, and herding.

Zuboff points out:

> *With this reorientation from knowledge to power, it is no longer enough to automate information flows about us; the goal is to automate us to achieve behavioural modification through the automated medium of an increasingly ubiquitous computational architecture of 'smart' networked devices, things, and spaces.*
>
> *(Zuboff, 2019, p. 8)*

## 18.9 Surveillance capitalism and libraries

Roger Clarke is another central, research-based voice critical of the foundations and role of the digital surveillance economy. Like Cesez-Kecmanovic and Zuboff, he also emphasizes the notion of a shift from the original optimistic idea that digitization and the Internet could make consumer marketing 'less intrusive and manipulative, and more collaborative'. However, the opposite took place and the web's architecture was inverted from its original, consumer-driven request-response pair into a marketer's data collection and consumer manipulation framework. Indeed, Web 2.0 features laid the foundations for the digital surveillance economy. Within less than a decade from 2005 onwards, consumer marketing became anything but the two-sided conversation that had been envisaged (Clarke, 2019, p. 61).

Clarke defines 'surveillance' as the 'systematic investigation or monitoring of the actions or communications of one or more persons' (Clarke, 2019, p. 61). Before the Internet, a number of visual and aural communications have been employed. Computerized surveillance, however, rapidly emerged as a more cost-effective alternative. One may here ask to what extent surveillance capitalism in Zuboff's understanding of the concept has any relevancy in a public and academic library context at all?

## 18.10 'Reunite supply and demand'—From mass to individual consumption

According to Zuboff's analyses, the digital era offered the tools to shift the focus of consumption from the mass to the individual, liberating and reconfiguring capitalism's operations and assets. Digitization and online communication, indeed, promised something utterly new, urgently necessary, and operationally impossible outside the networked spaces of the digital. As Zuboff emphasized: did digitization open the door to a 'new rational capitalism able to reunite supply and demand by connecting us to what we really want in exactly the ways that we choose'? (Zuboff, 2019, p. 30). At the same time, terms and psychological mechanisms like individualization and personalization entered the library literature. On the other hand, traditional library terms and processes were transformed into the complex and more or less covert and clandestine processes of data acquisition and data exploitation (Cecez-Kecmanovic, 2019). Companies which Zuboff emphasized as central surveillance capitalistic actors—Google, Facebook, and Microsoft—are also present in different public and academic library contexts. Indeed, the principles and practices of surveillance capitalism were deeply criticized by critical voices in the library world.

Next, we deal with the third research question concerning the extent to which user-to-user mediation and social navigation are related to the threats of surveillance capitalism.

## 18.11 User-to-user mediation in the participatory library

The Danish library researcher Lennart Björneborn has emphasized the importance of the library as an 'enabling space for creative practices like user participation and user-to-user mediation' and he sees the library as a 'participatory medium that can facilitate and support users to develop necessary participatory competences in all facets of … the life cycle of information behaviour' (Björneborn, 2011, p. 1). In his 2011 paper, he provides both low- and high-tech examples with rich potential for facilitating user-to-user mediation and social navigation.

Björneborn represents a positive and optimistic point of view of the future of digitization in libraries. It should be mentioned that he only deals with user-to-user mediation and social navigation and not with the role of administrative units or commercial actors. Surveillance capitalism does not appear in his universe. He concludes that

> *A higher degree of involving users' activities and skills in the mediation of information resources may create more engaging, inspiring, playful, and stimulating library spaces that can circulate more information resources among the users—and not least: this can also create more engaged users feeling more ownership of the library.*
>
> *(Björneborn, 2011, p. 1)*

It should also be noted that Björneborn's concept of behavioural traces not only include digital traces but also physical traces like 'worn covers, dog-eared pages, hand-written notes in books, and left-behind books on a table' (Björneborn, 2011, p. 1). Tagging, rating, editing, and re-mixing are examples of participatory activities and user-to-user mediation leaving behavioural traces that can be found and followed by other users. Björneborn points out that although many Library 2.0 approaches have focused on web-based solutions like blogs, wikis, tagging, and the like, his own model represents a 'holistic' approach, viewing human, physical, and digital information resources as supplementary parts of an integrated library platform. Björneborn's ideas of user-centred change are inspired by the 'Library 2.0' concept. According to its creator, Michael Casey, 'the heart of Library 2.0 is user-centred change' (Björneborn, 2011, p. 2).

An important element in Björneborn's thinking concerns his 'extended life cycle model of human information behaviour', which adds several verbs to the five facets of human information behaviour. The simplified 'life cycle' model contains five information behaviour facets: find-learn-create-store and share, whereas in the extended model, several verbs have been added. Instead of just 'create', verbs like 'produce, edit, remix, and copy' have been put together. The sophisticated conceptual framework allows more nuanced analyses and judgements concerning the social navigation in the library of users which can be, for example, direct and synchronous or indirect, asynchronous, and often anonymous.

This fruitful conceptual framework is elaborated through distinctions between spaces (digital or physical), and between intended and unintended contacts. The framework has been applied to study users' information behaviour in two Danish public libraries. Björneborn emphasizes the augmentation of the physical environments of the library with so-called ambient interfaces. As examples, visual cues, sound, and other sensory modes for representing aggregated behavioural patterns by users to other users in the library, are suggested. Also 'dynamic wall maps' visualizing how many users are present in the different library sections are mentioned (Björneborn, 2011, p. 5).

## 18.12 Associated inconveniences

In my 2017 book (Johannsen, 2017, pp. 75–76) about staff-less libraries, I described a related new concept, 'The Transformative Library'. The Transformative Library aims to enable a library unit to automatically adapt to the wants and needs of its present users.

The transformative library—based on user ID delivered at the entrance—automatically identifies the user groups that are within the library space, and then it transforms the space targeting those present at the library in that very moment. The users are identified by automatically collecting data, typically when they let themselves into the library during the staff-less hours or when they use the self-service kiosks for delivery and loan of books, or when they move in certain zones in the library equipped with motion sensors.

These data are then processed, and the results used to activate different 'modes' at the library. 'Modes' should be understood as a theme or a topic, chosen from the above input. The different modes can launch music playback, advertising on speakers, lighting changes, and presentations on large, dynamic wall maps. If you, as a user, for example, recently had ordered or delivered library materials on ornithology or on the travel destination, Costa Rica, you would probably be pleased when you see or hear relevant pictures on large screens and sounds, as, for example, Latin American rhythms on loudspeakers in the library. Probably, in cases where your ordered or delivered book titles deal with less innocent themes and topics than birds and travelling, the wall map experience could probably be embarrassing, especially when other library users are present. So, clearly, there could be a privacy concern associated with the transformative library.

To sum up, user-to-user mediation and social navigation is certainly different from digital surveillance models in many respects, for example, by including both low-tech, physical library and digital library hi-tech aspects. However, there are also serious ethical questions associated with some forms of user-to-user communication especially through modern, Library 2.0 media like 'dynamic wall maps' where there apparently exists a certain risk of unpleasant, indiscreet disclosure of personal preferences, and the like. Such risks are here associated with the use of a mix of personal and more or less public media and channels.

I now address the fourth question concerning the users' perceived need for pro-active, digital library services.

## 18.13 Do library users need or demand more pro-active digital services based on surveillance?

We now look at the role of surveillance in the recent digital strategies of public libraries. For that purpose, I have chosen a recent Danish report from 2017—*Digitale Biblioteksstrategier* (*Digital Library Strategies*, Moos and Schroeder, 2017) to examine the importance of surveillance and monitoring of library user behaviour. The report contains a survey of 7205 Danish adult inhabitants of their use/nonuse, perceptions, and preferences of the digital services of Danish public libraries. The survey is interesting because it utilizes a sophisticated approach to different library user segments, which enables separate pictures of digital use, preferences, and needs within eight different library user segments. The patterns of the use of digital library services vary, for example, between different user segments such as the 'male parent', 'the analogue women', the 'male cultural user', and the 'superdigital female'.

## 18.14 Platform-conscious vs entertainment-focused users

The report concludes that, in general, there is a great perceived demand for digital library services. Moreover, the report also emphasizes that there exists a considerable potential to further develop digital services in public libraries (Moos and Schroeder, 2017, p. 8). Indeed, 46% of Danes use the digital public library services more than once a year, whereas only 8% use it on a weekly basis. Besides the sociological framework of the *Digital Library Strategies* (2017), the survey makes an interesting distinction between users who are 'platform conscious' (platformsbevidste) and users who are 'entertainment-focused' (underholdnings-fokuserede). The former category emphasizes the use of a specific platform based on a relationship of trust, where the user gets inspiration and guidance towards new cultural experiences, whereas the entertainment-oriented users look for more specific materials and formats. Both categories—the platform conscious and the entertainment focused—are represented in public libraries and it is important that the digital services are consciously tailored towards the two different profiles.

## 18.15 Needs of inspiration vary within the eight library user segments

The sociological characteristics of user types that appreciate inspiration can help libraries to target their services, although the characteristics do not remove the need for estimates and judgements. Although it may be possible to deduce and assert that users who belong to the entertainment-oriented segment are likely to be less interested in being induced to read other book titles than expressly ordered than their platform-conscious colleagues, the logical library political consequence is not necessarily then that public libraries and librarians, in general, should stop to make suggestions as to new materials to entertainment-oriented users. First, it can be difficult for the librarian to determine to which category an individual user belongs, and second, public libraries typically also serve a higher cultural development perspective. Does the entertainment-oriented user, in reality, more than the platform oriented, need to be challenged in their literary preferences and choices?

The Danish survey indicates that the users' interest in pro-active library services varies a lot according to which particular library user segment the user belongs.

## 18.16 Summary

1. What has characterized the use of extended library services through digitization?
2. Should libraries get inspired by the pioneers of surveillance capitalism to obtain desired behavioural modifications of their users or should they oppose the development?

3. To what extent are user-to-user mediation and social navigation related to the threats of surveillance capitalism?
4. To what extent are library users interested in more pro-active technologies based on surveillance?

As to the first question, it seems—at least in certain academic libraries—that practices resembling those in the private sector have appeared where academic libraries have provided a research management unit at universities with bibliographic data concerning researcher performance, quality, and productivity. The commercial aspects, compared to private sector Internet activities, however, seem to be absent in public and academic libraries.

As to the second question, very few if any library literature authors seem to recommend pure surveillance capitalistic-oriented business models based on targeted and tailored advertisement to be introduced into libraries. On the contrary, library literature and information technology authors have warned against the dangers and threats of digital surveillance. However, it seems as if certain traits have been adopted by certain public libraries, such as recommendations based on the behaviour of other users like the type of recommendations applied by Amazon: 'users who have bought title X, also bought title Y'.

As to the third question, user-to-user mediation and social navigation in libraries are not seen as particularly related to surveillance capitalism; they rather confirm an adherence to old Library 2.0 dreams and visions of user-centred change and the creation of a new culture of participation catalyzed by social web technologies. Certainly, the 'burgeoning exhibitionist technologies like blogs, social networking sites, and photo-sharing sites' encourage a shift in privacy and what we consider private information. More of our private lives today are open to surveillance and new conceptions of how privacy works are reflected in terms like 'reciprocal transparency' (Halavais, 2009, p. 139).

What distinguishes traditional surveillance from 'reciprocal transparency' seems to be the type of interests and the underlying intentions behind them. User-to-user mediation and social navigation are, according to a reciprocal transparency point of view, considered as a positive feature in the library world although some users have 'explored and exploited other users' behavioural traces' (Björneborn, 2011, p. 6), whereas digital surveillance by FAANGs (Facebook, Apple, Amazon, Netflix, and Google) often appears to be more or less suspicious activities.

As to research question four, evidence from a recent Danish national user survey indicates that attitudes and preferences as to the application of pro-active technologies in libraries vary according to different library user segments. Especially relevant is the distinction between platform- and entertainment-oriented users, corresponding to a distinction between library users who expressively wish to be challenged and another segment of users who prefer to do without basic challenges. The survey does not reveal to what extent library users want to receive recommendations from other library users.

It is difficult to deduce from the conclusions just presented precisely what strategies modern libraries should follow regarding digital surveillance. Maybe transparency is a key word here. The library should take care that it's use of all kinds of user data from transactions and from other sources should be transparent to its users.

## References

Åström, F., Hansson, J., 2013. How implementation of bibliometric practice affects the role of academic libraries. J. Librariansh. Inf. Sci. 45 (4), 316–322. https://doi.org/10.1177/0961000612456867.

Björneborn, L., 2011. Behavioural traces and indirect user-to-user mediation in the participatory library. In: Proceedings of the International Conference Information Science and Social Media, ISSOME 2011, August 24–26, Åbo/Turku, Finland. Åbo Akademi University, Finland, pp. 151–166.

Cecez-Kecmanovic, D., 2019. The resistible rise of digital surveillance: a call for action. J. Inf. Technol. 34 (1), 81–83.

Clarke, R., 2019. Risks inherent in the digital surveillance economy: a research agenda. J. Inf. Technol. 34 (1), 59–80. https://doi.org/10.1177/0268396218815559.

Halavais, A., 2009. Search Engine Society. Polity Press, Cambridge.

Johannsen, C.G., 2017. Staff-Less Libraries: Innovative Staff Design. Elsevier/Chandos Publishing, Cambridge, MA.

Johannsen, C.G., 2019. Users, Technology, and Library Design: From Clients to Participants and Data Sources. Lambert Academic Publishing, Mauritius.

Moos, M., Schroeder, J., 2017. Digitale Biblioteksstrategier (Digital Library Strategies). Moos-Bjerre & Lange, Copenhagen, p. 108.

Whitley, R., Gläser, J. (Eds.), 2007. The Changing Governance of the Sciences: The Advent of Research Evaluation Systems. Springer, Dordrecht.

Zuboff, S., 1988. In the Age of the Smart Machine: The Future of Work and Power. Basic Books, New York.

Zuboff, S., 2015. Big other: surveillance capitalism and the prospects of an information civilization. J. Inf. Technol. 30, 75–89.

Zuboff, S., 2019. The Age of Surveillance Capitalism: The Fight for a Human Future at the New Frontier of Power. Profile Books, London.

# Conclusion

# Future directions: Emergent process; constant invention; sum total

**19**

*David Baker*[a,b] *and Lucy Ellis*[b,c]
[a]Plymouth Marjon University, Plymouth, United Kingdom, [b]David Baker Consulting, davidbakerconsulting.co.uk, [c]University of Exeter, Exeter, United Kingdom

## 19.1 Introduction

> *The future is not a destination, but an emergent process. It is not, to paraphrase, something we are all heading towards, but rather a constant process of invention. The future, in other words, is only the sum total of the decisions we make today.*
> *(Nick Poole, in Baker and Evans, 2016, p. xviii)*

> *There is no clear end state towards which we are inevitably headed.*
> *Mark Dahl (Chapter 10)*

This book has focussed on *future* directions in digital information. Having begun by looking at the recent past and current developments, the subsequent chapters have covered a range of themes to do with the core topic by means of analysis and synthesis, action research, social survey, case study, and a range of other approaches. Every author—including the writers of the thought pieces—has concluded their contribution with a forecast of the future and, more specifically, proposals for further work, next-stage actions, the likely impacts of current and intended developments, and the likely scenarios that will be evident and experienced over at least the next 5 years or more.

This chapter, then, looks to the future with the aid of the Delphi participants and the thought pieces, as a way of bringing the rest of the book together and providing possible scenarios, which library and information service leaderships can influence, shape, and manage. Not that any of this is easy. For as Mark Dahl (Chapter 10) comments, 'the information ecosystem will continue to shift in directions that are difficult to predict', especially—at the time of writing—in the light of the Coronavirus epidemic.

## 19.2 COVID and beyond

There is little doubt that life will never be the same after 2020 and the 'new normal' of the next 10 years at least is not necessarily what could have been predicted 12 months let alone 5 years ago. But that is not to say that all change from now on will be discontinuous. Many trends are already emerging to suggest that Coronavirus is

**Future Directions in Digital Information. https://doi.org/10.1016/B978-0-12-822144-0.00019-7**

only hastening what would be happening anyway, as our Delphi participants strongly suggest. Whatever the outcome by, say, 2030, the environment will be a digital one, root and branch.

The recent COVID-19 epidemic has shown technology is valuable for contingency in emergency situations, and as such, adaptation is becoming increasingly key.

### Whither the flexible future?

Until the coronavirus (COVID-19) pandemic of 2020 brought the workplace into many homes around the world and established a 'new normal' of solo remote working based on the technology, professional isolation had been a significant but largely unrecognized challenge facing knowledge and information management professionals for some years. It is a phenomenon I reluctantly call 'the majority of one' and has increasingly come about as our traditional workplaces and teams have become more fragmented and fluid—through societal and technological disruptions (not least signal events such as the 2020 pandemic), ongoing globalization trends, greater use of contractors, and increased opportunities to work remotely and contribute to projects and decision-making by virtual means.

At the same time, for corporate and government librarians in particular, and our higher education colleagues too, the move from physical spaces and collections to online delivery has driven many to re-think and question their professional identities, values, and purpose—the means by which we define ourselves as professionals. Thus, while many of us enjoy greater flexibility in our workplaces and enhanced capacity to juggle our working and personal lives, we must simultaneously guard against becoming self-absorbed and disengaged from our professional identity. In a world of increasing flexibility and uncertainty, the challenge for us as significant stakeholders in the digital economy is to remain professionally, socially, and culturally connected with our colleagues and the core values such as evidence-based practice we are all supposed to share and promulgate. We must also remain focussed on the projects and services that are our common and defining purpose, and that ultimately deliver meaningful value to our end users and clients.

The 2020 pandemic has brought many changes in traditional workplaces, not least libraries and other information services. I see these changes as opportunities enabling great gains in our professional practice if we work together to realize their potential. The global experience of coronavirus (COVID-19) has also reinforced, I believe, an important message for our profession and practice: none of us are islands—we cannot be majorities of one.

***Richard Sayers***
**Health Sector, Brisbane, QLD, Australia**

Flexibility, pragmatism, and openness to change will be key. There is no strategic value in locking information provision spending into 3- or 5-year content deals. Making arrangements that are too long-term risk locking users and staff into older, obsolete ways of working. Advertizing will be key to expanding impact, and also staying technologically relevant. Using technology in new ways to promote services, embracing the latest trends in technology, and surveying and staying current in the new and changing technological landscape will be important.

## Life after COVID

The COVID-19 pandemic has ushered in a new era of social distancing and separation. What will this change mean for the future of digital information use and delivery? Social distancing is a new term for most of us, and an apt metaphor for the current times, though in truth we have been steadily moving along this path for some years. Meeting and conducting research in physical proximity is no longer as important to our society. Many academic programmes at universities and colleges are taught online for learners, who earn their degrees at a distance. Our academic libraries have fewer visitors and no longer build extensive collections, and instead provide access to digital information as a premium service. New forms and use of OER materials, open scholarly communication, and peer review, all serve to distance us and eliminate the need for direct contact in physical space. Open, by its very definition, conveys a sense of distance. In truth, as a society we were already highly adept at social distancing long before the pandemic struck.

We will see more social distancing in the future, even after the current crisis ends, which will foster innovative and accelerated methods of information use and delivery. Witness the remarkable speed at which the genetic code of the novel coronavirus was released to researchers in the current digital information environment. Our separation will continue to accelerate information delivery, as our work continues to become more virtual. Information needs will increasingly be met at the point of demand, with a sense of immediacy and urgency, as the world responds to future crises. What other forms of evolution will digital information take? In the medical sciences, especially, we will see evaluation and treatment at a distance, which will require innovative systems and new methods of digital diagnostics and testing. Our mental health services will make use of distancing technologies, and our social interactions will be more reliant on sophisticated digital platforms. Indeed, even our physical environments will be predicated on evolving systems of digital information, as some of our most critical needs are met by remote delivery of goods and services.

In our new world, both this present and future reality, evolving digital information systems will necessarily become a part of our raison d'etre and permeate every aspect of our lives on a virtual level. Enhanced digital and social media systems will influence and challenge us in new and unpredictable manners. Digital media platforms will evolve to respond to the need to deliver unbiased, responsible, and reliable information and news. Intelligent, speedy, and efficient technologies to optimize our work and living environments, with the concomitant potential for both positive and negative outcomes, will be the hallmarks of the new digital information systems. Digital information will enhance our lives, and we will use information in new ways that empower us, but also to keep us safely at a distance.

***Paul Kelsey***
**Sims Memorial Library, Southeastern Louisiana University, Hammond, LA, United States**

---

Thinking of the current situation with COVID-19, there is the potential to collect and curate a wonderful archive of information from everyday life during this time, which would be useful for future generations of researchers. If libraries can help with the creation of this type of content, it could help to attract new users and create new services.

The COVID-19 epidemic has proved a baptism by fire for library systems and highlighted a serious need for sustainable off-premises (digital) access. While offering a physical space to read and study will remain important, current events are likely to trigger a significant shift towards off-site working and study, making online access to information crucial.

Yet despite all the developments, trajectories, opportunities, and successes in digital information provision and usage since the first *Digital Information Review* was published, and as noted in the discussions in Chapter 1 and this chapter in particular, there remains a vital need for the physical library, not necessarily to access collections (other than as an adjunct to remote use of digital materials or to use material that is only available as print on paper), but as that third space between home and work that continues to fulfil a basic human need, as Roumpani and colleagues demonstrate in relation to the UK public libraries. While social media have become powerful almost beyond measure in our global society, and have much potential for the common good, as described by Daniella Smith in Chapter 11 in relation to continuing professional development, it should be remembered that the library is itself a social medium; one that could have a vital role in rebuilding our economies, societies, cultures, health, and well-being in the new normal environment that we are planning for, expect, or hope for.

Many view and use the library as a social institution, to assist with needed services, like social services, or help filing taxes or applying for loans or assistance. These services may actually increase and play an even more important role over the next decade, depending on the political and economic climate.

## 19.3 Accessibility

As discussed in Chapter 1 and elsewhere, 'the user' will determine much of what is planned and implemented, underpinned by necessary responses to technology developments, resulting in the identification of library staff's future key roles. Due note will need to be taken of the fact that technology is not always the solution and that 'technical rationality' has many dangers. At its best, however, technology has the power to maximize accessibility and hence move towards minimizing inequality and inequity of provision.

All aspects of future research and innovation must ensure maximum accessibility through revisions to organizational behaviour, engagement with users both in consulting on need, and engaging them in the developmental processes. On that basis, marginalized groups should form a normal part of the research process through consultation and engagement to make sure that the barriers that they face are reduced as far as is technically and practically possible. A good current example of this is electronic legal deposit. Many groups have talked for some time about the accessibility issues inherent in the current approach of replicating a physical copy as a digital copy (therefore, only one user across an institution, and can only be read on designated machines). Now that the physical libraries are closed these titles are inaccessible. This represents a vast proportion of some collections and there is little that can be done without complex interventions. Had concerns from marginalized groups been listened to earlier this could have been avoided or lessened.

---

Large-scale digitization of specific collections is imperative. Libraries, by definition, are places of inclusion and equality and so minorities always have their place. E-books, in collaboration with technology such as tablets and screen readers, have allowed the traditional printed book to become far more accessible to those with special needs. Both archivists of older materials and publishers of new ones need to adapt their output to this technology (i.e. produce digital documents) to allow the greatest numbers of users to have access.

---

The potential for marginalization will increase in the future, due to the possibility of economic upheavals and other social and cultural problems. Access to information and technology are necessary to prevent this, and information providers and technical industries must adopt an ethos that will support marginalized people on many levels. This ethos is not yet universal.

---

Libraries need to move towards a model which prioritizes inclusion over exclusion as standard. Creating accessible digital content, curating diverse and accessible collections, and building accessible spaces are all things which can be done, bearing in mind the need to operate within certain restraints. A feedback mechanism should be provided for differently abled persons to evaluate the type of services provided for them. Through user analysis the needs of individuals can be identified, allowing, as far as possible, personalized adaptations. The principle is first recognized and then implemented according to the individual circumstances, on the understanding that making something accessible can improve the service for all.

## 19.4 Envisioning the future

Horizon scanning, trend analysis, and a proactive approach in response to change will all be essential skills. Library and information managers will have to be proactive by constantly studying evolving pedagogy of learning, the culture of the learner, and the development of technology. They will need to think outside the box and work to attract new audiences who do not usually make use of the library by using methods such as diversifying collections. Libraries will need to develop and integrate new services, especially as societies respond to crisis management.

---

Several chapters—as, for example, those by Hamilton and Roumpani and colleagues—not only envision possible futures but also describe how scenarios can be formulated using a range of techniques, the results of one of which, Delphi, underpins this chapter. While it is important within such approaches to provide robust narratives to accompany the result of any scenario planning exercises, it is also crucial to maintain maximum flexibility, as Richard Sayers stresses (above). For example, it is not so long ago—and still being proposed in this book—that physical space could be reduced in the wake of pervasive e-access to content, information, and services. Library managers are not so sure, in the wake of social distancing, that smaller building footprints are necessarily a good idea; perhaps existing space should be repurposed to meet the upcoming challenges. Having said that, it would also seem evident that, in a matter of months, the idea of the 'inside-out' library looks set to be part of the new normal.

### The online public library user

With the COVID-19 pandemic having forced the closure of physical public libraries, it has been shown that the online public library user is, potentially, anyone and everyone. Digital methods of communication, information access, and entertainment have experienced much higher usage during the lockdown, helping maintain a sense of normality during the severe measures.

Improved technology has allowed more and more stock, both fiction and nonfiction, to become easily and viably accessible in digital formats. Online databases in a variety of sectors, from genealogy to law, allow information to be accessed anywhere, at any time. Audiobooks can be streamed in a manner akin to music apps. Specialist reading devices have been developed for black-and-white textbooks and novels, while other tablets are ideal platforms to read colour graphic novels and comics.

The activity of sitting and reading a physical book will doubtless retain an appeal for many. The experience and engagement of 'touchy-feely' books aimed at young children is still currently not replicable by digital means. Yet the lockdown has, at the very least, shown the importance of digitized stock as a contingency measure. Libraries have a responsibility to preserve their stock, and the potential that modern technology offers can help it to remain safe and accessible regardless of what may come.

***Hannah Myers***
**Walker Morris, Leeds, United Kingdom**

### A future prediction from someone who will have to live it

I use the online college information page 'Moodle' every day. I am in college on average 5 days a week. I use this resource as it is very easy to navigate through subject content for my studies. However, I am drawn towards online articles when looking for information about real-world applications for my A level studies. For example, Business Studies requires external information, which is not available in the physical or virtual library. For instance, Chinese economic growth is forecast to slow to 4.5% in the first quarter of 2020.[a] Chemistry and Maths are not the same in this regard. When at university I expect this situation will change depending on the subject.

Measures of success of digital information services could involve comparison with other colleges and also questionnaires for students about their experiences with physical and online library services. For me, there is no correlation between social media and subject information. For instance, no-one would post publicly with information about their college subject. This would be done by private message.

In the next 10 years, there will be fewer physical library buildings and more online resources will be available for students. However, you could argue that there will be no change, as students only require a few generic study guides (dependent on subject). Social well-being will suffer as physical libraries decline. Fewer students will use libraries as resources can be found online and they do not need physical books. Online resources are easier to use. Therefore, there will be less social interaction.

***George Williams***
**A Level Student (Maths, Chemistry & Business Studies), Cornwall, United Kingdom**

a Editors: This thought piece was written pre-COVID-19.

## Producers and users of digital information: matches or mismatches?

In researching and putting together a collection of case studies on technology, change and academic libraries (Atkinson, 2020), I identified some important issues relating to the pace of change in the rapidly developing world of digital information. In the past, a common theme in papers on academic libraries was the use and nonuse of libraries and information resources. In 2020, everyone is a provider and consumer of digital information, but there are some important differences in the nature and extent of use, the systems and services used, and the perspectives, confidence, innovation, and flexibility of providers and users. The stakeholder 'pen pictures' that follow reflect some of these issues. They are intentionally provocative, simplistic, and generalized, but attempt to highlight some 'mismatches' that will require reflection and action, particularly in developing working partnerships.

**Commercial providers**: focused on system development and innovation that is not always centred on users or integration of different systems. Importance of efficiency and profit. Often capable of rapid change.

**18–21-Year-old students**: expert in digital content and platforms, up to speed with the latest offerings of commercial providers. Images often as important as text. Not always engaged with traditional teaching methods or traditional library services, or with attempts to provide new platforms such as online reading lists. Differences in subjects, but students not always reading in depth and preferring bite-sized information. Some students preferring to separate platforms used for leisure, such as social media, and those used for study.

**Academic staff and researchers**: more wedded to academic library services, but increasingly requiring services and provision that make their working lives easier, in both teaching and research. Great variations in digital skills. Multiple, complex, and bureaucratic online systems are the bane of their lives.

**Academic librarians**: with the advent of the electronic library, academic librarians have done well to reinvent themselves and create new roles. However, there are still some issues with agility vs stability. Digital skills vary and some are slow to react or engage with technological developments. Changes in library systems take much longer than those in the commercial sector. Current focus on digital literacy, but users may consider themselves to be adequately skilled. Use of an increasing range of digital communication channels, but users may not always want to engage.

***Jeremy Atkinson***
**Library and Information Services Consultant, Cardiff, United Kingdom**

### Reference

Atkinson, J., 2020. Technology, Change and the Academic Library: Case Studies and Reflections. Chandos Publishing, Oxford.

## 19.5 Strategy and design

> *With change as the only constant, an academic library should develop medium-term strategies and then continuously monitor the situation. This will lead to mission-driven, pragmatic choices that support institutional needs and align with long-term library values.*
>
> *(Mark Dahl, Chapter 10)*

Key factors in future strategies must include making clear how both the virtual and the physical are managed to deliver best value and engagement with collective research and innovation. There should be a preparedness to change significant parts of delivery priorities as external demands change. Sometimes success will require speedy action, sometimes not. Balancing radical change with the traditional incremental approach but ensuring that at all stages the processes of development, innovation, and research engage with current users and potential new audiences will be important.

The fixed stoic image of a library is no longer fit for purpose. It must be made flexible, modernized, and more accessible to meet the needs and demands of today's users. The sector must not shy away from nontraditional development and collaboration. If technology is able to perform menial tasks, then this frees up staff to specialize in research and other aspects of the profession, leading to a more useful and efficient front-line service overall. We will see more remote and virtual working, as social distancing becomes a normal practice. There will be improvements to information delivery services and digital meeting and sharing applications.

Much of this book has been concerned with strategy and design as it relates to future library and information systems. Clarity of roles—what the library does and does *not* do from now on—will be crucial. Once the foundations are laid in this respect, it will be possible to build evaluation mechanisms that demonstrate worth, benefit, and return on investment.

There must be clarity of mission and purpose, for without a clear sense of what the institution exists to achieve that is written down and agreed with the parent organization and all staff, it will be impossible to produce an evaluation able to demonstrate in a meaningful way whether those purposes have been achieved. If people do not agree about what it is that they are trying to evaluate and where their role fits into it then this almost renders the process of evaluation futile. Evaluation needs to link mission/purpose with user experience (and nonuser experience, ideally), so as to gauge success in delivering existing mission and inform the evolution/enhancement of that mission and its delivery.

A clear mission and purpose must underpin everything a library service does. Practices and ways of working must evolve to meet both user demands and new technological potential. This should lead to an appraisal of the institution within its environment to establish the external pressures, changes, and opportunities it will face through time. The institution must remain confident in its fundamental purpose and when necessary be fleet of foot, acting like an entrepreneur in responding to external change. The critical challenge of digital projects is the speed of change that can and does take place.

Critical to successful evaluation of value will be the relationship with users, using tools of engagement through market studies, focus groups, sampling, and studies on who within the community served is not using the service and why. Such approaches to evaluation are not new, but they are not widely used and are not consistent across institutions. To build a collective view of value delivered to individuals and across society would be a powerful message to present to parent organizations and, perhaps, most important for the future, could offer a stronger voice on the role of library and information services within national policy agendas. Engaging with users to ascertain what they want from libraries, and presenting this data to funding and managing bodies, is a good way to ensure libraries stay relevant and use their money wisely to best support the communities. If we reframe evaluation in terms of what we are not doing to attract these users, it could yield interesting results and help to inform our service delivery more than knowing what we are already doing well. Who is using the service, what for and its benefit/impact is also critical to evaluation.

The 'learning for life' that technology offers presents the greatest opportunities for increased value to individuals and to society at large. The ability to demonstrate the value of such a broad societal opportunity could position library and information services collectively more centrally within national policy frameworks. Value that is not valued is not valuable.

While demonstration of value to the user will be essential, it is highly likely that scale of use and success will continue to be significant. The future of public funding looks now more uncertain than ever and institutions wishing to protect (and grow) their budgets will have to show value at scale. This will be important in the exploitation of Internet technologies, where the possibility exists to reach the widest possible audience. Comprehensive measurement of online services will be developed to provide metrics for access points and use of resources. The question of value comes in, which can still be captured online. It will become less about the numbers, especially as user numbers drop when people bypass the library completely in search of online information. Instead it will become more about the quality of the information that people are using and the uses to which they put this information. Numbers will still play a role, but this will be vastly diminished when it comes to justifying services and projects.

The category of users of the library will determine whether the library will continue to remain open or start considering virtuality along with the types of resources and facilities provided. Organization of content and making content easily discoverable with necessary links to other relevant content will be the primary task of the librarian as more access is trafficked in the virtual environment. Technology will be a huge change agent in the coming years in a variety of ways. Greater bandwidth and mobile technologies will continue to raise expectations of anything, anywhere, anytime accessibility.

How can technology be used by all, not just those who are used to it? This includes both users and staff to ensure no one gets left behind. The development of online services should work with the development of in-person resources rather than as a separate thing. It is important to think about those who do not visit libraries in person but do not have access to personal technology.

> We should not automatically assume that technology is the solution to every problem: the danger of technical rationality—the extent to which seeking technological solutions dominates future research programmes. Technology is a key component, but research programmes should begin by considering carefully what is the core of the problem faced: problem setting rather than problem solving. The dangers of technical rationality and the need for policy frameworks for the future call for radical change both in the overall management and funding of research programmes and the behaviours and attitudes of institutions. This should take place within limits to set aside organizational identity and accept the value of collective action and advocacy in research and innovation with the aspiration that it will offer services that better meet the future needs of audiences of all types.

But financial pressures—no doubt at least partly as a result of fallout from the current pandemic—will also shape the future for library services, not least because of the commercial value (discussed extensively in this book) of information. Library responses will have to respond to the massification of provision by increased cooperation and collaboration in order to create necessary critical mass, building on perceived reputations as honest brokers, albeit ones who are not as visible as either they once were or they need to be in the future to maintain the vitality and essential nature of the services that they provide.

> Outside the public sector, Internet services show how scale can build success; successful services get bigger, and bigger services get more successful. Linking the matter of scale with the hunter-gatherer vs harvester behaviour model implies in the future far more emphasis across library and information services on cooperation and resource convergence, reducing the need for users to be digital hunters.

> There is already a great deal of discussion about the commercialization of information and who holds the power. We need to implement a system of checks and balances to ensure that the interests of all are protected. Libraries are traditionally good at collaboration; barriers are more to do with technology (systems do not interoperate) and organizational politics.

> The library is still seen as an optimal place for collaborative projects, because of the perception that libraries add value to almost every project involving learning and research. Libraries add a layer of service that is highly desirable, which is the provision, management, and delivery of information resources. It is not just about the core user groups but the wider user base who might need access to knowledge. We must think about both current and future users, especially when building technology-based collections.

> What will be called for is a far more collaborative and coordinated approach to innovation, where risks can be shared and where ideas can be incubated, and risk managed. It will be necessary to find ways for local institutions to give up some of their independence in service innovation for the greater good for truly effective service development in the digital landscape. Curated and trusted

resources should be promoted and advertized by libraries since these are stable and authoritative. By relying on these resources, but managing them internally for delivery, risk is then diminished.

---

The determination of authentic information and credible publishers will become problematic, especially as the promotion of open data, open science, and open access will be high. There is an honourable tradition of public institutions managing collections, whether museums, libraries, or archives, making every effort to ensure that their services can be trusted and are reliable. Library collections and services must hang on to that tradition. But at a time when fake news and information is on the increase, will people seek information from the library, which offers opportunities for services around education and evaluation training? We know from many studies that librarians are one of the lowest used sources of information, however, trusted they are as a professional group. And there is still a perception that users have to be educated rather than the systems designed to be user friendly.

---

## 19.6 Who are the users?

The future users of library and information services is a topic discussed in Chapter 1 and throughout the following chapters and the primacy of the user will remain central to future development. But who are the users? There is the potential for a much larger user base for library and information services than ever before, not least post-COVID, as discussed earlier. Nonhuman users will also need to be considered in future strategy development.

---

User demand should be key, especially with the development of collections. Libraries should focus on what they want to see and, perhaps crucially, what they do not want to see. Librarians risk offering both collections and services that they think users want as opposed to what they will actually find useful. They need drive to focus on what users actually want in conjunction with using their professional judgement.

---

Services should be user centred (a basic principle of service management) so that collections and services are more appropriate for them. In practice, this means consulting with and surveying users (and nonusers if possible), including user representatives in decision-making and undertaking user experience research. User-centred service delivery and design will be critical factors in future success.

---

Close involvement with users to understand their behaviours and needs should be fundamental to all developments. Because of the increasing role of technology in accessing and retrieving library resources, users can also suggest how best to display and retrieve them for use as well as suggesting the appropriate gadgets to have in accessing digital collections, since they are the key users. They can identify priorities for purchase or to unsubscribe, by engaging in patron-led acquisition processes, as well as providing recommendations and comments for other users.

An interesting question is the extent to which the majority of users are (or will be) 'bots' or programs that are already trying to harvest our content by fair means or foul, especially with the trend towards open access. We should not discount the originators of content being programs: machine-written articles, standards, etc. Information professionals will need to understand how these things work, review how their content behaves when harvested by these bots, and influence content providers to allow (or prevent?) this type of access to ensure users find the right information. What are libraries' responsibilities towards nonhuman users? If articles are written by machines, how do we approach our usual services such as referencing advice and plagiarism support? How far do we go in recommending this content to our human users? This raises interesting ethical questions: should all bots be allowed to harvest or only some? To what extent are librarians responsible for the use to which their collections are put? Arguably we are not.

Successful delivery of online resources will call for new relationships with users in terms both of the design of new systems and the constant monitoring of how services are received and revised in the light of experience. Success will depend on an organizational shift towards constant monitoring and engagement.

It will always be important that users of services are able to gain access and achieve what they aspire to. Use of the hardware and software are prerequisites; hardware should continue to be refined and simplified to be as intuitive as possible. Why do so many institutions maintain online services that are completely unlike those of any other institution? Why are there still so many different library, museum, and archive websites when the online searcher might wish to find a range of diverse resources on a theme without having to hunt to find where online those resources might be held? With online services designed with diverse audiences in mind, such barriers might be mitigated or even disappear. User friendliness and accessibility are essential to the survival of all digital systems, not just educational ones.

Learning literacy (LL—known more formally as heutagogy)—assisting users to understand how they maximize personal benefit from the knowledge and information they find—will become significant: how to interpret, how to test reliability and encourage the value of what they find in ongoing learning journeys, whether in formal education or in everyday life. Supporting LL, understanding the exchange relationship between the online collection resources and the user and modelling the value delivered must be core activities for library and information services.

## 19.7 Where formal meets informal

The division between formal and informal, home and work, job and leisure, and education and entertainment has been increasingly permeable for some time now and has almost been eroded in many areas in the recent months. As evinced by the responses from the Delphi study and many of the chapters in this book, this trend is set to continue, not least because of the ubiquity and pervasiveness of social media (SM) and mobile technology. Chapter 11 shows how SM can be vitally useful in continuing professional development. Opportunities already exist for library and information staff to act as facilitators and educators, helping users to navigate through the increasingly complex ecosystems that underpin the information environment and to help maximize accessibility. Many more will present themselves in the near future.

---

Social media will continue to be a path for information dissemination to digital natives who are always 'on the go'. There will be a thin line between 'work' and 'social' situations. Institutional information cannot and should not ignore the presence of users on social networks and digital media, but neither should it lose focus on its face-to-face services. Social and other digital media represent an opportunity for institutions to reach out to their users in a space they are already using. Rather than just broadcasting information, libraries should use these channels to interact on a more informal level. They can also use it to understand what users say about them but not to them. This can raise both good points and potential issues that need addressing. It should be a companion to, rather than a replacement for, face-to-face services.

---

The onus on supporting accessibility has switched to mobile device manufacturers rather than individual organizations. For engaging with marginalized groups, identifying relevant third sector enterprises to act as intermediaries is probably the most effective strategy. If companies have specialist knowledge and technology to offer that allow staff to work more effectively, it should be considered and embraced, so long as the library does not lose control over its own development and process. But there is still a role for libraries and professionals to advocate for accessibility and speak on behalf of users.

---

Social media and other digital tools allow connection with more people than ever before, on a global scale. Practitioners will need to adjust to the preferences of the users who use social media as a platform for communication. There will be more real-time (synchronous) delivery of results/answers to queries. Academic libraries have a crucial role in helping researchers share their outputs and other libraries have a role in making sure that their users can access these outputs. As more and more scholarly information becomes freely accessible online, these needs will only increase and help to contribute to wider economic and social well-being.

---

But the opportunities referred to above will not be simply be handed to library services; librarians' roles, status, and very presence will need to be justified and fought for. Justifications will best be made when they are underpinned by research, collaborative partnerships, and effective and comprehensive policy frameworks. The importance of being involved at the earliest stages of new developments should be self-evident.

---

The information field needs a body of current and cutting edge research to make improvements in design and delivery of digital information. Without this, true improvements cannot be made. Libraries need to push for greater collaboration with companies to ensure needs are met. Even having your say over something like the presentation and format of your own website and catalogue gives you influence over how resources are presented. Applied user behaviour research is used within information systems, publishing, and technology companies to improve their interfaces and algorithms, especially as the big publishers buy up more and more of the scholarly publishing cycle. The Oxford Internet Survey has done this every other year since 2003 and is a goldmine of information about social take up and uses of the Internet (https://oxis.oii.ox.ac.uk).

---

Text and data mining are new opportunities for libraries and if they can get involved at this developing stage then they will stand in a good position for the future. Continued emphasis on presenting content for data mining and text mining and semantic searching would be helpful to facilitate new forms of interdisciplinary research.

---

## 19.8 Applications and delivery

Much of this book has been about practical application and delivery, as demonstrated by the case studies in particular. Every one of those projects was, of necessity, grounded in, and strongly linked with, the relevant external environments. Their success has been at least partly attributable to the fact that there was a demonstrable value to the work being undertaken well beyond the specific host institution. Allied to this was the willingness to embrace risk and manage it effectively and coherently, without becoming inappropriately risk averse. Agility, openness, responsiveness, willingness to cooperate and collaborate, ability and desire to look ahead, and a fundamental engagement with 'the human factor' will be crucial.

---

The external political and economic environment will continue to influence what the institution can do. Library and information services should do even more to demonstrate their social learning and economic value at the highest level possible. It may not be possible to do this from within a larger parent organization but increasing cooperation and collaboration in developments could enable a *single voice* demonstrating social and economic value collectively.

---

Library managers need to be open to taking more risks, while weighing this against other concerns. They should think about both the positives and negatives of the action and how it might impact both their service and the people delivering it. In all of the planning for various projects, the human element is often forgotten, and it is important to remember that people only have so much capacity to complete work. The potential for human failure needs to be built into the project plan and catered for if needed. Beyond this, people should follow the basic sensible steps for implementing major projects and conduct an audit of potential risk so that they can create a backup plan. People may think that the worst will never happen, but they need to be well prepared if it does. This will be essential for dealing with the dynamics of IT and society but demands a radical shift both in professional worldviews and also how public organizations are generally risk averse.

---

Libraries will need to be open to consolidation of physical collections so they can focus on support services at a local level. This extends into the virtual collection space. They must ensure that everything possible is harvestable and discoverable in standardized formats and APIs so that new services can be built on top of them. They should be open to collaborating cross-functionally and across different institutions and be ready to use human beings where technology cannot substitute. They should be scanning the local and global environments of library and information services, actively responding to the dynamics of technology application in the provision of resources and reviewing and adjusting their digital content to meet real need.

---

Library and information services are used to planning for slow, incremental change. Sometimes a sector needs to move away from traditional roles in order to better serve its users. It will be necessary to find horizon scanning mechanisms to identify trends and monitor changing patterns of social use of digital technologies. Detailed planning is not always possible. Perpetual beta approaches enable agile working. Calculated risks allow for new ways of working and new developments. Library services will have to be even more agile in the future as they respond to ever changing technologies. Creating responsive, adaptable services will mean that libraries remain relevant.

## 19.9 New paradigms

The Delphi panellists spent much time formulating statements that could be used as the basis of new paradigms. This chapter ends with a summary of the key points that emerged from that work.

---

Libraries are safe places; spaces for comfort and well-being. These characteristics guarantee users the confidence to explore information freely and openly. This is at the basis of the development of ideas that in turn will foster new knowledge for society. They have an indirect impact through education, with a population who are better informed about the world and able to conduct themselves responsibly in the digital environment and more able to make social connections. If libraries continue to focus on free and open information, open buildings, and free services, then they will remain essential.

---

The trajectory of use of digital devices seems unlikely to lose momentum in the foreseeable future. There are many benefits in everyday life from always-on access, but at the same time we face the problems of fake news, scams, and the exploitation of children. This not an issue that is likely to go away any time soon and libraries need to take steps to promote themselves as able to teach the evaluation of information. They cannot and should not promote one view over the other but instead offer the tools for people to make informed decisions. This will not capture all of those who use misinformation but making it a core part of education can help in the future.

---

Information overload is a major implication, which can lead to confusion for the information illiterate. Some people will surrender accessing certain information because of the deluge of information flooding the media. Greater knowledge in the use of technology will lead to manipulation of news and information generally, with the resultant effect of not being able to separate authentic from fake and false news/information. People should be able to turn to libraries to access true, verified information. Then again, life under lockdown would be even more difficult without the ability to connect easily to loved ones at a distance; people can be mobilized (for good purposes) quickly and easily through services such as Facebook; messages can be disseminated quickly, so there is a good side also.

---

The development of, and increasing reliance on, AI may create a culture of misinformation. As large corporations develop AI products, there is the potential to lose valuable perspective on information sources. For collecting institutions, it will be important to recognize such risks and defend and promote public information and knowledge services as being reliable, unbiased, and trustworthy. Libraries will have a greater role to play if AI results in the creation of misinformation or intentionally misleading information. Libraries can serve as an essential source for reliable information and will benefit by promoting their services as authoritative and unbiased.

---

Changes to information and technology are inevitable. Libraries will promote new products and services, but their mission to meet the information needs of constituents will not change. Services and collections will look different, but over the next 10 years libraries will still manage and provide information to constituents. Developments such as the Digital Public Library of America and Europeana offer early insight into how resources may be gathered from a wide range of different information services, but significant change will call for a ubiquitous online service designed to be accessible to the widest possible range of audiences. Such services and collections also need to adhere to similar standards and improve their usability.

---

It is conceivable that there will be a consolidation of libraries into two broad categories: national and research-intensive hubs that offer learners space, facilities, and support services with most digital content provided via national licences or free as open access. This suggests a significant change in the way that collections and services might be provided which, while attractive, would require a transformation in national and local policies, and a radical shift in the professional values of libraries and their parent institutions.

---

Many people will access library collections in the future but not everyone will realize that this is what they are doing. As libraries have a role in helping to disseminate research outputs via repositories and other technologies, they will serve as the bridge between knowledge and their users. With the increase in available information, libraries will play a key role in educating users in digital literacy skills and curating good quality digital information which they can repackage for their users.

---

It is important that information ethics underpins everything that libraries do, especially if they are offering user training in digital literacy, which should include citizens' rights and duties and training in the good and ethical use of information. They should regularly question their practice and ensure that users do the same. In a world where other digital competencies and websites are questioned, libraries need to set the best possible example of good practice and use data responsibility, so users can learn from their example.

There are concerns about how technology might be used (or misused, deliberately, or otherwise) to influence opinion and behaviour. Information professionals have a role to play in raising awareness of this, delivering services which are as far as possible fair and unbiased, pursuing our values of equal and inclusive access to information, and consciously seeking to adopt ethical approaches to service delivery.

Libraries will continue to collect and enable access to quality sources of information. They will retain authority, organizing and enabling effective search and retrieval for end users, curating, acquiring, and delivering quality information sources for different user groups. They will save users time and effort, provide reassurance about information quality, provide guidance to users on how to make good choices about information, how to use information appropriately, and how to create and disseminate their own content in an appropriate and safe manner.

Finally, libraries bring a set of values to the broader information ecosystem that are particularly distinctive. Libraries value preservation of knowledge over the long term. They value access to information and are sometimes in a position to promote open access resources. They value a diversity of viewpoints and voices. As libraries make choices about their bought collection guided by these values, they will help to fill gaps and offset biases in the broader, more commercialized information.

There should be new approaches to change management. By tradition, library and information services have had a duty to collect, care for, and exploit their collections in whatever form over time. Radical, disruptive change brings with it significant risk. The incremental approach to change management is likely to be retained for aspects of service management and delivery. However, within the turbulent landscape of the Internet, while rapid change in service propositions has similar risks, there will be occasions when, to deliver effectively, quicker responses to outside forces will be needed. Those leading innovation and change may sometimes need to operate more as entrepreneurs than conventional public service managers. Flexibility and open mindedness are key when it comes to developing new approaches. If it does not work, try something else. Different ideas should be explored and monitored to help achieve success.

## 19.10 20 Absolute truths

One of the Delphi panelists suggested that at the end of the forecasting exercise, and once the summary of all the responses was complete, a list of '20 absolute truths' emerging from the project, and also perhaps the writing of this book, should be compiled. The following list is offered by the editors of this volume as a summation of future directions in digital information provision and how library and information services—and society more generally—should best respond to the challenges and opportunities that the next 10 years will bring.

1. The more things change, the more they can never be the same, but not all change is necessarily discontinuous.
2. Radical and organic change will both occur; the balance between them will need to be managed.

3. Digital ecosystems—like any ecosystem—develop organically.
4. Everyone and every system is a valuable source of data.
5. Access is all. Social media and mobile access will remain dominant.
6. Convenience and point of demand will continue to be the drivers of innovation.
7. Anywhere, anytime access to digital content and information is already the norm.
8. Institutions will move from digital first to digital only (though it will be a long time before we get there!).
9. Libraries and information services are social institutions. It is important that information ethics underpins everything that they do in the future.
10. There will always be a need for physical libraries as a third space.
11. Determining, and satisfying, user needs will be essential for the survival of library and information services.
12. Building collective views of value will be necessary; value that is not valued is not valuable.
13. Flexibility, pragmatism, and openness to change will be key.
14. Constant beta testing will be vital to ensure effective responses to environmental challenges.
15. Every member of a society will need to be learning and information literate if that society is to be successful in a digital world. The determination of authenticity and credibility in information provision will be more vital than ever.
16. Information inequity remains a serious problem that must be tackled. Inclusion should be prioritized over exclusion.
17. Radical thinking and bold yet measured risk taking will be required.
18. Technology is not always the solution to the problem.
19. There must always be clarity of mission and purpose.
20. Libraries' mission to meet the information needs of their constituents will not change; libraries bring a set of values to the broader information ecosystem that are particularly distinctive.

## 19.11 Endnote

This chapter began with a quotation from Nick Poole, Chief Executive of the Chartered Institute of Library and Information Professionals (CILIP). The text was taken from his foreword to the previous volume of *Digital Information Reviews*. Re-reading his words made us realize how prophetic they were, 4 years ago. We conclude with his last paragraphs. Given what has been written not only in this chapter but also the rest of the book, his forecast continues to be both true and vitally important for our future.

> *Looking into the further future, we can see already that the physical and the digital worlds are converging; social media is less a new technology and more a wave of technologically enabled translation of traditional human behaviours into a networked environment. Atoms and electrons are both physical phenomena, and the infrastructure required to compute, transmit, store, and repurpose information will come to change the physical landscape of our cities and nations as fundamentally as the industrial and agricultural revolutions which came before. Equally profound, but less immediately apparent in the sheer pace and noise of the connected age, is the shift*

*in cultural norms and practices that technology has enabled. The culture of 'rip/mix/share' has resulted in a practice of universal appropriation; generations today and in the future increasingly assemble their identity from many cultures and contexts. These behaviours are echoed in the rise of the 'Sharing Economy' in which the distinction between the personal and corporate is becoming less and less meaningful, with private citizens trading their knowledge, their time, and their space as commodities.*

*Libraries and librarians have a unique and trusted role to play in this emerging culture of sharing and appropriation. Trust and authority used to belong to organizations on the basis of their status and size. These organizations in turn, ensured their survival by controlling access to knowledge and information. In this new economy, organizations and individuals are equal, status is allocated on the basis of how much you share, how freely, and how good your knowledge is. Survival and growth are increasingly predicated on how much you share, how much you facilitate, and how much you enable other people to do with your knowledge. As the authors in these pages show, the channel shift is only the beginning. Following in its wake is a far larger cultural and economic shift, which will change the world forever. Libraries and librarians have two great and central roles to play. The first is in helping people to make this transition as openly and positively as possible. The second is to set the foundations, governance, and organizing principles of a truly equitable Information Society.*

## Reference

Baker, D., Evans, W., 2016. Digital Information Strategies: From Applications and Content to Libraries and People. Chandos, Oxford.

# Appendix: Delphi questions

A series of questions were developed according to the main themes of this book and are listed below. The answers to these questions were collated and turned into a series of statements, which were then sent back to the participants for further comments. These responses were then summarized, analyzed, and presented in Chapters 1 and 19.

## Strategy and design

1. What do you see as the main drivers of change in library and information provision over the next 10 years? This could include such areas as technology and demography.
2. What will be the best ways to evaluate libraries and information services over, say, the next 10 years?
3. How should library and information managers best take decisions on future provision of content and services for a changing user landscape in order to broaden and expand their impact?

## Who are the users?

1. Who are the 'users' of library and information services now and who are they likely to be over the next 10 years?
2. What roles could and should users play in the development of digital collections and services over the next 10 years?
3. Digital literacy is likely to be a pervasive theme of the book. Should it be? What do you take digital literacy to be and how should it best be taught/learned by users and embedded in information services and related provision?

## Where formal meets informal

1. What impact do you think digital and social media will have on working practices and outputs? What are the key factors to be considered in the development of future institutional information strategies?
2. How can research best support developments in digital information provision? What research approaches and methodologies are particularly appropriate for the future management of content and services? How should evidence best be collected?
3. How can organizations use technology to maximize accessibility? How do information providers foster meaningful participation with marginalized groups?

## Applications and delivery

1. How can and how do library and information services improve productivity, efficiency, effectiveness, and our economic and social well-being? How will they best do so in the future?
2. Equity if not equality of access to resources and services remains a challenge in an unequal world. For those who are differently abled, how do library and information services best recognize the rights of all to be included on the same terms?
3. How should risk best be managed in major information service projects?

## New paradigms

1. What are the main societal implications of current and likely future technology developments?
2. What will be the future role(s) of library collections and services in the wider digital information ecosystem?
3. How should information ethics best be developed and embedded in the future? What about digital rights?

# Index

Note: Page numbers followed by *f* indicate figures, *t* indicate tables, and *b* indicate boxes.

## B



## C

## H



## I

## U



## V



## W



## X



## Y



## Z

CPI Antony Rowe
Eastbourne, UK
October 21, 2021